D1242186

Making Islam Democratic

SOCIAL MOVEMENTS AND THE POST-ISLAMIST TURN

Asef Bayat

Stanford University Press
Stanford, California

Stanford University Press
Stanford, California

Printed in the United States of America on acid-free, archival-quality paper

Library of Congress Cataloging-in-Publication Data

Bayat, Asef.
  Making Islam democratic : social movements and the post-Islamist turn / Asef Bayat.
     p. cm.
  Includes bibliographical reference and index.
  ISBN-13: 978-0-8047-5594-8 (cloth : alk. paper)
  ISBN-13: 978-0-8047-5595-5 (pbk. : alk. paper)
    1. Democracy—Religious aspects—Islam. 2. Islam and social problems. 3. Social movements—Iran. 4. Social movements—Egypt. I. Title.
BP190.5.D45B39 2007
320.5'57—dc22   2006035451

Designed by Bruce Lundquist
Typeset at Stanford University Press in 10/14 Minion

Making Islam Democratic

Stanford Studies in Middle Eastern and Islamic Societies and Cultures

To Linda, Shiva, and Tara,
sources of inner joy.

CONTENTS

Abbreviations   ix

Chronology   xi

Preface   xviii

1 Islam and Democracy:
   The Perverse Charm of an Irrelevant Question   1

2 Revolution without Movement, Movement without Revolution:
   Islamist Activism in Iran and Egypt, 1960s–1980s   16

3 The Making of a Post-Islamist Movement:
   Social Movements and Sociopolitical Change in Iran,
   1979–1997   49

4 Post-Islamism in Power: Dilemmas of the Reform Project,
   1997–2004   106

5 Egypt's "Passive Revolution":
   The State and the Fragmentation of Islamism, 1992–2005   136

6 The Politics of Presence:
   Imagining a Post-Islamist Democracy   187

   Reference Matter

   Persian and Arabic Journals Cited   209

   Notes   211

   Bibliography   255

   Index   275

ABBREVIATIONS

ACC   Association of Combatant Clergy (moderate, Iran)
CSS   Center for Strategic Studies (a presidential think tank, Iran)
DTV   Dafter-e Tahkim-e Vahdat (the organization of Iran's student
        movement)
EPCSPI Egyptian Popular Committee for Solidarity with the Palestinian
        Intifada
NCSPO   National Center for the Study of Public Opinion (Iran)
NDP   National Democratic Party (Egypt)
OMIR   Organization of the Mujahidin of the Islamic Revolution (Iran)
SCC   Society of Combatant Clerics (conservative, Iran)

CHRONOLOGY

1796–1925: Iran is ruled by the despotic Qajar dynasty.

1798–1801: France occupies Egypt.

1805–1952: Egypt is ruled by a dynasty established by Muhammad 'Ali, a commander of the Ottoman army; a process of modernization begins, in education, industry, the army, and state institutions.

1869: The Suez Canal is opened to traffic.

1905–07: Iran's Constitutional Revolution establishes law; the first Parliament is organized.

December 1914: Britain declares a formal protectorate over Egypt. A nationalist movement for independence grows.

1922: The protectorate over Egypt is abolished, martial law removed, and independence declared. However, British influence remains.

1922–52: Egypt experiences a "liberal age."

1925: Reza Shah, the father of the late Muhammad Reza Shah, establishes the Pahlavi dynasty by ending the Qajar rule. Reza Shah begins an ambitious program of economic, social, and educational modernization through a secular autocratic state. Some of the policies anger the Shi'i clergy, notably Ayatollah Khomeini.

1928: The Society of Muslim Brothers (Ikhwan al-Muslimin) is established with a plan to Islamize the society, fight foreign influence, and eventually establish an Islamic state.

1946: Allied forces compel Reza Shah to abdicate in favor of his son, Muhammad Reza.

1946–53: A period of democratic experience. Nationalist and Communist movements grow in Iran.

July 23, 1952: Gamal Abdel Nasser and a number of young officers overthrow the Egyptian monarchy and establish an independent secular republic.

March 1951: The campaigns of the nationalist leader, Muhammad Musaddiq, lead to the nationalization of the oil industry; Britain threatens to invade Iran.

July 1956: Nasser nationalizes the Suez Canal, leading to tripartite (Britain France, and Israel) aggression against Egypt.

1952–70: The Nasser regime brings Egypt to a new "socialist" path; massive social programs and a welfare state follow, leading to nationalization of big industry and banks, land reform, educational expansion, and a foreign policy directed against Israel and with closer relations to the eastern bloc. The social change leads to the expansion of the modern middle classes.

June 1953: A coup engineered by the CIA and supported by Britain overthrows the democratic government of the secular nationalist Musaddiq in Iran. The Shah, who had left the country, returns to Iran, ending the democratic experience. Iran becomes the most crucial ally of the West, notably the United States, in the region. Systematic suppression of political parties, associations, and movements follows throughout the decade. Meanwhile, programs of modernization, industrialization, and westernization gain new momentum.

1961: President Nasser of Egypt abolishes religious courts, puts all the endowments under state control, and intensifies the integration of al-Azhar (the religious establishment sanctioned by the state) into the state apparatus.

January 1963: The Shah of Iran launches his White Revolution, including some significant initiatives such as land reform, the enfranchisement of women, a literacy corps, and profit-sharing schemes.

June 1963: A number of large-scale riots break out in Tehran and other cities. Ayatollah Khomeini emerges as a religious opposition leader and is sent into exile in Iraq.

1967: Israel defeats Egypt in the Six-Day War; Nasser offers to resign, but responds to popular demand to remain in office and retains power until his death in 1970.

1970: President Anwar Sadat takes over after Nasser's death. The government undertakes a new program of *infitāh*, or "open door policy," in economic and political domains.

1960s–1970s: In Iran, an increase in oil income supports economic development and social change. The new middle class and the industrial working class expand; youths become more modern and women more visible and active in public. The old classes—feudal, traditional petite bourgeoisie, and clerical—shrink or feel threatened. The Shah's regime remains strong and autocratic.

1970s: Egypt's Islamic militant groups mushroom under President Sadat, who wishes to undermine the Nasserists and Communists. Among these groups, al-Jama'a al-Islamiyya evolves from an activist student group to become an Islamist political organization throughout 1980s.

1978: Gradually, rallies for political reform in Iran escalate into massive street demonstrations, industrial strikes, and street clashes and lead to a revolutionary movement led by Ayatollah Khomeini to depose the Shah.

1979: Sadat signs the Camp David agreement with Israel, causing a furor in the Arab world, as well as among Iranian revolutionaries.

January 16, 1979: The Shah is forced to leave Iran, and Khomeini returns from exile in Paris a month later.

February 11, 1979: The Shah's regime is overthrown; jubilant armed youths take control of the streets.

February–March 1979: Nationalities in Iran demand autonomy; women demonstrate for democratic rights. The unemployed are mobilized. Homes, hotels, and urban lands are occupied by squatters.

November 4, 1979: The U.S. embassy in Tehran is seized and hostages are taken; the hostage crisis brings down the government of Prime Minister Mehdi Bazargan.

December 23, 1979: Following a referendum, Iran's Islamic Constitution is ratified.

January 25, 1980: Abul-Hasan Bani-Sadr is elected as Iran's first president. A "cultural revolution" begins to Islamize education, cultural institutions, and industrial workplaces.

September 22, 1980: Iraqi forces invade Iran. An eight-year war begins.

June 1981: Bani-Sadr is dismissed as both commander-in-chief and president following an escalating factional struggle. The Mujahidin-i Khalq declare an armed struggle against the Islamic regime. A guerrilla war begins.

September 1981: President Anwar Sadat is assassinated by the Islamist Jihad Organization. Scores of militant Islamists are taken into custody, among them Ayman al-Zawahiri who, following his release in 1984, moves to Afghanistan.

October 13, 1981: Khamanei is sworn in as the new president and Husayn Musavi as prime minister following the assassination of President Raja'i, the prime minister, and several other leaders in a Mujahidin-i Khalq bombing. A reign of repression begins in Iran, leading to suppression of almost all secular opposition groups in the following few years.

October 1986: The "Irangate" political scandal begins to surface in the United States.

June 1987: The Mujahidin-i Khalq declare the formation of the National Liberation Army in Iraq to fight against the Islamic Republic

July 1988: Iran agrees to end the war.

June 4, 1989: Ayatollah Khomeini dies; a period of "postwar reconstruction" begins under new President Rafsanjani.

1990s: Postwar reconstruction includes progress in economic areas and some openness in international relations. Significant social changes take place in education, the women's movement, youth activism, intellectual activities, publishing, culture, urban development, and the modernization of rural areas.

1992: Ansar-i Hizbullah is established to counter Rafsanjani's "cultural openness" and economic liberalism.

November 1992: Fourteen thousand security forces move into the Cairo slum of Imbaba to "cleanse" the area of the Jama'a militants who had established an "Islamic republic" in the heart of Cairo.

Early 1990s: Egypt's Islamism reaches its peak. It is expressed in the expansion of the Society of Muslim Brothers and al-Jama'a al-Islamiyya; an increase in the number of *ahli* (private) mosques, Islamic nongovernmental organizations (NGOs), syndicates, commodities, and publications, as well as Islamic fashion and language.

1993: Confrontations between militant Islamists and the Egyptian government leave more than 1,000 people dead and thousands others injured.

1995: The Egyptian government begins to put heavy pressure on the Muslim Brotherhood (MB) while intensifying its resolve to annihilate the militant Islamists. MB activists are arrested. The government is determined to control the "Islamic sector" in Egypt.

November 18, 1997: In Luxor, Egypt, al-Jama'a insurgents brutally murder and decapitate fifty-eight Western tourists and four Egyptians in the Temple of Hatshepsut.

March 1999: Al-Jama'a militants declare a unilateral end to armed struggle. Renouncing violence, they opt to establish political parties within Egypt's legal framework.

Late 1990s: A general decline in Egypt's organized Islamism coincides with a rise in active individualized piety among various segments of the population. Meanwhile social and class cleavages grow. The Egyptian state becomes more religious. Stagnation in religious thought and intellectual production characterizes the period.

May 23, 1997: Khatami is elected president of Iran on the promise of comprehensive political reform. A new optimism and political climate ensue.

1997–2001: In Iran, a period of widespread social mobilization among youth, women, and intellectuals takes root in both the cities and the provinces. Diplomatic relations with the Arab world and Europe improve markedly. In the meantime, intense factional struggles between the "reformists" and "conservatives" characterize Iran's internal politics.

July 1999: Paramilitary vigilantes storm a Tehran University dormitory, causing violence and destruction. A three-day national student uprising follows.

January 2000: Reformists take control of the Iranian Parliament after a landslide electoral victory.

Early 2000: Egyptian television preacher 'Amr Khalid rises to stardom in Egypt and beyond, attracting scores of well-to-do women and young people to his lectures; weekly gatherings of women (halaqāt) expand.

April 2000: The participation of several Iranian reformist intellectuals in a Berlin conference leads to a wave of persecution and to the closure of reformist publications by the conservative judiciary.

2001: The United States invades Afghanistan following the September 11 terrorist attacks.

June 8, 2001: Khatami is elected president of Iran for the second time.

2002: A poll shows that over 74 percent of Iranians favor ending hostilities with the United States. Pollsters are arrested.

October 2002: President Khatami introduces "twin bills" to the Parliament attempting to empower the president and limit the power of the Council of Guardians.

March 2003: British and American forces invade Iraq. The reformists in Iran lose in city council elections.

2002–2004: A new wave and style of "street politics" develops in Egypt following the Israeli incursions into Palestinian territories and the British and American invasion of Iraq.

June 2003: The Council of Guardians rejects Khatami's "twin bills."

January 2004: The Council of Guardians disqualifies about half of the candidates (mostly reformists) in the parliamentary elections. A massive political row takes over the country.

February 1, 2004: Members of the Parliament in Iran, mostly reformists, collectively resign. Parliament falls back to the conservatives.

2004: Egypt experiences a "new dawn" following the emergence of a nascent democracy movement. A new constitutional amendment allows for multicandidate presidential elections. The push for democratic reform continues.

June 2005: Reformists in Iran lose the presidency; a hardline conservative, Mahmud Ahmadinejad, comes to power, hoping to turn back the tide of social and political change in the Islamic Republic.

September 2005: Hosni Mubarak is elected to a fifth consecutive term as president of Egypt. Political reform stagnates.

PREFACE

THIS BOOK IS A MODEST RESPONSE to a great anxiety of our time—the global march of "Muslim rage." It examines the contemporary struggles within and on behalf of Islam by exploring the relationship between religion and societal trends and movements. As a point of departure, I interrogate the infamous question of "whether Islam is compatible with democracy" by demonstrating that the realization of democratic ideals in Muslim societies has less to do with the "essence" of Islam than with the intellectual conviction and political capacity of Muslims. For it is individuals, groups, and movements who give meaning to "sacred" injunctions; the disposition of a faith, whether tolerant or repressive, democratic or authoritarian, is determined primarily by the attributes of the faithful. The question of democratic polity is then one of political struggle rather than religious scripture, even though religion is often deployed to legitimize or to resist political domination.

Focusing on the Muslim Middle East, the book explores the struggles of multiple movements, movements that construe religion to unleash social and political change, to legitimize authoritarian rule, or, in contrast, to construct an inclusive faith that embraces democratic polity. By contrasting histories of religious politics in Iran and Egypt over the past three decades, my goal is to demonstrate in detail how and under what conditions specific societal movements may, or may not, be able to render Islam to embrace a democratic ethos.

In 1979, Iran experienced the first "Islamic revolution" in modern times, spearheading a global movement currently described as the "age of Islam."

Yet it is also an Islamic republic entangled in a profound identity crisis and has been struggling to transcend its legacy in a bid for a "post-Islamist" order. Egypt, on the other hand, has been home not to an Islamic revolution, but to the oldest Islamic social movement in the Muslim world, one that, since the 1980s, has left an enduring imprint on society, polity, culture, and international relations. I examine these processes within the historical period between the late 1970s, when new Islamist movements rapidly proliferated, and 2005, when Iran's reformists lost the Parliament and the presidency to the conservative Islamists and when Egypt's "reform initiative" from above seemed to stagnate while a nascent democracy movement heralded a new turn in Egypt's political and religious landscape.

I have written this book with an odd sense of obligation to narrate the tale of two lands where I grew up, lived, and have worked, and whose cultures and peoples I deeply internalized. I was born in and studied in Iran through my early adult life in the late 1970s. As the revolution unfolded, I, like so many others, became deeply involved, not as an observer but primarily as a participant. The revolution had become an all-embracing obsession, the subject of unending discussions, arguments, and anguish; a source of profound happiness and enduring despair. In the turbulent years of the early 1980s, almost every Iranian was a participant, either for or against or somewhere in between. Few took the time to reflect, to place the events in scholarly perspective. It is not surprising, then, how few memoirs, diaries, or even simple descriptions of intimate moments, events, and moods are available from those early revolutionary years, other than some that have appeared very recently in the West. It is as though everyone was there to change things, with little time to interpret them. It wasn't until the 1990s that I consciously decided to merely observe— to record, narrate, and analyze rather than participate. Consequently when the dramatic social and discursive change of Iran's postwar years culminated in the reform government of 1997, I knew I wanted to write this book.

During the years when I followed Iran's postrevolutionary developments with great passion, I happened to reside in Egypt, a land of remarkable people, culture, and history, where I had moved in the late 1980s. My initial two-year appointment at the American University in Cairo entailed a long-term and profoundly rich experience of living, working and researching in contemporary Egypt, while traveling between Cairo and Tehran. Egypt, notwithstanding its enormous problems of poverty and pollution, captivated me. Like Iran, it became part of my intellectual and political conscience. Happy for its achievements and worried by its misfortunes, I could not help caring about it. Thus what follows is more than a benign scholarly treatment. It reflects an intense association with these lands and their people. In writing this book, I have not forsaken my scholarly voice, but traces of sentiment—admiration as well as irritation—have been unavoidable.

As a social scientist, I favor scholarship that not only produces nuance as well as intimate and empirical knowledge about the geographical areas of our inquiry, but also contributes to the central domain of our profession, social theory. At the same time, I have taken seriously the observations of colleagues that many of us scholars "are accustomed to writing to one another" rather than to the general public. So, reacting to a great "anxiety of our time," I have tried to write in an idiom and a style that is accessible to educated lay readers and to the public at large. I do hope, however, that this book also says something worthwhile to professional colleagues, members of scholarly communities, and policy makers.

This book is a historical sociological text grounded in a *broad* comparative vision. I use comparison not for its own sake, but as a methodological enterprise necessary to address specific analytical questions. The logic of comparison follows the imperative of responding to our central research inquiry, which in turn determines which aspects of the comparable cases need or need not be considered. Because a tight, detailed, and integrated comparison would upset the integrity and flow of historical narratives and deprive the reader of the historical flow in each country, I have refrained from pairing every aspect of the countries under study in a detailed fashion. A more integrated comparison was possible for Chapter Two, but not for the subsequent three chapters, whose history has been written in much greater detail. In short, my aim is to examine Islamism and post-Islamism in Iran and Egypt within a broad comparative framework as a means of addressing the central questions of this book, while also maintaining the integrity and flow of the historical accounts unique to each experience. Tackling the relationship between Islam and democracy both demands and offers an opportunity to narrate histories of social movements and Islam in Iran and Egypt over the past three decades.

.   .   .

Over the many years spent working on this book, I have gained significantly from the intellectual assistance and practical guidance of so many friends, colleagues, students, and institutions that I regretfully cannot acknowledge them all within the limits of these pages. Yet I must mention some. I am grateful to my colleagues and to staff members in the Department of Sociology and Anthropology at the American University in Cairo (AUC) for providing a congenial work environment in which to conduct my research in Egypt, Iran, and neighboring countries. It was at AUC that I grew and matured in my professional life over some sixteen years. I hope that I also made some contribution to this institution and to Egypt at large. Numerous students and research assistants were a source of inspiration and knowledge. They are too many to name individually, but I wish to record my appreciation of their friendship and kindness.

Inspiration did not come only from within academia, but especially from outside, in the complex and colorful Egyptian society. Without the trust and intellectual exchange provided by numerous Egyptian NGOs, Islamists, women's groups, youth centers, and ordinary people in poor neighborhoods, this book could not have taken its present shape. I extend this acknowledgment equally to similar institutions and constituencies in Iran—colleges, neighborhoods, libraries, civil society institutions, researchers, young persons, and especially ordinary Iranians. I am thankful to them all.

I wrote much of the manuscript during a year at the Middle East Center of Oxford University's St. Antony's College. In addition, the University of California, Berkeley, has generously offered working space during summer terms. I wish to extend my gratitude to friends and colleagues Professors Sami Zubaida, Khaled Fahmi, Shahnaz Rouse, and Richard Bulliet, as well as to the anonymous reviewers for Stanford University Press who read the manuscript and provided very constructive comments. I owe a great deal to Kaveh Ehsani, an astute observer of contemporary Iran, for his critical reading and informed comments. Mohamed Waked, Annelies Moors, Joe Stork, Kamran Ali, Dennis Janssen, Shahrzad Mojab, Eric Denis, and Lee Gillette helped in different ways, by reading, lending, and editing. I thank them all. My new appointment has landed me in the Netherlands, at the International Institute for the Study of Islam in the Modern World (ISIM) and Leiden University. It was in Leiden that the book eventually came to a conclusion; I thank all my ISIM colleagues and the staff for their enthusiasm and support. I am grateful to the journal *Comparative Studies in Society and History* for allowing me to reprint "Revolution without Movement, Movement without Revolution" here; it appeared in that journal under the same title (vol. 40, no. 1 (1998): 136–69). In addition, a significant part of the section "Post-Islamist Women's Movement," in Chapter Three, draws on my article "A Women's Non-Movement: What It Means to Be a Woman Activist in an Islamic State," published in *Comparative Studies of South Asia, Africa and the Middle East,* vol. 27, no. 1 (2007).

Kate Wahl, my editor, and Judith Hibbard, the production editor at Stanford University Press, exhibited unusual efficiency and professionalism in bringing this book to publication; the series editors, Joel Beinin and Juan Cole, were extremely helpful and enthusiastic. All translations from Arabic and Persian are mine. Finally, I owe Linda, Shiva, and Tara my greatest debt for their life-long affection, patience, and camaraderie. I hope they know that I am truly grateful.

Making Islam Democratic

1 ISLAM AND DEMOCRACY
The Perverse Charm of an Irrelevant Question

A MAJOR PREOCCUPATION of nineteenth-century social theorists was to dispel the distinction between the religious and the *non*religious. Now, after over a century of modernization, we are compelled to differentiate between the religious and the *more* religious. This "over-religiosity," couched in various terms as fundamentalism, revivalism, conservatism, fanaticism, or extremism, appears to represent a global trend that involves most of the world's major religions. Yet it has shaped a particular negative thinking about Muslim societies in particular.

Undoubtedly, the terrorist attacks in the United States on September 11, 2001, and the subsequent developments have greatly intensified Western anxiety over the "threat" of "Islamic fundamentalism" and have reinforced more than ever the notion of the "peculiarity of Muslims." Of course, the notion of "unique" Muslims is not new; it has been the hallmark of the "Orientalist" outlook that Edward Said and others have so remarkably and critically taken up.[1] For Said and other critics, Orientalism represented a discursive apparatus that produced knowledge as an instrument of power, as a means to maintain domination. It is the story of how a host of travelers, novelists, artists, diplomats, scholars, and now the media depict the Muslim Middle East as a monolithic, fundamentally static, and therefore "peculiar" entity. By emphasizing the exceptionality of Muslim societies in general, they focus on the narrow notion of a static culture and religion as the context of historical continuity and on individual elites or external forces as the source of change. Consequently, group interests, social movements, and political economies as internal sources of change are largely overlooked.

But how "peculiar" are Muslim societies, if they are at all? Are they so different as to require different analytical tools? Can we speak of such a thing as "Muslim societies" at all? By employing such a broad category are we not in a sense "re-Orientalizing" Muslim societies and cultures, constructing homogeneous entities where they do not exist? Does the category "Muslim societies" not imply religion as the defining characteristic of these cultures? Would this category not exclude and "otherise" the nonreligious and the non-Muslim from citizenship in nations with a Muslim majority? While such questions address legitimate concerns, I believe nevertheless that "Muslim societies" can serve as a useful analytical category.

I have proposed elsewhere that the terms "Islamic world" and "Islamic society," used in *singular abstract* forms, may indeed imply that Islam is the central factor that shapes the dynamics of these societies.[2] "Islamic society" becomes a generality constructed by others to describe Muslims and their cultures. It tells how others imagine what Muslims are and even how they should be. This worldview has been perpetuated in part by some Muslim groups (mainly Islamists) who themselves construct a unitary Islamic landscape. In contrast, the designation "Muslim societies," understood as *plural* and *concrete* entities, allows a self-conscious Muslim majority to define their own reality in an inevitably contested, differentiated, and dynamic fashion. Here the emphasis is not on Islam but on Muslims as agents of their societies and cultures, even if not of their own making. And "culture" is perceived not as static codes and conducts but as processes that are flexible, always changing, and contested. These are the societies in which aspects of Islam, interpreted and adopted in diverse ways, have influenced some domains of private and public life—including the realms of morality, family relations, gender dynamics, law, and sometimes (but not always) politics and the state. What is common to this differentiated whole is the claim of all Muslims (liberal or conservative, activist or layman) to "true" Islam, to the sacred texts.

Yet in reality "Muslim societies" are never monolithic and never religious by definition; nor are their cultures confined to religion alone. Indeed, national cultures, historical experiences, political trajectories, and the element of class have often produced distinct cultures and subcultures of Islam, as well as different religious perceptions and practices. In this sense, each "Muslim" (majority) country comprises an ensemble of people with varying degrees of religious affiliation: political Islamists, the actively pious, the ordinarily religious, and secular or non-Muslim minorities. Degrees of religious affiliation among these groups can even change at different historical junctures. In this sense, Muslim societies resemble their counterparts in the developing world. Similarities are particularly compounded by the relentless process of globalization, which tends to produce not only differentiation, but also parallel structures and processes between the nations of the globe and without regard to religion.

Despite structural similarities, the Muslim Middle East (and by extension the Muslim world) is still measured by the "exceptionalist" yardstick of which religio-centrism is the core. Thus the region's authoritarian regimes, "weak civil societies," or political cultures are often attributed to its main religion, Islam. Although "exceptionalism" is not limited to the Muslim Middle East—we have also "American exceptionalism," "European exceptionalism," and the "peculiarity of the English," as E. P. Thompson called it—it has often led to the marginalization of this region from mainstream scholarly perspectives.

At least three factors have contributed to the "exceptionalist" streak in the perception of the Muslim Middle East. The first is the continuing prevalence of Orientalist thought in the West, particularly in the United States, which seems to converge well with interventionist foreign policy objectives in the Middle East. The second is the persistence of authoritarian rule by local regimes (for example, the Shah's Iran, Saddam's Iraq, Saudi Arabia, Jordan, and Egypt) that have often been supported by Western states, especially the United States. The third factor has to do with the regional emergence and expansion of socially conservative and undemocratic Islamist movements. These positions and processes have given rise to countless claims and counterclaims that revolve around the infamous question of whether Islam is compatible with democracy—the question to which this book is devoted.

ISLAM, DEMOCRACY, AND SOCIAL MOVEMENTS

Prevailing media and intellectual circles in the West view Islam as being at the root of authoritarian polity in the Muslim Middle East. To them Islam is patriarchal and lacks any concept of citizenship and freedom, since its belief in God's sovereignty has diminished popular power.[3] The religion of Muhammad, instead of being a private matter, is essentially political. Islam embodies, it is often claimed, a "world in which human life doesn't have the same value as it does in the West, in which freedom, democracy, openness and creativity are alien."[4] Such views have been energized by many home-grown Islamists who, in the name of their religion, suspect democracy as a "foreign construct" and suspend popular will in favor of God's sovereignty (see Chapters Four and Five). In contrast to advocates of this "incompatibility thesis," others tend to present an *inherently* democratic spirit of Islam and claim it as a religion of tolerance, pluralism, justice, and human rights.[5] "Islamic rule is by nature democratic," according to Rashed al-Ghannoushi.[6] The Qur'anic notion of *shura* (consultation), in this perspective, ensures the compatibility of Islamic doctrine with democracy, and its valuation of human beings by degree of piety implies equality in race and gender and free will. The God-given sovereignty of the *umma* (community of Muslim believers) underlies democratic governance based upon pluralism, difference, and human rights.[7]

In their methodological approach, both "skeptics" and "apologists" share an exclusive commitment to texts, drawing their arguments from the literal reading of sacred scriptures (the Qur'an and *hadīth*), and pay astonishingly little attention to what these texts mean to the fragmented Muslim citizenry in their day-to-day lives. What is more, rarely is there discussion of how these meanings change over time.

A central argument of this book is that sacred injunctions are matters of struggle, of competing readings. They are, in other words, matters of history; humans define their truth. The individuals and groups who hold social power can assert and hegemonize their truths. Historical narratives in this book demonstrate how societal forces, notably social movements, play a decisive role in changing and shaping the "truth" of holy scriptures. The plurality of various theological genres—liberation theology, feminist theology, "queer theology," and, I would add, "republican theology"—reveals how different social groups (the poor, women, homosexuals, the religiously oppressed) define their religious meanings by and large according to their social existence.

Is Islam, then, compatible with democracy (assuming that "democracy" is free of ambiguity, which it is not)?[8] My contention is that this is the wrong question to pose in the first place. The question is not whether Islam is or is not compatible with democracy or, by extension, modernity, but rather under what conditions Muslims can *make* them compatible. Nothing intrinsic to Islam—or, for that matter, to any other religion—makes it *inherently* democratic or undemocratic. *We*, the social agents, determine the inclusive or authoritarian thrust of religions because, from this perspective, religion is nothing but a body of beliefs and ideas that invariably make claims to authentic meaning and a "higher truth." Regardless of whether religious beliefs and experiences relate to supernatural reality, in the end, according to James Beckford, "religion is expressed by means of human ideas, symbols, feelings, practices, and organizations."[9] In a sense, religious injunctions are nothing but our understanding of them; they are what we make them to be.[10]

Some fifty years ago many social scientists believed that Christianity and democracy were incompatible.[11] But today the most deep-rooted democracies are in the Christian heartland, even though fascism also emerged, and was associated with the church, in the heartland of Christianity. Indeed, authoritarian and exclusivist ideologies coupled with Christianity have not been uncommon. Early Christian sects promoted loyalty to authoritarian rulers, so long as they were not atheists and did not harm the believers. Obedience was at the heart of Christian political thought, based on the belief that higher powers were ordained by God. "Those who sit in the office of magistrate sit in the place of God, and their judgment is as if God judged from heaven," Martin Luther proclaimed. "If the emperor calls me, God calls me."[12] Indeed, early Christian accommodation of authoritarian power led to a tragic anti-Semitism enshrined by biblical interpretation of the Crucifixion for which the Jews, not the Romans, were claimed to be responsible.[13] Even today, some staunch Christians proclaim democracy is the "cause of all world problems" because, as the invention of Satan, it rules not by God's will but by the will of "sinful humans" who demand "abortion laws, anti–death penalty laws, gay rights," and the like.[14] This might represent the voice of Christian extremists or "outlaws," but in September 2000 the Vatican itself lashed out at the idea of "religious pluralism," pronouncing non-Christian creeds as flawed and "defective" and their believers as being in a "gravely deficient situation."[15]

Despite this history, today few lay Christians would probably read the Bible in the authoritarian terms of Luther and "Christian outlaws" or treat their creed as exclusively as the Vatican. In other words, *we*, as social forces, render a religion inclusive or exclusive, monovocal or pluralist, and democratic or authoritarian.[16] Resorting to mere literal readings of scripture to determine the democratic thrust of a religion will not take us very far, not only because ambiguity, multiple meanings, and disagreement are embedded in many religious scriptures (as the scholars Nasr Abu Zayd and Khalid Mas'ud have shown in the Qur'an and *hadīth*), but because individuals and groups with diverse interests and orientations may find their own, often conflicting, truths in the very same scriptures.[17] Rather than resorting to the Qur'an or Shari'a to make sense of Osama bin Laden, or of Islamist radicalism in general, we need to examine the conditions that allow social forces to make a particular reading of the sacred texts hegemonic. And this is closely linked to groups' capacity to mobilize consensus around their "truth." Mere reference to scriptures may not serve as a useful analytical tool, but it is at the core of the political battle to hegemonize discourses. Stating that "Islamic rule is by nature democratic" might be naïve analytically, but it is an expression of the struggle to *make* Islamic rule democratic. At any rate, efforts to make a religion democratic undoubtedly begin at the intellectual level. The challenge is to give democratic interpretations material power, to fuse them with popular consciousness.

Foucault's emphasis on the power of words, the power of discourse, is well known and instructive. Yet we can also dispute Foucault's unqualified claims by arguing that power lies not simply in words or in the "inner truth" expressed in words, but primarily in those who utter them, those who give truth and thus power to those words. In other words, discourse is *not* power unless it is given material force. Perhaps we should look not simply for what the discourse is, but more specifically for where the power lies. The idea of, say, "Islam being compatible with democracy," carries different weight depending on who expresses it. It is not enough to utter "right" ideas; those ideas must be given material force by mobilizing consensus around them. This inevitably leads us into the realm of social movement theory and practice, which, I suggest, mediates between discourse and power, between the word and the world. The compatibility or incompatibility of Islam and democracy is not a matter of philosophical speculation but of political struggle. It is not as much a matter of texts as it is a balance of power between those who want a democratic religion and those who pursue an authoritarian version. *Islamism* and *post-Islamism* tell the story of these two social forces.

ISLAMISM: MOVEMENT AND WORLDVIEW

In its high degree of generality, Islamism emerged as the language of self-assertion to mobilize those (largely middle-class high achievers) who felt marginalized by the dominant economic, political, or cultural processes in their societies, those for whom the perceived failure of both capitalist modernity and socialist utopia made the language of morality, through religion, a substitute for politics. In a sense, it was the Muslim middle-class way of saying no to what they considered their excluders—their national elites, secular governments, and those governments' Western allies. They rebuffed "Western cultural domination," its political rationale, moral sensibilities, and norma- tive symbols, even though they shared many of its features—neckties, food, education, and technologies. In contrast, those who enjoyed and prospered under the modern socioeconomic and cultural conditions of globalization, if they were not secular, adhered to a different kind of Islam, the so-called moderate Islam, or more precisely, "passive piety."

In a quest to operate within an "authentic" nativist ideology, Islamists tried to articulate a version of Islam that could respond to their political, eco- nomic, and cultural deficits. Thus Islamism imagined Islam as a complete divine system with a superior political model, cultural code, legal structure, and economic arrangement—in short, a system that responded to all human problems. More important, this Islam offered Muslims a sense of self-respect, self-confidence, and a wide-ranging autonomy. Accompanied by strong popu- list language and heavy-handed social control, this interpretation of Islam would inevitably marginalize and even criminalize those who remained out- side its strictures: nonconformists, seculars, non-Islamist Muslims, religious minorities, and many women. At the core of the Islamist paradigm, then, lay a blend of piety and obligation, devotion and duty.

Contemporary Islamism, as a movement and discourse, has grown since the 1970s against the backdrop of cold war politics and is clearly a histori- cal phenomenon. Two simultaneous but contradictory processes pushed Is- lamism toward its hegemonic position: opportunity and suppression. The opportunity for massive educational expansion, economic development, an abundance of wealth (oil money), and social mobility went hand in hand with continuous political repression, marginalization, a sense of humilia- tion, and growing inequality (see Chapter Two). In the 1950s, ten universities existed in the entire Arab world; by 2003 that number had increased to over 200.[18] The crucial point is that members of this now widely educated but still marginalized middle class became acutely aware of their marginalization, experiencing a strong "moral outrage" that they directed at their own elites and governments, which had allied with Western powers, particularly the United States, the very government that had, ironically, favored Islamic op- position as a bulwark against both communism and secular nationalism. In the Arab world, the political classes considered the long-standing U.S.-backed Israeli occupation of Palestinian lands as evidence of their subjugation at the global level. Intransigent Israeli occupation (in particular under the rightist Likud governments) assumed such a central place in Arab/Muslim popular sentiment that the people's struggle to regain "dignity" by freeing Arab lands often overshadowed their quest for democracy. In other words, freedom from foreign domination took precedence over freedom at home.[19]

Induced by Islamist populist language, some observers tend to associate Middle Eastern Islamist movements with Latin American liberation theology. Although religion frames each movement, they have little else in common. Liberation theology began as an attempt to reform the church from within and evolved into a social movement in which the concerns of the dispossessed assumed a central place. Liberation theology aimed at transforming the oligarchic disposition of the Catholic church and its neglect of the poor, in conditions where socialist movements (notably the Cuban revolution), by raising the banner of social justice, had pushed the church to the brink of social irrelevance. Led by socially conscious theologians, liberation theology's strategic objective was the "liberation of the poor"; its interpretation of the Gospels followed from this strategic ambition.[20]

In contrast, Islamism, despite its variation, has had broader social and political objectives. Its primary concern has not been social development or the plight of the poor but rather building an "ideological community"—establishing an Islamic state or implementing Islamic laws and moral codes. Only then could the poor expect to profit from a kind of Islamic moral trickle-down effect. In short, Middle Eastern Islamist movements and Latin American liberation theology represent two quite different social and political trajectories. If anything, Islamist movements, especially radical Islamism, resemble the Latin American guerrilla movements of the 1960s and 1970s—not, of course, in their ideologies, but in the social profile of their adherents and the conditions under which they emerged. The rise of both movements can be traced to simultaneous conditions of social transformation (rapid urbanization, mass schooling, higher education, and an expectation of mobility) and social exclusion of those whose dream of economic mobility had been dashed by unjust social and political structures. Of course, different global and regional contexts gave each movement its own ideological framework: secular leftism in the case of Latin American guerrilla movements and radical religion among Middle Eastern Islamist movements.

In the Muslim Middle East, the political class par excellence remains the educated middle layers: state employees, students, professionals, and the intelligentsia who mobilized the "street" in the 1950s and 1960s with overarching ideologies of nationalism, Ba'athism, socialism, and social justice. Islamism is the latest of these grand worldviews. With core support from the worse-off middle layers, Islamist movements have succeeded for three decades in activating large numbers among the disenchanted population through *cheap Islamization*: by resorting to the language of moral and cultural purity (e.g., calling for the banning of alcohol or "immoral" literature, or raising the issue of women's public appearance), appealing to identity politics, and carrying out affordable charity work. However, by the mid-1990s it became clear that Islamists could not go very far when it came to a more costly Islamization: establishing an Islamic polity and economy and conducting international relations compatible with the modern national and global citizenry. Consequently, Islamist rule faced profound crisis wherever it was put into practice (as in Iran, Sudan, and Pakistan). At the same time, violent strategies and armed struggles adopted by radical Islamists (in Egypt and Algeria, for example) failed to achieve much. Islamist movements were either repressed by authoritarian states or compelled to revise their earlier outlooks. Many departed from totalizing discourses or violent methods and began to develop a more democratic vision for their Islamic projects.

These changes did not terminate the political role of Islam. Global and domestic social and political conditions have continued to generate appeals for religious and moral politics, especially in nations that had not experienced Islamism. Anti-Islamic sentiment in the West after the September 11 terrorist attacks, and the subsequent "war on terrorism," reinforced a profound feeling of insecurity and outrage among Muslims who sensed that Islam and Muslims were under an intense onslaught. This increased the appeal of religiosity and nativism, and Islamic parties that expressed opposition to U.S. policy in Afghanistan scored considerable success in several national elections in 2002. The Justice and Development Party in Morocco doubled its share to forty-two seats in the September 2002 elections. In October 2002, the Islamist movement placed third in Algerian local elections, and the alliance of religious parties in Pakistan won fifty-three of the 150 parliamentary seats. In November, Islamists won nineteen of the forty parliamentary seats in Bahrain, and the Turkish Justice and Development Party captured 66 percent of the legislature.[21] However, these electoral victories pointed less to a revival of Islamism (understood as a political project with national concerns) than to a shift from political Islam to fragmented languages concerned with personal piety and a global, anti-Islamic menace. Indeed, many Muslim societies were on the brink of a *post-Islamist* turn.

WHAT IS POST-ISLAMISM?

The term *post-Islamism* has a relatively short history. In 1996, I proposed in a short essay the "coming of a *post-Islamist* society"[22] where I characterized the articulation of the remarkable social trends, political perspectives, and religious thought that post-Khomeini Iran had begun to witness—trends that eventually coalesced into the "reform movement" of the late 1990s. My tentative essay dealt only with societal trends, for there was little at the governmental level that I could consider post-Islamist. Indeed as originally used, post-Islamism pertained only to the realities of the Islamic Republic of Iran, and not to other settings and societies. Yet the core spirit of the term referred to the metamorphosis of Islamism (in ideas, approaches, and practices) from within and without.

Since then, a number of observers in Europe have deployed the term, often descriptively, to refer primarily to what they see as a broad shift in attitudes and strategies of Islamist militants in the Muslim world.[23] Given the different ways it has been used by individual authors, the term seems to have confused more than it has clarified. For some, such as Gilles Kepel, "post-Islamism" describes the departure of Islamists from *jihādi* and *salafi* (conservative and scripturist) doctrines, while others, such as Olivier Roy, perceive it as a "privatization" of Islamization (as opposed to the Islamization of the state) where emphasis is placed on how and where Islamization takes place rather than on its content. Others tend to employ the term without defining it. Yet it has usually been presented and perceived primarily as an empirical rather than analytical category, representing a particular era or a historical end.

The term's poor conceptualization and misperception have attracted some unwelcome reactions. Critics have correctly disputed generalizations about the end of Islamism (understood mainly in terms of the establishment of an Islamic state) as premature, though they acknowledge a significant shift in the strategy and outlook of some militant Islamist groups.[24] What seems to be changing, critics argue, is not political Islam (doing politics within an Islamic frame), but only a particular revolutionary version of it.[25] "Post-Islamism," others have argued, signifies not a distinct reality but simply one variant of Islamist politics.[26]

In my formulation, post-Islamism represents both a *condition* and a *project*, which may be embodied in a master (or multidimensional) movement. In the first place, it refers to political and social conditions where, following a phase of experimentation, the appeal, energy, and sources of legitimacy of

Islamism are exhausted, even among its once-ardent supporters. Islamists become aware of their system's anomalies and inadequacies as they attempt to normalize and institutionalize their rule. Continuous trial and error makes the system susceptible to questions and criticisms. Eventually, pragmatic attempts to maintain the system reinforce abandoning its underlying principles. Islamism becomes compelled, both by its own internal contradictions and by societal pressure, to reinvent itself, but it does so at the cost of a qualitative shift. The tremendous transformation in religious and political discourse in Iran during the 1990s exemplifies this tendency.

Not only a condition, post-Islamism is also a project, a conscious attempt to conceptualize and strategize the rationale and modalities of transcending Islamism in social, political, and intellectual domains. Yet Post-Islamism is neither anti-Islamic nor un-Islamic nor secular. Rather it represents an endeavor to fuse religiosity and rights, faith and freedom, Islam and liberty. It is an attempt to turn the underlying principles of Islamism on its head by emphasizing rights instead of duties, plurality in place of singular authoritative voice, historicity rather than fixed scripture, and the future instead of the past. It strives to marry Islam with individual choice and freedom, with democracy and modernity (something post-Islamists stress), to achieve what some scholars have termed an "alternative modernity." Post-Islamism is expressed in acknowledging secular exigencies, in freedom from rigidity, in breaking down the monopoly of religious truth. In short, whereas Islamism is defined by the fusion of religion and responsibility, post-Islamism emphasizes religiosity and rights.

Whether or not Islam corresponds to democratic ideals depends primarily on whether proponents of the above perspectives are able to establish their political hegemony in society and the state. The history of socioreligious movements in Iran and Egypt since the 1970s offers a fitting ground to examine the logic, conditions, and forces behind the politics of making Islam democratic or undemocratic. In Iran, the 1979 revolution and establishment of an Islamic state set conditions for the rise of opposition movements that aimed to transcend Islamism in society and governance. The end of the war with Iraq (1988), the death of Ayatollah Khomeini (1989), and the program of postwar reconstruction under President Rafsanjani marked a turning point toward post-Islamism. It expressed itself in various social practices and ideas, including urban management, feminist practice, theological perspective, and social and intellectual trends and movements. Youths, students, women, and religious intellectuals, as well many state employees, among others, called for democracy, individual rights, tolerance, and gender equality, but they refused to throw away religious sensibilities altogether. Thus daily resistance and struggle by ordinary people compelled religious thinkers, spiritual elites, and political actors to undertake a crucial paradigmatic shift. Scores of old Islamist revolutionaries renounced their earlier ideas and warned of the dangers of a religious state to both religion and the state. Adversaries from both without and within the Islamic state called for its secularization but stressed maintaining religious ethics in society.

Egypt, however, followed a different course. Instead of an Islamic revolution, there developed a pervasive Islamic social movement with a conservative moral vision, populist language, patriarchal disposition, and adherence to scripture. By the early 1990s, through *da'wa* and associational work, the movement had captured a large segment of the civil society moving to claim space in state institutions. Although it failed to dislodge Egypt's secular regime, the movement left an enduring mark on both society and the state. Engulfed by the pervasive "Islamic mode," major actors in Egyptian society, including the intelligentsia, the new rich, al-Azhar (the institution of establishment Islam), and ruling elites, converged around a language of nativism and conservative moral ethos, thus severely marginalizing critical voices, innovative religious thought, and demands for democratic reform. In the end, threatened by expanding Islamism, the authoritarian state appropriated aspects of conservative religiosity and nationalist sentiment (generated by the continuing Arab-Israeli conflict) to configure Egypt's "passive revolution." This Islamic passive revolution represented a managed Islamic restoration in which the state, the real target of change, succeeded in remaining fully in charge. Even though a nascent democracy movement (Kifaya) in 2005 pointed to some change in the political climate, political structure remained authoritarian, religious thought stagnant and exclusive, and political class nativist. Little in Egypt resembled Iran's post-Islamist trajectory.

Is post-Islamism an exclusively Iranian phenomenon? While the Islamic revolution bolstered similar movements in other Muslim countries during the 1980s, Iran's post-Islamist experience has likewise contributed to an ideological shift among some Islamist movements (as in the Tunisian al-Da'wa Islamic Party led by Rashed al-Ghannoushi).[27] Nevertheless, since the early 1990s, internal dynamics and global forces have played a greater role in instigating post-Islamism among individual movements in the Muslim world. The pluralist strategy of Lebanese Hizbullah in the early 1990s leading to a split in the movement; the mid-1990s emergence in Egypt of the Al-Wasat Party as an alternative to both militant Islamists and the Muslim Brothers; the inclusive policies and practices of religious parties in Turkey (the Rifah, Virtue, and Justice and Development Parties); the discursive shift in India's Jami'at-i Islami toward more inclusive, pluralistic, and ambiguous ideological dispositions;[28] the emergence in Saudi Arabia in the late 1990s of an "Islamo-liberal" trend seeking a compromise between Islam and democracy[29]—all are signs of post-Islamist trends in Muslim societies today. The Turkish Islamic movement of Fetullah Gulen is a typical example, in which Gulen and his followers have tried to produce a political movement that favors modernism, nationalism, tolerance, and democracy while cherishing religious precepts.[30] In each of these cases, post-Islamism expresses itself as a departure, albeit to varying degrees, from the Islamist ideological package of universalism, monopoly of religious truth, exclusivism, and obligation, toward acknowledging ambiguity, multiplicity, inclusion, and compromise in the movement's principles and practice. I should stress that "Islamism" and "post-Islamism" serve primarily as conceptual categories to signify change, difference, and the root of change. In the real world, however, many Muslims may adhere eclectically and simultaneously to aspects of both discourses. But the advent of post-Islamism, as a trend, should not be seen necessarily as the historical end of Islamism. Rather, it should be viewed as the birth, out of Islamist experience, of a qualitatively different discourse and politics. In reality we may witness simultaneous processes of both Islamization and post-Islamization.

Although post-Islamist movements have succeeded, in varying degrees, in shifting the religious and political discourse, they have yet to transform authoritarian political arrangements in Muslim societies. Iran's post-Islamism, despite its inroads in early 2000, failed to fully democratize the Islamic Republic. Its project of "political reform," which was poised to become an indigenous model of democratic transformation in the Muslim Middle East, was thwarted by the reformists' own blunders and the coercive power of the ruling clerics to cripple the reform movement. In other words, the obstacles to democratic governance in Muslim societies have little to do with religion as such; they are more closely tied to the material and nonmaterial interests of those who hold power. To what extent, then, are social movements able to bring about political change in the Middle East, where the Muslim majority is caught between authoritarian governments, Islamist oppositions, and the threat of foreign domination?

A discursive shift alone is clearly insufficient to cause real institutional transformation. Movements need to win over the political power. But how can social movements committed to nonviolent strategies outmaneuver the coercive power of states? As I discuss in the final chapter, pervasive social movements are not single-episode expressions that melt away under an act of repression. Rather, they are prolonged multifaceted processes of agency and change, with ebbs and flows, whose enduring "forward linkages" can revitalize popular mobilization when the opportunity arises. Through their cultural production—establishing new lifestyles and new modes of thinking, being, and doing things—movements may be able to recondition and *socialize* states and political elites into the society's sensibilities, ideals, and expectations. *Socialization of the states* might offer a clue to understanding the effect of social movements and an "active citizenry" to bolster a democratic turn in Muslim societies.

.   .   .

To elaborate on these propositions, I begin in the following chapter by providing historical background to the two different political trajectories in Iran and Egypt. The comparative analysis starts with a key question: Why did the Iran of the late 1970s undertake an Islamic *revolution*, while the Egypt of the early 1980s, with more or less similar socioreligious settings, experienced only an Islamist *movement*? The subsequent three chapters examine the implications of these different trajectories for the relationship between Islam and democracy. Chapter Three chronicles the making of Iran's post-Islamist social movements in the 1990s, those embodied in the collective activism of young generations, students, Muslim women, and religious intellectuals who pushed for a more inclusive understanding of Islam. I attribute the rise of post-Islamism to the contradictions of the Islamic state and to the profound social changes (mass literacy, expansive urbanization, transnational flows, and individuation) generating new urban individuals and collective agents whom the Islamic state was unable to integrate. Chapter Four addresses the workings of post-Islamism at the state level, when the reform movement moved to share the political authority; it scrutinizes the agony and anomalies of a social movement that had one foot in state power.

The Iranian post-Islamist strategy of cumulative reform reflected what mainstream Egyptian Islamism undertook during the 1980s. Islamic reform in Egypt achieved remarkable results at the societal level, to the extent that it was poised on the state's doorstep. As the government struck back with a blend of repression and appropriation, Egypt experienced a salient instance of Gramscian "passive revolution," embodied in the fragmentation of Islamism, political closure, and stagnation in religious and intellectual thought (discussed in Chapter Five). Thus the dynamics of the relationship between Islam and democracy in Egypt differed radically from those in the Islamic Republic. While Egypt underwent a profound Islamization of society, Iran experienced a post-Islamist turn. Yet in neither country did social movements succeed in radically transforming the political regimes.

In what way can social movements alter the states and political elites into society's sensibilities? I conclude by suggesting that Muslim citizens may be able to forge a sustained movement calling for an inclusive political and moral order if they master "the art of presence."

2 REVOLUTION WITHOUT MOVEMENT, MOVEMENT WITHOUT REVOLUTION
Islamist Activism in Iran and Egypt,
1960s–1980s

WHY DID THE IRAN OF THE LATE 1970S, with its thriving economy, wealthy middle class, repressive political system, massive military might, and powerful international allies, experience an Islamic revolution, while the Egypt of the early 1980s, with similar international allies but a weaker economy, large impoverished middle classes, and a more liberal political system, fell short of revolution and experienced only an Islamist movement?[1] What do their experiences tell us about the trajectories of political change in general and the nature of Islamism in particular?

EXPLAINING THE ISLAMIC REVOLUTION

Mainstream scholarship views the Iranian revolution as the culmination of an ideological process: an Islamic movement that had been evolving since the late 1960s. Hamid Dabashi's impressive work seems to suggest that in this "deeply religious society" Islamists had long prepared for an Islamic takeover. Through the institutions of the mosque, the hawzeh (the religious seminary in Shi'i Islam), preaching, and publications, they were busy with recruiting, organizing, training, and mobilizing resources so that they would be able to act when the opportunity arose.[2] Similarly, for Mansoor Moaddel, the emergence of the "Islamic discourse" during the "episode" lasting from 1953 to 1977 culminated in the Islamic revolution.[3]

While Moaddel and Dabashi focus on internal factors, Anthony Parsons and Nikki Keddie regard Islamic revival as the popular assertion of "Muslim identity" against Western political and cultural penetration.[4] According to Parsons, the Iranian revolution was unique in that the "bulk of the Shi'a population of Iran knew both what they did not want (the continuation of Pahlavi rule) and what they did want (a government controlled by religious leadership, the historical guardians of the Islamic Iranian tradition)."[5] For Keddie, a growing association between secularism and Western control, demonstrated by the government's ties to Western powers, also played a role.[6]

Others have explained the revolution as a breakdown of traditional social order caused by "social dislocation and normative disturbance." Sa'id Amir Arjomand views this as the result of socioeconomic changes initiated by the state. Unable to integrate the dislocated and disoriented groups into its own structure, the state pushed them into the arms of Shi'a clergy who since the 1960s had been ready to mobilize them. The Islamic movement acted as the "rival integrative movement," offering moral and spiritual community.[7] What happened in 1979, according to Arjomand, "was destined to be an Islamic revolution with the goal of establishing a theocracy."[8]

Structural factors and class interests are emphasized by yet another group of scholars. Ervand Abrahamian, Fred Halliday, Mohsen Milani, and Nikki Keddie (in her later writings) consider the contradiction between socioeconomic development and political autocracy to be the main source of conflict, and social classes as major players in the revolution.[9] Misagh Parsa, meanwhile, places special emphasis on the role of the state—the high degree of state intervention in capital accumulation eroded the mediating role of the market, rendering the state the target of all conflict and opposition.[10]

I do not intend to offer a thorough assessment of each of these explanations. Undoubtedly these authors have on the whole shed valuable light on the complexities of the Iranian revolution. But there are two problems. First, despite their differences, they overestimate the role of a supposedly strong Islamic movement, which is said to have evolved since the 1960s or earlier, in ultimately carrying the revolution to victory. This is an assumption that I question in this chapter. Second, the proposed models explain not the revolution per se, but rather the major causes of popular resentment and mobilization, for it still remains to be seen exactly how popular resentment and mass mobilization develop into a revolution. Indeed, as Henry Munson argues, most of the factors suggested by the above-named authors—resentment of foreign domination, authoritarian rule, violation of traditional values, social dislocation, economic downturn, inequality, and state intervention—also existed in some other Middle Eastern countries but did not materialize into revolution.[11] For Egypt, David Snow and Susan Marshall maintain that cultural imperialism and globalization were the underlying causes of the Islamist movement.[12] Similarly, François Burgat and William Dowell see Islamism in Egypt and North Africa as the third phase of decolonization—cultural and discursive independence—after political and economic independence.[13] Meanwhile, Saad Eddin Ibrahim (and to a certain extent Gilles Kepel), among others, focus on national crisis caused by foreign influence (in particular, defeat in the 1967 war with Israel), class incongruity, and alienation among educated rural migrants as major contributors to the rise of the Islamist movement since the 1970s.[14] In Egypt, as in Iran, both internal (socioeconomic and political) and external (resentment of Western domination and Israel) factors helped spawn Islamist activism. So why did Iran and Egypt follow two different trajectories? Why revolution in Iran but not in Egypt? Mere structural causal analysis cannot answer these questions, but explaining the link between popular mobilization and revolutions might.

SOCIAL MOVEMENTS AND REVOLUTIONS

None of the major models of collective action has theorized the dynamics of the transformation from collective action to revolution. They are concerned mainly with explaining causes of social discontent and revolutionary crisis.[15] For James Davies, "Revolutions are most likely to occur when a prolonged period of objective economic and social development is followed by a short period of sharp reversal."[16] According to Ted Gurr's "relative deprivation" thesis, what seems to mediate between these objective processes and the occurrence of revolution is the psychological mood of the people, their expectations and frustration.[17] But as the "resource mobilization" theorists have pointed out, the people's mood may not lead to action unless they are able to mobilize the necessary resources by creating appropriate opportunities. In this context, Charles Tilly's concepts of "opportunity" (factors that facilitate collective action) and "suppression" (factors that restrict it) are particularly useful.[18] So are the degree of the authorities' legitimacy, the dynamics of the use of violence, and the amount of division among the elites, as discussed by Quee-Young Kim.[19] Yet they fail to capture the complex dynamics of the interaction between the contenders and the state during the revolutionary process.

Popular discontents, whatever their cause, may give rise to two types of mobilization. One type, protest or insurrectionary movements, as occurred in Iran in 1978, aim solely to negate the existing order; they may or may not be able to build an alternative structure. A second type is social movements. While they aim to alter the dominant order, they also attempt to establish alternative institutions and value systems before a total change. European socialist movements, Poland's Solidarity, and some Islamist movements are examples. In general, social movements are fairly structured and durable efforts by a relatively large number of people to produce social change. They may be composed of diverse activities with pervasive institutional ramifications in civil society. Because they represent constituents of alternative institutions and cultural settings, they differ from such free-form collective actions as riots and street demonstrations and from practices by rigidly structured interest groups that concern only their own members. Social movements also differ from power-seeking political parties, small clique-like secret discussion groups, and underground guerrilla organizations without mass support, though they may be connected to these groups, share some of their features, or even transform into one (the Rifah Party in Turkey, for example). But they are distinct from revolution, which involves processes of pervasive change, usually violent and rapid, where the political authority collapses and is replaced by the contenders.[20]

In contrast, protest movements, which may culminate in insurrections, are usually transitory and do not last long. They either achieve their goal or are suppressed. Since they directly challenge the political authority, the most critical element of a protest movement is sustainablity. Nevertheless, in some rare cases, a protest movement may transform into a more structured and institutionalized social movement or even into an interest group. Jadwiga Staniszkis referred to Solidarity's transformation, during September 1980 and March 1981, from a national movement into a trade union as "Poland's self-limiting revolution."[21] After the military regime's crackdown in 1981, Solidarity regained its original status and reemerged in the late 1980s following the "Gorbachev revolution."[22]

Because of their institutionalization within civil society, social movements can persist longer than protest actions and insurrections when confronted by the state. However, precisely because of their civil institutionalization, social movements are likely to shy away from revolutionary or insurrectionary activity and struggle instead within the existing arrangement. Many factors contribute to this. The first has to do with the temporal element. Unlike an insurrectionary movement, which has a short lifespan (because it either crushes or is crushed), social movements function over a longer time span, during which people can ask questions, debate key issues, and clarify the movement's aims. Often various ideas develop, and divergent tendencies emerge. While clarity and differentiation are salient features of a social movement, ambiguity and unity are the hallmarks of insurrections. Second, because of the positive change they can generate, social movements may transform the conditions of their own existence. For instance, the "unemployed movement" in Iran in 1979 undermined itself partly by achieving some of its goals.[23]

Unlike protest movements or insurrections, which only negate the prevailing order, social movements tend also to construct alternative institutions and value systems. In this process, they might develop alternative credit systems for the poor, clinics, factories, mutual aid, housing, and social welfare systems, all of which fulfill some of the needs of their constituencies. They also create social and cultural subsystems that usually coexist, albeit contentiously, with the dominant order. Alternative electoral systems in autonomous unions, syndicates, neighborhoods, and associations for excluded groups are a few of their institutional expressions. Finally, alternative religious and cultural organizations, schools, holidays, charities, social gatherings, music, art, and even laws are established, forming a moral community in which the excluded people feel at home. The Austrian socialist movement in the 1920s and Egyptian Islamic activism are two examples.

Some neo-Durkheimian social theorists, such as Arjomand, view such institutions as the embodiment of an "integrative community" that breeds opposition to dominant institutions and value systems (as in Iran). However, instead of political opposition, integrative communities are likely to lead to what Guenther Roth (in an analysis of Social Democracy in Imperial Germany) calls "negative integration"—partial economic and political inclusion combined with alternative cultural and social existence.[24] On the other hand, integration theorists Reinhard Bendix and Seymour Martin Lipset (referring to the Western European trade union movement) have argued that institutionalization of this nature helps contenders develop interests and work within the prevailing system.[25] However, I wish to emphasize that social movements do not simply integrate contenders into the prevailing system; they also produce real change and generate subsystems within which their actors operate and reproduce themselves. Instead of leading to a sudden revolutionary transformation, social movements often coexist and compete with the dominant social arrangement. Unlike insurrections, they do not and cannot undo political authority, but this does not necessarily doom them to "integration" in the sense of ideological and political co-optation, because the very operation of the movement signifies considerable change for its members.

This conjures up the Gramscian strategy of the "war of position," which aims not simply to capture state power (as the insurrectionists do in their "frontal attack") but focuses on the capture and possession of the society by gradually exerting moral and intellectual leadership over civil institutions and processes.[26] A true revolution, for Gramsci, is not just about taking over the state, but about winning over society by establishing institutional, intellectual, and moral hegemony: "A social group can, and indeed must already exercise "leadership" before winning governmental power (this indeed is one of the principal conditions for the winning of such power)."[27] Although, the war of position represents a conscious strategy, its consequences are similar to those of social movements. Whereas frontal attack or insurrection is likely to occur in a society that lacks sufficient civil institutions to mediate between the government and the people, the war of position happens where a strong civil society prevails. But the war of position, this "revolution of the spirit," would be prolonged, "complex," and difficult," and calls for "exceptional qualities of patience and inventive spirit."[28]

The reformist core of social movements and the "war of maneuver" must be evident both from their "integrating" impacts and from the conscious strategy of the movements, which gives priority to changing the society rather than to capturing governmental power. This is radically different from insurrectionary movements whose aim is frontal attack against the government (the war of maneuver), and which produce a different outcome. Iran experienced an insurrectionary movement aimed at capturing state power; but Egypt, in relative political openness, developed a pervasive Islamic social movement that brought about significant changes within civil society but failed to alter the political structure. In other words, Iran experienced an Islamic revolution without a strong Islamic movement, and Egypt a movement without a revolution. Three major differences between the two countries contributed to this contrast of experience: the political and social status of the clergy; the way in which Islam was articulated and practiced; and the degree of political control over the citizens.

THE ISLAMIC REVOLUTION IN IRAN

On February 11, 1979, Tehran radio announced with feverish jubilation the triumph of the Iranian revolution and the end of a 2,500-year-old monarchy. An ecstatic populace flooded the streets en masse. Women milled through the crowds handing out candies and *sharbat*, sweet drinks. Vehicles sounded their horns in unison, flashing their headlights as they drove down main streets that only days earlier had been the scene of bloody clashes between protesters and the army. Now these same streets were being patrolled by revolutionary militias, the Pasdaran. For those present, it was a day of incomparable victory.

The victory day was the culmination of more than eighteen months of mass demonstrations, bloody confrontations, massive industrial actions, a general strike, and political brinksmanship. Yet the revolution's origin can be traced farther back to the structural changes that had been under way since the 1930s, when the country began undergoing a process of modernization. It was accelerated after the CIA-sparked coup of 1953 that toppled the nationalist prime minister, Muhammad Musaddiq, and reinstated the Shah. These structural changes resulted in many conflicts, chief among them the contradiction between socioeconomic change and political underdevelopment.[29] In addition, certain accelerating factors were also involved: state inefficiency, corruption, and a sense of injustice in many sectors of Iranian society.

Modernization policy initiated during the reign of Reza Shah (1925–41) and continued by his son, the late Shah Muhammad Reza Pahlavi, spawned the growth of new social forces while dismaying the traditional social groups. By the late 1970s, a large well-to-do middle class, a generation of modern youth and publicly active women, an industrial working class, and a new impoverished class of slum dwellers and squatters dominated the social scene. Except for the poor, most groups benefited from economic development and enjoyed higher social status and a superior quality of life. However, the persistence of the Shah's autocracy prevented these thriving social layers from participating in the political process. As their resentment mounted, so did that of the older traditional social groups—merchants, the former urban middle class, the clergy, and those dedicated to Islamic institutions—who were frustrated by a modernization strategy that undermined their economic interests and social status.

Quelling any expression of discontent, mired in corruption and inefficiency, the state increasingly alienated the people, instilling in them a collective sense of injustice and moral outrage. During the tense 1970s, the height of the Shah's authoritarian rule and yet also a period of remarkable economic growth, many (except perhaps the upper class and landed peasantry) were discontented, and they found unity in blaming their discontent on the Shah and his Western allies. It is not surprising, then, that the language of dissent and protests was largely anti-monarchy, anti-imperialist, Third Worldist, and even nationalist, turning in the end to religious discourse.

The opportunity for popular mobilization arrived with what we used to call the "Carterite breeze" (*Nasim-i Karteri*). President Carter's human rights policy of the late 1970s forced the Shah to allow a limited degree of expression that snowballed and in less than two years' time swept aside the monarchy. It all began with a limited relaxation of censorship, allowing some literary and intellectual activities (at the Goethe Institute and Tehran universities) and public gatherings by political Islamists in the Quba Mosque. As intellectuals and liberal politicians used this breathing room to publish open letters critical of high officials, a state-sanctioned daily newspaper, the *Itila'at*, ran an article insulting Ayatollah Khomeini. It triggered a violent demonstration in the shrine city of Qum that left several dead. In commemoration of these deaths a massive demonstration in the northern Azeri city of Tabriz inspired still more demonstrations that snowballed into a nationwide protest movement in which diverse segments of the population—modern and traditional, religious and secular, men and women—massively participated, and in which the ulema, or clerical class, came to excert its leadership. How did the clergy come to lead this revolution?

For over twenty-five years of autocratic rule, all effective secular political parties and nongovernmental organizations (NGOs) had been neutralized. The 1953 U.S.-backed coup crushed both the nationalist and communist movements; trade unions were infiltrated by the secret police, SAVAK; publications were strictly censored, and very few effective NGOs remained.[30] Underground guerrilla organizations, Marxist Fida'iyan and radical Islamic Mujahidin, organized most political dissent, but their activities were limited to isolated armed operations.[31] Student activism remained restricted to campus politics or to universities abroad. In short, secular political entities were organizationally decapitated.

Unlike secular forces, however, the clergy possessed invaluable institutional capacity that included its own hierarchy, more than 10,000 mosques, *husayniyya*s (ad hoc religious establishments), *hawzeh*s, and associations that acted as vital means of communication among revolutionaries. Young Islamists, both girls and boys, and junior clerics formed a link between the ulema and the people, while the clergy's hierarchical order facilitated unified decision-making and a systematic flow of order and information, with higher-level decisions disseminated from mosques to both activists and the general public. In short, given the lack of a credible alternative, the institutional capacity and remarkable *ambiguity* in the clergy's overall message pushed the ulema to rise above all other contenders. That leadership was maintained owing to the relatively rapid conclusion of revolutionary events; there was little time for debate or dissent to germinate, or for other social movements and alternative leaders to emerge. Thus the nascent Islamic movement of the 1970s rapidly transformed into a state form. "Islamization" unfolded largely after the victory of the Islamic revolution and was enforced largely from above by the Islamic state. It was manifested in the establishment of the *vilāyat-i faqīh*, or the rule of clergy, the Islamic legal system, restrictive policies on women, and "Islamic" cultural practices and institutions.

SOCIOECONOMIC CHANGE AND THE DECLINE OF ISLAM

This is not to underestimate the significance of political Islam before the Islamic revolution. Indeed, as in Egypt, the history of political Islam harks back to at least the late nineteenth century. The Iranian ulema played a role in the tobacco movement—the first nationalist-religious movement against foreign influence—in the Constitutional Revolution of 1905–1906, and in the Jangali movement of the mid-1920s.[32] Yet their legitimacy, political orientations (largely owing to their social heterogeneity), and thus political efficacy fluctuated markedly in different periods. To preserve their special interests as a status group, their judiciary prerogatives, and economic benefits, the clerical figures such as Shaykh Fadlullah Nuri became staunch opponents of the 1906 Constitution, leading "the vast majority of the constitutionalist ulema"[33] into *mashrū'a*, or to an Islamic constitution. *Mashrū'a* politics failed, but the Russian and British occupation during World War I motivated Islamic leaders to foment uprisings and movements by combining nationalism with anti-government sentiment. Many local uprisings and movements emerged throughout the country. From 1917 on, Mirza Kuchek Khan, a dynamic Islamic preacher from Rasht, along with secular revolutionaries such as Khalu Qurban and Ihsanullah Khan, led a spectacular movement (Jangali) that controlled much of the Caspian Sea province of Gilan.[34]

After World War II the grand cleric Ayatollah Kashani and the Fida'iyan-i Islam intensified their political involvement in the nationalist movement led by Muhammad Musaddiq. Out of the urban riots of July 1963—the last major showdown between Islamists and the state until 1979—Ayatollah Khomeini emerged as a resolute politico-religious figure.[35] Following the riots, the Shah forced Khomeini into exile in Turkey. From there he traveled to Iraq and then to Paris, where, as events unfolded in Iran, he became the exiled leader of the revolution. Throughout these episodes Islam played such an effective political mobilizing role because both Islam (as a faith, an identity, and a discourse) and Islamic leaders enjoyed a great deal of legitimacy among their followers, even though its role had begun to decline since the reign of Reza Shah (after 1941).

Reza Shah, the father of Muhammad Reza Pahlavi, emerged in conditions of remarkable political instability and social insecurity caused by years of upheavals, civil war, foreign occupation, and nomadic uprisings, all of which bred a desire for "strong leaders." Brought to power by a British-engineered coup, he set out to establish a strong state on the image of the West and its Third World variant, the Turkish Republic of Kemal Ataturk, and founded on principles of secular nationalism, educational development, and state capitalism.[36] Many of these measures seriously undermined the institutions of Islam and the ulema.

To begin with, the judiciary, up to then under the influence of the clergy, was entirely restructured; modern educated lawyers replaced traditional judges; French civil codes took the place of most Islamic laws; and secular judges determined whether cases should be tried in secular or religious courts. Reza Shah restricted religious festivals, commemorations, passion plays, and other practices that affected public life. The establishment of modern taxation and the Ministry of Awqāf (Endowments) deprived the clergy from a sizable segment of religious tax income and threatened the economic independence that it had enjoyed during the previous two centuries. But of all Reza Shah's secular dreams, none had more lasting impact than educational reform. Establishing a unified system of state-run schools undermined traditional institutions of learning controlled by the clergy and dominated by the teaching of the Qur'an, grammar, rhetoric, and logic in *maktab*s and *madrasa*s. While the number of students in modern primary school and college grew more than fivefold between 1925 and 1941,[37] the number of students, or *talabeh*s, in *madrasa*s fell from more than 5,500 in 1929 to fewer than 1,340 in 1937. Even the children of prominent ulema preferred and moved into jobs in the modern administration.[38]

The social and intellectual impact of modern schooling was far-reaching. Emphasizing diverse subjects, scientific rationality, and secular practices, it offered alternatives to religious paradigms. Moreover, modern schools and other public places such as parks, cinemas, cafes, factories, and offices drew urban women out of their domestic seclusion and into the world of men.[39] In seeming contradiction to his patriarchism, Reza Shah outlawed the *chador*, the single-piece veil, and required high officials to bring their wives to public events.

These measures, while drastic and often brutal, profoundly undermined but did not neutralize the clergy. Nor did they kill religious sentiment among the people. They did, however, make alternative, secular ways of living, thinking, and reasoning accessible and offered diversified role models and sources of legitimacy. It is not perhaps surprising that after the Allies removed Reza Shah, during an unprecedented democratic period between 1941 and 1953, secular nationalist, radical, and Marxist ideologies flourished. Islam as a faith, discourse, and mobilizing force continued to decline. Few women who had been forced to unveil under Reza Shah returned to wearing the *chador*; most, including the younger generations, retained their new identities.[40] Although the number of *talabeh*s increased,[41] political Islam declined dramatically. Under Ayatollah Borujerdi, the *marja'-i taqlīd* (source of emulation), the *hawzeh* remained apolitical. While a segment of the ulema together with bazaar merchants supported the nationalization of oil, the Ayatollah chose to remain neutral. In the end, fearful of the Tudeh Communist Party's growth under secular Prime Minister Musaddiq, the clergy allied with the 1953 coup that toppled the nationalist leader.[42] In the words of a leading Ayatollah, "the clerical class following the Constitutional Revolution went through a period of isolation and demoralization until the emergence of imam Khomeini."[43]

While it is likely that popular religious sentiments remained, new venues of popular expression sprouted in the form of political parties, artistic circles, associations, and trade unions. Now millions of ordinary men and women joined or sympathized with movements known to be secular, radical, and Marxist. In the early 1950s, Musaddiq led the struggle to nationalize the Iranian oil industry and became a national hero. His National Front, an alliance of secular nationalist parties, was rivaled only by the more cohesive Tudeh Communist Party. With over 25,000 members, and some 300,000 sympathizers, Tudeh enjoyed support among workers, women, intellectuals, artists, military officers, students, teachers, professionals, the urban underclass, and even some peasants. Despite police restrictions, it became the most effective organization in the country,[44] leading the most powerful communist movement in the Middle East.[45]

THE POST-COUP ERA: ACCELERATING CHANGE

The coup d'état of 1953, planned by the CIA, terminated the premiership of Muhammad Musaddiq and reinstated the authority of the Shah. It ended the democratic experience, crushed both the secular nationalist and communist movements, pushed political Islam to the sidelines, and empowered a regime that was to be a model of modernization in the developing world. The post-coup era, notably the 1960s and 1970s, saw remarkable economic growth, integration into the world market, urbanization, and social change—all initiated primarily by the Shah's autocratic state, itself safeguarded by the notorious secret police, SAVAK. This new phase of modernization enhanced many programs that Reza Shah had initiated. It promoted the ascendancy of modern classes—the professional-bureaucratic and technocratic intelligentsia, the industrial working class, publicly active women, and modern youth—at the expense of traditional social structure and authority: the feudal class, bazaar merchants, the ulema, and Islamic institutions in general.

The Shah became America's closest regional ally and joined Western military, political, and economic treaties. In 1963, to accelerate modernization, the Shah inaugurated the "White Revolution," in which land reform, female enfranchisement, and the Literacy Corps were the most important elements. They had far-reaching social consequences. Land reform, in particular, curtailed the power of feudal lords, converted the peasantry into either small landowners or rural proletariat (who subsequently migrated to cities), enhanced capitalist relations in the countryside, and expanded communications between villages and cities and throughout the countryside itself.

In the meantime, rising oil prices contributed to a remarkable annual growth rate of 11 percent for the entire 1963–72 period, a rate that jumped to a staggering 30 percent during 1974 and 1975. Oil income was able to finance impressive programs of industrialization and national education. Between 1963 and 1978, industrial output rose almost twelvefold, with an average annual growth rate of 72 percent.[46] By 1977 the industrial working class grew to one-third of the total work force.[47] The modernization strategy also boosted a large and fairly prosperous new middle class through expanded modern education. Urban literacy rates grew from 33 percent in 1956 to 65 percent in 1976; half the country's women could read. In 1978, some 175,000 students—one-third of them women—enrolled in 236 institutions of higher education, in addition to some 80,000 abroad.[48] Education enabled social mobility and contributed to the growth of the modern middle class: the number of students, professors, teachers, writers, doctors, lawyers, technocrats, and bureaucrats increased from 16.5 percent of the urban labor force in 1966 to over 33 percent, or more than 1.9 million people by 1976, including 300,000 women. A strong modern middle class had been created.[49]

Meanwhile, traditional social classes were losing ground. The feudal class, which included many grand clergy, had virtually withered away, its members gradually migrating into commerce, speculation, and industry. A large segment of the bazaar, well over 500,000 retail and wholesalers, felt the impact of modern financial institutions, trade companies, shopping centers, large factories, and new tastes.[50] Some resisted this invasion of the new, others battled and lost, and many more conformed to the reality of modernization by trading foreign goods and employing modern trade relations and language.[51] By the eve of the revolution, the bazaar was sociologically divided.[52] The political divide came only after the revolution: modernist and well-off bazaaries supported President Banisadr, while the clergy backed traditional, small-scale traders.

The clerical class, more than anyone, was put on the defensive on economic, political, and social fronts. In economic terms, land reform and the establishment of the Ministry of Endowments cut back the main source of clergy's income from *awqāf*. Earlier, Reza Shah's administrative reform had already diminished the fees the ulema were entitled to for performing their legal and clerical duties.[53] What remained were *haqq-i-imām* and *khums*, contributions from the faithful. In political terms, the historic allies of the clergy, the traditional bazaaries and the feudal class, were both seriously debilitated. At the same time most of the new middle class, women in the public sphere, and youth expressed little affinity with the institutions of Islam, undermining the social legitimacy of religious institutions. I can recall that, in the 1960s, my village classmates would question the village mullahs' lack of modern knowledge, while the mullahs expressed dismay over youth who, they felt, no longer listened to their preaching. By 1968 the number of *madrasas* had declined to only 138, most of which had only a handful of students. "[S]ome continued to exist as monuments or landmarks more than instructional institutions."[54] Hence, Ayatollah Mutahhari's acknowledgment as early as 1963 of the sad truth that "materialistic philosophy has its appeal among Iranian youths."[55] He blamed this on the ulema and on their dated practices.[56]

Indeed, this onslaught of secular ideologies made some Muslim leaders rethink their practices and modernize their strategy. The opportune time came when a vacuum was created following the death in 1961 of Ayatollah Borujerdi, the *marja'-i taqlīd*. A group of like-minded ulema and Islamic intellectuals began to present Islam in an attractive modern language, mixing Islamic discourse with rational scientific concepts and paying particular attention to the concerns of everyday life.⁵⁷ Instead of jurisprudence or religious rituals, they discussed Darwin's theory of evolution, Sartre's existentialism, and Marx's materialism. As an engineer, Mehdi Bazargan insisted that hard scientific evidence be used to arrive at religious conclusions. Like-minded clergy followed suit. The leaders of the Freedom Movement, a remnant of Musaddiq's National Front (including Mehdi Bazargan, Murtaza Mutahhari, Beheshti, Allameh Tabataba'i, and Mahmud Taleqani, most of whom would become leaders of the Islamic Revolution), organized monthly seminars around the theme of *marja'iyyat va vilāyat dar Islām* (the source of emulation and leadership in Islam). These seminars continued under the rubric of a group named Maktab-i Tashayu', but still paid little attention to strictly Qur'anic teachings or traditional Shi'i texts; instead, they maintained their emphasis on modern scientific language. The group published a journal, *Maktab-i Tashayu'*, which printed articles on such themes as "leading the young generation," "the law of causality in human science and religion," and "Islam and the proclamation of human rights." A similar publication, *Guftār-i Māh*, also carried comparable contributions.

These reformist Muslim leaders even resorted to sociological surveys to learn what youth thought about Islam. This was the beginning of what came to be known as *ihyā-yi fikr-i Islāmī* (reviving Islamic thought), which characterized political Islam throughout the 1960s and the early 1970s, until it was overshadowed by the Muslim intellectual 'Ali Shari'ati. Islamic revival found expression in Islamic publications, Islamic study groups, and Islamic schools that differed from *madrasa*s in that they combined regular curriculum with extracurricular religious activities, including *tafsīr* and Qur'an-reciting sessions, Islamic entertainment, daily collective prayers, and alternative leisure. Their mission was to create "true" Muslim individuals.

This trend represented a significant shift in the socialization and politicization of Islam, but it fell short of a mass social movement, with little resemblance to the Egyptian or Algerian versions of the 1980s and early 1990s. In Iran, the Maktab-i Tashayu' and similar groups remained weak, isolated, and elitist. Only three issues of its periodical were published. As historian Reza Afshari points out, Ayatollah Khomeini's most significant contribution to Islamic ideology, *vilāyat-i faqīh* (guardianship of jurists), was unknown to some of his most ardent followers.⁵⁸ Contrary to the prevailing assumption, there is not adequate evidence to suggest that the ulema resorted to the appeal of the masses.⁵⁹ Indeed, none of the major leaders paid particular attention to the *mustaż'afin*, the poor, as a special class. A review of eighty-eight sermons, messages, and letters by Ayatollah Khomeini attests that in the fifteen years before the revolution he made only eight passing references to lower-class people, as compared to fifty references to educated youth, students, and universities.[60] Ayatollah Mutahhari's elitist approach is clear through his warnings against *'avām zadegui* or populism;[61] for 'Ali Shari'ati, intellectuals, not the popular masses, constituted the revolutionary force.[62] For these Muslim leaders, then, the critical mass was not the masses, but the educated classes.

Indeed, some evidence seems to point to the proliferation of Islamic books, tapes, and associations during the late 1960s and 1970s. Some accounts given in 1976, for instance, claim the existence in Tehran of 12,300 "religious associations," of which 1,800 had formal titles; forty-eight publishers of religious books and the sale of 490,000 copies of *Mafātih al-Jinān* (*Keys to the Heavens*); and thirteen centers for the recording and distribution of tapes.[63] Despite serious doubts about the accuracy of these figures,[64] many scholars take this as "firm evidence" of a "religious movement" in the 1960s and 1970s, presumably auguring the Islamic Revolution.[65]

To begin with, the censorship policies after 1966 caused a general decline in published works on nonreligious subjects and increased the relative proportion of religious books.[66] After the revolution, when censorship was removed, secular periodicals, books, pamphlets, and tapes immediately flourished. According to the Iranian Publication Association, more than 2 million books were published within the first six months of 1979.[67] Whereas the highest circulation for the largest daily in Tehran (*Kayhan*) was 300,000 in 1978, the circulation of Tehran's two major evening dailies (*Kayhan* and *Itila'at*) reportedly surpassed 1.5 million in the early months of the revolution, while the leftist morning newspaper, *Ayandigān*, hovered at around 400,000. In Tehran alone, over 100 newspapers and periodicals started or resumed publication in the postrevolutionary months.[68]

Moreover, most religious publications disseminated before the revolution hardly represented *political* Islam; rather, they were either "practical guides" on religious rituals or preaching on morality or scholarly inquiries into mysticism or theosophy.[69] Although *Maktab-i Islam*, a journal of the *hawzeh* in Qum, reportedly had a large circulation in the late 1960s, it always refused to publish reformist or political materials.[70] And *Mafātih al-Jinān* represented, according to 'Ali Shari'ati, no more than "the most other-worldly aspect of fossilized traditional Shi'ism."[71]

One should also be cautious in considering the success of the Islamic schools in spreading religious messages, or, for that matter, political Islam. During my own three-year experience in an Islamic school in the 1960s, the Islamic programs were the least attractive to most students[72] and the clerical instructors the least popular to many of us who felt pressured by institutional indoctrination and as a result left the school for secular equivalents. On the other hand, there is a widespread assumption that the *mustaż'afin* knew the mullahs and joined the revolution through such Islamic institutions as *hay'at*s, ethnic-based and ad hoc religious establishments. Contrary to what some claim,[73] while the *hay'at*s did bring together many Shi'i poor, they were hardly the sites of political mobilization. My own observations confirm a young squatter's view that the functions of the *hay'at*s remained limited to "socializing," "sacrificing Imam Hussein, and weeping [for his dead body]."[74] The urban poor gathered under the political banner of the ulema only just before the insurrection of February 1979. In short, the significance of religious publications and institutions for political Islam lay not as much in their ideological impact during the 1960s and the 1970s as in their networking capacity and mobilizing role on the eve of the revolution.

More important, taking these as a sole indication of Islamic revival, especially in retrospect, downplays a significant parallel phenomenon—that is, the strong *secular tendency* that was developing at the very same time—a subject that has been overlooked by postrevolutionary scholarship. Above, I indicated the historical foundation of secular behavior in Iran—widespread modern education, the expansion of communication, and a clergy whose economic and social position had been undermined.

The secular trend reached its peak in the same decade as the Islamic revolution. Unlike the 1940s, when communist, nationalist, and intellectual movements found expression in major secular institutions, the Shah's dictatorship of the 1970s largely deprived the society of comparable establishments. Instead, there was a tremendous boost in the production and consumption of secular journals and in the popularity of Western cinema, popular music, youth centers (*khānih-i javānān*), bars that served alcohol, Caspian Sea holidays, and Western television programs.[75] The number of movie viewers increased by over 50 percent between 1969 and 1975, nearly twice the rate of urban population growth in the same period. Every year during the 1970s, Iranian cinemas showed more than 500 foreign films, one-quarter of which were American. By 1975 half of urban families owned television sets, in comparison with less than 4 percent in 1960, and 65 percent of households owned radios.[76] By the late 1970s, the media had molded a highly secular popular culture, embodied in the songs and performances of dozens of popular singers and actors, such as Gougoush, Fardin, Aghasi, and Sousan. This was at a time when cinema, radio, and television, were condemned by religious-minded people, since in Ayatollah Khomeini's views, they were used "to corrupt our youth."[77]

It was such a backdrop that made Islamic leaders skeptical about the feasibility of political change. While many scholars writing after the revolution magnified the extent of an "Islamic movement" in the late 1960s and early 1970s, a letter from 'Ali Shari'ati to his son (in the late 1960s) shows how he was frustrated, pessimistic, and bitter toward the people who had remained disinterested in his mission.[78] Even Ayatollah Khomeini, in 1970, thought it might take two centuries to overthrow the Iranian monarchy.[79]

Indeed, it was through the popularity of 'Ali Shari'ati, a modernist Islamic intellectual, that an Islamic movement seemed to begin during the mid-1970s. It remained limited to political discourse among the Muslim intelligentsia and hardly assumed any institutional form within civil society—associations, NGOs, syndicates, schools, neighborhoods, workplaces, and media—as would movements in Egypt during the early 1990s. The Mujahidin-i Khalq Organization was influenced by Shari'ati's ideas, but it did not gain a mass following until after the revolution.[80] In short, the Islamic movement in prerevolution Iran proved to be a late bloomer. There remained no time for political Islam to evolve into a mass social movement. In Iran, an Islamic movement was in the making when it was interrupted by an Islamic revolution.

THE EGYPTIAN ISLAMIST MOVEMENT

Unlike Iran, however, by the early 1990s Egypt had developed a strong and pervasive Islamist movement. The popular image of the Islamist movement in Egypt was represented by the protracted war of attrition between militant Islamists, notably members of Egyptian Islamic Jihad and al-Jama'a al-Islamiyya, and the state, beginning with the assassination of President Sadat in September 1981. It was also manifested in attacks on Christian Copts, Western tourists, secular Muslim thinkers, and in the image of Shaykh 'Umar 'Abd al-Rahman, the spiritual leader of al-Jama'a al-Islamiyya who was detained in the United States for his alleged involvement in the bombing of the World Trade Center. Indeed, in 1993 alone, confrontations between Islamists and government forces left 1,106 killed or wounded and resulted in 17,191 arrests.[81]

Several attempts were made on the lives of politicians, security heads, and public figures. Cinemas, cafes, video shops, Nile cruise ships, and banks became the targets of bombing campaigns. Despite the attention its violence attracted, the militant trend was far less influential and pervasive than the gradualist, nonviolent trend responsible for spreading political Islam within civil institutions.

Born of a bottom-up social movement in the 1920s, the Islamic revival in Egypt spread rapidly during the 1970s and reached its peak in the early 1990s. Its vast spectrum included militant groups, the nonviolent and gradualist Islamic coalition (of al-Ikhwan and Hizb al-'Amal), individualist Sufi orders, al-Azhar, and institutions of the secular state including the Ministry of Awqāf and the Supreme Islamic Council.

By the early 1990s, the number of *ahli*, or private mosques, numbered some 40,000, an increase of more than 100 percent since the mid-1970s; in contrast, the number of government-controlled mosques had grown by a mere 40 percent. Between 1975 and the late 1980s, the number of Islamic associations also grew by over 100 percent, to more than 4,000. The production and sale of Islamic books, pamphlets, and religious cassettes flourished. In 1994, more than a quarter of all books published were religious, a 25 percent increase since 1985,[82] and Islamic books constituted 85 percent of those sold during the 1995 Cairo book fair.[83] Recordings of Islamic figures such as Shaykh Kishk, which numbered over a thousand, sold in the millions. Dozens of Islamic newspapers, weeklies, and monthlies were in high circulation.[84] Radio Qur'an, devoted entirely to religious matters, maintained its highest ratings during this period.

In contrast, the number of moviegoers and domestically produced films dwindled.[85] Self-censorship emerged in the production of television programs in response to popular pressure on the state, and religious programming increased by 50 percent between 1975 and 1990.[86] Islamic sentiment was particularly evident in a marked decline of alcohol consumption and patronage of bars, liquor stores, and nightclubs for Egyptians. Even the Mubarak government could not escape acknowledging the prevalence of the idea of an "Islamic solution." The interior minister, claiming that all laws were based on Shari'a, publicly denounced the notion that Egypt was a secular state.[87]

At the same time, Islamic activism after the 1970s penetrated a variety of civil institutions, mass media, formal education, and community social services. By the late 1980s, the Muslim Brotherhood had control of Egypt's major professional unions: doctors, engineers, pharmacists, lawyers, dentists, commerce, and college professors, as well as students. In general, the 4,000 Islamic NGOs were more active than the 9,000 secular ones, because they were financed, managed, and functioned better.[88] During the early 1980s, until a government crackdown, the Muslim Brotherhood also created Islamic investment companies which, with returns as high as 20 percent, were able to subsidize low-income groups. In addition to civil activism, the Islamic coalition of the Muslim Brotherhood and the Labor Party made considerable headway in local and national elections. Together their seats in Parliament increased from twelve in 1984 to thirty-eight in 1987.[89]

Support for the Muslim Brotherhood came from diverse groups: the business community, the lower classes, young and old, men and women. But its backbone was the modern middle class. Militant groups, in contrast, relied mostly on college-educated young men between 20 and 30 years old with a rural or provincial background, who were professionally employed and resided in Cairo's lower-class neighborhoods or in the large villages of central Egypt. This changed in the early 1990s, when younger, less well educated members joined their ranks: their average age was 21, and only 30 percent had a university education, compared with 64 percent in the 1970s.[90] Lower-middle-class youth became the newest players in radical Islamism.

While organized labor remained largely beyond the reach of Islamists, the latter's relationship with the urban poor was more complex. Contrary to common perception, Islamic social welfare organizations were not bastions of Islamist political activism. While it was true that many radical activists in greater Cairo, for instance, came from or resided in slums or shantytowns, this in itself did not mean they insisted on mobilizing the poor. High rent and the need to maintain a low profile were sufficient reasons for the militants to live on the fringes of society.[91] In fact, a pervasive housing crisis had made a spatially "marginalized" middle class a peculiarly Egyptian urban phenomenon, a tendency currently on the rise in other countries in the region.

Although the Cairo earthquakes of 1992 and the northern Egypt floods of 1994 inspired the Islamists to build a social foundation among the poor, their attempts to do so were sporadic. The educated classes remained the central focus of Islamist politics. At the same time, the fall of the lawyers' syndicate, traditionally Egypt's most liberal and secular association, to the Muslim Brotherhood, demonstrated the extent to which modern professionals embraced Islamism. But this did not occur in a void. President Sadat's *infitāh*, or economic openness, beginning in the 1970s boosted interest in commerce, engineering, and construction to the detriment of liberal arts and law. Law schools, once the destination of bright children of old liberal elites, swelled with the mediocre and often conservative children of lower-class families. Many law professors, in search of better pay, flocked to the rich Gulf states, leaving college curricula to their less enlightened replacements. They in turn trained a generation of conservative lawyers to whom *fiqh* (Islamic jurisprudence) became the central authority.[92] Upon graduation, many of these young lawyers faced either unemployment or low-paying jobs, joining the Bar Association which, instead of providing benefits, had fallen prey to internal conflicts and corruption. To address this grave deficiency, the Islamist-oriented lawyers in the Bar Association established Shariʿa Committees as venues for professional and political activities, thus attracting many to their cause. By 1992, lawyers supporting the Muslim Brotherhood led by Ahmad Sayif al-Islam Hasan al-Banna (son of Hasan al-Banna) had taken control of the syndicate, turning it into "an Islamic Association whose members abide by Shariʿa and fear of God in their activities."[93]

Thus political Islam in Egypt during this period reflected the rebellion of the impoverished and morally outraged middle class.[94] Their higher education fueled high expectations of a job market that offered few prospects for economic success. A product of Nasser's welfare-state boom, they were the losers of Sadat's *infitāh* policy that opened the country to Western economic, political, and cultural influence and sought rapprochement with Israel.ʿTo them Islamism represented an ideological package that negated all the perceived causes of such a state of deprivation: economic dependency, cultural selling-out, and national humiliation (embodied in the 1967 defeat to the Israelis and the Camp David Accords). In view of all the failed ideologies, chiefly Nasserite socialism and Sadat's capitalism, and the Western cultural, political, and economic onslaught, they saw Islam as the only indigenous doctrine that could bring about genuine change. "ʾ

Such an articulated ideology in political Islam clearly belonged to the core—cadres and activists. Beyond them, there were many others in the outer concentric circles of the movement, such as the lower classes, who were attracted to Islamism not for its ideology, but because it was the only viable alternative to the status quo. These "free riders," or fringe groups, often articulated no coherent ideology of their own, and did not even rehearse that of the leadership. They would have turned to almost any social force they felt offered them the prospect of a dignified future. Similar strata had followed the Wafd in the 1920s and 1930s, then Nasser in the 1950s and the 1960s, both of which were secular to the bone but offered credible alternatives.[95]

POLITICAL VERSUS SOCIAL ISLAM

Why did Islamic activism in Egypt assume the character of a social movement while in Iran it was narrowly politicized? It is often noted that Shi'ism is a tradition that, unlike its Sunni counterpart, mixes religion with politics and, as an oppressed sect, constitutes an inherently revolutionary tradition. Careful analysis does not support such a claim, but the Iranian revolution, led by the Shi'i clerics, created that popular image, which faded in the glare of Sunni radicalism in the late 1990s and early 2000, as the reform movement gained ground in Iran and after the al-Qa'ida culprits of the September 11 terrorist attacks all proved to be Sunni Arabs. The Shi'i and Sunni branches each take a different approach to the issue of rule, or *hākimiyya*, but both equate Islam with politics, and there is nothing inherently revolutionary about Shi'i doctrine.

In Sunni Islam, the community determines political authority. In Shi'ism, however, only imams can rule the *umma* (the community of Muslim believers). Historically, this kind of rule came into existence in the time of Shi'i imams. After the occultation of the last twelfth imam, the issue remained in controversy for over a century until the Qajar period in Iran, when Shi'i scholars were divided into two schools, *akhbāri* and *usūli*. The former stressed the literal following of the Prophet's traditions; while the latter recognized the concept of *ijtihād*, which granted power to the ulema to interpret the Prophet's sunna and stipulate new injunctions, if deemed necessary. Although the clergy gained unprecedented prominence, they were not yet entitled to exercise full authority on behalf of the imams. As such, Ayatollah Khomeini's concept of *hukumat-i Islami* (Islamic government), written in 1971, simply represents a new invention in the Shi'i tradition,[96] and its invocation after the revolution was largely the result of political circumstances at the time that ensured clergy leadership.[97] Yet certain historical and institutional aspects of Shi'i Islam contributed to the political rather than social character of Islamist activism in Iran.

In both Iran and Egypt, the clergy constituted a distinct status group who, despite internal differentiation (according to seniority and economic status), shared common interests in income security and social and spiritual legitimacy. But their political and social positions in the two countries differed. Unlike in Iran, where traditionalist Shi'i clergy (who later became opposition leaders) were solely responsible for religious affairs, in Egypt lay activists augmented clergy efforts by spreading their message through associational work in civil society. In the eighteenth century, the ulema of Egypt were integral to the ruling elite and acted as intermediaries between them and the people. By the time Muhammad 'Ali consolidated his power, the ulema had become a formidable authority that the Egyptian leader could not ignore. He first bought their support by offering them income from farm taxes and endowments and a prerogative of consultation on political matters; later he subordinated them by denying such privileges and making them paid employees of the state. Nevertheless, the ulema remained a significant force in the anticolonial movement.[98] Al-Afghani and Muhammad 'Abdu, and later Rashid Reda, continued ulema opposition to British rule. As Islamic reformers, they struggled not only against foreign domination, but to reformulate Islam in order to rival Western progress—a measure that some modernist ulema in Iran began as late as the 1960s.

As a component of the state, however, the political role of the ulema remained limited to nationalistic posturing. Except for some individual clerics, the ulema remained by and large complacent on domestic matters. The ulema's dependence on the state was further intensified by Nasser, who in 1955 abolished religious courts, put all endowments under state control, and, in 1961, took over al-Azhar and Islamic education. Similar actions in Iran during the 1960s seriously curtailed the clergy's control over shrines and *mawqūfāt* (endowments), but the former maintained a measure of autonomy by relying on themselves (many were landowners), on bazaars with which they had close ties, and on small religious donations.[99]

Thus in Egypt, lay Islamic activists, not the ulema, raised the banner of opposition politics. Hence the emergence of the Society of Muslim Brothers (MB), in 1928, during Egypt's liberal era (1919 to 1952), when the secular-nationalist Wafdist Party and the royal family ruled the country. The Muslim Brotherhood was founded by Hasan al-Banna, a school teacher from Isma'iliyya who was dismayed by imperialist economic domination of his country, corruption, the decadence of the kings, and the degradation of Muslims, especially the younger generation. His messages found appeal among a vast array of Egyptian citizens who came to believe that theirs was a society of *jāhilīyya*, characterized by the worship of man by man and the sovereignty of man over man. The Brotherhood grew rapidly, from only four branches in 1929 to 2,000 branches in 1949, with about 1 million activists and sympathizers at its peak. They came from various walks of life, but most were from the rising urban middle classes who felt the crunch of "foreign economic control which limited the prospects for the new bourgeoisie."[100] Hasan al-Banna was assassinated by police in 1949 and was replaced as spiritual guide by Hasan al-Hudaybi.

Despite close ties to the Free Officers (the military men who, along with Nassser, toppled the monarchy), the Muslim Brothers were subjected to suppression after the 1952 Revolution by Nasser, a nationalist leader committed to modernization, secularism, nationalism, and later to socialist ideas.[101] Such Muslim Brothers figures as Sayyed Qutb, a major ideologue, were executed and the organization was banned. The movement survived but split into a "revolutionary" wing that subscribed to the views of Sayyed Qutb and the gradualist wing of Hasan al-Hudaybi. Both sides agreed that Egyptian society and polity was one of *jāhili*. While both strived for an alternative Islamic state and society, they disagreed on how to attain it. Sayyed Qutb advocated political action and movement, charging the passive and complacent with being non-Muslims. Hudaybi, however, called for *da'wa*, or discourse and preaching. Both wings eschewed crusaders and shared notions of anti-Zionism, anti-communism, anti-secularism, and anti-Nasserism. This schism was to mark the origin of the split between the later revolutionary and the reformist Islamic coalition (with Muslim Brothers). From the revolutionary trend emerged al-Takfir wa al-Hijra, Jama'iyya al Islamiyya (both crushed under Sadat), al-Jihad, and al-Jama'a al-Islamiyya, and from the reformist line the Islamic coalition that included the Muslim Brotherhood.[102]

In the 1960s, small groups of young activists, among them Ayman al-Zawahiri, found recourse in the ideas of Ibn Taymiyya, a fourteenth-century Muslim jurist who authorized "jihad" against "infidel rulers." Jihadi groups mushroomed mostly in the 1970s aftermath of Israeli's victory over the Arabs, as an alternative to the peaceful politics of the Muslim Brotherhood; they included Shukri Mustafa's puritanical al-Takfir wa al-Hijra, Shawki al-Shaykh's al-Shawqiyyun, Ayman al-Zawahiri's al-Jihad and Tali'at al Fatah (Vanguards of the Conquest), and the Military Academy group led by Salih Saraya, a Palestinian émigré who argued that the defeat of the Zionist enemy would be dependent on the establishment of an Islamic state in Egypt. Although most of these groups vanished, al-Jama'a al-Islamiyya, called simply Jama'a, remained and became the most powerful militant group until the late 1990s.[103]

The Jama'a had orgininated from the "religious family" of al-Jama'āt al-Islamyya, the Islamic Student Associations, which President Sadat encouraged to grow as part of his policy to undermine communists and Nasserists. Dominating Egyptian universities, these associations went beyond student welfare activities, also promoting moral discipline, and opposing music, theater-going, dancing, and mixing between sexes. With the advent of the Iranian revolution and Camp David Accords in 1979, two trends emerged in these associations. Moderates, based largely in Cairo and Delta universities, aligned with the Muslim Brothers; and the radical trend, dominant in upper Egypt, evolved into the Islamist al-Jamaʿa al-Islamiyya led by ʿAbd al-Salam Faraj, ʿAbud al-Zumur, and Karam Zuhdi.[104] By assassinating President Sadat in 1981, the group hoped to launch an Islamic revolution in the image of Iran.[105] But this naïve initiative instead resulted in the arrest of some 1,200 (5,000 according to Jamaʿa) culprits and the execution of their leaders.[106] The blunder sparked a heated debate in prison cells over the nature of leadership, underground versus open activities, the conditions necessary to launch an Islamic revolution, and whether to pursue daʿwa before or after an insurrection. Those who favored open daʿwa to mobilize for insurrection followed the spiritual leadership of ʿUmar ʿAbd al-Rahman, a blind salafi shaykh, and united within the Jamaʿa. Supporters of a more secretive and militaristic activism sided with al-Jihad led by Ayman al-Zawahiri and ʿAbud al-Zumur. The Jihad militants, once released from prison in 1984, transferred their operations to Afghanistan to fight alongside the Mujahidin and Osama bin Laden against the Soviet Union, in the meantime training new recruits to carry out military operations back in Egypt.

But the Jamaʿa stayed behind. The new leaders and cadres, mostly trained while in prison, returned to their native land, rejoining their families, neighborhoods, villages, and colleges, where they began to reorganize, mobilize, and gradually broaden their hold over southern Egypt. The Jamaʿa militants openly agitated against the state, preaching moral discipline on campus and in towns, and organized welfare services, literacy classes, transportation, work co-operatives, and arbitration of local disputes, while police watched and gathered intelligence. In a quest for security, the Jamaʿa sent its leaders Ala' Muhiddin, Safwat ʿAbd al-Ghani, and Talʿat Yasin Humam to live less visibly in the anonymity of Cairo. When their operatins failed to survive in the integrated old and modern Cairo (Jamaliyya and Zamalek), the militants penetrated the crowded squatter slums of ʿAyn al-Shams and Imbaba, where they could blend into the maze of opaque spaces that were not mapped and had no street names, house numbers, police, or state presence. Ironically, it was in Imbaba that Jamaʿa made international headlines in the early 1990s.

In Imbaba, the al-Jamaʿa began by recruiting youths with roots in the Saʿid, organized meetings, discussed its "charter," and gradually took control of mosques and *ziwāyā*. The militants divided the area into ten subdistricts, each managed by a Jamaʻa leader who trained new cadres and gave political lectures. They went door-to-door to hand out newsletters (*Kilāmāt Haqq* and *al-Jamaʻa al-Islamiyya*), cassettes of religious teachings, revolutionary music, and videos (showing, for instance, how they killed President Sadat). Weekly meetings held in mosques and on street corners began with prayer, followed by discussion of the day's news facilitated by speakers standing in front of large Jamaʻa flags. Nonconformists did not remain immune from the Jamaʻa's moral wrath. Vigilante groups led by Shaykh Jaber set fire to video shops, threatened unveiled women with acid, closed down beauty shops, banned music from weddings, and forbade social mixing of the sexes.[107] In this fashion, the Jamaʻa ruled over such towns as Dayrut for more than a decade, and by the early 1990s they had established the "Islamic Republic of Imbaba" in the heart of Cairo.[108] Army intervention abruptly ended the "republic" in November 1992, when 14,000 soldiers seized the area for three weeks and arrested some 600 suspects.

Despite its political drama and revolutionary posture, militant Islamism was insignificant and fragmented, and it began to decline. Some abandoned violence and worked through peaceful methods, while others gravitated toward Afghanistan's Taliban and Osama bin Laden (see Chapter Five). More significant was the gradualist trend represented by the outlawed Muslim Brotherhood, which in pursuit of legal cover aligned with the Islamized Labor Party, led by Ibrahim Shukri, who after years of persecution under Nasser, had resurfaced under Sadat and set up the Socialist Labor Party in 1978.[109] Responding to the tremendous appeal of an "Islamic solution" during the 1980s, the party gradually adopted Islamist ideology. ʻAdel Husayn, an ex-Marxist-turned-Islamist, pushed the party to form an alliance with the Muslim Brothers under the slogan "Islam is the Solution."[110] In 1987 the alliance captured seventy-eight seats, making the Islamists the largest opposition group in Parliament. But the party lost momentum in 2000 after being outlawed by the state for its ferocious campaign against secular values and government corruption.

The comparative advantage of Egypt's Islamism was due primarily to its associational and social movement character. Crucial to its success was the Muslim Brothers' commitment to social mobilization in civil society through its organization of cells, alternative mosques, schools, youth associations, athletics, women's organizations, clinics, work co-operatives, and paramilitary groups. These activities consolidated the grassroots and turned the Muslim

Brothers into a mass social movement that imbued everyday life with Islamic sensibilities. In turn, the spread of Islamic sentiments (enhanced by both the failure of the liberal experiment and the mistrust of secular liberalism, which in the 1940s was associated with colonialism) pushed the Egyptian secularists to give way to Islam.[111] As Ira Lapidus notes, in this period, the secular intelligentsia "accepted an Islamic framework, and attempted to compromise between Islam and modernity. The net effect was not so much to rescue secularism as to legitimize the Muslim revival."[112] Yet it was a peculiar kind of revivalism, as the infusion of Islamic symbols into everyday life helped produce a somewhat "secularized" religion.

Whereas in Egypt the "secularization" of religious symbols has been a feature of Islam, in Iran religion and its symbols hold an exalted position that emphasizes the sacred and esoteric nature of Islam. An Iranian, for example, would treat the Qur'an with great deference, placing it in assigned holy locations where it is protected until being taken out to be read on a special occasion. In Egypt, however, it is not uncommon to see a taxi driver switching between playing Egyptian pop music and reciting the holy book. In contrast to Egypt, where religious occasions are by and large popular festivals (*'iyd*), for an Iranian Muslim, they represent sober, sad, and serious events, often associated with death and mourning. The playful and highly festive mood of Egyptian Ramadan is comparable in Iran only to the *nuruz*, or new year festivities. Islamic pop music is a common feature of Egypt's cultural landscape, where popular singers perform songs about the Prophet Muhammad, accompanied by a full backup band with synthesizer and electric guitar. But it would be unthinkable for an Iranian Muslim to imagine pop singer Gougoush singing about Imam Husayn. In short, in contrast to Iran, where modernity and religion and the mundane and the sacred were treated as mutually exclusive, Egypt experienced a kind of cultural hybridity in which religion remained by and large dominant.[113] Consequently, "religious/traditional" versus "secular/modern" identities were far more pronounced in the Iran of the 1970s than in the Egypt of the 1980s and 1990s. Like Turkey in the 1990s and unlike Egypt, Iranian society was deeply divided along secular and religious lines. The implications of these different religious practices for the social and political status of the clergy in the two countries was highly significant.

During the 1950s and 1960s, the Iranian ulema were frustrated by the overall cultural change, rapid Westernization, and secular behavior that threatened their social and cultural legitimacy. Modern educated youth in particular began to dismiss the clergy and the institution of religion in general. The source of this "evil" was perceived by the ulema as the corrupt regime and its Western allies. These conditions then turned the ulema to oppositional politics that targeted the state. The experience of clergy in Egypt, however, was different. Despite the rise of modern ideas and social groups (such as the middle classes, educated youth, and women in public roles), al-Azhar (and nonclerical Islam) still enjoyed a great deal of respect and legitimacy among Egyptian Muslims; and despite the surge of political Islam, al-Azhar continued to represent religious orthodoxy in the country. During the 1980s and 1990s, modern youth did not shy away from embracing traditional Islam. As someone who had observed the religious laxity of Iranian youths during the early 1970s, I was astonished by the extent of religiosity among Westernized middle- and upper-class Egyptian youths, who spoke with reverence about Islamic precepts and the clergy's authority. Consequently, not only had different segments of Egyptian society—the youth, the traditionalists, the ulema, and the state—found something to cherish about their Islam, the clergy did not experience as much frustration, resentment, and political dissent as their Iranian counterparts. They maintained a strong social following and religious legitimacy.[114] Similar to political Islamists, the ulema remained committed to Islamizing society, not by seizing political power, but through *da'wa*.

REFORMIST OUTCOME

Strategically, Iran and Egypt presented two different approaches to Islamic change. The Iranian experience demonstrated Gramsci's "frontal attack" or insurrectionary approach, whereas Egyptian Islamists pursued a "war of position" with "reformist" consequences. Hardly familiar with Antonio Gramsci, Hasan al-Banna echoed this strategy many years ago:

> Our duty as Muslim Brothers is to work for the reform of selves [*nufus*], of hearts and souls by joining them to God the all-high; then to organize our society to be fit for the varied community which commands the good and forbids evil-doing, then from the community will arise the good state.[115]

Mustafa Mashur, Ikhwan's leader (who died in 2002) referred to the same approach: "All we ask is an Islamic state based on Shari'a. . . . It may take us a century to establish an Islamic state. Our principles should be bequeathed to future generations and there should be no deviation from these principles."[116] In an encounter in a Cairo mosque, I observed a militant young man charge the shaykh with political complicity. The shaykh, a young man dressed in a suit and tie, replied that the task was not anti-government political agitation but "building an ideological infrastructure" and creating a truly Muslim society as its foundation.[117] The Muslim Brothers had begun their "war of position" years earlier by building an ideological infrastructure through extensive networking and grassroots activities. Not only did these networks spread Islamic sentiment; they also served to fulfill fundamental material and spiritual needs of ordinary Egyptians. In doing so, the movement unintentionally provided conditions for a "negative integration" of its constituency, since those networks and activities had coping mechanisms and a moral community in which many contenders felt at home. Guilain Denoeux's argument that reformist outcomes occur only when the leaderships of such institutions adopt a conciliatory strategy is partly true, but it disregards the objective (reformist) impact these networks often have on the perception of the constituency and on the movement's dynamics.[118] In Egypt, for example, Islamic associations played a crucial role not only in this process of integration but in overall change.

During 1980s and early 1990s in Egypt, shortcomings in traditional top-down planning and in implementing development objectives boosted the expansion of local and small-scale development projects, especially by NGOs. Islamic associations jumped on the opportunity to grow extensively, accounting for over one-third of the country's 12,832 NGOs in the late 1980s,[119] and half of all welfare associations, or some 5,000 private voluntary organizations (PVOs), in the early 1990s.[120] During the early 1990s, about 5,600 PVOs (most were probably Islamic) provided charitable and health services to over 5 million Egyptian poor.[121] Indeed, it appeared that mosques began to provide alternative support services to the low-income to compensate for the government retreat from social welfare provision after the implementation of neoliberal economic policies. A typical association, the Islamic Community Development Association in Ezbat Zein in Cairo, offered classes in the Qur'an and sewing, as well as day care, medical care, remedial tutoring, a food cooperative, and septic tank cleaning.[122] Others offered video clubs, computer training centers, and services that catered to high school graduates—the potential recruits of radical political Islamists. The availability of both funding (in the form of *zakat*, or Muslim charity from businesses and migrant workers in the Persian Gulf) and volunteers (who are scarce in today's Egypt) made these associations comparatively successful. The government supported these grassroots activities only to the extent that they shouldered some of the burden of providing social services.[123]

What made these practices "Islamic"? A combination of things: *zakat* funding; reduced service fees in the name of religion; they were alternatives to the state and the private sector; and some of their activists held firm religious convictions. But for many, Islamic NGOs simply provided a job or another way to conduct a business. As already mentioned, Islamic social welfare organizations were not places for Islamist political mobilization; they simply acted as service organizations. The vast majority of these NGOs had no link to political Islam. Only a few were affiliated with the Muslim Brothers and a handful with radical Islamists.[124]

However, unlike Islamic associations, Islam-dominated professional syndicates were all allied with the Muslim Brotherhood. By the early 1990s the Ikhwan controlled the major professional syndicates and constituted formidable opposition in the rest. Under Islamist influence, syndicate membership surged; the Teachers Union, for example, grew from 250,000 in 1985 to 750,000 in 1992.[125] Syndicate leaders fought corruption, increased members' incomes or found them jobs, created social welfare systems, set up consumer co-operatives, subsyndicates, and social clubs, and were extremely active politically.[126] Their rapid mobilization during the Cairo earthquakes in 1992 and the flooding in upper Egypt in 1994 reflected their efficiency. In fact, the syndicates became so powerful that the government limited their activities both by legal means and by arresting their leading members.[127]

The Muslim Brothers were not alone in providing social services. Indeed, their grassroots activities compelled other groups, such as al-Azhar, to offer similar services in the hope of maintaining legitimacy and gaining poltically.[128] In addition, the government's measures to upgrade slums and squatter areas in the early 1990s clearly responded to the creation by militants of an Islamist safe haven in the Cairo slum of Imbaba. Similarly, secular groups, NGOs in particular, worked hard to offer their own piecemeal alternatives. The net result of this intense competition was the mobilization of a critical mass and the creation of coping mechanisms of a political, economic, and spiritual nature.

Beyond improving material conditions, the Islamist movement offered the alienated constituencies an alternative social, cultural, and moral community within which the rival secular Western culture appeared less threatening. Facing rapid globalization and Western cultural penetration, these communities provided the traditionalists both a way to express their discontent and a moral safety net. In cities of every size, ritualized weekly gatherings (*halaqāt*) reflected not only a cultural protest but also Durkheimian social solidarity, security, and moral integration—paradoxical conditions that Arlene MacLeod, referring to the new veiling among Cairene women, called "accommodating protest."[129] The Young Men's Muslim Association, with over 2,000 members in Tanta alone, for instance, offered young people libraries, sports facilities, language and computer classes, video and television access, lectures, tours, and retreats.[130] Women from diverse socioeconomic backgrounds met not only to learn about Islamic precepts, but also to feel a sense of community.

Islamic-dominated syndicates also provided assistance beyond the material. They became known as organizations where those excluded from national political processes could participate in decision-making and feel confident that their votes counted. They rallied behind human rights, political prisoners, and the Palestinian cause. Activists collected donations for war victims in Bosnia, Iraq, and Chechnya,[131] and organized pilgrimages to Mecca. Even young adults could avoid opulent Egyptian hotel marriage ceremonies by organizing "Islamic weddings."

The Egyptian Islamic private school became yet another institution of both dissent and integration. In addition to providing a decent education (*ta'līm*)—which, it was believed, could not be obtained from the feeble and "morally misguided" national education system—private schools socialized pupils according to morality and the virtues of Islam (*tarbiyya*). Different from Azhari institutions, they resembled my own Islamic school in Tehran in the late 1960s, where daily collective prayers, religious classes, camps, and alternative leisure activities defined its Islamic identity. But their scale in Egypt was much larger than in Iran.[132] Islamism also managed to penetrate the national education system. Islamist students and teachers dominated many universities, notably in the south. But the Islamists' greatest feat was their infiltration of the Dar al-'Ulum, or Teachers Training College, which produced future school teachers who would wave the flag of Islamism in their classrooms.

So in the early 1990s, contestation over culture and moral virtues had grown even fiercer than the competition to improve material welfare (perhaps because it was less costly). In Egypt, "true Islam," both in idea and in deed, became a subject of intense competition among various contenders, including the seculars, which resulted in further concessions by secularists and the spread of Islamic discourse. This included not only variants of political Islam, but also "modernists" (e.g., Mustafa Mahmood), as well as the secular state, which had already made significant concessions to Islamic revivalism. Beginning in the 1980s, the state cut "immoral" television shows and increased Islamic programming, "nationalized" many mosques, and hired thousands of shaykhs to offer sermons during Ramadan. The number of imams working for the Ministry of Awqāf increased from 6,000 in 1982 to 22,000 in 1996. In the same period, Qur'an study groups jumped from 900 to about 1,200.[133] Al-Azhar expanded its grassroots activities tremendously; in 1995 it controlled more than 10,000 mosques and 6,000 educational institutions, ranging from primary and Qur'anic schools to university branches, and taught close to a quarter-million students.[134] Each year thousands of al-Azhar and local *kuttāb* (traditional religious school) graduates were added to the ranks of the ulema.[135] Meanwhile, the ruling National Democratic Party (NDP) and secular elite figures began to incorporate Islam into their political agendas: the NDP created the Islamic weekly *al-Liwa' al-Islami*, and a Westernized publisher, Sami Rajab, established *'Aqidati* to "spread correct Islamic thought and culture among Egyptian youth."[136] Ironically, both publications exhibited traditionalist and at times remarkably "fundamentalist" interpretations of Islam.[137] The national army also joined in the race in 1989 by publishing the Islamic monthly *al-Mujahid*. Such competition fueled popular religiosity of a traditionalist type in which, unlike Iran's nascent Islamic revivalism of the Shari'ati type, modernists became rather isolated (see Chapter Five).

The prevalence of Islam-inspired communities, conduct, and sentiment gave the Egypt of the early 1990s the partial appearance of an Islamic society. Along with great strides toward building an "Islamic infrastructure," the integrationist and even acquiescent consequences of these measures became ever more apparent. This angered and even demoralized some revolutionaries. The latter expressed concern about "conciliatory" ulema and their "apolitical" preaching. Although police surveillance was partially to blame for this, the reformist consequences of Egypt's Islamist movement played a crucial role.[138] The growing conservative religiosity of the state further complicated the countours of Islamist change.

These concerns signified not only a widespread debate in Egyptian society but also considerable differentiation and division within its Islamist movement: various militant groups, reformist Muslim Brothers and its factions, al-Azhar and its internal discontents, certain state institutions such as courts and the various sufi orders. The intense competition for "true Islam" and a "correct strategy" for change espoused a heated controversy; it offered an opportunity for people to put hard questions not only to politicians but also to the Islamic opposition—a phenomenon totally absent from the Iranian political scene before its Islamic Revolution. These debates owed much to the relative political openness of Egyptian society; the space available for political parties, the press, and NGOs during the 1980s, however limited, was far greater than what existed under the Shah during the 1970s.

But competition and controversy within the Islamist movement were also important in another respect: they implied relative clarity on political views, a diversity of positions, internal dissent, and thus disunity—all of which are characteristics of a social movement and anomalous to a revolutionary scenario. Revolutions, unlike social movements, depend on a high degree of unity, generality, and ambiguity. Unlike in Egypt, these were strongly present in Iran. The autocracy of the Shah, the sole leadership of the clergy resulting from the Shi'i clergy's hierarchical structure, the swift unfolding of events that allowed no time for debate or dissent, and thus a remarkable generality and ambiguity in the language of the revolution provided that astonishing unity.[139]

In the meantime, in Egypt, the perseverance of both the Islamists and the state created a political equilibrium in which the state succeeded in taking advantage of the increasing piety and religiosity in the country. While the Islamic revolution in Iran, just like the socialist revolution in Russia, surely bolstered similar movements in other parts of the world, its victory in Iran may have prevented similar scenarios in other countries, principally because it made incumbent states more vigilant while carrying out some reforms. Thus, the Egyptian political regime not only remained intact, but in the mid-1990s it intensified pressure on even the moderate Islamists, while simultaneously presenting itself as a pious state. State pressure exacerbated controversies and rifts already present in the Islamist movement. Internal division within the Ikhwan led to the 1996 split that spawned Hizb al-Wasat. And yet Islamic moral reform and religiosity from below continued unheeded. Egypt by the early 1990s was undergoing a level of Islamic social change that would have been unthinkable for the Iranian clergy under the Shah. Thus Egypt experienced the persistence of an Islamic movement without an Islamic revolution, whereas Iran underwent a revolution without a strong Islamic movement.

By the late 1990s, when Iran was experiencing its "post-Islamist" turn, Egyptian Islamism faced growing fragmentation, accelerated economic and cultural globalization, and a "seculareligious" state pushing for a "passive revolution." These differential trajectories had crucial implications for the conditions under which Islam could be made to embrace democratic ideals and an inclusive social order.

3 THE MAKING OF A POST-ISLAMIST MOVEMENT

Social Movements and Sociopolitical Change in Iran,
1979–1997

THE IRONY OF IRAN was that its Islamic revolution emerged not out of a strong Islamist movement but because of the absence of one, and that by the mid-1990s, the revolution that had so intensified the process of Islamization from above led to one of the most remarkable reform movements (*junbish-i islāhāt*) in the Muslim world. This chapter unravels the logic behind the contours of sociopolitical change in Iran since the revolution, highlighting the emergence of *post-Islamism* both as the engine and embodiment of this change.

In the following narratives, instead of focusing merely on ideas, I attempt to connect ideas with practices, movements, and structures. Driven primarily by students, women, youths, and religious intellectuals, as well as state employees and the professional class, post-Islamism heralded a new vision of society and polity that was expressed in a new outlook on public space, youth culture, student politics, gender relations, the state, and above all religious thought. At the heart of the post-Islamist project lay a blend of republican ideals and religious ethics, with "religious democracy" as its political mission. Through this prism, the association of Islam and democracy was not only possible, it was imperative. Post-Islamist republicanism was a response to popular disenchantment with a revolution that had come to recognize its own deficits and discrepancies. It embodied widely held dissent against a religious polity that had denied many of individual liberty, gender equality, and meaningful participation in public life. Reform (*islāhāt*) became the strategy, or method, sought out by emerging popular forces and social movements to realize the post-Islamist goals of democratizing the polity and religious thought, separating religious affairs from the state. It manifested struggles among the unfolding social movements in society to make Islam compatible with democratic and inclusive social order.

ISLAMIZING THE STATE, SPACE, AND SOCIETY

Whereas in Egypt Islamization spread because of a bottom-up Islamic movement, in Iran it was largely a top-down process driven by the state. The establishment of the first Islamic Republic in modern times following the revolution set the stage for a concerted strategy to "Islamize" the nation, state apparatus, public space, and individual behavior. Accordingly, national symbols, the flag, and the national anthem were all altered to correspond with the Islamic spirit, and the internationalization of Islamist order, or pan-Islamism, assumed a special significance.

The Islamist order was expressed most visibly and immediately in urban public space. In the early 1980s the regime launched a "cultural revolution" to transform the nation's education system. It shut down the universities, which until then had offered American-style programs, for three years to reorganize them around a "religious" curriculum and extracurricular activities, and to purge non-Islamic faculty and recruit committed personnel. Aiming to produce an "Islamic man," it abolished prerevolution youth centers, turning them over to the Revolutionary Guards or the police. Workplaces, factories, offices, banks, and hospitals became sites of moral prescription: sex segregation and daily collective prayers were imposed by law and enforced by hard-line Islamic associations established within most public institutions. Revolutionary posters and slogans adorned all public spaces, and the constant blaring of religious recitation from loudspeakers reminded citizens of the new social order.

The urban social scene and street culture went through a dramatic transformation. Revolutionary zealots, radical clergy, and leftists took over luxury hotels, previously the hangouts of foreigners and wealthy Iranians, and gave them to the homeless or turned them into office buildings. Western names, logos, and symbols were dramatically diminished, and cinemas and theaters ceased to attract audiences. Bars, cabarets, and nightclubs had already been shut down during the revolutionary turmoil, their derelict facades all that was left of their past energy and glory. The red-light district in south Tehran was deliberately set ablaze, forcing sex workers, now literally undercover, to operate in the streets.

The visual legacy of the revolution—political graffiti, huge murals, posters, and placards—embellished every urban street and back alley. The old street-corner culture, or *sar-i kuchih*, where young men would assemble, socialize, form gangs, and ogle young women, faded away rapidly, demonized by revolutionaries as vanity and idleness. In their place the *pāsdārān*, or Revolutionary Guards, and the dozen groups of male vigilantes, or *hizbullahies*, wielded clubs and guns and patrolled the streets to enforce the new moral order.

The escalation of the war with Iraq further militarized the mood in the public sphere. The brutality of the war had produced heroes and martyrs in almost every urban street. The dramatic increase of street names beginning with *shahīd* (martyr) became a testimony to this new geography of violence. Temporary but elaborate altars mushroomed on streetcorners, where voices blared Qur'anic verses from loudspeakers in mournful tribute to the fallen. But no sight was more jarring in the new public space than the sudden disappearance of bright colors. Black and gray, reflected most spectacularly in women's veils and men's facial hair, dominated the urban visual scene, mirroring an aspect of Islamists' draconian control of body, color, and taste. Probably not even Foucault could have imagined the extraordinary credence his concept of power and discipline would receive in the aftermath of what he had cherished as the "first postmodern revolution of our time."[1]

Granted that the public space of the 1980s was informed by redistribution, egalitarian ethos (in terms of class), and new spatial solidarities induced by war and new urban migration. It nevertheless represented a regimented, masculine, and exclusionary space. It was severe, sad, and sober, with little color, compassion, or fun. The dark public ambience celebrated death and bravery, valued manliness and moralizing, and bred suspicion.

The public aura in this "republic of virtue" stood in sharp contrast not only to prerevolutionary culture, but also to Egyptian street life, even at the height of its Islamism in the 1980s. In this paradoxical spatial order, large city centers and squares turned into highly controlled, enclosed, or "interior" spaces of the "ideological self" that excluded nonconforming people, styles and behaviors.[2] Although spatial distinctions based on class and privilege were diminished, the gender spatial division surged. Managers and workers, or professors and students, could commingle in more egalitarian common spaces; they were, however, forcibly segregated along gender lines. Thus men and women were barred from mixing in libraries, refectories, and sports centers, as *basīji*s and top personnel systematically humiliated women for "improper" dress or behavior.

Moralizing public space virtually eliminated the bustling Caspian Sea resorts, leading either to the domestication of recreation (in private villas of the rich) or to the institutionalization and regimentation of leisure. In the state-run resorts assigned to government employees, large murals of martyrs, slogans, and loudspeakers constantly warned the vacationers about the consequences of their moral wrongdoings. Such institutionalized leisure provided little relaxation or fun for many middle-class urbanites, women in particular, who wished to get away from a domestic space that itself had been transformed. Older residential architecture with features such as courtyards, terraces, and rooftops (*ayvān, zīrzamīn,* and *sardāb*) that had provided privacy and places for neighborly sociability gave way to boxlike apartment buildings. Such architecture lent itself to the seclusion and surveillance of women, who were forced indoors by the new regime's colonization of neighborhoods and back under the thumb of husbands, fathers, and brothers.[3] These new spatial arrangements forged new types of identities, the political implications of which were expressed a decade later.

Compulsory veiling was the most severe measure designed to give religious identity to postrevolutionary Iranian women. Indeed, many liberal laws that had favored women under the Shah, such as the Family Protection Law, were annulled. The legal age of maturity declined (to 9 for girls and 14 for boys). Day care centers and family planning programs were devalued, polygamy and temporary marriage assumed renewed legitimacy, and men lawfully received custody of children and the automatic right to divorce. The imposition of a quota system effectively barred many women (among others) from studying in some colleges and restricted their enrollment in others.

The first days of the revolution launched a quest for an "Islamic economy"—neither capitalist nor socialist but based on "Islamic justice," *qist-i Islāmi.* Its cornerstone was a redefinition of property rights compatible with the undefined notion of *mashrū',* or legitimate capital accumulation, to safeguard both property rights and the interests of the *mustaż'afīn,* the downtrodden. Dozens of seminars were held to discuss "Islamic economics," to determine the limits of *mashrū'* capital, but only the least controversial policies were implemented. Banking interest was removed (in theory), the labor laws were changed, Islamic prayers were enforced in workplaces, "un-Islamic" businessmen were jailed or had their capital confiscated, and foreign investment was discouraged.

Such measures caused business insecurity, led to a sharp drop in investment and production, and instigated a public debate between the "specialists" (*takhassusgirāyān*) and the populist Islamists known as *maktabies*. The former, representing President Abul-Hasan Bani-Sadr, emphasized expert knowledge in dealing with economic and technical issues, while the *maktabies* stressed the importance of Islamic ideological commitment. The populist view remained dominant during the 1980s, dismaying free-market Islamists (those close to bazaar merchants with the backing of the Qum Seminary) whose economic visions ironically invoked Milton Friedman's unfettered laissez-faire.[4] By the early 1990s, President Rafsanjani's technocratic government had seriously undermined the hegemony of *maktabism*. Although Shari'a was the law of land, much of the prerevolution legal code continued unaltered, and only eighteen articles of the civil code changed; labor law was altered considerably, but not necessarily in an "Islamic" direction, and commercial law remained almost intact. The most dramatic changes occurred in the penal code.

Central to Iran's Islamism was the establishment of an Islamic state based on *vilāyat-i faqīh*, or the supreme rule of jurists. The constitution, written for the most part by the ulema, or clergy, granted the *faqīh*, or supreme jurist, the power to govern the *umma* (Muslim believers) in the absence of the Twelfth Imam, who, in Shi'i tradition, is believed to be in occultation. It stipulated that all laws of the land be in accordance with Islamic principles. Although the "people's sovereignty," which God had transferred to them, was institutionalized in the Western-style Parliament, parliamentary decisions were subject to the approval of a Council of Guardians, a twelve-member jury appointed by the *faqīh* and the head of the judiciary (see Figure 1).

But the *faqīh*, the most powerful political and religious figure—he appoints the head of the judiciary, commands the security forces, oversees the heads of state radio and television, and could dismiss the president of the republic—was not elected directly by popular vote. In fact there was no systematic method of selecting the *faqīh*; he was to be the highest *marja'-i taqlīd* (source of emulation) although he was customarily recognized by clerical peers. Khomeini's *marja'iyyat* (religious leadership) was defined by both his religious and political charisma. However, owing to the lack of a "suitable" *marja'* (religious leader) to replace Khomeini, the constitution was amended in 1989 to give power to the Assembly of Experts to elect the *vali-i faqīh* for an unlimited period, but not necessarily from among the grand ayatollahs. The Assembly of Experts supervises, and, if necessary, suspends the *faqīh*. But the members of this assembly are, in turn, screened and effectively sanctioned by the Council of Guardians,

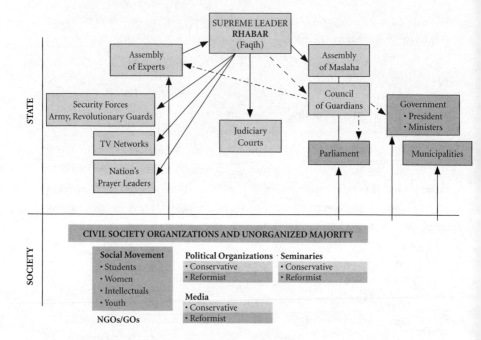

Figure 1. Distribution of power under the reform government, 1997–2004.

whose members are appointed by the *faqīh* himself. So in effect, the Assembly of Experts, which elects and is supposed to supervise and, if necessary, dismiss the *faqīh*, is effectively sanctioned by him. The establishment of this circular exchange of support and loyalty, in addition to the *faqīh*'s disproportionate power, resulted in a semi-patrimonial Islamic state.[5]

In short, Islamism was in general based on a reading of Islam that interpreted it as a complete social, political, economic, and moral system that had answers to all human problems. It was up to the "true" Muslims, through resiliency and commitment, to discover them. The Islamists' monopolization of truth meant that there was little room for the coexistence of competing worldviews. Islamism appeared exclusionary, monovocal, and intolerant to pluralism, representing an absolutist and totalitarian ideology. Infighting within the Islamic state showed disagreement over such an Islamist vision. Yet polarity, enmity, and binary opposition marked the salient features of this political discourse, espoused by a regime that secured support among segments of the urban poor, traditional petite bourgeoisie, rural youth, and the middle classes.

Revolutions often generate short-term value systems expressed by solidarity, loyalty, and generosity. While some found vested interests in the prevailing system, other Iranians upheld Islamist policies out of loyalty to the revolution. Segments of urban youth were integrated into the Islamic system through the war effort and the revolutionary institutions, or *nahādhā-i inqilābi*, such as the *pāsdārān, basīj*, and *jihad-i sāzandigi*. The state hoped that the Islamization of schools would expand this critical mass of supporters, and indeed the Islamist discourse and its support base prevailed throughout the 1980s, though it was inspired considerably by the charisma of Ayatollah Khomeini.

Nevertheless, it would be a mistake to assume that Islamism was fully internalized by the populace, or even by the "true" Muslims. Scores of ordinary people, and even some grand ayatollahs, resisted totalitarian Islamism, especially Khomeini's concept of *vilāyat-i faqīh*. Many Muslim women contested forced veiling, while the secular-leftist and liberal-religious opposition vehemently fought religious rule. However, this early opposition was soon repressed. The war with Iraq, where Islamic symbols were fully utilized (the war of *haqq* against *bātil*, of Islam against unbelief), contributed to the Islamic vision.

However, with the end of the war (in 1988) and the death of Ayatollah Khomeini (in 1989), a new phase began. The program of postwar reconstruction under President Rafsanjani marked the beginning of what I call "post-Islamism." As both a condition and a project, post-Islamism characterized a series of remarkable social and intellectual movements driven by younger generations, students, women, and religious intellectuals, and a new perception of urban space that would shape Iran's political and social course in the years to come. By embracing a fusion of faith and freedom, religion and rights, post-Islamism transcended the Islamist polity. It called for individual choice, pluralism, and democracy, as well as religious ethics.

TRANSFORMING URBAN PUBLIC SPACE

An early and more visible sign of the post-Islamist trend appeared in urban public space, beginning first in Tehran in 1992 and spreading to other cities. By the late 1980s, Tehran had reflected a crisis of governance that afflicted the nation as whole. The city had become overgrown, overpopulated, polluted, unregulated, mismanaged, and exhausted by war. Its Islamist (exclusionary, masculine, harsh, segregating, and highly regimented) spatiality had alienated the majority of youth, women, and the modern middle classes. In 1989 the pragmatist President Rafsanjani appointed Ghulam Husayn Karbaschi, a former theology student turned urban planner, to fix the capital city. In the course of eight years (1990–98), Tehran assumed a new character that had little to do with the image of an "Islamic city." Its new aesthetic, spatial configuration, symbolism, freeways, huge commercial billboards, and shopping malls emulated Madrid or even Los Angeles more than they did Karbala or Qum.

All of the hurriedly written revolutionary slogans and imposing posters that had covered almost every empty wall gave way to commercial advertisements and a handful of officially sanctioned slogans adorned impressively with colorful designs and portraits. Splendid cultural centers, beginning with the Bahman Cultural Complex, were established, largely in poor south Tehran, catering to the arts, music, and modern technology. In the course of four years, the municipality built 138 cultural complexes and 27 sports centers and turned 13,000 vacant lots into recreation areas. It also built 600 new public parks—three-and-a-half times their previous number—and transformed thousands of barren acres on the city's periphery into forest plantations.[6]

The scores of shopping malls and *shahrvand* (citizen) department stores, with high ceilings, wide aisles, and parking lots, were the first of their kind in Iran's urban history. Not only did they offer a more modern and efficient distribution system, undercutting the black market, but they also aimed to diminish the influence of the traditional bazaar, which had been the major support base for the conservative clergy. The mayor became one of the most popular public figures in Iran, and the municipality's daily, *Hamshahri*, re-styled in color, outsold all other dailies by accumulating a circulation of half a million within two years. The social, symbolic, and political implications of these changes can hardly be overestimated. Most visibly, glimpses of bright colors returned to the city's landscape. Green parks, trees, boulevards lined with flowers, and painted shops and offices brightened up the gloomy and grim mood of the city.

The city had always been home to an internal "other": during the Shah's reign it had been the "traditional" and poor south, while under the Islamist regime it was the rich (*tāghūti*) and westernized north. Indeed, this image of the "internal other" fit well with the Islamists' discourse of blame and enmity, separation and antagonism. However, the new municipality was determined to eliminate the sociocultural (though not economic) divide between north and south that starkly marked the capital. It was as though Karbaschi had invoked the Olmstedian view of a "central park," a vision of public landscapes and parks as social safety valves that induced social classes and different ethnicities to mix in common, morally safe recreational spaces. Karbaschi achieved this by undertaking urban renewal, creating a large number of public parks, establishing cultural complexes in the south, and constructing expressways that linked north and south. For the first time, members of the upper class, celebrities, and foreign dignitaries living in the north would attend concerts and cultural events in the south.

The new cultural complexes bolstered the tremendous popularity of Western and Iranian classical music among the youth. Over 75 percent of concertgoers were young boys and girls, and 65 percent of the visitors to cultural centers were women. Perceived as morally secure, cultural centers drew young women from traditional families, who would otherwise be secluded at home or in controlled religious spaces, to engage in secular activities and artistic recreation.[7] These new mixed social spaces became havens of relative freedom and accelerated the emergence of new social actors.

While the wearing of headscarves and gender segregation were still enforced by the state, the municipality's newly constructed 600 public parks brought men, women, boys, and girls together in public places. Recreational activities facilitated a less restricted mingling of the sexes, including mountain climbing, skiing in north Tehran, and biking in the forest plantations on the city's outskirts. City dwellers who previously spent their leisure time in the seclusion of their homes or those of relatives and friends, or attending religious gatherings, now flocked to public places. The Islamist control over body and color, space and mobility revealed its paradox—the largely imposed black *hijāb* generated a homogeneity, anonymity, and "invisibility" that women used to enjoy mobility and a presence in the masculine public space.

Whereas the urban space of the 1980s fostered domesticity, kinship, and worship, the new spatial logic embraced civility, citizenry, and secular pursuits. It was a space of relative inclusion, dialogue, and agonistic interactions. The policy of removing fences from around public parks collapsed boundaries between different worlds, facilitated an unimpeded flow of space from streets straight to greenery, fountains, and flowers, and invoked a sense of openness and freedom that stood in sharp contrast to the rigid and regimented geography of Islamism.

The municipal leadership did not want to "westernize" youth but to protect them from unregulated and corrupting behavior, aiming for an alternative, hybrid modernity, efficient but responsive to certain ethical sensibilities. The effect was the creation of an urban individual, which angered many Islamists.

'Ali Akbar Natiq Nuri, the head of Parliament, declared constructing expressways and overpasses to be against Islamic urban values. Muhsin Reza'i, the former commander of the Revolutionary Guards, deplored the energy spent after the war on building freeways and factories instead of a nation-wide cultural (meaning Islamist ideological) movement.[8] And the supreme leader, 'Ali Khamenei, warned the municipality about the erosion of the city's "Islamic identity." In 1995, therefore, in order to give an "Islamic identity" to the city, the authorities approved a massive project to build the world's largest mosque in the center of Tehran. The colossal $100 million edifice, with 6,000 toilets for 1 million worshipers, is larger than the holy sites in Mecca and Medina.[9] A reminder of flamboyant Stalinist architecture, it evoked the image of the Islamic revolution in this post-Islamist era.

Meanwhile, the populist weekly *Payam-i Danishju* and the vigilante groups of *Hizbullah* attacked the mayor and municipality not only about the increasing commercialism, conspicuous consumption, and speculation, which indeed marked urban life in 1990s, but also about the spread of music, moral laxity in public parks, and "Western-style urbanization." Likewise, colorful women's clothing, biking, skiing, women athletes, and the mere presence of women in public provoked outcries from the hard-line publications *Haftih Namih-i Subh*, *Jumhuri-i Islami*,[10] and *Farhang-i Āfarīnesh*. The last summed up the "problems" it claimed the new thinking had caused:

> The growing presence of women in public places, freedom to wear fashionable and colorful outfits, legitimizing interaction between men and women, assertiveness [of women] in public, [women's] expression of independent opinions in the household, their activity in the male domain, the right [of women] to have jobs despite the opposition of family or husband, and education as the first priority under any circumstance—these are some of the ideas that are being fed to society.[11]

Although conservative Islamists took their revenge in 1998 by putting the popular mayor behind bars on charges of embezzlement, the drive for post-Islamist spatiality continued, as other cities followed Tehran's lead. Muslim women and youths were clearly the integral players in this new urbanity. Indeed, the post-Islamist urban space was both a product and a producer of post-Islamist youths. For more than any other social category, as agents of a movement and cultural politics, youths were shaped by and expressed themselves primarily in urban public places.

POST-ISLAMIST YOUTHS

The post-Islamist youths who injected spirit into the new urban spatiality had departed from the Islamism that stifled "youthfulness," a disposition associated with idealism, individuality, and spontaneity. By their simultaneous adherence to faith, freedom, and fun, Iranian youths created one of most remarkable youth movements in the Muslim world. The drive to reclaim youthfulness melded with the struggle for an inclusive religion and democratic ideals.[12]

The spectacular activism of youths in the revolution,[13] in the war, and in the new revolutionary institutions altered their public image from "youth-as-trouble" to "heroes and martyrs." Nevertheless, the young remained "vulnerable" to corrupting ideas and temptations, thus requiring protection, surveillance, and reeducation. Through sweeping institutional engineering in the media, schools, and universities, and through a "cultural revolution," the Islamic regime strived to create an ideal "Muslim man": austere, controlled, and selfless, with an extraordinary personality that negated the expression of levity, individuality, or a free spirit. The young were subjected to draconian social control in public places.

What sustained the regime of surveillance for a decade or so were a revolutionary fervor, a preoccupation with the war, and the repression of dissent. Young men were either on the war fronts caught up in its destructive consequences, or fleeing the country, preferring the humiliation of exile to the "heroic martyrdom" of a "meaningless" war. Anxiety, gloom, and depression haunted many of those who remained in the country: one out of every three high school students suffered from some kind of behavioral disorder. Girls were particularly susceptible to stress, fear, and depression.[14]

Few officials noticed the inner despair of the young. Postwar media stories about "degenerate behavior" shocked the public: boys disguised as women walked the streets; girls wore male attire to escape the harassment of the morals police; college students refused to take religious studies courses,[15] while others were arrested for playing loud music on their car stereos or for establishing underground popular music groups.[16] Boys crashed cars for fun, drag-raced toward cliff edges while handcuffed to the steering wheel, or danced in the streets beside self-flagellation ceremonies on the religious mourning day of 'Ashura.[17] Drug addiction raged among schoolchildren, and the number of prostitutes skyrocketed by 635 percent between 1998 and 1999.[18]

Beyond individual escape and rebellion, the young took every opportunity to assert their youthful dispositions, forming open and clandestine subcultures that often defied moral and political authority. Surveillance did not deter their pursuit of Western classical music, or their smuggling of cassettes and music videos by exiled Iranian singers. Music blaring from speeding cars dismayed Islamists. Underground pop, rock, rap, and heavy metal bands thrived across Tehran, performing at covert late-night parties. With the music came fashion and a globalized youth subculture—tight or baggy pants, vulgar English slang, tattoos—and a general sense of group belonging.[19] Some had run away from home to join such youth groups, and many ended up in prison. Indeed, by the late 1990s, Tehran faced an "escalating crisis of runaway girls frequently becoming victims of prostitution rings and human trafficking." In 2002, officials reported some 60,000 runaway girls, of whom 4,000 had been found or arrested.[20] Most had left home to escape family surveillance or to pursue male partners.[21]

Although the freedom to date openly had become a casualty of Iran's republic of virtue, the young found ways around the surveillance. The children of the well-to-do met at private parties, in underground peer groups, and even in public parks, shopping malls, and restaurants, often communicating by cell phone. In these distanciated datings, Muslim girls and boys eyed one another from a distance, flirted, chatted, or expressed love through electronic waves. Seeking privacy in the legitimate public, young couples hired taxis and drove together for hours in the anonymity of the city; they held hands, romanced, and enjoyed the delight of each other's company.[22] The popularity of Valentine's Day testified to the widespread practice of "forbidden love" and relationships, in which sex, it seemed, was not excluded. An academic claimed that one out of three unmarried girls and 60 percent of a sample in north Tehran had experienced sexual relations. Out of 130 reported AIDS cases, ninety were unmarried women.[23] An official of the Tehran Municipality reported "each month at least ten or twelve aborted fetuses are found in the garbage."[24]

Clearly, sexuality had challenged the capacity of the Islamic state to integrate youths and their subversive sensibilities. To address the problem, President Rafsanjani, in the early 1990s, advocated *mut'a*, or temporary "marriage of pleasure." Ayatollah Hā'iri Shirazi proposed allowing "legitimate courtship" (without sex), an openly recognized relationship approved by parents or relatives.[25] Others called for some kind of official document confirming the legitimacy (*halāliyyat*) of such relationships.[26] And in 2000, conservative Islamists came up with the idea of establishing "chastity houses" where men could "temporarily marry" prostitutes to "legitimize" their encounters. None of these desperate measures offered an adequate solution. If anything, they expressed a growing moral panic.

Anxiety over the increasing frequency of *bad hijābi* (laxity on observing veil) among school and university girls alarmed officials. "We are encountering a serious cultural onslaught. What is to be done?" they lamented.[27] Over 85 percent of young people in 1995 spent their leisure time watching television, but only 6 percent of them watched religious programs; of the 58 percent who read books, less then 8 percent were interested in religious literature.[28] A staggering 80 percent of the nation's youth were indifferent or opposed to the clergy, religious obligations, and religious leadership,[29] and 86 percent of students refrained from saying their daily prayers.[30]

Official panic notwithstanding, youths however did not abandon Islam altogether. Most of them exhibited strong "religious belief" and "religious feeling," even if they neglected religious practice.[31] Their Islam seemed to have little impact on their daily lives; God existed but did not prevent them from drinking alcohol or dating. Few attended mosques, but most filled the lecture halls of "religious intellectuals" who preached a more inclusive Islam. The young were forging new religious subcultures that embraced the sacred and the secular, faith and fun, the divine and diversion. Given harsh social controls, they resorted to legitimate norms and institutions to assert their youthful claims, and in doing so they creatively reinvented and subverted the meaning of those norms and institutions. This *subversive accommodation* was expressed, for instance, in the way some youngsters turned the highly charged ritual of Muharram into evenings of glamour, fun, and sociability. At these "husayn parties," as they were called, boys and girls dressed up, strolled the streets until dawn, chatting, flirting, exchanging phone numbers, making the best out of what was allowed. Similarly, the *sham-i gharībān*, the most sorrowful Shi'i ritual in Islamic Iran (the 11th night of the month of Muharram) became a blissful night of socializing for the north Tehrani youths who assembled in public squares until dawn.[32] Even the *nowhih*, the sorrowful recitation mourning the death of Imam Husayn, acquired a pop-music orientation.

Contestation over youth culture at times spilled over into the streets and turned into spectacular public protests. Soccer matches often became occasions of political defiance, expressed through both collective fun and fury. In 1998, for example, when the Iranian team defeated the United States in Paris, youngsters in every major Iranian city took over the streets for five hours to cheer, dance, and sound their car horns. When the same team lost to Bahrain in 2001, hundreds of thousands again poured into the streets, only this time to direct their deep-seated anger at Islamist authorities. In Tehran and the provincial cities of Karadj, Qum, Shiraz, Kashan, and Isfahan, they marched, chanted political slogans, threw rocks and hand-made explosives at police, vandalized police cars, broke traffic lights, and lit candles in mourning. By the time the protestors went home, 800 had been arrested.[33] Earlier in the city of Tabriz thousands of young spectators had raged against *basīji* bands in reaction to the latter's objections to the "improper behavior" of a few in the crowd.

Authorities remained deeply divided over what to do about such subversive behavior. Hard-liners repeatedly called for the vigilante supporters to take to the streets to fight against "cultural invasion," "hooliganism," and "anti-Islamic sentiments."[34] They punished people whom they saw as promoting immorality, "depravity," and "indecency," closing down boutiques, cafes, and restaurants.[35] In July 2002, some sixty "special units," including several hundred men wearing green uniforms and toting machine guns and hand grenades, drove up and down the streets of Tehran chasing young drivers who were listening to loud music, women wearing makeup or loose veils, partygoers, and alcohol drinkers.[36] Yet the crackdown did little to change behavior. Instead, it caused a public uproar in which the fundamentals of the Islamic penal code came under attack, as scores of reform-minded clerics questioned its application in this modern age.[37] The reformists attributed the youth rebellion to the regime's "suppression of joy."

In a unique public debate in the late 1990s, they called for a "definition" and even the "management" of joy in order to develop a culture of festivity that people had been denied and who were thus ignorant of its rules.[38] Seminars and essays debated the meaning of "leisure" and the modalities of "fun among women" who had been suffering from depression more than other groups.[39] Reformists called for a "love of life" and a "right to happiness," because "a depressed and austere society cannot have a solid civility."[40] By declaring that "laughter is not deviance," the reformists lashed out at hard-line Islamists who had shunned fun and laughter, which were, after all, human experiences that invigorated the society.[41] In so doing, reformists supplied the young with a political platform, support and moral courage, unintentionally sparking Iran's youth movement.

The movement challenged the moral and political authority and subverted the Islamist dream of producing "true Muslim youth," an image emulated by those lower-class youngsters who had joined the hard-line *basījis*, *pāsdārān*, and *Ansar-i Hizbullah* groups. The young generation, however, were children of the postrevolution and barely remembered the revolution's fervor. Unlike their parents, who had been concerned with social justice, cultural authenticity, and anti-imperialism, the young rejected traditional hierarchies and yearned for autonomy and individual freedom. Through innovative interpretations of Islam that suited their youth habitus, the young pluralized religious perceptions and practice and projected a more inclusive and tolerant Islam. Through their everyday struggles to reclaim joy, fun, and individuality, they enforced a reading of Islam that came to be known as the "religion of life." The post-Islamist call for the fusion of faith and fun owed its logic not simply to an essential doctrinal truth, but also to the resistance of young Muslims.[42]

Did this mean Iranian youths were collectively agents of democratic change? Only to the degree that claims of youthfulness clashed with political-moral authority. Otherwise, many of their mannerisms differed little from those of youngsters elsewhere in the world. The defiant behavior of Iranian youths was similar to that of post–World War I behaviors in America and Europe or post-Franco Spain. A rebellious, belligerent, deliberately anti-moralist and hedonistic backlash seem to be common features of most post-crisis societies.[43] Nor were the quest for self-expression, a counterculture, and global cultural products peculiar to Iranian youth. "Across the world," as Doreen Massey notes, "even the poorest of young people strive to buy into an international cultural reference system: the right trainers, a T-shirt with a Western logo, a baseball cap with the right slogan."[44]

Youth activism may pose little challenge to authoritarian states unless youths become part of a political movement. For a youth movement is essentially about *claiming youthfulness*; it embodies a collective challenge whose central goal is defending and extending the youth habitus, the conditions that allow the young to assert their individuality and creativity and to diminish their exclusion, anxiety, and insecurity. Curbing or curtailing these dispositions, as in Iran, Saudi Arabia, or, to a lesser degree, Egypt, might cause collective rebellion. Yet, unlike in Egypt or Saudi Arabia, only in Iran did a pervasive youth movement develop. Why?

Their simultaneous valorization and severe social control, coupled with the opportunity for expression in the new post-Islamist conditions, offered

Iranian youth a strong sense of self and the latitude to act collectively. Still, *young people* (as an age category) might not be able to forge a collective challenge without first turning into *youth* as a social category.

When I was growing up in a small village in central Iran during the 1960s, I had, of course, friends and peers with whom I talked, played, agreed, and fought. However, then we were not "youth," strictly speaking; we were simply young persons. In the village, most young people had little opportunity to experience "youthfulness." They moved rapidly from the vulnerability and dependence of childhood to adulthood, to the world of work, parenting, and responsibility. Many never went to school. There was little "relative autonomy" (the sociological element of being young), especially for most young women, who passed swiftly from the sphere of their fathers' or brothers' authority to that of their husbands. "Youth" as a social category is essentially a modern, indeed an urban, phenomenon. It is in cities that "young people" turn into "youth" by developing a particular consciousness about being young. Schooling prolongs the period of youthfulness and cultivates status, expectations, and critical awareness. Cities, the locus of diversity, creativity, and anonymity, open up opportunities for young people to explore alternative role models and choices, and offer venues in which they can express their individuality. Such conditions were present in Iran.

By 1996 the number of young people had increased dramatically. Two-thirds of the population was under 30, and a staggering 20 million, one-third, were students. Most lived in cities, exposed to diverse lifestyles and public spaces that allowed for relative autonomy, extra-kinship identities, and social interactions on a broad scale. In the meantime, an "urbanizing" rural youth was taking shape, as urbanity sprawled into the countryside. The spread of Open University branches throughout the country, for instance, meant that on average every village was home to two university graduates, a very rare phenomenon in the 1970s. As meritocracy began to undermine ageism, the young moved into decision-making positions. Sweeping rural social changes and expanding communications facilitated the flow of young people, ideas, and lifestyles, and the social barriers separating rural from urban youth began to crumble, giving the country's young a broader, national constituency. In the meantime, the weakening of parental authority (resulting from the state's valorization of youths) and the reinforcement of "child-centeredness" in the family (an outcome of the rising literacy among women and mothers) contributed to the individuation of the young and their militancy.[45]

By the mid-1990s, Iran's postrevolutionary young had turned into "youth," a collective social agent. Their movement did not embody a coherent organization, ideology, and leadership (unlike the student movement), but rather "collective sentiments" in asserting youthful, albeit fragmented, identities. Theirs was a movement whose principal expression lay in the politics of presence, tied closely to everyday collective being, cultural struggle, and normative subversion. This mass of fragmented individuals and subgroups shared common attributes and expressed common anxieties in demanding individual liberty and in asserting their collective identities. Individuals were linked by dispersed subgroups, such as youth magazines, peer groups, streetcorner associations, and NGOs (400 youth NGOs existed in 2001, 1,100 in 2003,[46] plus thousands of informal groups throughout the country), and through cultural, artistic, charity, developmental and intellectual activities, lectures, concerts, and charity bazaars. The more common venues in which to forge identities were, however, "passive networks. Passive networks point to instantaneous and undeliberate communications between atomized individuals, which they establish through gaze in public space by tacitly recognizing their common traits. The young built collective identities spontaneously by recognizing shared symbols, styles (T-shirts, blue jeans, hair), activities (attending concerts, shopping in music stores), and places (sports stadiums, shopping malls, hiking trails).

Unlike Iran's Muslim women, who caused change by making incremental claims, the youth did so by their very collective being. Through their central preoccupation with cultural production or lifestyles, the young fashioned new social norms, religious practices, cultural codes, and values without needing a structured organization, leadership, or articulated ideology. This was so because youth movements, I would suggest, are characterized less by *what the young do* (networking, organizing, deploying resources, mobilizing) than by *how they are* (expressed in behavior, clothing, slang, mannerisms). The youth movement's identity is based not so much on collective *doing* as on their collective *being*; and they make their claims less through collective protest than *collective presence.*

The power of Muslim youth movements lay in the ability of their seemingly dispersed agents to challenge the political and moral authorities by their mere alternative, but persistent, *presence.* As a national social category operating in uniquely simultaneous conditions of both repression and opportunity, Iranian youth reclaimed their youthfulness in a battle in which the state became the target.

THE STUDENT MOVEMENT

At the core of post-Islamist youth lay Iran's student population, including 1 million college-goers. Student activism of the late 1990s, which reflected their triple identities of being young, schooled, and increasingly female, had come a long way to become the backbone of the post-Islamist reform movement. Things were different earlier on.

In my college years in the late-1970s, student politics had been dominated by Marxist and Islamist revolutionary discourse. Expressed grievances about teaching conditions, tuition, dorms, or cultural clubs often led to political mobilization. Many activists had links with the leftist, Islamist, and liberal National Front underground organizations. At that time, Iran's student movement resembled in many ways those in post-colonial countries, notably Latin America, marked by political radicalism, a revolutionary strategy, nationalism, Third-Worldism, and an anti-imperialist orientation. The Islamic Revolution politicized students even further, splitting them into clusters aligned with the dozens of leftist and Islamist political groups that had proliferated during the last weeks of the Shah's regime.

In the period immediately after the revolution, the student movement retained much of its ideological character but became overwhelmingly Islamist and male. University campuses virtually turned into headquarters of the radical Islamist and leftist groups, whose radicalism often disrupted academic life. It was then, in November 1979, that the Muslim Student Followers of Imam Line, led by such Islamists as 'Abbas 'Abdi, Muhsen Mirdamadi, Ibrahim Asgharzadih, and Habibullah Bitaraf, seized the U.S. embassy in Tehran and took American diplomats as hostages for 444 days.

In 1980 in the midst of this new chaotic order, Islamic authorities backed the creation of Islamic student associations, which with the help of vigilante Hizbullahi groups, proceeded to "cleanse" campuses of political factions and nonconformist faculty and students. Islamist students occupied and closed several universities, and eventually all higher education was suspended by order of the Revolutionary Council for three years. This paved the way for what came to be known as Iran's Cultural Revolution, which aimed to purge and Islamize universities.

The student movement was deeply divided between pro-regime Islamist students gathered around *Daftar-i Tahkim va Vahdat-i Anjumanha-yi Islami* (the Office of Consolidation and Unity of Islamic Associations), or DTV, and secularists, nationalists, leftists, and regime opponents—in a word, nonconformists. When they reopened in 1983, universities were dominated by the DTV, which along with members of the *pāsdārān* and *basījis*, acted on campuses as agents of the regime, mobilizing for war efforts or the Construction Crusade (institutions of rural development), using surveillance to drive nonconformists into hiding or jail, or into apathy and demoralization.[47] DTV, mirroring the government itself, was split over what economic strategy to deploy. The majority, Imam Line, sided with "leftist" clerics, such as Karrubi and Khatami, who advocated state intervention in the economy and in 1988 formed the Society of Combatant Clerics (SCC) of Tehran. The minority, led by Hashmatullah Tabarzadi, aligned with pro-market and socially conservative clerics, notably Hashemi Rafsanjani and 'Ali Khamenei, who organized the Association of Combatant Clergy (ACC). Even though Tabarzadi's group, which soon broke with the DTV, extended its membership to alumni, workers, and civil servants, and published its own newspaper, it remained insignificant. When the regime consolidated itself in the mid-1980s, its need for student mobilization decreased, thus severely diminishing the earlier clout of the Islamist student groups. The presidency of the pragmatic Hashemi Rafsanjani (1989–96), following the death of Ayatollah Khomeini, reinvigorated Islamist students into populist opposition to the government's free-market policies.

As the rivalry grew between the Islamist "left" and "right," the rightist Rawhaniyat-i Mubariz and allies established the partisan Islamic Society of Students to undermine the leftist DTV, but the initiative went nowhere. The Islamist-leftist DTV attacked Rafsanjani's economic liberalization policy, which it felt had hurt the poor, opened the country to foreign capital, and spread immoral practices. Even Tabarzadi's group, once an ally, lashed out at the government's "cultural lenience." By 1996 Tabarzadi had fallen from the grace of both the president and the supreme leader. For the first time student leaders began speaking of democracy; but rather than being a genuine ideological shift, this was no more than mere posturing derived from their declining influence under Rafsanjani.

Expectedly, these new developments did little to trigger the interest of the mass of students who had remained distant from such political bickering. Between the early 1980s and mid-1990s, the official student organization, DTV, was still an extension of the state, allied with the Islamic-left factions, with student leaders acting like state officials.[48] A handful of independent student groups (such as Daftar-i Mutali'at-i Farhangi of Sharif University and Jame'y-i

Mustaqil-i Danishjuyi) initiated cultural work, including reading groups and open lectures, but their scope remained limited. The Cultural Revolution stipulated that only students with ideological allegiance to the *vilāyat-i faqīh* could form or gain membership in the student associations. The inclusion of representatives of the supreme leader and *basīji*s in these associations reinforced ideological conformity.[49]

For Islamists, student activism was an obligation, not a right, and was meant to solidify the Islamic state's legitimacy.[50] Thus DTV's exclusivist ideological approach, Islamist rhetoric, populist disposition, and patriarchal propensity deeply alienated the vast majority of students, who were not only increasing in number (at an annual rate of 13 percent throughout the 1980s), but also going through an intense transformation. For one, more and more students were women and from rural and provincial backgrounds.[51] And unlike students of the 1970s, who had prolonged their studies because they cherished the carefree and enjoyable campus life, the 1990s generation were interested in college primarily for the degrees it offered. Compared to my student experience in the late 1970s, or the college environment in Cairo, the highly repressive feel at universities in the Iran of the mid-1990s was shocking.

The private Azad University in particular, with branches nationwide, a privileged and apolitical student body, suffered exceptionally under the management of Islamist free-marketer Jam'iyat-i Mu'talifiyyih Islami.[52] Above all, college education had lost its exclusivity and prestige, owing to its mass expansion and the noncompetitive or quota-based entry of thousands of pro-regime war veterans, *basīji*s, and *pāsdārān*. The campus's previous centrality in student life, its vitality and vigor, had faded away—no more was it a place of socializing, fun, and freedom, or of cultural, athletic, and political life. Instead, draconian social control pushed students to spend much of their time off-campus. They also had to work. The economic downturn and higher cost of education meant having to earn money to pay for study, particularly for the half of the student population who attended the private Azad University. These students were deprived of the carefree spirit of my generation, and they wished to graduate and leave as quickly as possible.[53]

So 1990s student activism was concerned not with conventional politics and ideological squabbles as in the 1970s or just after the revolution, but with economic and social issues that directly affected the students themselves. Grievances relating to food quality or the lack of instructors, laboratories, and classrooms could trigger sporadic protests involving 50 or 500 students.[54]

The student body was a potential social force, but one whose desire for a better material life and political participation had been dashed by the sluggish economy and the clergy's tight control over political institutions and everyday life. The poor economy turned their expectations into outrage, while moral surveillance and political suppression stifled the expression of their youthful dispositions and made them ever more frustrated. Indeed, this has been a familiar scenario in some Muslim countries where, in the absence of other credible alternatives, morally outraged youth turn to Islamic politics. What ideological inclinations would these Iranian youngsters pursue when they were already experiencing Islamism?

Far from being radical, Third Worldist, anti-West, utopian, ideological, or even Islamist, this new generation of students became pragmatic and nonideological with a clear aversion to violence, a distrust of officials, and a dream of living in the West. They admired the West for its openness, advances, and comforts, internalized its affordable cultural imports (fashion, music, cinema, dating games), and aspired to become as much a part of it as millions of their compatriots had become. In short, students of the 1990s had departed from radicalism and ideological orientations, Marxist and Islamist alike. They had become ordinary—they lived their lives, studied, worked, and worried about their future. The older generation had demanded social justice; the younger generation yearned for individual liberty.[55]

It was this newer rank-and-file, their political apathy and noncompliance, that compelled DTV, the official student leadership, to call for a gradual revision of its outlook. The Islamist students who had accepted the charismatic Khomeini as a supreme *faqīh* (who stood above the law) now began, in this post-Khomeini era, to view the law above the *faqīh* and favored a more open and democratic polity.[56] Some began to call for the limitation of power, more accountability, and direct election of the supreme leader. Assisting DTV's ideological break were the increasing intellectual criticisms in the media—for instance, in the post-Islamist monthly *Kiyan*—of revolutionary and Islamist politics (in 1995 one out of three regular readers of *Kiyan* was a college student).[57] In addition, the "defeat" of the war and of its early utopian goal ("to establish a world Islamic government")[58] had pushed many committed Islamists toward pragmatism and political rationality. Some abandoned politics altogether and simply tried to live their lives, but many joined the Islamic left, notably the Organization of Mujahidin of the Islamic Revolution. They worked in tandem with the leftist Islamic weekly *'Asr-i Mā* and the SCC's daily *Salam*, and were among those who came to be known as "religious intellectuals." Former student leader Ibrahim Asgharzadih, who had worked for the rightist daily *Kayhan*, became a parliamentary deputy of the Islamic left (1988–92). He abandoned engineering in 1992 to study politics at Tehran University and began to call for more political and economic openness.[59] Hashim Aghajari, after admitting the harm his earlier activities had done to the nation's politics, followed a similar academic career. 'Abbas 'Abdi edited the SCC's daily *Salam* and later, in 1995, published a post-Islamist magazine, *Bahar*. And Hashmatullah Tabarzadi went through a dramatic ideological transformation; in his new weekly, *Huviyyat-i Khish*, he lashed out at the "political despotism" of conservative clergy who used religion to gain power. Tabarzadi called for the direct election of the supreme leader by popular vote to a limited term. In June 1999, after publishing only three issues, his weekly was banned and he was imprisoned.

By 1997, DTV had mobilized its members, not in the name of Islamization, anti-imperialism, or class disparity, but in the name of the centrality of liberty, democratic participation, and the intrinsic dignity of student and teacher.[60] While there had emerged a new subjectivity among both students and DTV leaders, student mobilization remained sporadic, localized, and small scale, until the presidential election of 1997 pushed the student population into a spectacular return to national politics. Their renewed participation had more to do with suddenly being released from a long suppression than it did with an organized pursuit of a political goal. Khatami's victory and reform government, however, provided a new structure in which a novel student movement with a post-Islamist identity, reformist outlook, and pluralistic orientation was born almost overnight. With its focus on "democracy," the movement developed an elaborate organization and network structure. In May 2000, the first national student paper, *Azar*, was published, and by summer 2001, the number of college student newspapers topped 700. By that same year 1,437 scientific, cultural, artistic, and professional organizations had been established in the universities. They were the movement's grassroots.[61]

The presence of female students in the movement contributed to this new "democratic" orientation. Women, who made up half the total student population, linked student concerns with those of young women who were suffering more than their male counterparts, owing to gender inequality, which inflicted even more draconian social controls and moral patronizing on them. Still, confirming the social status of women, the student movement remained overwhelmingly male in disposition and policy. Few women attained leadership rank, and those who did refrained from raising "women's issues" for fear of causing "division" or "meaningless commotion."[62] Even during Khatami's term, while the student movement was preoccupied with notions of "civil society" and democracy, it paid only lip service to gender questions. Women needed to express their claims and concerns in their own feminist circles. A "post-Islamist feminism" was articulated by Iran's women's movement of the 1990s.

THE POST-ISLAMIST WOMEN'S MOVEMENT

Like student activism, Iran's women's movement of the 1990s departed radically in discourse and strategy from the early revolutionary years. Women's simultaneous mobilization and suppression under the Islamic Republic rendered them both morally outraged and remarkably active. Perhaps no social group felt so immediately and pervasively the brunt of the Islamic revolution as middle-class women. Only months into the life of the Islamic regime, new misogynous policies enraged women, who only recently had marched against the monarchy. The new regime overturned the Family Protection Laws of 1967, and overnight women lost their right to be judges, to initiate divorce, to win child custody, and to travel abroad without permission from a male guardian. Polygamy was reintroduced, and all women, irrespective of faith, were forced to wear the *hijāb* (veil) in public.[63] In the early years, social control and discriminatory quotas against women in education and employment compelled many women to stay at home, seek early retirement, or go into informal and family business.[64] Many sought life in exile.

The initial reaction to these drastic policies came from secular women. Thousands demonstrated in Tehran on March 8, 1979, vilifying Khomeini's imposition of the veiling requirement. Even though Khomeini retreated temporarily, the decree was gradually enforced. Shocked by the onslaught on their limited civil liberties, secular women desperately organized dozens of organizations, most of them affiliated with sectarian leftist trends for whom the gender question was subordinated to the "class emancipation" project.[65] All these groups were put down by the Islamic regime once the war with Iraq began in 1980. Then followed a decade of repression, demoralization, and flight. While secular women in exile continued with feminist education and activism, those in Iran began to emerge slowly from their tormenting abeyance and into the world of arts, literature, journalism, and scholarship only at war's end.

Although traditionalist clerics favored keeping women at home and away from "moral dangers," others, compelled by the remarkable presence of women in the revolution, adopted a discourse that exalted Muslim women as both guardians of the family and active public agents. This broad discursive framework guided a spectrum of "Muslim women activists." Inspired by the writings of ʿAli Shariʿati and Murtaza Mutahhari, they set out to offer an endogenous, though abstract, "model of Muslim women" (olgu-yi zan-i Musalman)[66] in the image of the Prophet's daughter Fatima and his granddaughter Zeinab, who were simultaneously "true" homemakers and public persons.[67]

Out of dozens of Islamic groups and organizations, the Women's Association of the Islamic Revolution (WAIR) gathered prominent Islamist women including Aʿzam Taliqani, Firishtih Hashimi, Shahin Tabatabaʾi, Zahra Rahnavard, and Gawhar Dastgheib. Most were members of prominent clerical families and held that the East treated women as merely "working machines" and the West as "sex objects," while only Islam regarded them as "true humans."[68] Instead of equality, these activists pointed out the complementary nature of men and women. Some justified polygamy on the grounds that it protected widows and orphans. Although some objected to forced hijāb and the abrogation of the Family Law, they stopped short of any concrete protest but contended that wearing the veil should be enforced through education, not by coercion. Most refused to acknowledge, let alone communicate with, secular Western feminists, whom they saw as "provoking women against men" and questioning religious principles and the sanctity of Shariʿa.[69]

Indeed, alarmed by the danger of gender debates, Shahla Habibi (President Rafsanjani's advisor on women's issues) declared herself "against overstating women's oppression" and identity politics. Instead, she emphasized the "family [as] the heart of the society, and women [as] the heart of family."[70] Thus day care centers were said to be "harmful for children,"[71] even though their closure would throw many women out of work. Muslim women activists accepted the "tradition" (the Qurʾan, hadīth, Shariʿa, and ijtihād) as an adequate guide to ensure women's dignity and well-being.[72] "In an Islamic state led by vilāyat-i faqīh, there would be no need for special organizations to defend women's rights," argued Maryam Behruzi, a female member of Parliament.[73] While the moderates agreed with "women's freedom to study, choose suitable jobs, and have access to various social and administrative fields,"[74] the more conservative Islamists (such as the parliamentarians Marziyih Dabbagh, Rejaʾi, Dastgheib, and Maryam Behruzi) viewed gender division in occupations, functions, and activities as a divine order.[75] In their paradigm, women, as Muslims, had more obligations than rights.

With the onset of the war with Iraq (1980–88) debate about women's status was suppressed. The authorities continued to project women primarily as mothers and wives, whose purpose was to produce manpower for the war, for the glory of Islam, and for the nation. But by the late 1980s dissent simmered in women's "politics of nagging." Women complained in public daily, in taxis, buses, bakery queues, grocery shops, and government offices, about repression, the war economy, the war itself. In so doing, they formed a court of irrepressible public opinion that could not be ignored. And a certain iconic moment shattered the illusion of the "model of Muslim women," when on national radio a young woman expressed her preference for Osheen, a Japanese movie character, over Fatima, the Prophet's daughter. Only then did authorities realize how out of touch they had become regarding women's lives in Iranian society. Some ten years into the Islamic Republic, A'zam Taliqani admitted bitterly that "poverty and polygamy are the only things that poor women have obtained from the revolution."[76]

War and repression had surely muted women's voices, but had not altered their determination to assert themselves through the practices of everyday life, by resisting forced Islamization, pursuing education, seeking employment, engaging in the arts and music, practicing sports, and socializing their children in these pursuits. Mobilization for the war effort had already placed them in the public arena as "model Muslim women," making them conscious of their power. In a mere twenty years, women's unprecedented interest in education had more than doubled their literacy rate: in 1997 it stood at 74 percent.[77] By 1998, more girls than boys were entering universities, a fact that worried some officials, who feared that educated women might not be able to find men with equal or higher status to marry. But for young women, college offered not only education but also a place to socialize, gain status, and have a better chance to pursue a career and find a desirable partner.

While for some the sheer financial necessity left no choice but to seek employment in the cash economy,[78] most middle-class and well-to-do women chose to work outside the home in order to be present in the public realm. After an overall decline in female employment, largely in industry, of 40 percent between 1976 and 1986, the share of women at work in cities rose from 8.8 percent in 1976 to 11.3 percent in 1996. This excluded those who worked in informal occupations, family businesses, or part-time jobs.[79] By the mid-1990s,

half of the positions in the government sector and over 40 percent in education were held by women. Professional women, notably writers and artists,
reemerged from domestic exile; at the first Book Fair of Women Publishers in
Tehran, in 1997, some forty-six publishers displayed 700 titles by women authors. Over a dozen female filmmakers were regularly engaged in their highly
competitive field, and more women than men won awards at the 1995 Iranian
Film Festival.[80] But few of their internationally acclaimed productions helped
elevate the underdog image of Iranian Muslim women in the world.

The economic conditions of families made housewives more publicly visible than ever before. Growing economic hardship since the late 1980s forced
many middle-class men to take multiple jobs and work longer hours. Consequently, most of the chores (taking children to school, dealing with the
civil service, banking, shopping, and fixing the car) that had previously been
shared by husbands and wives shifted to women.[81] A study confirmed that
women in Tehran, notably housewives, spent on average two hours per day in
public places, at times until ten at night, traveling by taxi, bus, and metro.[82]
This public presence gave women self-confidence, new social skills, and city
knowledge, and encouraged many to return to school or to volunteer with
NGOs and charities. One impressive example of volunteerism was the Ministry of Health's mobilization of some 25,000 women in Tehran in the early
1990s to educate urban lower-class families about hygiene and birth control.
Mounting population growth (3.9 percent between 1980 and 1985 and 3.4 percent between 1985 and 1990) had caused the regime great political anxiety,[83]
and these women contributed to decreasing the rate of population growth to
a low of 1.7 percent between 1990 and 1995.[84]

Women did not give up sports, even though women's bodies (and as a consequence, sports) had been at the center of the regime's moral crusade. The
hardship of sweating under a long dress and veil did not deter many women
from jogging, cycling, and target shooting, or from playing tennis, basketball,
and climbing Mount Everest. Nor did they avoid participating in national and
international competition—albeit exclusively for women or Muslims.[85] They
also defied the state policy banning women from attending male competitions; some disguised themselves in male attire,[86] while the more assertive
simply forced their way in. In 1998, hundreds of women stormed into a massive stadium full of jubilant young men celebrating a national soccer team victory. From then on women were assigned to special sections in the stadium.
Their demand to play soccer in public bore fruit in 2000, when the first wom-

en's soccer team was formally recognized.[87] Faezeh Rafsanjani, the president's daughter, played a crucial role in promoting and institutionalizing women's sports. The first College of Women's Physical Education was established in 1994 to train school athletics staff.

While the new moral order and imposition of the *hijāb* had a repressive effect on secular and non-Muslim women, it brought some degree of freedom to their socially conservative counterparts: traditional men felt at ease allowing their daughters or wives to attend school and appear at public events.[88] Moreover, the regime's mobilization of the lower classes for the war effort, street rallies, or Friday prayer sermons dramatically increased the public presence of women who would have otherwise remained in the seclusion of their tiny homes.

Meanwhile, the women who felt stifled by the coercive moralizing of the government resisted patiently and persistently. Officials invariably complained about *bad hijābi*, or young women neglecting to properly wear the veil. The jail penalty for improperly showing a few inches of hair (between 10 days and two months) sparked daily street battles between defiant women and multiple moral enforcers such as Sarallah, Amr bih Ma'ruf, and Idarih Amakin. During a four-month period in 1990 in Tehran, 607 women were arrested, 6,589 were forced to submit written affidavits that they would obey the law in the future, and 46,000 received warnings.[89] Nevertheless, by the late 1990s, "*bad hijābi*" had become an established practice.

Women's daily routines and resistance to the Islamic government did not mean that they abandoned religiosity. Indeed, most displayed religious devotion, and many were willing to wear light head coverings if they were not forced to do so.[90] Yet they insisted on exerting individual choice and entitlement, which challenged both the egalitarian claims of the Islamic state and the premises of orthodox Islam. Women wanted to play sports, work in desirable jobs, study, listen to or play music, marry whom they wished, and reject grave gender inequality. "Why are we to be acknowledged only with reference to men?" wrote one woman in a magazine. "Why do we have to get permission from Idarih Amakin [the moral police] to get a hotel room, whereas men do not need such authorization?"[91] These seemingly mundane desires and demands, however, were deemed to redefine the status of women under the Islamic Republic, because each step forward would encourage demands to remove more restrictions. The effect could snowball. How could this dilemma be resolved?

The women's magazines *Zan-i Ruz*, *Payam-i Hajar*, and *Payam-i Zan* were the first to reflect on such dilemmas. At the state level, the Social and Cultural Council of Women and the Bureau of Women's Affairs were established in 1988 and 1992, respectively, to devise concrete policies to address such issues. Even Islamists such as Ms. Reja'i, wife of a former prime minister, expressed reservations about the "model of Muslim women," attacking "narrow-minded" anti-female ideas and obsession with the *hijāb*.[92] Interestingly, many of these women worked in public office, including Parliament, and had been given a taste of discrimination by their traditionalist male colleagues. WAIR, the Women's Association of the Islamic Revolution, was shut down and its views attacked; the Islamic Republic Party incorporated the magazines *Zan-i Ruz* and *Rah-i Zaynab*; and once her parliamentary term ended the prominent female Islamist A'zam Taleqani fell out of the government's favor. In the end, the rather abstract philosophical approach of Islamist women proved insufficient to accommodate women's desire for individual choice within an Islamist framework. Post-Islamist feminists, however, emerged to take up the challenge.

Post-Islamist Feminism?

In a departure from Islamist women's activism, post-Islamist feminism articulated a blend of piety and choice, religiosity and rights. It set out a strategy for change through discussion, education, and mobilization in a discursive frame that combined religious and secular idioms. With a clear feminist agenda, the post-Islamist strategy derived not from an abstract model but from the reality of women's daily lives.

Activists held Islam in its totality as a system that could accommodate women's rights only if it was seen through the feminist lens. These feminists valued women's autonomy and choice, emphasizing gender equality in all domains. For them, feminism, irrespective of its origin (secular, religious, or Western) dealt with women's subordination in general. They no longer saw the West as a monolithic entity imbued with immorality and decadence (a view held by secular revolutionary and Islamist women); it was also home to democracy and science, to feminists and exiled Iranian women with whom they wished to establish dialogue. This position transcended the dichotomy of "Islamic" versus "secular" women. Post-Islamist feminists were different from Islamist women activists, such as the Egyptian Heba Rauf, who were primarily Islamist but happened to be women and raised women's issues. Post-Islamist feminists were feminists first and foremost, who utilized Islamic discourse to push for gender equality within the constraints of the Islamic Republic. They did not limit their intellectual sources to Islam, but also benefited from secular feminism.[93] The women's magazines *Farzānih*, *Zan*, and *Zanan* spearheaded this trend by running articles on, for instance, how to improve your sex life, cooking, women's arts in feminist critical discourse, the deconstruction of patriarchal Persian literature, and legal religious issues, written by Muslim, secular, Iranian, and Western authors, including Virginia Woolf, Charlotte Perkins Gilman, Simone de Beauvoir, and Susan Faludi.[94] *Zanan* appealed in particular to educated young urban women.[95]

The major challenge to post-Islamist feminism was to demonstrate that the claims for women's rights were not necessarily alien to Iranian culture or Islam. But, as secular feminists wondered, would operating within the Islamic discourse not constrain endeavors for gender equality when "all Muslims, from the very orthodox to the most radical reformers, accept the Qur'an as the literal word of Allah, unchanging and unchangeable"?[96] Post-Islamist feminists responded by undertaking women-centered interpretations of the sacred texts, similar to the way in which early European feminists such as Hildegard of Bingen (1098–1179), Christine de Pizan (1365–1430), Isotta Nogarola (1418–66), and Anna Maria von Schurman (1607–78), to name only a few, deconstructed the Bible-driven perceptions of the "sinful" and "inferior" disposition of Eve/woman.[97]

Zanan set out to deconstruct the "patriarchal readings" of the scriptures, offering gender-sensitive perceptions that would allow women to be equal with men, to take on social and political positions as judges, presidents, *marjaʿ*, or *faqīh*. "There are no deficiencies in Islam [with regard to women]. Problems lie in political and patriarchal perceptions," they contended.[98] Within this emerging "feminist theology," interpreters questioned misogynist legislation and the literal reading of Qur'anic verse; they emphasized instead the "general spirit" of Islam, which, they argued, was in favor of equality. If in his twenty-three years of struggle the Prophet of Islam changed many anti-women practices of his time, post-Islamist feminists were to extend this tradition of emancipation to modern times. Methodologically grounded on hermeneutics, philology, and historicism, women interpreters transcended literal meanings in favor of tangential deductions. To refute the "innate superiority of men" that orthodox readings deduced from Qur'anic verses (such as Sura 4:34 Nisa', where men seem to be favored over women), *Zanan* writers shifted the basis of hierarchy from sex to piety by invoking gender-free verse: "The noblest among you in the sight of God is the most God-fearing of you" (S. 49:13).

Accordingly, child custody should not automatically be the right of men (as the Shari'a authorizes) but determined by the well-being of children, which Islam stresses highly.[99] Against a 1998 parliamentary bill that called for the separation of men and women in medical treatment, *Zanan* argued not only that the Qur'an ruled against any forced guidance in general (because people are responsible for their choices, good or evil), but also that in Islamic theology religion exists to serve humans rather than the other way around. Instead of obligation, it concluded, the bill should recognize the patient's choice over her medical treatment.[100]

Building on linguistic analyses, post-Islamist feminists deconstructed the verse *"al-rijāl qawamūn 'ala nisā"* (men are protectors and maintainers of women) (Nisa', 4:34), on which many of the misogynist deductions are based.[101] Feminist theologians attributed the word *qawam* not to the Arabic root *qym*, meaning "guardianship over other," but to *qwm*, meaning "rising up," "fulfilling needs," or "protecting."[102] In the same fashion, they said that the verb *darb* in the Qur'an should be understood not simply as "to beat," but also "to put an end to" or "to go along with."[103] Consequently, they argued, the Qur'an did not authorize the right to divorce to men alone or deny such a right to a woman.[104] Indeed, the gender-neutrality of the Persian language, as reflected in the Constitution of the Islamic Republic, offered much discursive opportunity for women to campaign for equal rights.[105] For example, eligibility requirements for the country's presidency, such as *rijāl-i mazhabi* (religious personalities) or *faqīh-i 'adil* (being a just jurist), can apply to both men *and* women. While the word *rajul* was generally accepted as meaning "a man" in Arabic, in Persian, they contended, it referred to (political) "personality" in general; thus they argued that women were also eligible to run for president.[106] The major novelty of these gender-sensitive theological debates was that, beyond a few enlightened clerics,[107] women were waging them, and they were doing so on the pages of the popular daily press.

The new women's activism alarmed the clerical establishment, ordinary men, and conservative women. A male pathologist commented with dismay that "the freedom of women in Iran has been misconceived. . . . In the past few years some women who apparently became protagonists in the struggle for equal rights have gone astray. They talked so much about men's domination that people became enemies, and this was a blow to our society."[108] Ayatollah Fadhel Lankarani of the Qum Seminary warned the activists "not to question Islam's principles by your intellectualism. . . . Who says there is no difference between men and women?" he challenged. "Who are you to express opinions[. . .] before God and his prophet?"[109] The Friday prayer leader in Rasht denounced women who "questioned religious authorities on the *hijāb* and Shari'a," warning them "not to cross the red line, not to dismiss the Qur'an and Islam."[110] Others, such as Ayatollah Mazahiri, were outraged by the activists' demand that the Iranian government endorse the UN Convention on the Elimination of Discrimination Against Women because this would reflect Western domination of the nation.[111] Munirih Nubakhat and Marziyih Wahid Dastjerdi, Islamist women members of the Majlis, proposed to curtail feminist debates in the press and public because they "create conflict between women and men" and undermine Shari'a and fundamentals of the religion.[112] Such attacks became intellectual justifications for hard-line mobs and media to harass *bad hijāb* (improperly dressed) women on the streets, denounce women's sports and recreation, and fight against the return of "decadence, fashion, and individual taste."[113] *Zanan* was taken to court in 1998 on charges of inciting women against men and "spreading homosexuality."[114] The cleric Muhsen Saidzadih, whose woman-centered essays on theology and Islamic law had dismayed the conservative clergy, was jailed in June 1998.[115]

Despite all this pressure, the movement made considerable inroads, empowering women through education, employment, family law, and greater self-esteem. The opportunity for equal education with men made a comeback after the official restrictive quotas that favored men were eliminated. Polygamy was seriously curtailed, men's right to divorce was restricted, and religiously sanctioned *mut'a* (temporary marriage) was demonized. At its height in 2002 (1381), only 271, or one out of 1,000 marriages, were *mut'a*, or "temporary."[116] In cases where husbands initiated divorce proceedings, women won *ujrat al-mithl*, a financial reward equal to the value of their involuntary housework during marriage, even though enforcing such rulings proved to be difficult. New laws authorized financial rewards to widowed working women, increased maternity leave to four months, reestablished nurseries for the children of working mothers, and decreased the length of women's workday to 75 percent of the time required of men. New legislation also made *mahr* (bride price) payable in the current value, allowed early retirement after twenty years of work, offered financial protection for women and children deprived of male support, obliged the government to provide women's sports facilities, and authorized single women over age 28 to study abroad without a male guardian.[117] In 1998, a pilot project to prevent wife abuse was launched.[118] Child custody was intensely debated, and the struggle for women to be judges led to their appointment as judicial counselors in lower courts and co-judges in high courts. In 1997, fifteen female deputies sat on the Women's Affairs Commission of Parliament.[119]

These struggles also led to changes in power relations between women and men in the family and society. Female suicide and the rising divorce rate (27 percent in 2002, 80 percent of which were initiated by women) were seen as what an Iranian sociologist called the "painful modernization of our society."[120] Meanwhile, opinion polls on women's public role showed that 80 percent of respondents (men and women) were in favor of female government ministers, and 62 percent did not oppose a female president.[121] The Western perception of Iranian women as helpless subjects trapped in the solitude of domesticity and hidden under the long black *chador* proved to be a gross oversimplification.

A Non-Movement?

This is not to overstate the status of Iranian women in the Islamic Republic. Indeed, as late as 1998, feminist lawyer Mihrangiz Kar warned against reading too much into what women had achieved. She listed a dozen areas in Iranian law where flagrant gender inequalities persisted,[122] as they did in most political, legal, and family institutions imbued with patriarchal relations. Men still retained more rights in divorce and child custody; they were allowed multiple wives and could make sexual demands of their wives. In addition, the amount of a man's blood money was still twice that of a woman.

Yet it is also true that the daily struggles of women in the public domain not only changed aspects of their lives, but also advanced a more democratic interpretation of Islam. Women's most significant achievement was subverting the conventional gender divide between "public man" and "domestic woman." Against much resistance, Iranian women imposed themselves as public players. The paradoxical status of women under the Islamic Republic perplexed many observers, as well as activists themselves, who were trying to grasp the nature of women's activism. Activists unequivocally characterized it as a social movement,[123] but some qualified it as a "silent movement,"[124] while others argued that women's sporadic activism did not go beyond being a "social problem."[125]

How do we characterize Iran's women's activism? Was there such a thing as a "women's movement"? If not, how did fragmented yet collective and undeliberate activities lead to some tangible outcomes? By the late 1990s women's involvement in hundreds of women's NGOs, solidarity networks, and discourses pointed to some degree of organized activism. Women's groups held rallies, participated in international women's meetings, lobbied politicians and clerical leaders, and campaigned in the Majlis. Women's Weeks, book fairs, film festivals, and sporting events were sites of their mobilization. In 1995 independent activists together with moderate officials such as Shahla Habibi (president Rafsanjani's advisor on women's issues), coordinated a Women's Week Festival that included 62 seminars, 3,000 celebrations, 230 exhibits, and 161 contests.[126] Over two dozen women's magazines (among them *Zanan, Farzanih, Huquq-i Zan, Zan-i Ruz, Nada, Rayhanih, Payam-i Hajar, Mahtab, Kitab-i Zan,* and *Jins-i Duvvum*)[127] and an increasing number of websites (such as those of *bad jins* and *Zanan-i Iran*) communicated ideas, advertised events, and established solidarity networks. Between 1990 and 2002, thirty-six new women's journals were published. Feminist ideas permeated universities, where female student groups printed newsletters on gender issues; and by the late 1990s four Iranian universities had established Women's Studies programs, though their operation left much to be desired.[128]

All of these activities and networks, however, fell short of generating a structured movement capable of large-scale, organized protest. Iran's women's activism embodied an aggregate of dispersed collective sentiments, claim-making, and everyday practices related to diverse gender issues, chiefly the assertion of women's individuality. Collective identities were formed less in women's institutions than in (albeit controlled) public spaces: workplaces, universities, rationing lines, shopping markets, neighborhoods, informal gatherings, and mosques. Although there was some deliberate network-building, "passive networks" acted as the crucial medium for the construction of a collective identity.[129] As they did among youth, passive networks allowed instantaneous and unspoken communication to pass between individual women who tacitly recognized their commonalities of style, behavior, and concerns. Nonconformist women wearing similar "improper" clothing on the streets, for instance, would feel a common threat from the morals police and solidarity with one another.

Occasions of intense political tension, threat, or opportunity would often turn women's passive networks into active communicative groups. Thus the housewives or mothers of war victims, since they lacked institutional settings to express discontent, would often take their grievances into the streets while standing in long rationing lines at bakeries or butcher shops, or at bus stops, where they perfected the irrepressible practice of "public nagging." Women successfully deployed their gender-based comparative advantage, *maternal impunity*, or their power as mothers and homemakers, to protest and yet remain immune from backlash. While the protests of men and the young were often suppressed, women's maternal status offered them protection. The wives of war victims compounded this maternal impunity with their political capital as the family of martyrs to launch successful campaigns against the patriarchal interpretation of Shari'a that granted the custody of their now fatherless children to their grandfathers.

Yet public protestation of this kind made up only an insignificant aspect of women's struggles. They rarely articulated shared demands about gender inequality; instead they went ahead on their own to claim them directly where they could—in education, work, sports, and courts. Theirs then was not the conventional social movement so often associated with the images of solid organizations, known leadership, banners, and marches. Iranian women's activism represented a *movement by implication*—a sort of structural encroachment, an incremental and imperative process of claim-making rooted in their *power of presence* and tied intimately to the practices of everyday life. Against Islamist gender bias, the mere public presence of women was an achievement, but it also acted as a stepping stone which women could use to encroach on or negotiate with patriarchal politics. Women got involved in the war effort and volunteer work and sought paid jobs; they pursued education and sports, jogged and cycled, and participated in international athletic competitions; they worked as professionals, novelists, filmmakers, and bus and taxi drivers, and they ran for high public office.

And these very public roles beset the social and legal imperatives that had to be addressed: restrictive laws and customs needed to be altered to accommodate the requisites of "public" women within the prevailing patriarchal system. College education, for example, often required young women to live independently from their families, something that would otherwise be deemed inappropriate. Women's public activity raised the issue of the *hijāb* (of its compatibility with the nature of their work), their association with men, sexual tensions,[130] and equality with men in society. If more women than men entered and graduated from universities, more women might (though would not necessarily) occupy positions supervising men, who would have to accept if not internalize their authority. Playing similar public roles as men would open the way for women to demand equal rights in personal status laws, in divorce,

inheritance, blood money, or child custody. As Zahra Shujaʻi, President Khatami's advisor on women's issues suggested, "Now that women have become
breadwinners, is it not time to read the *'al-rijāl qawamūn 'ala nisā"* with new
eyes?"[131] Why should women not be elected president or supreme leader? If
women could serve as high officials in business or government, would they still
need to obtain their husbands' permission to attend a foreign conference?

In this structural progression, women performed similar mundane activities (working in the public domain, playing sports, studying, or doing
chores); but these very ordinary doings compelled the authorities to acknowledge women's role in society, and thus their rights. It was the imperative of a meaningful, but persistent public *presence* that would further
enhance women's claims, entitlement, and choices, for it would progressively
necessitate breaking further patriarchal constraints. Each step forward
would justify the next, creating a cycle of opportunity for further claims,
and ultimately leading to more gender equality and individual rights. This
"non-movement" drew its power not from activists' threat of disruption or
uncertainty, but from their *power of presence*: their ability to assert collective
will, despite all odds, by circumventing constraints, utilizing what was possible, and discovering new spaces within which to make themselves heard,
seen, and felt. Yet progress relied on more than just everyday practices; in
addition, feminist activists deployed sophisticated legal, theological, and
theoretical means to take advantage of the opportunity that women's public
presence had offered them.

It was the "danger" of such "incremental encroachment" that alarmed
the conservative clergy, who had some thirty-five years earlier opposed the
Shah's granting of voting rights to women in local elections. "Voting rights
for women, in addition to its own troubles, would lead to their participation
in the parliamentary elections; then this would lead to equality of men and
women in divorce, in being judges, and the like. . . . No doubt these practices
would stand against our religious principles."[132]

Women's drive for a public presence was fueled by the memory of their
prerevolution status, economic necessity, and the globalization of women's
struggles. But the more immediate factor was the *discursive opportunity* that
women's own struggles had already generated. Their massive participation in
the revolution of 1979 had compelled many religious leaders, chiefly Ayatollah Khomeini, to publicly acknowledge women's social and political agency.
Khomeini's appeal to women voters during the first referendum of the Islamic

Republic established their public power. "Women do more for the [revolu-tionary] movement than men; their participation doubles that of men," he admitted.[133] He continued, "That Muslim women are to be locked up in their homes is an utterly false idea that some attribute to Islam. Even during early Islam, women were active in the armies and war fronts."[134] Later, Muslim fem-inists would invoke Khomeini's statements to defy conservative clerics who wished to drive them back into the private realm. At the same time, women's pervasive publicness was bound to challenge many of patriarchal structures of the Islamic state and gender relations, establishing for them a new autono-mous identity. This in turn framed women's demands for gender equality and rejection of many "traditional" roles.[135] Women's daily resistance and pres-ence deepened contention within religious discourse and enforced a different, post-Islamist, and woman-centered interpretation of the sacred texts. And in this, women obtained vital insights from yet another emerging movement, that of "religious intellectuals."

THE MOVEMENT OF "RELIGIOUS INTELLECTUALS"

The main intellectual source of the post-Islamist practices discussed above (the new concept of urban space, student and youth movements, and post-Islamist feminism) lay in a major discursive shift articulated by a group of "religious intellectuals," the rawshanfikrān-i dīni. They generated one of the most remarkable intellectual movements in the Muslim world with far-reaching implications for religious thought and democratic practice. Com-pelled by concerns expressed by dispersed activists in fragmented movements, the post-Islamist "religious intellectuals" gave coherent voice to Iran's social movements by creating an altogether new discourse. Labeled "digar andishān" or "alternative thinkers," they offered the ideological foundation for a post-Islamist master movement.

At the height of religious control of the state and society, a group of in-tellectuals initiated a discursive campaign against orthodox interpretations, opening the way for a significant rethinking of sacred texts. This was neither heresy nor a secular campaign against theocracy, but an attempt by a number of clerics and religious-minded intellectuals to secure both the sanctity of re-ligion and the rationality of the state in a society whose primary religion had been used as an instrument of political domination. Somewhat reminiscent of the European Reformation against the Catholic Church, the post-Islamists' ideas navigated through theology, jurisprudence, clerical institutions, and the fusion of religion and state. As in the Reformation, the dissent came from both within and, more significant, outside the religious establishment.[136] The term *rawshanfikrān-i dīni* first appeared in a speech by Muhammad Khatami in 1993, long before he became president, in which he deplored the fact that Islam and Muslim revolutionaries suffered from a "vacuum of [social] theory."[137] He felt that a new type of intellectual was needed to replace both the "religious fanatics who were preoccupied with God but neglected humans," and the "secular intellectuals" who focused on man alone and ignored God. The religious intellectual "respects reason and appreciates freedom," but perceives the body as more than mere matter and the human as greater than mere nature.[138] He ignores neither the divine nor the human but takes "the divine human" (*insān-i khudâ'i*), human beings with rights, as his point of departure.[139] Reason, rights, and religion became fundamental elements in the discourse of these thinkers.[140]

Scores of seminars and essays about "religious intellectuals" reflected a deliberate attempt to forge an identity that distinguished the group from both the seculars and their own Islamist past.[141] This identity was also instrumental in establishing an intellectual self-confidence to counter the challenge of the West and the weaknesses of the self.[142] The core of the group came from a middle-class, revolutionary, Third-Worldist, and above all, Islamist background. They had been invariably influenced by the thoughts of Muslim modernists 'Ali Shari'ati, Murtaza Mutahhari, and Ayatollah Khomeini. During the 1980s, most of them were functionaries of the Islamic state, having been appointed to sensitive positions or having worked in revolutionary institutions, such as Sepah-i Pasdaran, or in theological seminaries.

Muhammad Khatami, the president of the reform government, was a member of Parliament (1980–82), director of the state-run daily *Kayhan*, and then minister of culture (1982–89). 'Abd al-Karim Surush, the leading post-Islamist figure, had been an early ideologue of the Islamist state and a member of the Cultural Revolution Council (which in the early 1980s planned to Islamize the universities and the education system). Sa'id Hajjariyan, editor of the reformist daily *Khurdad* and later advisor to President Khatami, was a young pro-Shari'ati activist before the revolution. After the revolution, he worked in the Intelligence Office under the prime minister until 1984, when he helped establish the Ministry of Intelligence, in which he held a position until 1989.[143] Hamidreza Jala'ipur, editor of three banned reformist dailies, had been an Islamist revolutionary when he was appointed governor of the

Kurdistan towns Naqadih and Mahabad at the age of 22; after the war he worked in the Foreign Ministry.[144] He lost his two brothers in the war, one of whom was killed by the Mujahidin-i Khalq. Akbar Ganji, editor of the weekly *Rah-i Naw*, had joined the Revolutionary Guards, working as a *pāsdār*, until he volunteered to serve in the war; upon his return he rejoined the *pāsdārān* as an instructor of political-ideological classes. Muhsin Sazgara, publisher of the dailies *Jāmi'iyyih* and *Taws*, had been a companion of Khomeini in Paris; once in Iran, he drafted statutes for the *pāsdārān*, became the head of Iran Radio, and then, at age 28, the deputy minister of industry. After the revolution, the cleric Muhsin Kadivar gave up studying electronic engineering, joined the Qum Seminary as a student of Ayatollah Muntazari, and concurrently began a Ph.D. program in theology at the University of Qum. Hashim Aghajari, a post-Islamist academic, was a leader of Mujahidin Inqilab-i Islami, who had lost a leg in the war.

And there were the student leaders who had seized the U.S. embassy and taken American diplomats hostage in 1980: Muhsin Mirdamadi, editor of *Nuruz*; Ibrahim Asgharzadih, a reformist member of the Tehran City Council; 'Abbas 'Abdi, editor of the reformist *Bahar* and *Salam*; and Masumih Ibtikar, a leading "Islamic feminist" and head of an environmental organization.

Over the course of more than a decade, these individuals "matured" intellectually,[145] expressing ideas that radically distinguished them from their own past and from their predecessors, notably from those associated with Mehdi Bazaragan, Yadollah Sahabi, or 'Ali Shari'ati.[146]

First, the religious intellectuals self-consciously embraced modernity, emphasizing such notions as "critical reason [*'aqlāniyāt-i intiqādi*] as the essence of modern life," rationality, human rights, liberty, plurality, science, and free-market economics. But they also espoused faith, spirituality, and religious ethics. Of course, many of the earlier "Muslim reformers," notably al-Afghani, 'Abd al-Rahman al-Kawakibi, Muhammad 'Abduh, Murtaza Mutahhari, and even their conservative opponents, also considered science and reason to be compatible with Islam. However, for the post-Islamists modernity required embracing not only science and technology (hardware), but also, as Surush, the mentor of Iran's post-Islamists suggests, a new mentality, new attitudes, and new concepts (software).[147] In addition, older Muslim reformers hailed from anti-colonial and Third World persuasions. Jalal Al-i Ahmad's celebrated essay "Westoxication" represented Third Worldism par excellence to which most prerevolution Islamists and Marxists adhered.

In contrast, and this is the second point, the religious intellectuals espoused generally "post-nationalist" orientations. They no longer blamed the nation's problems exclusively on foreign powers and Western imperialism. Iran's underdevelopment, they believed, originated in its own historical despotism.[148] Therefore, the focus should not have been on some abstract Western conspiracy but on institutionalizing the ideals of freedom and democracy in society. Revolutionary intellectuals, Islamists, and secular Marxists alike rarely cherished the ideal of liberty. To them, "freedom" often meant freedom from foreign domination.

Third, religious intellectuals were "postrevolutionaries," post-idea-of-revolution, that is. They had experienced and transcended the revolutionary discourse of martyrdom, bravery, discipline, militancy, war, and especially violence,[149] the kind of idioms that conservative Islamists continued to embrace. The absence of a populist language markedly distinguished religious intellectuals from the Islamists. Instead, they emphasized reform, tolerance, acknowledging differences, and peaceful coexistence. Finally, religious intellectuals were "post-ideological." Ideology, understood in the Marxian sense of "inverted truth," was seen as rigid, the antithesis of free critical thinking, and as needing to create "enemies." "Ideologizing religion," something commonly practiced by 'Ali Shari'ati, Murtaza Mutahhari, and Mehdi Bazargan, was fiercely critiqued by the post-Islamist intellectuals.[150] Like Surush, Akbar Ganji warned that "ideologizing religion opens the way for a totalitarian system; and by its tendency toward violence, war-mongering, and restricting freedoms, it inevitably encourages secularism and apostasy [*ilhād*]."[151] Thus, they read and were inspired by Marx, Popper, Lakatos, Thomas Kuhn, Habermas, and Rawls, as well as Giddens, David Held, Huma Katuzian, and Husayn Bashiriyyih. However, they made little attempt to establish dialogue with marginalized Iranian secular intellectuals, whose ideas on politics, culture, and society circulated in *Gardoun, Adinih, Rawnaq, Itila'at Siyasi-Iqtisadi*, and *Guftugu* and contributed considerably to this intellectual shift.[152]

The religious intellectuals represented perhaps the first significant post-colonial intellectuals in the Muslim world.[153] Post-colonial thought rejects the essentializing attitude that both Islamists (similar to most Arab nationalists) and the Orientalists take toward "self" and the "other," positions that end up reproducing each other. Post-colonial intellectuals discarded "orientalism in reverse," refusing to view either the Muslim world or the West as an undifferentiated, unitary, and unchangeable entity, or in binary opposition. Rather, they discerned differentiation, change, and hybridity within these worlds, and flow and dialogue between them. According to *Kiyan*, "The West is not just a place of 'night life' but also the locus of intellectual, technical precision. It is here that fundamental human questions are raised and addressed. The proliferation of philosophies and schools of thought is a witness to this phenomenon."[154] We are living, in Jala'ipur's view, in a globalized world where boundaries between countries have been broken; the world has been decentered, countries are interdependent, and the classic dichotomy of imperialism versus the Third World no longer holds.[155] We must confidently shed our "foreignphobia," and discover our location in this global system.[156]

The West is not merely a dominant power, Khatami argued. It is also the locus of modernity, freedom, and democracy, of Marx, Goethe, and Hegel.[157] East-West relations should be seen in the same sense that both Goethe and Muhammad Iqbal saw them, as "being of divine origin." But dialogue does not mean pretending sameness; rather, differences as well as a common thread must be acknowledged.[158] Muslims should challenge Western views on freedom and humanity not through violence, indignation, or contempt, but through the language of logic and fairness.[159] In Kadivar's view, the "dialogue of civilization" means simply an exchange between the Islamic world and the West. "We give something, and take something else."[160] We take industry, modernization, philosophical, and social science categories, and we offer concepts in ethics and mysticism. Surush insisted that Muslim intellectuals needed to learn from the West without necessarily being its slave. By insisting on autonomy and interaction in the social sciences, religious intellectuals explicitly departed from thinkers associated with the "Islamization of knowledge," a notion prevalent in some Muslim communities.[161]

Republican Theology

Deeply influenced by social and political conditions in the 1990s, the post-Islamist intellectuals sought to redefine the capabilities of religion in the modern age in order to address complex human needs. Thus their intellectual efforts centered on constructing a *republican theology* by blending the ideals of modernity, democracy, and religiosity. Fundamental to their thinking about religion was the role of reason and rationality (*'aqlāniyyāt-i dīni*). The Qur'an, according to the cleric 'Abdullah Nuri, frequently invites humans to think, reason, and discover, rather than to imitate.[162] Thus religious texts are to be understood only through reasoning and deliberation. Indeed, faith and freedom are two sides of one coin: "People are free to choose a religion, and free to leave it."[163] Religious faith cannot be forced on people; compulsion merely produces hypocrites. Deliberately hostile apostates may have to respond to God only in the hereafter; otherwise "apostasy does not have punishment in this world."[164] People believe according to their own reading of religion.

Epistemologically, the "religious intellectuals" called for a hermeneutic reading of the religious texts, including the Qur'an, rejecting a single "true reading," or for that matter an exclusive "expert reading" by the ulema.[165] In fact, many wished to end the professionalization of religious interpretation by the clergy, who subsist financially on religion and who monopolize religious knowledge and spiritual property.[166] In fact, a singular "official reading" of the Scriptures was seen as detrimental to free interpretation and perception, and therefore was rejected.[167] This epistemology later inspired the monumental call for a project of "Islamic Protestantism." In a devastating critique of the "clerical establishment," Hashim Aghajari, a war veteran, dismissed the ulema's role not only in politics but also in religion. In Lutherian spirit, he called for the individual Muslim to seek his own religious truths without the medium of clerics. But unlike Lutherian or Wahabi obsession with scripturism, religious intellectuals favored interpretation, reason, and innovation. "Islamic humanism," informed by "rationality, science, and respect for human dignity," was at the heart of this Protestantism. Since the Qur'an recognizes human dignity (karāma), then people are God's vice-regents on earth. Religious intellectuals urged the revival of humanist Islam, which clerical officialdom had sidelined.[168]

The question of religious or divine truth is a fundamental issue in the philosophy of religion. As individual believers of a particular faith, our truths may be different from one another. Does that mean that there is more than one divine truth? The question is pertinent both within a faith and between faiths. How can one justify the different truths of different religions? Does this mean that religious truth is relative?

The cleric 'Abdullah Nuri was confronted with precisely such questions during his prosecution in a religious tribunal in 1999. "Relativity of truth is one thing, and epistemological error is something else," he replied; "simply, truth is not obvious." It is imperative for believers to acknowledge that they might not know the entire truth, he suggested, and that their opponents possess at least part of the truth: "Even if truth is absolute, it does not mean that it is at the disposal of a particular group."[169] And as far as Islam is concerned, "except God, there is nothing absolute."[170] In sum, "the idea of religion is complete, truthful, and sacred, but our perception of it is not. The idea of religion is not subject to change, but our perception of it is."[171]

In the view of post-Islamists, the significance of religion, notably Islam, lay neither in *fiqh* (the lowest order) nor in rituals (though they are not totally useless), but rather in its ethics and moralities. *Fiqh*, or religious jurisprudence, which has assumed such prominence among Islamist groups in general, is far from being the core of the religion. In the view of post-Islamists, instructions based upon *fiqh* should not be mandatory unless they become law. And laws should reflect social necessities that may conflict with Shari'a. Therefore, *vilāyat-i faqīh*, the doctrinal foundation of Iran's Islamic state, is no more than an idea, and a minority one, among Shi'a political thinkers;[172] it is subject to debate, scrutiny, and change. Although sovereignty belongs to God, he has bequeathed it to people, empowering them to enact laws to govern their society. In view of religious intellectuals, the *vali-i faqīh*, as a spiritual leader, was to be elected by and accountable to the people, if his role was necessary at all. His power should be limited by law.

Indeed, as their ideas evolved, many post-Islamist intellectuals later discarded the idea of *vilāyat-i faqīh* as an "undesirable" and "undemocratic" and thus unacceptable model of government. Surush explicitly argued that the management of modern societies was both possible and desirable, not through religion, but through scientific rationality in a democratic structure.[173] Not only are Islam and democracy compatible; their association is inevitable. In fact, religious intellectuals called for the establishment of a secular democratic state that was compatible with "religious society,"[174] an idea that later came to be known as "religious democracy" (*mardum sālāri-yi dīni*). It was described in the most general terms as a government that "emanates from a religious society and serves the interests of the people."[175]

Gender relations did not escape the attention of this new religious thought. Beyond directly advocating gender equality, "religious intellectuals" equipped the post-Islamist feminists with the conceptual resources necessary to sustain their struggles. The cleric Sayyed Muhsen Saidzadih offered a thorough "woman-centered" reading of Islamic sacred texts. Muhsin Kadivar and 'Alireza 'Alavitabar criticized Shari'a's discrimination against women but argued that it could be interpreted in such a way as to support women's rights. Although women and men are different in their biological makeup, they argued, they should be equal in their social roles.[176] The feminist monthly *Zanan* was in essence the sister publication of *Kiyan*, the journal of the religious intellectuals.

These thinkers, in sum, explicitly rejected "*Islām huwa al-hal*" (Islam is the solution), the popular slogan among contemporary Islamist movements in the Arab world. For Iran's religious intellectuals, Islam had limitations as the solution to all of humanity's problems. In fact, religion was seen not as the domain of mundane concerns but of mystery, perplexity, love, and devotion. Nevertheless, they believed that religious faith must be encouraged, not only because it makes life tolerable by enabling humans to cope with the harsh realities of life, but also because it can provide mechanisms for internal control against individual abuse of others, just as democracy facilitates external control.[177] Surush made it clear that democracy, with its emphasis on rights, was essentially different from and preferable to the feeble Qur'anic notions of *shura* (consultation) or *bey'a* (allegiance), which are informed by obligation. "Democracy," according to the cleric Kadivar, "is the best system in today's world."[178]

The new religious thinking found currency not only among the literate public, but also in seminaries, or *hawzeh*s; and not among the established ulema, but primarily among younger clerics. The monthly *Kiyan* established a substantial following in Qum, the city of Islamic seminaries.[179] The younger ulema began to critique the cultural and epistemological legacy of their *hawzeh*s.[180] Religious knowledge ceased to draw merely on the traditional texts and relied increasingly on literature from outside the seminary, including that produced by Western philosophers. *Fiqh* lost its authority to theology and philosophy, while scripturist method gave way to the centrality of reason and hermeneutics. The new critical reflections were debated in such innovative journals as *Naqd va Nazar*, *Ma'rifat*, and *Hawzih va Danishgah*, all published in Qum. Ghulamreza A'wani, Mustafa Malakian, Mujtahid Shabastari, and others led the debates, contributing to what the religious intellectuals had already spearheaded: a republican theology, or a theology that embraced democratic ideals, religious pluralism, critical rationality, and rights.

Ideas as a Social Force

The ideas expressed by the religious intellectuals were neither flawless nor utterly original. They also had little to say about economics. Indeed, the ongoing debates and differences within the group, disclosed in the monthly *Kiyan*, chronicled the group's intellectual evolution. For instance, the notion of a "religious society" remained ambiguous, since it immediately brought to mind the United States, one of the most religious societies in the world. Was the U.S.

administration then a "religious government"? Some of the main philosophical contentions of Surush and Nuri were based simultaneously on both logic and faith. If the idea of religion is truthful but our perception of it is not, as they suggest, then how do we know about its truthfulness in the first place? It seems that the truthfulness of religion was simply a statement of faith rather than a logical deduction. It is in the same spirit of faith that Nuri excepted God from relativism ("Except for God, nothing is absolute in Islam") while making a logical argument. On the other hand, the epistemology adopted by religious intellectuals could be found among other Islamic modernists in the Muslim world such as the Algerian Muhammad Arkoun, the Egyptian Hasan Hanafi, the Syrian Shahrur, and the secular Egyptian Nasr Abu Zayd, not to mention in the rich scholarship on religious pluralism.[181]

Yet the significance of these ideas in the Iranian context lay not in their originality but in their popular appeal under a self-conscious Islamic state. Not only did these views shake up the conceptual foundation of the traditional clergy and theological seminaries, forcing them to rethink their perspectives; their convergence with the people's political grievances rendered them a social force. It was as though what the younger generation wished to express had found its way into the intellectuals' elegant language. These ideas gathered support primarily among the young, educated, and largely religious-minded individuals, but also among secular Iranians, especially the modern middle classes, many of whom had been politically marginalized.[182] *Kiyan*, the protagonist publication of new religious thought, for example, claimed 100,000 readers in 1995. But the ideas assumed wider circulation through lecture halls, mosques, and the daily press. Perhaps more remarkably, they secured a significant following among theology students. The cleric Muhammad Mujtahid Shabastari reported a significant shift in the religious worldviews of the younger generation of ulema, reflected in new interest in "religious pluralism."[183] The debates launched in *Kiyan* had managed to penetrate the Qum Seminary, so that even students of the conservative Ayatollah Misbah Yazdi contributed to the journal.[184]

As the nucleus of a movement, the formation of the group went back to 1991, when Muhammad Khatami, just out of the Ministry of Culture, had expressed the need for "religious intellectuals." Earlier, some of these thinkers had begun to publish essays in *Kayhan-i Farhangi* with the aim of "rationalizing religious studies, bringing it into public debates." Although Khatami's Ministry of Culture (1988–90) had encouraged intellectual publications, their scope was still limited.[185] The year after *Kayhan-i Farhangi* was closed down by Rahbar Khamenei in 1990, the group established the monthly *Kiyan* (under Reza Tehrani and Mashallah Shamsulva'izin) and its sister magazine, the feminist *Zanan*. Then other scholarly works on new epistemology and religious thought published in the Qum Seminary, such as *Naqd va Nazar, Ma'rifat, Hawzih va Danishgah, Farārāh*, found their way into intellectual circles. But it was the Tehran headquarters of *Kiyan* that became the intellectual salon of post-Islamist thought: college students and lay thinkers flocked to weekly lectures, seminars, and discussions to which Surush and some forty other Muslim writers contributed.[186] Reading groups, in which Khatami was an active participant, read Machiavelli, Dante Alighieri, and Galileo's essay on religion as Queen of Science (*Letter to Grand Duchess Christina*). Others discussed Christopher Hill's *God and the English Revolution*. Parallel gatherings were organized in mosques, *husayniyya*s, and homes. When Surush was banned from lecturing in university halls, he organized lessons in the *Husayniyyih-i Shuhadā'* and in private gatherings.[187] Although Surush remained the intellectual mentor of the group, others (such as Alavitabar, Burqani, Muhajirani, Kadivar, Nuri, and Mujtahid Shabastari) later joined in to carry the nascent movement. In the meantime, liberal-religious activists (*milli mazhabiha*) rallied around the monthly *Iran-i Farda*, while new circles in the Qum Seminary, with participants such as Mustafa Malakian and students of Ayatollah Muntazari, worked through *Naqd va Nazar*, and the secular intellectuals established *Guftugu* and a number of literary social publications.[188]

The religious intellectuals were soon to encounter a strategic question: where to go from here? Some, such as Shamsulva'izin and Jala'ipur, believed they should bring their ideas to the mass of the people by establishing daily papers and a political party. To this end, they applied for official authorization to set up a "Coalition of Religious Intellectuals." Although official authorization was denied, progress was made on the press front. Ata'ullah Muhajirani established the weekly *Bahman* in 1995, 'Abbas 'Abdi published *Bahar* a few months later, and the quarterly *Kitab-i Naqd*, covering themes on secularism and religious pluralism, appeared in bookstores during the winter of 1996. Yet *Bahman* published no more than seventeen issues and *Bahar* only three before they were forced by the conservative judiciary to close down. Consequently, the early pressure from conservative Islamists confirmed the concern of others in the group that it was premature to engage in such radical measures because they would provoke a backlash. To spread its discursive project on a mass scale, the group felt it needed to wait for a more open political climate. But to create such an opportunity, the problem of political power had to be addressed.

THE POST-ISLAMIST POLITY:
FROM "RELIGIOUS DEMOCRACY" TO DEMOCRACY

At the same time that Muslim women, student activists, intellectuals, and state employees were mobilizing their constituencies for social and ideational change, "religious intellectuals" began to ponder how such civil society movements could be sustained, and how the tremendous energy of the citizenry could be translated into political change at the state level. Thus "political development" became the group's preoccupation, and their ultimate objective democratizing the patrimonial Islamic state. While wishing to maintain the "Islamic" thrust of the system, they stressed enhancing its "republican" dimension, hoping to realize what later came to be known as a new model of "religious democracy."

The idea of "political development" (*taws'i-yi siyasi*) originated in the early 1990s from religious intellectuals' reexamination of Iran's closed political structure. It was formulated in a systematic fashion by a research team headed by Sa'id Hajjariyan, probably the most innovative strategist of the religious democratic left. Hajjariyan, a follower of Shari'ati's ideas, had become active in his local mosque in south Tehran during the 1970s. After the revolution, he worked for the counterintelligence unit until 1984, when he established the first Intelligence Ministry and worked as its deputy minister. In 1989, following the war, he created the Political Bureau of the President's Center for Strategic Studies (CSS). Launched under President Rafsanjani, the CSS became the organizational and intellectual hub for political reformers. Hajjariyan brought together the most talented post-Islamist political strategists, assigning to each a particular project. Musavi Khoiniha (a cleric who had led students seizing the U.S. embassy) became the center's general director; Bahzad Nabavi acted as a leading strategist; 'Abbas 'Abdi, Mohammad Reza Tajik, and Khusru Tahrani were in charge of "cultural studies"; and Muhsin Kadivar directed the "Islamic political thought" program, which included some seventy projects.[189] In the meantime, Mustafa Tajzadeh, Muhsin Aramin, 'Alireza 'Alavitabar, Majid Muhammadi, and Hashem Aghajari (who were linked to the Organization of Mujahidin of the Islamic Revolution), among others, developed projects on such themes as Iran's political culture, the nature of the state, modernization, political and strategic theory, and theories of revolution.[190]

Within the CSS, Hajjariyan launched a project of "political development" at a time when President Rafsanjani had begun his "economic development" or structural adjustment program.[191] The team worked on various aspects of political reform, beginning with political theories that, ironically, were rooted in North American modernization theory. Political development was crucial, Hajjariyan concluded, first, because it was a precondition for economic development (similar to the notion that democracy is good for economic growth),[192] and, second, because it could contain the repercussions of economic growth— inequality and social unrest.[193] In addition to conceptual work, the team was also concerned with practical matters, beginning with the establishment of a college to train intellectuals and cadres; promoting civil society organizations, chiefly the Organization of the Mujahidin of the Islamic Revolution (OMIR); and launching the daily *Salam*. Study findings were covered in the monthly *Rahburd*, and later in *'Asr-i Mā*.

The group unleashed an unprecedented debate on the nature of the religious state in Iran, often questioning the relevance of the concept of *vilāyat-i faqīh*, the Islamic state's doctrinal foundation. In this new reading, the "religious state" receives its legitimacy from the will of the people, God's vice-regents on earth.[194] And "people" should not be taken as a homogeneous *umma*. Rather, the plurality of their views, orientations, and lifestyles must be recognized.[195] Both religion and the state reach their ideal forms only when they play the minimalist roles of attending to their own specialized functions.[196] Thus, "separation of the institutions of religion and the state" was advocated as a precondition for an ideal religious republic.[197] For the group, the idea of *vilāyat-i faqīh* was nothing but an innovation by Ayatollah Khomeini, and was thus subject to modification or removal if people decided to do so.[198] To begin a process of modification, they favored the election of the supreme leader to a limited term by direct popular vote (rather than by the Assembly of Religious Experts). In addition, the *faqīh* should remain accountable and his powers reduced. Simply, the supreme leader should serve as the spiritual, not political, leader.[199] In this fashion, Iran's Islamic Republic could be as democratic as British monarchical democracy, where the state would have no business telling people what or how they should believe, wear, eat, or act in their private lives.[200]

The post-Islamist polity called for "secularization" (institutional separation of religion and state), but not "secularism," which meant diminishing the significance of religion in society. Broadly, the projected political order was to blend "Islam and republicanism, religion and democracy, the Revolution and reform, unity and diversity, participation and competition, independence and liberty, strong state and strong society, ethics and politics, this world and the afterworld, God and people."[201] These hybrid elements were summed up in Khatami's notion of "religious democracy" (*mardum sālāri-yi dīni*), which was to guide national policies on culture, economics, and international relations. Policy on such taboo issues as relations with the United States, the Middle East peace process, Israel, and foreign investment was to be formulated only according to "national interests" determined by popularly elected representatives.[202] President Khatami's "dialogue of civilization" and subsequent improvement of relations with many Arab, Asian, and European countries represented that new vision.

Notwithstanding more than a decade of talk about "religious democracy," the exact meaning of the term remained ambiguous.[203] In general, it referred to the quest to democratize the patrimonial Islamist system without losing sight of religious ethics. For in addition to their intrinsic value, the post-Islamists argued, religious sensibilities needed to be respected if modernity and democracy were to succeed in Muslim societies like Iran.[204] Yet the precise place of religion within their projected democratic system remained contested, and with the changing political circumstances perspectives were still evolving. Whereas it was enough for some that their ideal democratic state not be hostile to religion, others, such as Surush, perceived a religious state as one that responded to the sensibilities and interests of a religious population. A few believed that the Islamic character of the state included "ethics and our ruler's moral standards"; otherwise, "99 percent of it [religious democracy] will resemble any other democratic state in the world."[205] For the cleric Mujtahid Shabastari, "religious canons" regulate the relationship between individuals and God, but democracy grounded on human rights would be sufficient to organize the relationships between individuals in an Islamic society. "There aren't such things as Islamic and non-Islamic democracies. There are either democracies or dictatorships," he concluded.[206] Eventually, following Akbar Ganji's celebrated *Republican Manifesto*, Jala'ipur, later Alavitabar and others, called for deleting the word "religious" from "religious democracy," not only because democracy alone would fulfill the desires of a religious society, but because the conservative Islamists might appropriate the term and make it meaningless.[207]

But who would this democracy include? Many opted for an inclusive polity summed up in the dictum, "Iran, for all Iranians," irrespective of individual religious, political, or ideological affiliations. "Unconditional citizen rights," wrote Sa'id Hajjariyan, "would require me to worry about the human and citizenry rights of Reza Pahlavi [the son of the late Shah]. But I would also retain my right to oppose his notion of the nation."[208] Muhammad Khatami often invoked Rosa Luxemburg's idea of democracy to mean "freedom of the opposition" and the protection of the minority.

The question of how to realize such a polity was more challenging. It was to be achieved through a nonviolent strategy, via social mobilization and social movement activism—"mobilizing from below and negotiating from above." Mobilization from below was well under way through the expanding activism of the young, students, women, and middle classes. Negotiation at the top had to win over elements of state power. Hence, the idea of nominating a post-Islamist intellectual to run for president in 1997. The campaign strategy led by Sa'id Hajjariyan, based on years of social research at CSS, produced a decisive victory. In May 1997, Muhammad Khatami was elected president of the republic in a landslide. This triumph of the new thinking drew many of its intellectuals into the new government as ministers (Nuri, Muhajirani, and Habibullah Bitaraf), deputy ministers (Tajzadeh and Burqani), advisors (Hajjariyan), and dozens of parliamentary deputies. Others turned to journalism and within two years created "the freest, most professional, and socially effective press in the region's history."[209]

The ideas developed by the religious intellectuals and institutionalized by President Khatami's election led to the formation of the Reform Movement. For the first time in Iran's history, intellectuals had converged with both the grassroots and the state. Ascending to political power on the shoulders of persistent social movements, they cultivated the promise of a home-grown model of democracy in a Muslim society.

EXPLAINING THE CHANGE

Why did post-Islamism, as a condition, project, and movement, come into existence? At least three factors were broadly responsible: first, the failures and contradictions of the Islamist project that entailed a rethinking of Islamism from within; second, social changes (increasing literacy, urbanization, and an economic shift) that generated actors (educated middle classes, the young, increasingly literate women) who together formed a collective urban consciousness that pushed for social and political transformation; and third, the global context within which these changes were taking place.

The Islamist project unleashed by the Islamic state was bound to eventually generate dissent, for it was brought about not by pervasive social movements from below but from above, by a divided political elite under constant pressure from the zealous grassroots. Created from scratch, it was a crash course in experimentation, trial, and error. The system of *vilāyat-i faqīh* was opposed from the start by the majority of Shiʻi grand clergy,[210] and the patrimonial nature of the Islamic state excluded many people from political participation. Although the *faqīh* ruled alongside an elected Parliament, restrictions on forming political parties and the Council of Guardians' veto power marginalized other political tendencies. Even some of the ardent supporters of the system became demoralized by the government's excessive political control and factional infighting. Former allies (such as Ayatollah Kazim Shariʻatmadari, Mahdi Bazargan, Sadiq Qutbzadih, Ayatollah Husayn ʻAli Muntazari, and Abul-Hasan Bani-Sadr) turned into enemies, and secular leftist groups, ethnic political organizations, and the Mujahidin-i Khalq Organization, which had waged armed struggle against the regime in the early 1980s, were harshly repressed.[211] Surveillance, jail, and summary execution of opponents became the order of the day.

Also, the economy did not deliver. "Islamic economics" remained a "disputed utopia"[212] and in the end settled for an often disrupted and distorted capitalist economy. Income distribution improved slightly: in 1977, the top 20 percent of the population earned 57.3 percent of the country's income while the lowest 40 percent earned 11.28 percent; in 1991, the top 20 percent earned half of all income while the bottom 40 percent earned 13.4 percent.[213] Nevertheless, during the same period per capita income dropped by half. Economic blockades, the devastating cost of war (some 90 billion dollars),[214] and a major decline in international oil prices contributed to this decline, but economic mismanagement and lack of security for capital accumulation also played debilitating roles. The alarming development indicators of the First Five-Year Plan (1989–94) heralded the end of a golden age of the rentier state. Subsequently, idealistic and still young Islamic war veterans, disenchanted by the populist rhetoric of the Islamic state, rioted in Islamshahr, Shiraz, Mashdad, Arak, and Khoramabad.[215]

Industrial workers barely managed through strikes to maintain their purchasing power, while professionals and the salaried middle classes—the privileged prerevolution groups—were ravaged by inflation and recession. Chic middle-class families, like their Egyptian counterparts, took on several informal jobs to maintain their standard of living. State control of individual behavior and leisure, and moral regulation of females in particular, frustrated middle-class women and urban youth. In the universities, the "Cultural Revolution" dismissed 180,000 students and two out of every three faculty members.[216] Economic pressure, political repression, and social control of bourgeois lifestyles induced the biggest "brain drain" in Iran's modern history. An estimated 3 million Iranians left the country.[217] The rich and skilled headed for the West, and working-class men to the East: Japan, Southeast Asia, and the Persian Gulf states.[218] By early 2000, Iranian immigrants had invested over $50 billion in Turkey and Arab countries and a staggering $400 billion in the United States, Europe, and China.[219]

With the end of revolutionary exceptionalism and the beginning of normalization after the Iran-Iraq war, the mundane realities of wages, food, housing, and individual liberty pushed aside ideology and altruism. "The system of *vilāyat-i faqīh* showed its limitations," acknowledged a hard-line Khomeinist who had defected from his revolutionary past.[220] "It became clear that [despite] many of the slogans . . . like justice, and the defense of toilers and the deprived . . . the country was, instead of approaching its utopia [i.e., a world Islamist system] was pushed back."[221] By the early 1990s, social problems associated with crime, divorce, deviance, exclusion, apathy, a growing population, and the daily women's quarrels with the morals police, had confronted Iranian Muslims with a sobering question: "Is this the kind of Islamic society we are building?" If in Egypt, defeat in the war (with Israel) bolstered sentiments for Islamism, in Iran it caused many to rethink this very same project. Islamic leaders feared people might associate all these social ills with Islam and turn away from it. This moral panic did have some strong objective grounds. Self-critical leaders acknowledged, "we have progressed only in religious appearances . . . but not in essence."[222] "By our wrongdoings," admitted the prominent Ayatollah Musavi Ardabili, "we have alienated three-fourths of the people. . . . We are responsible for creating a violent, detestable, terrifying, inflexible, irrational, anti-science, unethical, and inhuman image of Islam"[223]

A survey by the Tehran Municipality painted a grim picture of private religiosity under the Islamic state: 73 percent of Tehranies did not recite their daily prayers and 17 percent did so only occasionally. Drug use and divorce were sharply rising, and moral vices increased by 635 percent in 1999.[224] Up to 2 million Iranians were reportedly addicted to narcotics. In 1996 half of all Iranian households filed over 3 million criminal and legal suits in the courts of a nation that promised social peace and harmony.[225] "Islamic solidarity" was merely a myth.

Youth, the children of the revolution, caused the most concern. By 1996 Iran had one of the world's youngest populations: two out of three were under the age of 30. The regime's control of leisure and suppression of youthful desires alienated them from the Islamist authorities. Officials panicked when surveys unveiled the growing indifference and hostility of the young toward religion, the clergy, and the religious state. The state faced the formidable challenge of integrating youth into religious politics, from which they were exiting en masse. It became clear that in this new post-Islamist era, mainstream Iranian youth were experiencing an ideological void: they had tried many ideologies but had not gained much. And pushed by the horror of war, the absence of normalcy, constant control, and humiliation in public, and trapped in tiny, overcrowded apartments with little privacy, some turned to nihilism or fell into depression. Medical reports claimed 20 percent of those over age 15 suffered from a psychological disorder.[226] Soccer matches became formidable security problems, as many were followed by mass violence and riots, while others chose passive resistance, expressing fragmented subcultures. Those more ambitious fantasized about migrating to the West. What ideological alternative was there to offer the young who were departing from Islamism?

Then "the first sparks of self-examination surfaced and intellectual debates found space in society."[227] Post-Islamism emerged as a way out, as a worldview to integrate such alienated and marginalized segments of society, in particular the young. "Today more than any other time," a *Kiyan* editorial proclaimed in 1993, "the Islamic revolution needs to formulate a new vision in order to rescue our current generation from mental disorder, nihilism, and degeneration."[228] This paradigm shift resulted not simply from intellectual self-discovery, but also from societal pressure. The new discourse would not have become dominant had it not been backed by the rising social movements.

What facilitated these post-Islamist ideas to emerge and assume currency even among the ulema were the paradoxes of the Islamic state. First, the very Islamization of the state had led to a growing secularization of Shari'a, because the latter largely failed to respond to the demands of complex modern life. The crisis exploded in 1987 during the debate over the new labor law and Islamic penal code (*ḥudūd va taʿzīr*). Could individual *qādi*s, court judges, authorize different penalties on identical offenses? Forced to disregard Shari'a, Ayatollah Khomeini opted for legal uniformity, a clear encroachment on the *qadis'* authority. When questioned by ulema, the charismatic Khomeini invoked the "absolute" rule of the supreme jurist (*vilāyat-i mutlaqih-i faqīh*), according to which the supreme *faqīh* held the absolute power to change or disregard any law, precept, or religious injunction in the interest of the state. Even the constitution, religious obligations, daily prayers, and attending *hajj* were not excluded. For in this view, *vilāyat*, or governmentality embodied in the state, took precedence over all other obligations.[229] Earlier, Khomeini had authorized an Assembly of *Maslaha*, a secular body, to mediate between the Majlis, the secular assembly, and the Council of Guardians, the religious body that could veto any parliamentary law it deemed anti-Islamic. But Khomeini's new ruling not only broke the invincibility of Shari'a; it also showed that the *vilāyat-i faqīh* was a man-made reality, "just as the monarchy, or secular states, or any other conventional positions in society,"[230] and therefore just as Shari'a itself was subject to change.

This innovation in *fiqh* or "dynamic *ijtihād*" (the ulema's power to interpret the Prophet's sunna and stipulate new injunctions) as it came to be known, had far-reaching unintended consequences. First, it created political and intellectual opportunity for others, particularly the post-Islamists, to present their own interpretations based on religious pluralism. If Ayatollah Khomeini could offer his distinct reading of Islamic rule (and it could be opposed by other ulema), why not others? At the same time, the absolute *vilāyat-i faqīh* granted almost unlimited power to the *faqīh*, contradicting the republican tenets of the constitution[231] and pushing the state toward patrimonialism. Such power enabled Ayatollah 'Ali Khamenei to prevent the reformist Parliament from passing a bill in support of a free press in the summer of 1999. In addition, Khomeini's ruling further secularized the state, creating a new crisis in the *marja'iyyat*.[232] For it subordinated religious sanctity to mundane concerns and encroached on the clergy's prerogative to an autonomous interpretation of Shari'a. To their further dismay, the ulema's fatwas, or verdicts, on public affairs became subject to approval by the supreme *faqīh*, and their access to *haq-i imam*, or donations from the faithful, conditional on the *faqīh*'s permission. Because the state (Assembly of Experts) took charge of disbursing *khums* and *zakat* (religious taxes), the mujtahids lost their power of distributing stipends to their student clientele. Still further, the Special Clerical Courts, in which a number of dissident clerics (such as Kadivar, 'Abdullah Nuri, Muhsin Ruhami, and Ashkevari) have been prosecuted for expressing unorthodox ideas, eroded the clerics' intellectual immunity. And all this occurred in conditions where the fusion of the state and religion had stained the spiritual and social legitimacy of the clergy, as many Iranians tended to equate the failures of the state with those of the ulema.[233]

For the first time in their modern history, the mainstream Shi'i ulema were losing their independence and much of their traditional power, and this was happening, ironically, under a self-conscious Islamic state. Increasing ulema dependency on the state, itself ruled by a few powerful clergy, caused many younger clerics to worry about their future and that of the institution of the ulema. Many expressed their concerns publicly. "If we tie religion to politics," one said, "all the mundane and everyday troubles will be identified with religion, removing religion from its sacred plain of spirituality and turning it into an everyday political game. Religion should be saved for the days when politics fail." So "for the sake of both religion and the state, they should be kept separate."[234] Others felt that the heavy involvement of clerical students in state administration had harmed the academic dimension of the seminary[235] and began to feel that they might be better off if they left politics to politicians. In a sense, post-Islamism sought to save Islam as a faith by undoing Islamism as politics.[236]

Although post-Islamism had indigenous roots, it had developed within a particular global context: the collapse of the Soviet Union and its allies, the "triumph" of liberalism, and the globalization of the languages of civil society, pluralism, and human rights. Closing political doors could not prevent the information revolution from seeping into the Islamic Republic. Media images of Iranian mullahs wearing robes and turbans while surfing the Internet embodied the fragility of political barriers against such integration. Post-Islamist activists adopted many of the popular idioms of the day (civil society, rule of law, transparency, democracy, accountability) and blended them with religious ethics to generate their own hybrid alternative for a society that was yearning for change.[237]

But how was the social foundation of the movement built? Spectacular social changes since the 1980s had produced social actors, notably educated but impoverished middle classes, urban youth, and women, who aspired to social and political transformation. First, Iran had emerged from being a semi-literate country (48 percent in 1976) to become a literate society (in 1996, 80 percent of the population over age 6 could read; in cities the rate was 86 percent and in villages 74 percent). Within that same twenty-year period the student population had increased 266 percent to a staggering 20 million, or one-third of the populace. The nation's universities multiplied from twenty-six in 1976 to eighty in 1994. The number of college students tripled while faculties only doubled; one out of every five households produced a college student or graduate.[238] Education expansion affected almost all sectors of society: men and women, urban and rural, rich and poor. Traditional families in particular felt that it was morally safe to allow their female members to attend school, a practice that increased female literacy from 36 percent in 1976 to 74 percent in 1996. In cities 82 percent of women were literate. Literacy spread rapidly in rural areas as well (70 percent, including over 60 percent of women), to the extent that every village had on average two university graduates. Given the high value Iran's culture places on modern education, these rural graduates played a crucial role in social change.

Second, Iran was rapidly becoming an urban society. In 1996 over 60 percent of its people were living in cities, compared to 47 percent twenty years earlier. Mass urbanization spawned urban individuality, self-expression, and demands for urban citizenship. It created social space for subcultures, media exposure, diverse tastes and styles, extra-kinship identities, and extended social interactions. At the same time, urbanity crept into rural areas, changing occupational structures, the division of labor, literacy rates, and consumption patterns, while new means of communication, expanding electronic and print media, and college education drew the rural world into the urban trajectory. By 1996, more of the rural population worked in industry, construction, and services (51 percent) than in agriculture, with services employing 23 percent of the labor force, compared to 10 percent in 1976.[239] For example, in the village of Guyom (with 4,200 inhabitants in 1996), twenty kilometers from Shiraz, 90 percent of households had been dependent on agriculture in 1978; twenty years later no more than 10 percent were. Instead, the inhabitants worked as government employees, shopkeepers, factory workers, and rural entrepreneurs, or had simply retired.[240] Electricity, paved roads, day care centers, means of communication and transportation, newspapers, diverse occupations, television sets (some with satellite dishes), modern administration, and village councils largely run by young people—all became salient features of rural life. According to the 1996 census, of the 12.2 million households in Iran, only 1 million lacked a television set. By 2002, 99 percent of rural households had electricity.[241]

One key outcome of this social change has been the decline in traditional sources of authority and the emergence of new ones. The rural mullah, or clergyman, is no longer a dominant village figure. Indeed, in my own small village close to Tehran I observed the growing authority of the young relative to the traditional elders. Ageism, it seemed, was finally giving way to an appreciation of competence. In the view of one Iranian observer, this trend at the national level was reflected in the declining authority of parents over children, fathers over sons, teachers over students, religious experts over laymen, and husbands over wives.[242] In other words, the prevailing hierarchical dichotomies were subverted, giving rise to new social division and conflicts, and the structure of the family at the national level had begun to change. Survey after survey suggested that extended families were crumbling and nuclear families were consolidating. Matriarchal and "child-centered" perspectives were gaining influence over the traditional power of fathers,[243] while women were acquiring a new "autonomous identity."[244] Compared to youth in the Muslim Middle East, Iran's young people were adopting a notable trend of individualism.[245] The expansion of new urban lifestyles and "apartment living" both reflected and intensified this process of individuation. These remarkable social changes pulled urbanizing rural areas into the orbit of national politics.

Finally, the class structure experienced a profound change characterized by a relative de-proletarianization, a greater informality, and the rise of middle-class occupations.[246] From 1976 to 1996, when the total private labor force (consisting of those over 10 years old) increased only 37 percent, the number of small business entrepreneurs tripled and public sector employees expanded by a startling 254 percent. In the meantime, while the number of private wage earners remained virtually stagnant (6.5 percent), self-employed (independent) workers in the informal sector increased by 190 percent. Women's share of the workforce declined slightly, but more women were in occupations with higher pay, power, and prestige. In general, more people were employed in more flexible work conditions and middle-class occupations, displaying a wide range of choices in consumption. Yet the economic downturn and low income frustrated the realization of middle-class lifestyles.[247]

Thus, by the mid-1990s, a new type of middle class was in the making—one characterized by enormous size, educational capital, and global dreams, yet economic hardship. Their high expectations, tastes, and desires demanded, according to some estimates, a per capita GDP of $8,000, when the actual average income did not exceed $3,000.[248] For while Iran's social structure had changed considerably, economic arrangements remained "traditional," with low productivity and dependence on oil and agriculture. The highly educated but economically worse-off middle class felt inferior to its affluent prerevolution counterparts, but they became remarkably similar to the Egyptian middle layers. Frustrated and morally outraged, the middle class constituted the core of the social base for the post-Islamist movements, pushing the "reformist" Muhammad Khatami into the office of president. The movement had finally come to power. Could it spearhead a democratic transformation?

4 POST-ISLAMISM IN POWER
Dilemmas of the Reform Project, 1997–2004

ON THE PERSIAN SECOND OF KHURDAD 1376, or May 23, 1997, a post-Islamist candidate for president of Iran, Muhammad Khatami, defeated the well-established cleric Ayatollah Nateq Nuri, who had enjoyed the full backing of the entire conservative establishment: the state-run media, the military, most Friday prayer leaders (or imams), and Supreme Leader Ayatollah 'Ali Khamenei.[1] The ecstasy, jubilation, and optimism that followed this triumph brought back the memory of the postrevolution days. In fact, many described the victory as Iran's "second revolution." Euphoric crowds danced in the streets and passed around candies, and mothers invited their exiled children to return home.

The second of Khurdad was the beginning of a new era in the life of the Islamic Republic. Now that it had captured the executive branch, was the post-Islamist movement poised to lead Iran into a democratic future? This chapter discusses the dilemmas of a social movement that had one foot in state power. On the one hand, the movement found opportunities to institutionalize and extend its objectives; on the other, it was constrained by the imperatives of the undemocratic institutions of the state, which thwarted those objectives and eventually led to the loss of the support base. Working simultaneously both within and against the state—that seems to be the greatest challenge of a social movement.

NEW OPPORTUNITY, NEW HOPE
Khatami came to power on the promise of political and cultural "reforms" (islāhāt). This meant establishing the rule of law, a meritocracy, tolerance, and above all, democracy within the framework of the existing constitution.

The fundamental requisite for political reform was to empower civil society. Khatami's manifesto reflected the basic tenets of the post-Islamist polity, which informed the ideological foundation of what came to be known as the "reform movement" (*junbish-i islāhāt*). As the political dimension of post-Islamism, the reform movement represented both the collective desire for change and the coalition of political and civil groupings that had lent support to Khatami. This broad based-coalition, later called the "Second of Khurdad Front," aimed to consolidate and ensure political and cultural reform.

Partially in power, the reform movement began to pursue its strategy of mobilizing civil society from the bottom up while carrying out institutional and legal reform at the top, with Khatami and reformist ministers working as liaisons between the two domains. The Ministries of the Interior and of Islamic Guidance (Culture) were the most crucial state agencies for the execution of political and cultural reform. Conservative Islamists still controlled Parliament, the judiciary, and nonelected but powerful bodies such as state-run television, the security forces, the Council of Guardians, the Council of Exigency, and the influential Friday prayer leaders (see figure 1, p. 54). The cleric 'Abdullah Nuri was put in charge of the Ministry of the Interior to ensure popular participation in the public sphere, which until then had been controlled by the Islamist right. The ministry was also to appoint provincial governors and mayors who would extend reform to regional towns where hardline Friday prayer leaders had spread their influence. Ata'ullah Muhajirani of the Karguzārān Party took over the Ministry of Culture, which aimed to transform the culture by encouraging arts, literature, and a free press. Given that the Islamic state had restricted room for alternative modes of thinking, behaving, and being, the cultural realm was exceptionally critical.

Katami's victory offered an opportunity for already existing social forces to evolve. Thus after years of exclusion and intimidation by the Ansar-i Hizbullah, youths regained their presence in the public space—in streets, parks, cafes, shopping malls, cultural centers, concerts, and stadiums. Indeed, the continuing surveillance by hardliners, together with the reform government's sympathy, further politicized the young, fueling one of the most remarkable youth movements in the Muslim world. Most young people were students, who blended youthful dispositions with student aspirations to create a spectacular student movement with a new identity and vigor almost overnight, for they had already changed their perspective and had been awaiting the opportunity for a collective expression of discontent. As the ally of the students, the reform government offered that opportunity. With an organization (the Office of Consolidation and Unity of Islamic Student Associations, or DTV) in place, the student movement grew rapidly, expanding its nationwide networks, publishing a national student paper (*Azar*) and 700 local student magazines, and establishing an impressive student news agency (ISNA, the Iranian Students News Agency), and 1,437 cultural, scientific, and social associations.[2]

With a new generation of students at its helm, the movement shifted ideologically away from utopian Islamist and Third-Worldist revolutionary politics and toward a pragmatist post-Islamist paradigm based on democracy and civil liberties. Under the reform government, it matured further, from providing unconditional support for and integration into the reform government into a more critical and independent force. "The fundamental role of the student movement is to critique power," declared Reza Delbari, the Islamic Association leader at Amir Kabir University. "The student movement is not a political party, an institution, or a political actor; on the contrary, it is the antithesis of such powers. Its objective is to mobilize for democracy and human rights, and to reform power." This new vision underlined the DTV's decision to disengage from state power—to cease to nominate student candidates for parliamentary or local council elections—and remain independent.[3]

This was an extraordinary time for a society reborn, where an immense sense of vitality and energy animated every sector of society to stand up and assert itself. Within this "social movement animation," female students bonded through growing feminist circles, contributing to an already flourishing activism among Muslim women.[4] Women had already established a large social presence through their mass support for Khatami. Now they expanded their networks, created publications and organizations, and voiced both feminist and political aspirations.[5] Not just women, youths, and intellectuals, but also many local grassroots networks had emerged throughout the country to organize Khatami's electoral campaign (*setad*). These activists made up the bulk of the new governors, mayors, and local officials. Meanwhile, marginalized groups—the Freedom Movement, secular activists, Kurds, and many Iranians in exile—returned to the political scene. The likes of Ayatollah Muntazari, the dismissed heir of Khomeini, emerged from house arrest and lashed out against the "repressive and unjust practices of religious leadership" and against Supreme Leader 'Ali Khamenei for having made people "sick of seeing mullahs."[6] Some 385 opposition clerics had demanded his release and the resumption of his teachings,[7] while the merchants of Najaf-Abad Bazar, Muntazari's home town, followed suit by staging a strike.[8]

Leading reformists knew that this tremendous, unwieldy activism had to be consolidated in institutions. Their objective was to turn a shapeless mass into a civil society, creating a public that could internalize both their rights and their responsibilities. Khatami's advisor Sa'id Hajjariyan urged Khatami to move beyond being merely a symbol of the reform movement and to act as its leader by establishing and heading a political party.[9] Although Khatami failed to follow the advice, his Interior Ministry pushed for civil society institutions, promoting rallies and public meetings in the face of hostile security forces that remained loyal to the conservatives. Journalists led the way by forming their own professional associations in September 1997, including the Association for the Defense of a Free Press, born amid widespread rightist hostility toward critical media. By the end of 2000, ninety-five new political parties and organizations had registered; in 1997 there had been only thirty-five.[10] A year later there were 110 employers' guilds and 120 workers' guilds,[11] while one out of three workers belonged to Labor House, the main workers' organization.[12] Despite NGO inexperience and a dearth of expertise, younger reformists pushed through legislation that promoted the formation of modern NGOs, increasing the number of associations to 2,500 by 2001.[13] Environmental NGOs multiplied from five in 1994 to thirty in 1998, and to over 200 by April 2002. Women's organizations numbered 230 by 2000 and 330 by 2003.[14] Unlike in the Middle East, Iran's NGOs developed largely in the areas of advocacy, women, youth, environment, and professional associations. NGOs were valued more for their political and democratizing potential than for charitable and developmental roles.

Nothing was more visible than the energy around newsstands. Khatami chose the young journalist Ahmad Burqani to spearhead the development of a free press. During his brief tenure in the Ministry of Culture, Burqani issued hundreds of press permits. The reformist daily *Jami'yyih* (headed by Hamidreza Jala'ipur and Shamsulva'izin) and the weeklies *Subh-i Khānivadih* and *Rah-i Naw* (edited by Akbar Ganji) sparked an explosion of relatively free and independent print media unprecedented in the previous hundred years. Within a year, 880 new publications came to life, pushing up circulation of the dailies to 3 million, an annual increase of 100 percent. By April 1998, a thousand publications, including twenty-one major dailies, filled the newsstands,[15] and total daily readership swelled to more than 12 million.[16] Women and students initiated their own specialized press: at the first-ever Student Publication Fair in 1998, students from sixty colleges exhibited more than 200 titles,[17] and two years later there were 286; the number of women's publications reached forty by 2002, including the daily *Zan* published by Faezeh Rafsanjani, the former president's daughter, which was devoted primarily to women's issues.[18] While reformist papers such as *Jami'iyyih*, *Taws*, *Nishāt*, and *Subh-i Imrūz* flourished in sale, range, and quality, the leading conservative press—*Kayhan*, *Jumhuri-i Islami*, *Risālat*—struggled to keep up, clinging to the market largely because they received subsidies from hardline institutions.[19] The reform era would spawn 2,228 new titles, including 174 dailies.[20] In addition to the flourishing local press in the provinces, national dailies found their way into remote areas, including small villages, serving as a crucial vehicle for broader political mobilization.

The new press was no longer the voice of the state but a choir of diverse viewpoints, including those of the politically marginalized. They became relentless in reporting on what had been previously too sensitive: urban riots, official scandals, and Islamists' involvement in political murders. They sparked debate about taboo subjects such as the legitimacy of the *vilāyat-i faqīh*, the separation of religion and state, religious pluralism, and relations with the United States. The new print media became the most effective means of defending and extending the freedom of expression, safeguarding their own sovereignty, and cultivating a new culture of reading. However, as the nation became politically fractured, newspapers often assumed the function of political parties, mixing news and analysis with political posturing.[21] Nevertheless, the new press gave rise to a political glasnost that not only embodied unfolding social struggles but also made people aware of factional conflicts within the state. This awareness, in turn, broadened the social struggles that streamed from the pages of newspapers into the streets.

By fostering a social mobilization and a vibrant public sphere, the reform government helped its position at the state level. The mobilized public delivered resounding electoral victories to the reformists. In the first nationwide elections for city and village councils in February 1999, reform candidates won 90 percent of the 200,000 seats.[22] Many city councils became both a support base for reformists and institutions of grassroots social development.[23] In January 2000, the reformists took control of Parliament in a landslide. By the time Khatami was reelected the following year, the reform movement had gained control of almost all elected institutions.

These remarkable developments projected a fresh, intellectually vibrant, socially active, and democratic image of Iran abroad, thus facilitating the reform government's foreign policy of detente. Khatami opted for a rapid improvement of relations with other nations on the basis of mutual respect and a "dialogue of civilization." In 1997, Iran hosted the eighth Conference of Islamic Countries, the largest gathering of Islamic leaders in Tehran since the 1979 revolution. Millions around the world, including U.S. president Bill Clinton, watched on CNN as the smiling President Khatami cited Alexis de Tocqueville in praise of American democracy and called for dialogue with the United States.

Relations continued to improve until soon after September 11, 2001; despite Khatami's condemnation of the terrorist attacks in the United States and vigils organized in Tehran in memory of the victims, President George W. Bush shocked Iranians by declaring that their country was part of an "axis of evil." On the European front, Iran's Foreign Ministry formally terminated the dispute over Khomeini's infamous fatwa against the author Salman Rushdie, which angered hardline Islamists (the 15th Khurdad and the Hizbullah Student Union continued to offer rewards for the killing of Rushdie). Nevertheless, the establishment of full diplomatic ties with Britain and other European countries went forward.[24] To boost a dialogue of cultures, attempts were made to encourage foreign, notably Western, tourism by easing visa restrictions.[25] In less than four years, relations with pro-West Arab states improved, even though the democratic thrust of the reform movement had alarmed authoritarian Arab regimes. With its "model of democracy," Arab headlines warned, "Iran this time is exporting free elections instead of Islamic Revolution."[26] To the Western intelligentsia, Iran was no longer identified by its oil or Persian carpets, but by its highly acclaimed film production and its new "promise of democracy."

THE REFORMIST POLITICAL FORCES

The reform project was to be pushed forward by a current of diverse social forces that shared the goal of ending the semi-patrimonial clerical rule. The organized forces of the reform movement consisted of the Second of Khurdad Front, liberal-religious groups (*milli mazhabiha*), notably the Freedom Movement, and secular democrats. Organization of the movement centered on the Second of Khurdad Front, a broad coalition of eighteen political groups that included professional associations, student organizations, women's activists, and intellectuals, with ideological-religious tendencies ranging from those of socially conservative clerics to moderate, liberal, and secularist. At its core lay the more strategy-centered Islamic Participation Front (IPF) led by the president's brother Muhammad Reza Khatami, and the Organization of the Mujahidin of the Islamic Revolution (OMIR), to which many "religious intellectuals" belonged. Also included in the IPF were the Association of Combatant Clergy (ACC), whose members had split from the conservative Society of Combatant Clerics (SCC) of Tehran, the students' DTV; the Workers' Party; the Hambastigi Party; and the technocratic Karguzarān Party (led by Ghulam Husayn Karbaschi). The Islamic Participation Front brought together three general trends: the "religious traditional left," such as the SCC; the "religious new left," represented by intellectuals like 'Alireza 'Alavitabar; and the "pragmatists," such as the Karguzarān Party. Beyond Muslim democrats (Akbar Ganji, Sa'id Hajjariyan, and President Khatami), the IPF accommodated social conservatives and ex-hardliners (Yusif Sani'i, Hadi Ghaffari, and Sadiq Khalkhali, a former "hanging judge"), though the latter remained on the sidelines.

The reform movement in general had been dominated by more radical, democratic-minded tendencies. Most post-Islamist intellectuals wished to do away with the vilāyat-i faqīh, even though elements within OMIR and ACC insisted on retaining it and making it subject to popular supervision.[27] As the reform movement became more radicalized, the pragmatist Karguzarān Party shifted to a centrist position, and its support of Rafsanjani in the 2000 parliamentary elections widened the gap between itself and the left of the reformist coalition, whose radicalism pushed Rafsanjani into the conservative camp. As differentiation and debate within the reformist camp intensified, many began to fear a breakup of the reformist coalition. Yet there was also a sense that differences were the natural child of a free and unreserved exchange of ideas, and that candid but bitter exchanges represented a novel practice of democratic dialogue in a political landscape that had long cherished deference and double meaning.

With a mobilized society longing for change, and a reformist Parliament, local government, president, and cabinet devoted to political reform, Iran was poised to become a model of democracy in the Muslim world. But the path was far from smooth. Not only was Khatami's an era of immense public vitality in activism and intellectual production; it was also a period of tremendous instability, crisis, and struggle for power. The reform government embodied a formidable but fragmented movement that had a share in political power, but also one that was surrounded by hostile interests, institutions, and relentless intrigue. Conservative Islamists were determined to reclaim what they had lost.

COUNTERREFORM

Beaten and bewildered by their crushing defeat, the conservative Islamists sought every opportunity to regain confidence and fight back. The earliest arose when Ayatollah Muntazari publicly denounced the supreme leader for "promoting dictatorship." Conservative dailies and Friday prayer leaders, fearing that reformist governors would erode their regional power, waged a nationwide campaign against the ayatollah and his allies. Conservatives called for a day of national allegiance to the supreme leader, sending their supporters into the streets to bolster their own self-confidence and to apprehend reformist enemies. Seminary students, *basījis*, and Ansar-i Hizbullah groups organized street marches and attacked Muntazari's residence. Inciting "ordinary people" to violence such as this characterized the conservative counterreform strategy throughout Khatami's presidency. If the reform movement focused on "mobilization from below and negotiation from above," the conservative backlash aimed to do the opposite, to impair the reformist mobilization in society, and to paralyze the reform government at the top. To this end, the hardliners combined a discursive campaign with everyday violence, instigating crises, and using legal channels to suppress dissent and decapitate reformist-controlled institutions.

Discursive Campaign: Saving Their Islam

A conference organized by conservative clerics at the Qum Seminary in 1996 had attempted to confront the "ideological crisis" and head off the post-Islamist challenge. Participants had called on the grand clergy and supreme leader to articulate and disseminate through textbooks rebuttals to post-Islamist theological "flaws" (*shubahāt*).[28] The opponents targeted the elements of post-Islamist discourse—religious pluralism, secularization, tolerance, and above all democracy—that were wrecking the Islamist paradigm. Both the theological and the social status of Islam (including religious truth, Shari'a, religious freedom, the clergy, and religious politics) became matters of intense verbal struggle. With Khatami's election, however, the debate turned hostile. "Nothing is dirtier than [the idea of] a pluralist reading of religion," declared Ayatollah Khaz'ali of the Council of Guardians, warning Khatami to avoid using such terms in public.[29] For Rahim Sawafi, the commander in chief of the *pāsdārān* (revolutionary militias), these ideas were "produced by our enemies to cause uncertainty among Muslims."[30] The SCC warned, "We must not permit the sacred principles of Islam to become the subject of diverse interpretations of this or that individual."[31] And Ayatollah Misbah Yazdi declared, "We must shut the mouth of those who call for new reading of Islam."[32]

The conservatives realized the grave implications of a "pluralist reading of Islam" for the clerical establishment; it would inevitably deprive clerics of their monopoly of spiritual property and of "expert" interpretation of scripture. For the conservatives, post-Islamism unmistakably evoked the "horror" of Luther's crusade. "Europe got fooled by it, but we shall not," vowed Ayatollah Khaz'ali.[33] Indeed, much earlier, in 1995, the Ansar-i Hizbullah had disrupted a lecture by the post-Islamist 'Abd al-Karim Surush and reminded him of the "lethal fate of Martin Luther and Cromwell for their disruptive ideas."[34] Ayatollah Misbah Yazdi, then head of the judiciary, blasted lay "religious intellectuals" for expressing views on doctrinal matters. "I want to say that [Surush] cannot talk about religion from a Western perspective. The Qur'an is the source of Shari'a. . . . You cannot simply raise these matters and publish them in daily papers."[35]

Hardline clerics claimed exclusive expert knowledge of *fiqh*, discounting the opinions of lay thinkers in this area, and yet many of them took charge of diplomacy, public administration, or economics, about which they had little expertise. To legitimize their battered position, Ayatollah Khaz'ali and rightist Jam'iyyat-i Mu'talifih declared obeying the ulema to be a religious obligation: "Disobedience from clerics is tantamount to disobedience from Imam 'Ali, and thus from God."[36] Ayatollah Misbah Yazdi went as far as declaring the *vilāyat-i faqīh* to be the "continuation of divine rule. Opposing it would be equal to apostasy and the negation of Islam."[37] The Ansar-i Hizbullah blatantly warned, "we will chop the pencils of those who unknowingly write against the *vilāyat-i faqīh*; and will shed their blood if they do so deliberately."[38]

It was clear that for hardline Islamists, "Islam does not accept democratic government . . . [and] does not accept majority rule."[39] "Democracy is nothing but the dictatorship of capital, exploitation, consumerism and selfishness," according to the Islamist quarterly *Mashriq*. It continued, "Democracy is reactionary; it is a return to *jāhilīyya*, paganism, and disbelief. . . . Realization of democracy would mean negating noble human desires, man's true freedom."[40] Hardliners often equated freedom with moral laxity,[41] and therefore only the supreme leader could determine its boundaries.[42] Ironically, after years of advocating elections and political participation, Islamists began to reconsider their views about elections and majority rule once they had lost to the reformists. "Elections do not exist in Islam," declared Friday prayer leader Mullah Hasani, adding, "they are an imported category."[43] Some claimed the "people cannot develop deep analysis about things; they are usually influenced by newspapers and rumors."[44] Others argued for the primacy of "quality" (*ahsaniyyat*) over "majority" (*akthariyat*).[45] According to this logic, a government's legitimacy lay not in popular support but in its abiding by the "prevailing values," meaning Islam. "People? What people?" the cleric Khaz'ali wondered; "people are good only to obey God's commands, not to interfere in them." Most Islamists explicitly preferred "theocracy" (*khudā sālāri*) over democracy (*mardum sālāri*).[46] They seemed unaware that they were speaking the language of traditional Western Orientalism, which views Islam and Muslims as essentially hostile to democracy. This became invaluable evidence for their staunch discursive enemies.

The mass appeal of "reform" compelled most conservative factions to appropriate the term, often subverting its intended thrust. For the hardline *Kayhan*, the "good reformers" were the "fundamentalist reformists" who aimed to "tackle the nation's economic and social problems." Demanding a political change, however, was seen as a Gorbachev-like "revisionist" project desired by foreign powers.[47] The supreme leader assumed a centrist position, proposing "revolutionary reforms" to promote "progress and innovation" in religious thought consistent with the "values" of the Islamic revolution.[48] Only a "just *faqīh*," he stressed, could unite the two diverging orientations ("reform" and "values").[49] Far from Gramsci's notion of "revolutionary reform"—or, as Garton Ash puts it, "refolution," referring to Eastern Europe, where the reformists' hegemony was established by changing the political structure and economic rationale[50]—Khamenei's version invariably opposed the political thrust of Iran's "reform movement." He framed it, instead, as a populist campaign "against poverty and corruption."[51] In short, the supreme leader sought not Gramsci's "revolutionary reform" but his "passive revolution." He wanted to incorporate and pacify the reform movement by offering concessions in order to maintain clerical rule.

Violence and Chains of Crisis

Most conservatives perceived post-Islamist reform as the latest Western plot to dismantle Iran's Islamic system. After the failure of the Mujahidin-i Khalq and the Iraqi invasion, conservatives argued, enemies had infiltrated the system to encourage alternative thought and change perceptions. This "cultural meta-morphosis," according to them, paved the way for undermining Islam and the sacred canons, and aimed ultimately to dismantle the system.[52] If the Islamists' "passive revolution" failed to contain the post-Islamist quest for genuine change, then it should be stopped by violence, they argued. "If the situation gets out of hand," the Ansar-i Hizbullah warned, "Iran will turn not into another Turkey but another Lebanon."[53]

History and the subsequent activities of undercover hardline Islamists confirmed the seriousness of the threat. Indeed, the use of everyday violence in the name of "safeguarding Islam and the revolution" had become an effective way of doing politics. Through repression by proxy—"ordinary people" used as pawns—hardliners aimed to recapture the public sphere. Hundreds of semi-clandestine "cultural" groups associated with the Ansar-i Hizbullah and *basīji* vigilantes found fertile ground for activism after the reformists had come to power. The Hizbullah Cultural Front, the Shalamchih Cultural Group, the Shahid Avini Cultural Group, and the Maw'ūd Cultural Front represented only a few of them.[54] Many operated in conjunction with the Front for Islamist Resistance led by Mas'ud Dihnamaki, the editor of the extremist weeklies *Shalamchih* and *Jabhih*, who had links with the *pāsdārān*. They held political and ideological meetings, obtained combatant training, and published tracts in the hardline *Kayhan, Harīm, Partaw, Fayziyyih*, and *Yālithārāt*. They organized demonstrations, circulated petitions, attacked crowds, and disrupted meetings, lectures, and rallies of opposition forces. Amir Farshad Ibrahimi, a member of Maw'ūd group and a leading "plain-clothesman" who ransacked a Tehran University dormitory in 1999, disclosed in videotaped confessions the astonishing intrigues of rightist secret societies to cause terror, intimidate, and assassinate. Ibrahimi revealed his connections to the Qum Seminary, to the Fida'iyan-i Islam group, and to such prominent clerics as Ayatollah Misbah Yazdi, Mahdavi-yi Kani, and Ayatollah Jannati of the Council of Guardians.[55] Reminiscent of fascist vigilantes, the Ansar-i Hizbullah violently disrupted scores of reformist and secularist rallies, lectures, and events, ransacking offices and beating up individuals, while police stood by and watched. Those who were arrested were set free by the judiciary.[56] In 1999 vigilantes stormed a mosque and assaulted the respected pro-reformist Ayatollah Tahiri of Isfahan, who resigned from his post in 2002 in protest against clerical rule. Even cabinet ministers Ata'ullah Muhajirani and 'Abdullah Nuri were not immune from their violent wrath. Vigilantes terrorized foreign tourists (to subvert Khatami's policy of openness)[57] and fomented violence at a Tehran University dormitory in 1999 and at a student movement national congress in Khuramābād in 2000. On average during Khatami's first presidency, one small- or large-scale incident was plotted every nine days.[58] Some of them put Hollywood suspense dramas to shame.

In late 1997, Khatami paid a visit to the Ministry of Intelligence, where he reminded the intelligence officials, "while we should be concerned about the security of the state, we must, in the same manner, protect the security of society."[59] At the time, only a few people knew that a mafia among that audience was plotting to overthrow his government. In the fall of 1998 the brutal murders of Daryush Furuhar, a pro-Musaddiq ex-minister, and his wife in their home shocked the nation. Soon after, the writers Muhammad Mukhtari and Muhammad Ghaffar Puyandih disappeared, until their lynched bodies were found in a desolate neighborhood on the city's outskirts. Investigations revealed the involvement of Intelligence Ministry agents. In a startling plot the same mafia had attempted to force a bus full of Iran's best-known intellectuals down a mountainside; the group was on its way to the Republic of Armenia in 1996 to attend a cultural event.[60] Iranians then began to learn who had been behind the assassination of over a hundred political and intellectual dissidents at home and abroad over the preceding years.[61]

Public outrage over these murders put conservatives on the defensive. The reformist press relentlessly pursued the matter, using the opportunity to launch a spectacular debate on the evil of violence and the nobility of tolerance. A few people were arrested for the murders, but little was revealed about any larger network. The ringleader, Saʻid Imami (known as Saʻid Islami), was found dead in mysterious circumstances in prison, fueling public speculation that hardliners were behind the murders. The identities of the ultimate perpetrators remained unknown in the face of pressure from top clerics, and the lawyer for the victims' families, Naser Zarafshan, was incarcerated. Although Khatami went ahead with cleansing the ministry of such "cancerous tumors" by appointing a new minister and changing personnel, the *pāsdārān* set up its own parallel intelligence service.

To win back the public sphere, hardliners instigated a chain of national crises to demonstrate the "disruptive" consequences of reform policies. These crises often followed a similar pattern. Vigilante groups were first dispatched in the name of the "masses" to disrupt reform rallies, meetings, and offices, or to incite violence. Then state television, conservative dailies, and most Friday prayer leaders publicized, sensationalized, and demanded more of the same actions. Among other things, they lamented that "civil society" led to instability, that a free press spread anti-Islamic sentiments, that intellectuals who questioned the Islamic system opened the way for secularists and Western enemies. In the final stage, the judiciary ordered the security forces to stop certain activities, ban newspapers, close offices, and jail activists.

The April 1998 trial of Ghulam Husayn Karbaschi, the popular mayor of Tehran accused of corruption, was the first link in a chain of crises despite the general perception of the trial as a ploy to punish the mayor for supporting Khatami. Karbaschi's trial, in which he acted as his own defense lawyer, became the most watched daily program in Iranian television history. During the trial, pro-Karbaschi students battled *pāsdārān* and Hizbullah vigilantes in the streets, resulting in scores of injuries and detainments, and as night fell people rushed home to watch the mayor's spectacular performance, presided over by an imposing clerical judge. The entire nation was emotionally involved, politicized, and polarized in a crisis that many saw as a sinister conspiracy against the reform project. To prevent this national crisis from worsening, the mayor was released on the order of Khamenei. But serious and systematic confrontations were to follow.

In September 1999, a college student magazine, *Mawj* (Wave) published a two-page satirical play that told the story of a student who tried to convince the Twelfth Imam to delay his return from occultation because he had an exam! The daily *Kayhan* cited this obscure work, which allegedly showed disrespect to Shi'i Islam, to spark a national uproar on the eve of parliamentary elections. Senior clerics called for author's execution and a *pāsdārān* commander said he would carry it out. Islamists attacked Khatami for promoting the "unfettered freedom" that had spawned such "insults to the sacred." The incident eventually entailed the resignation of the minister of culture, Muhajirani. The hardliners inflicted more such crises on the reform government (arresting participants at a Berlin conference, ransacking Tehran University dormitories, and disrupting a student conference in Khuramābād), but their legal onslaught was more damning.

Fighting Civil Society by Law

Conservatives had felt "grave danger" from a free press that popularized dissenting ideas such as the "republican theology," activated the public, and connected that public to the leadership of the reform movement. The backlash against the reformist press began only few months into the reform govern-ment. In 1998 *Jamiʿiyyih* (Society), the first daily of civil society, was shut down and its publishers jailed only four months after its establishment. The paper reappeared three more times under different names (*Taws, Nishāt*, and *ʿAsr-i Azādigān*) following successive closures by the court. Others suffered the same fate: *Zan*, a women's newspaper; *Jamiʿiyyih Sālim*, a daring intel-lectual magazine; *Khānih; Navīd Isfahān; Tavānā; Akhbār; Āftābgardan*—the list went on. Often the charges very vaguely worded, accusing the publica-tions of "misleading people" or "insulting" Islam, the revolution, or prom-inent personalities. In a seeming war of attrition, almost daily the Culture Ministry issued press permits and the judiciary voided them. In its last days, the conservative-controlled fifth Majlis passed a law limiting the more liberal issuance of press permits, which the pro-reform daily *Salam* reported was the idea of Saʿid Imami, the intelligence agent behind the political murders in 1998. Salam was immediately banned. And more closures soon followed.

The first mass closure came in April 2000 after a conference in Berlin where a number of secular and post-Islamist intellectuals had spoken of in-evitable change in the Islamic Republic. The conservatives pounced. The su-preme leader declared in a speech that pro-reform journalism was "a grave danger to us all" giving the green light to the judiciary to shut down fourteen reformist newspapers and magazines, including *Bāmdād, Azād, Fath, Aryā, ʿAsr-i Azādigān, Abān, Arzish*, among others.[62] In the following days the court closed down the president's brother Muhammad Reza Khatami's *Mushārikat* and the influential *Subh-i Imrūz* published by Saʿid Hajjariyan, who had barely survived an assassination attempt by a group of hardline Islamists. The monthly *Kiyan*, the "salon" of post-Islamist intellectuals in the early 1990s, eventually fell victim to this wave of crackdown.

The onslaught crippled the reformists only three months after they had taken Parliament in a landslide election, though the Council of Guardians was still insisting on a recount, claiming fraud. In these nerve-wracking mo-ments, the hardline combination of refusing to accept the election results and banning the reformist press raised the specter of a social explosion. Eager to open Parliament but not wishing to give the defeated conservatives any reason to annul the results, reform leaders called for calm and self-restraint. They promised that the new Majlis, once in session, would amend the press law and reinstate the victimized press. Eventually, Khamenei validated the elections, the crisis subsided, and Parliament began its work. But when Parliament began to amend the press law, in August 2000, the supreme leader intervened to block debate on the proposed bill and subsequent attempts to reinstate the press. In fact, the judiciary continued its assault. Between 1997 and 2002, the courts banned 108 major dailies and other periodicals,[63] placing thousands of journalists, publishers, editors, and writers in detention or out of work. More than the restrictive press law, the intervention of the supreme leader was a devastating blow not only to the press but to parliamentary authority. It transformed the public's joy in the reformists' victory into deep cynicism about the system's republican thrust.

With the increasing crackdown on the print media, activists resorted to the Internet. Within three years, hundreds of quality news and networking websites and an estimated 100,000 weblogs sprang up. By 2003, student organizations, women's groups, NGOs, political parties, and private individuals were supplying uncensored news, analysis, and poor-quality political satire to a domestic Internet audience that had grown to more than 3 million. This free flow of information frustrated the judiciary, which desperately sought recourse by cracking down on Internet cafes, filtering websites, and arresting bloggers, though often to little effect.

It fared much better in the conventional world. By 2002, hundreds of pro-reform journalists, intellectuals, and activists of both secular and religious orientations had been arrested on "anti-religion" and "anti-state" charges. Hardline thugs forced 'Abd al-Karim Surush, the mentor of post-Islamist intellectuals, to withdraw from his academic position and cease lecturing in public. Immediately following the reformist parliamentary victory in 2000, Sa'id Hajjariyan, the movement's top strategist, was gunned down by a group of Islamist assassins that included members of the *pāsdārān*.[64] The man convicted of the plot was originally sentenced to fifteen years in jail, but he was back on the streets sooner[65] and disappeared until his rearrest during the attacks by Ansar-i Hizbullah thugs against student demonstrations in June 2003. Journalists Ibrahim Nabavi, Shamsulva'izin, and Mas'ud Bahnud, publishers Hamidreza Jala'ipur and Shahla Lahiji, student leader 'Ali Afshari, feminist lawyer Mihrangiz Kar, the academic Hashim Aghajari, and scores of others were put behind bars on such vague charges as distributing propaganda against the Islamic state. Journalists Akbar Ganji and Imdad al-Din Baqi were detained for their relentless investigation of serial political murders (without naming names, Ganji repeatedly said that a "key actor" (*shah klīd*) in the conservative establishment was behind the murders).[66]

Husayn Qaziyan, Bahruz Giranpayih, and 'Abbas 'Abdi, former student leaders and directors of social research centers, were detained and their organizations closed down for publishing survey results that often delegitimized conservative policies. One of their nationwide surveys found that in 2002 over 74 percent of Iranians favored ending hostilities with the United States. Outspoken clerics 'Abdullah Nuri (the interior minister), Hasan Yousefi-Ashkivari (who was initially sentenced to death), Muhsin Kadivar, Muhsin Ruhami, Asadullah Bayat, Ahmad Qabil (who criticized the supreme leader), and others prosecuted in the Special Clerical Courts.

The aura of such jury-less tribunals, their design and discourse, and their clerical "judges" acting simultaneously as righteous and belligerent prosecutors evoked the Inquisition of the medieval Catholic church. Indeed, many of the defendants pointed to this historic parallel. More than anyone's, Hashim Aghajari's trial in November 2002 brought home the horror of religious tribunals. Yet these "criminals" often emerged as heroes. For many, Surush, Nuri, Kadivar, and especially Aghajari became Muslim Galileis. Reminiscent of Oscar Wilde's biting rebuttal to his moral prosecutors, Akbar Ganji turned his courthouse and its clerical judges on their head. Ibrahim Nabavi deployed his satirical genius to disparage the entire operation. "Your honor!" he sarcastically pleaded with the judge, "I am *so* guilty, and you are *so* just that if I were to try myself, I would give myself far heavier sentences than you have!" The trial transcripts, a new genre in the Islamic Republic, became national bestsellers.[67]

If the "religious intellectuals" were the brains of the reform movement, students were its backbone. Students' spectacular activism during and after the revolution had earned them a reputation that conservative Islamists could not ignore. Student dissent needed to be contained. Student rallies and demonstrations had already been the subject of everyday violence by the Ansar-i Hizbullah and the university *basij* who had been given (by the conservative fifth Majlis) legal power to impose moral and political surveillance within the colleges.[68]

Although students' enclosure in the campus had given them a measure of protection, they did not remain immune from assaults. The most devastating attack occurred on July 8, 1999, the day after 200 students staged a peaceful demonstration in protest of the closure of the pro-reform daily *Salam*, which had followed the passage of a restrictive new press law by the conservative-dominated fifth Parliament. The day after *Salam* reported that Sa'id Imami had been behind the passage of the new press law, 400 plainclothes vigilantes and Special Security Forces wielding clubs and chains stormed student dormitories, looted

800 rooms, and beat up hundreds of students, killing one. The brutality engendered an outburst of popular support for the victims, entailing the most spectacular student protest since the revolution. Calling for democracy and protesting unjust rule, hundreds of thousands of students throughout the nation seized city streets for three consecutive days. They denounced the supreme leader and demanded the removal of the police chief, an official apology for the attacks, and the prosecution of the assailants. The *Economist*'s front page heralded the coming of "Iran's second Revolution."

The drama, however, subsided with a conservative backlash. On the fourth day, agents provocateurs and *basīj* militias concealed their identities (by shaving their beards and changing their attire), infiltrated student ranks, and began looting and attacking government offices. Recognizing the deception, the pro-reform DTV and Khatami called for an end to the demonstrations, but others continued. In the end, the street violence and chaos brought the defensive conservatives to an offensive position. Overnight, hardliners shuttled thousands of people from provincial towns into Tehran to stage a day of allegiance, *bey'a*, to the supreme leader. An air of an impending repression appeared on the horizon;[69] 1,500 protestors, among them the student leaders Manuchir Muhammadi, Akbar Muhammadi, and 'Ali Afshari, were incarcerated. Wary of a further uprising, hardliners attempted to contain the movement through detention and division. Student activities, meetings, and rallies were closely watched and often disrupted, while the violent disruption of DTV's national congress in Khuramābād in 2000 demonstrated the hardliners' resolve to dismantle the student movement; an attack on dormitories sparked public outcry and led to the arrest of some perpetrators, but they were later released for "lack of evidence." The victims' lawyer, the reformist cleric Muhsin Ruhami, was jailed on charges of conspiring, through the Amir Farshad Ibrahimi affair, to defame hardline clerics.

The backlash demoralized students, who were already suffering from fragmentation, lack of focus, and an absence of clear strategic goals. In November 2002 Hashim Aghajari's death sentence sparked new, albeit more prudent, protests. And half a year later, in June 2003, following the Anglo-American invasion of Iraq, and under increasing international pressure on Iran to abandon its nuclear program, a student protest against the privatization of higher education turned into four days of anti-regime unrest in Tehran and other major cities. Once again, the Ansar-i Hizbullah and the *pāsdārān* violently put down the protests and arrested 4,000, including student leaders.

DILEMMAS OF RESISTANCE

The educated and the ordinary reacted to hardline violence and legal provocations with a deep sense of resentment and frustration. Social groups, student organizations, university professors, journalists, intellectuals, and unions issued public statements of condemnation. Within two years, more than 8,100 legal suits against the judiciary were filed with a special parliamentary commission in the Majlis.[70] Even the singer Muhammad Reza Shajarian disallowed the broadcast of his videos on conservative-controlled television. Intellectuals around the world—from Ann Mary Schimmel, Muhammad Arkoun, and Muhammad Ayoub to Abdul-Aziz Sachedina and Juergen Habermas—issued statements in defense of intellectual freedoms in Iran. Exiled royalists, the far left, and the Mujahidin-i Khalq organization, threatened by the popularity of the reform government, pursued a campaign of destabilization. Others, such as the Kurdistan Democratic Party, the Fida'iyan majority, and the Socialist Party, gave tacit support to the reformists.[71]

But what could and did the "reform government," with its executive and legislative powers, do to offset the onslaught against the reform movement at the base? Astonishingly little. The reform government had effectively been squeezed between the encroaching nonelected bodies, the security apparatus, ideological institutions, and paralegal vigilante groups. The rival faction had already begun to paralyze those parts of the government controlled by reformists, which, after all, accounted for no more than a fraction of real political power. By creating parallel institutions in strategic fields, they pushed the reformist power centers into disarray. The *pāsdārān* created their own intelligence service, and parallel to the Foreign Ministry (which favored negotiating with the United States), the judiciary established the Special Committee to Oversee Correct Implementation of the Leader's policies, which checked Khatami's vision toward the United States, especially after its invasion of Afghanistan in 2001. Even the city police remained out of the Interior Ministry's jurisdiction. More important, the Majlis, the reformist power base par excellence since 1999, was rendered virtually paralyzed by the veto power of the Council of Guardians. Between 2000 and 2003, the Council of Guardians vetoed over fifty major parliamentary bills. The Parliament had been reduced from a law-making body to a mere forum for free speech, where deputies could lash out against counterreform hardliners. But even this prerogative was not tolerated by the judiciary.

In December 2001, when the deputy Husayn Luqmaiyan attacked the judiciary for "decapitating freedom of expression and attempting to threaten and intimidate the lawmakers," he was given a ten-month prison sentence for "slander." Reportedly, the courts had been investigating some sixty reform deputies on similar charges.[72] It was only by a sustained campaign that deputies managed to discharge Luqmaiyan and retain their parliamentary immunity.[73] But in the summer of 2002, reformists were shocked to hear a hardline plan to give the supreme leader the power to dismiss the president and dissolve Parliament. One Friday prayer leader launched the campaign by asking, "If the leader is able to appoint the head of the judiciary, why [would he] not dismiss the president? Why not dissolve the Parliament?" Others called for the supreme leader to have the power to change the constitution.[74] Then came news of a more serious threat: the Council of Exigency, which arbitrates between the Majlis and the Council of Guardians, was to legally empower itself to dismiss the president and dissolve Parliament. This would practically eliminate the republican dimension of the Islamic state. Conservatives backed down only after reformist deputies threatened to resign en masse from Parliament.

Counterreform Conservatives

The conservatives' resistance to reform was formidable and predictable. Indeed, the tremendous popular support that the reform project enjoyed obscured the power of conservative Islamists within the state and the economy. But who were the conservatives? This broad trend consisted of diverse clusters at the core of which lay the Society of Combatant Clerics (SCC) and its affiliates, such as the Society of Islamic Mu'talifih, the Islamic Society of Engineers, Islamic Associations of Bazaar Guilds, and dozens of smaller associations.[75] Some twenty-seven groups formed the conservative faction in the reformist-dominated sixth Majlis.[76]

The conservative camp also enjoyed the support of the Ansar-i Hizbullah. Established in 1992, the latter was made up of disillusioned young war veterans whose utopian sensibilities had been betrayed by the seeming opulence of urban life, directing them to embrace anger and extremism. While Ansar-i Hizbullah defended economic populism and social justice, most conservatives pursued a free-market economy. The hub of Islamist elites came from a network of 11,000 families with extensive kinship, friendship, and clientelistic ties.[77] They constituted a 'rentier class' which benefited from political access and bequeathed it to "aghazade-ha," or their privileged "clerical offsprings"—a phenomenon symbolized entrée to material interests imbedded in the political ties. Some top merchants of the influential Tehran Bazaar had kinship relations to many conservative leaders, although by 2002 it was clear that Islamists' support in the Bazaar was fading.[78]

Conservatives controlled the revenue of religious taxes and donations from 59,000 mosques, 6,000 shrines, and 15,000 other religious places,[79] as well as foundations—most notably, the Foundation of the *Mustaż'afīn*. This gigantic industrial and financial conglomerate controlled a major segment of Iran's economy but was accountable only to the supreme leader. With an annual budget of $10 billion, it employed some 150,000 employees and managed thousands of industrial, commercial, and cultural enterprises and real estate units. Muhsin Rafiqdust, from a *bazaari* family and a member of the Jam'iyyāt-i Mu'talifih, ran the foundation with almost absolute power from 1988 to 1998, when rumors of corruption forced the supreme leader to replace Rafiqdust. But conservatives continued to control it and used its immense financial resources to extend their political patronage.[80]

Patronage came also from other sources. Through their influence in thousands of informal credit associations (sandūq qardh al-hasanih), the Committee of Imdād Imām, Būnyād-i Jānbāzān, and local mosques, conservatives were able to generate and maintain loyalties at a time when their popular support was waning. Their control of revolutionary institutions (such as the Construction Crusade and the Revolutionary Guards) and dozens of official religious organizations, including the seminaries,[81] cemented ideological allegiance by providing jobs and status to hundreds of thousands of supporters. Only the management of Azad University, which housed some 500,000 college students, gave the hardline *Jam'iyyat-i Mu'talifih-i Islāmi* much political, financial, and social leverage.[82] The directors of "informal" credit associations forged a powerful economic block, political lobby, and support base on the Council of Guardians. Stationed mostly in local mosques, these associations operated like large banks and were involved in speculation, money laundering, and distorting the financial market, and they vehemently resisted supervision by the central bank.[83]

Despite holding different economic and political positions, conservative factions were fairly united in their opposition to reform and their desire for a closed political system and culture. Some of them believed in outright theocracy mediated through the supreme leader. Man-made laws were legitimate so long as they conformed to divine canons determined by the Supreme *faqīh* or the institutions he appointed. The more hardline conservatives believed in strict religious government, rejecting any concept of democracy, including "religious democracy." They saw democrats equating humans with God, and considered them apostates. Thus not only could popular will be ignored, but also the use of terror and assassination against liberal opponents could be justified. However, unlike hardline theocrats, pragmatist theocrats (the supreme leader, the Assembly of Experts, the daily *Risālat*) insisted on people's support. Yet people mattered not as sovereign beings, but primarily as defenders of the Islamic state; not as rightful citizens, but as "participant subjects." In sum, "religious democracy" meant the *obligation* of people to "participate" in supporting the religious state.[84]

It is important to stress that only a minority of the Shi'i clerics upheld the Islamic state modeled on the *vilāyat-i faqīh*. Indeed, as democratic thought swept the nation, many clerics modified their positions, suggesting that a religious state should be subject to popular will (Ayatollah Muntazari's idea), and the role of religion in the state diminished.[85] A clear sign of this change was the emergence in 2000 of a "center right." Led by cleric Taha Hashimi, and represented by the daily *Intikhāb*, it was backed by the Association of Islamic Scholars (Jami'yyih Islāmi-yi Pazhūhishgarān) and the Bureau of Islamic Propaganda of Qum Seminary. Despite a hardline campaign to publicize a list of 300 such *digār andishān* (alternative thinkers) for "causing doctrinal confusion,"[86] the trend continued. But radicals continued to dominate the political leaderships of the conservative factions.

The role of the supreme leader, Ayatollah Khamenei, was extremely crucial. Although at times he appeared to mediate between the two factions, supporting Khatami and uttering the language of *islāh* (reform), the supreme leader still overwhelmingly upheld conservative Islamist ideals. By simultaneously supporting Khatami and lashing out at reform activists, Khamenei attempted to separate and co-opt Khatami from the more radical reformists, and to be seen in a favorable light by a public who revered their president. Otherwise, Khamenei's idea of reform had little to do with that of the reformists. People's opinions were valued so long as they sided with Islamic orthodoxy; otherwise, they were to be guided by religious rulers. Conservatives tried to elevate the supreme leader's stature by reviving the cult of personality and supralegal powers, trumping reformist calls for the "rule of law" and accountability.[87] They tried to make the leader unaccountable to any body, thereby allowing him to intervene in any public issue or veto any decision.[88] Khamenei became stronger as factional struggles intensified, since rivals sought his approval for their positions. Thus his power derived not only from his constitutional position (which was contested by post-Islamist intellectuals), but also from his "extraordinariness," a status that was generated by Islamists and reproduced by acquiescent reformists. Consequently, the movement that had emerged to curtail his power was put in a position where it unintentionally contributed to its legitimacy.

What granted the conservatives formidable power was not only their financial resources, networks of clientelism, and control of nonelected state institutions, but that all of this power was safeguarded inside an enclosed political structure that was designed to reproduce its dominance. The constitution granted more power to the supreme leader than it did to the president. The supreme leader appointed the Council of Guardians, the head of the judiciary, and the commanders of the security forces, and he could dismiss the president. Yet he was not chosen by the people, but was elected for an unlimited period of time by the Assembly of Experts (which was also to supervise, and if necessary, suspend the *faqīh*). The members of this assembly were screened and sanctioned by the Council of Guardians, whose members were appointed by the *faqīh* himself. In other words, the Assembly of Experts that elected and was supposed to supervise and, if necessary, dismiss the *faqīh* was effectively sanctioned by him.

How could such a rigid political structure be reformed to allow for popular control, rule of law, and democratic governance? In a sense, Khatami's government found itself the prisoner of the legalism that it cherished so dearly. His climb to office exhibited the classical dilemma of a social movement that had a share in power. How could such a social movement act within and yet against the state, having to abide by the very rules that were used to undermine it? To their credit, the reformists continued to call for the "rule of law" even when they were its victim. If the laws were unjust, they would argue, the solution was not to violate them but to change them. However, the trouble was that the law-making body, Parliament, had been virtually crippled by the veto power of the Council of Guardians. To realize political reform, the reform government had to break this self-perpetuating cycle of power.

THE TWIN BILLS AND THE DESTINY OF REFORM PROJECT

Khatami tried. In October 2002 he introduced two crucial bills to Parliament. Their fate was to symbolize the destiny of the reform project in the Islamic Republic. The bills first authorized removing the Council of Guardians' prerogative to screen candidates standing for the Majlis, the presidency, and the Assembly of Experts (*nizārat-i istiswābi*); and second, they empowered the president to suspend rulings that he deemed unconstitutional, in particular those of the judiciary and other nonelected bodies. If ratified, "the president would be able to strip judges of their office and stop practices such as trials from occurring without a jury or behind closed doors."

This was not an easy task. Almost everyone predicted that the Council of Guardians would veto the bills once Parliament had passed them. For most reformists the twin bills represented the defining test of whether the reform project could succeed under the Islamic Republic. In the likelihood that the bills were rejected, the reformists planned to either resort to a referendum or simply relinquish state power en masse. The threat of Khatami's possible resignation reverberated in conservative circles like an earthquake, because it would bring the country to the brink of its most profound crisis at a time when the military forces led by the United States and Britain had moved in next door to occupy Iraq. Predictably, hardliners launched a massive campaign to kill the twin bills. Rightist circles, dailies (*Kayhan, Risālat*), Friday prayer leaders accused Khatami of wanting to create a "dictatorship" and allow "counterrevolutionaries and secularists" to hold public office. *Kayhan* charged Khatami with plotting a coup, while the weekly *Harīm* implicitly warned about his assassination.[89] The Council of Guardians distributed thousands of pamphlets defending its veto power and denounced its critics,[90] while the supreme leader spoke out clearly against the bills. Once again, the rumors of a widespread crackdown on reform leaders spread. To keep up the pressure, the judiciary closed down two social research institutes and arrested their directors: Ayandih, led by 'Abbas 'Abdi, a former student leader and one of the key leaders of the Mushārikat Front; and the National Center for the Study of Public Opinion (NCSPO), directed by Bahruz Giranpayih and Muhsin Gudarzi. The NCSPO had just published a poll that showed over 70 percent of Iranians favored negotiations with the United States. The directors and others were charged with acting against national security. By charging 'Abbas 'Abdi, the hardliners aimed to implicate the Mushārikat Front, the core organization of the reform movement, and eventually dissolve it.

The more devastating surprise was yet to come. The day after Parliament passed the twin bills on November 7, 2002, a hardline judge in Hamadan sentenced Hashim Aghajari, a prominent post-Islamist intellectual, to death. The charges: denouncing the clerical class and advocating an "Islamic Protestantism" by saying that Muslims did not need clerics to communicate with God. The news of the death sentence sparked worldwide protest, shifting attention from the bills onto Aghajari. The entire reformist camp, members of Parliament, students, and international human rights organizations launched a campaign to overturn what the reformist Parliament speaker called a "disgusting" sentence.[91] Student protests, demonstrations, open forums, and petitioning continued for weeks, the momentum building every day and spreading from Tehran to the provincial cities of Tabriz, Isfahan, Urumiyih, Shiraz, Ahwaz, and Hamadan, causing an unprecedented split in the conservative camp. Only Ansar-i Hizbullah and a few Friday prayer leaders supported the death penalty. Indeed, some rightists angered their colleagues when they equated Aghajari with Martin Luther, ignoring the brutality of Luther's enemies.[92] Even *Kayhan* and state television director Larijani criticized the ruling.[93]

After three quiet years, since the dormitory attack of 1999, students reawakened and revived their power to protest. At Amir Kabir University, protestors demanded the separation of religion from the state and that the supreme leader be held accountable for his actions or resign.[94] The DTV called for a general student and faculty strike and a street march. The focus of protests shifted from Aghajari's retrial to his release, and finally to a demand for "free speech." The ten-day nationwide demonstrations compelled the supreme leader to order a retrial of Aghajari "with considerable care." In late February 2003, the appeal court rescinded Aghajari's death sentence and asked for a retrial, in which he received a four-year sentence.

While this was undoubtedly a victory for the protest movement, the supreme leader's intervention once again firmly established him as an extralegal arbiter. The insistence by *Risālat* that Aghajari seek clemency from the supreme leader was an effort to make him acknowledge the very power the reform movement was struggling against as, indeed, supreme. But Aghajari refused, angering conservatives, some of whom openly called for the implementation of his death sentence.

As the judiciary shut down three more reformist dailies (*Hayat-i Naw*, *Yas-i Naw*, and *Nuruz*) in early 2003 and jailed more activists, reformists suffered a more devastating blow: they lost in the local council elections. The defeat, caused by people's growing apathy, showed the erosion of the reformists' social power and encouraged conservatives that the idea of reform was finished. Thus, after months of delay and provocations, the Council of Guardians in April and June 2003 threw out the twin bills. Even the national student day on which 2,500 Tehran University students, along with 10,000 Tehranies, chanted "Death to Dictatorship" and "Khatami, Resign" failed to deter the ruling. Now, the target of demonstrators was not only the conservatives but also Khatami's government.[95]

As the Anglo-American occupation took its precarious hold on Iraq, Iran's reform project came to a standstill. The initial strategy of "mobilizing from below and negotiating from above" seemed to have failed; the reform movement was instead the target of onslaught from above and popular disenchantment from below. The "street" remained deeply demoralized and dangerously indifferent to the upcoming seventh Majlis elections, giving hope to conservatives that they would regain Parliament. Even though the earthquakes that devastated the historic city of Bam in late 2003 triggered an outpouring of energy and national solidarity, political apathy gripped the society. January 2004 brought the latest blow from the Council of Guardians. In what was described as a coup d'etat, it disqualified half of all, mostly reformist, candidates in the parliamentary elections, including more than eighty incumbents. The news devastated the reform camp and caused what came to be known as Iran's "political earthquake." Hundreds of parliamentary deputies staged a three-week sit-in and hunger strike. Khatami sided with the parliamentarians, as did dozens of political groups. Provincial governors announced their impending resignations. Even the supreme leader called for reviewing the disqualifications. But ordinary Iranians, even college students, kept their distance, shattering reformist hopes and expectations for mass support.[96] A popular outcry of the Yugoslavian type, when activists stormed Parliament to oust Slobodan Milosovic, would not happen. For ordinary Iranians, the deputies' strike seemed like political bickering at the top, which did not concern them. People seemed to long for more radical measures or simply chose to wait.[97] Popular disenchantment, which had begun in local elections one year earlier, allowed the conservatives to complete their coup de force and finish off the reform process.[98] Even though the Council of Guardians, through some lobbying, reinstated one-third of the disqualified candidates, the indignant deputies submitted their collective resignation on February 1, 2004. Major reform parties, though not President Khatami himself, boycotted the elections and Parliament fell back to the conservatives. This buried any hope of an agreement over the twin bills, which President Khatami formally withdrew on April 13, 2004.

The collective resignation of 122 parliamentary deputies will remain a turning point in Iran's struggle for democracy, but it signaled the end of an era in the life of the reform movement. In the months that followed, a sense of despair overtook the public. Many activists braced for reprisal; a few were jailed, some settled for exile, others found solace in their private lives. Pre-reform methods of surveillance returned, aiming to subjugate a society that had been drastically transformed.

RESTORATION?

Was the attempt to establish a democratic polity a failure? Did the Iranian experience prove the incompatibility of Islam and democracy? By 2002 most analysts had declared political reform in Iran dead, and the U.S. government adopted a policy to topple the Islamist regime. The reasons for the failure ranged widely: the weakness of Khatami's leadership, the absence of a real political party and a long-term program of change, constitutional constraints, the movement's elitism, the idea that democracy in Iran remained a philosophical debate rather than an institutional reality.

These handicaps notwithstanding, the reform movement did make some significant institutional and discursive advances. Under the reform government, a number of ministries (Foreign Affairs, Intelligence, Higher Education, and Culture) changed in order to facilitate reform strategies. Civil society institutions expanded, and the somber, repressed mood in the streets and in government offices relaxed. More important, the post-Islamists in power managed to establish the language of reform and the idea that Islam and democratic ideals could be compatible. Never before in Iranian political history did such fundamental concepts as democracy, pluralism, accountability, rule of law, and tolerance become so pervasive, and all this in a political culture that nurtured seniority and patronage. The remarkable awareness and expectations that the citizens developed in this period threatened not only the conservative establishment, but also a reform government whose structural constraints to advance political reform betrayed popular hope.

Thus as the reform process unfolded, the movement experienced signs of differentiation. Many of the earlier critical ideas about the *vilāyat-i faqīh* or the religious state, became explicit. Known post-Islamists moved toward more liberal and secular ideals in the political domain. In August 2003, Husayn Khomeini, the grandson of Ayatollah Khomeini, went into exile in Iraq and launched a political campaign to dismantle the religious state in Iran. To him, Iran's religious state was the "worst dictatorship in the world." While the move toward secularization facilitated a broader coalition for secular republicanism (such as the new Front for Republicanism, which linked exiled and home-grown republicans), the more religious-minded reformists, notably from the ACC, were dismayed.

The student movement, more than other collectives, underwent change. At first passionate supporters of Khatami's government, students adopted a more independent, secular, and critical position. Earlier, the DTV had followed Khatami's strategy of "active calm" to neutralize the conservatives.[99] However, this position caused an initial unease and eventual split within the DTV. While a minority wished to act like a pro-government political party, the majority insisted on maintaining the independence and social movement character of the student organization.[100] Pressured by the rank and file's quest for radical change, DVT leaders, before Khatami's second term, launched a "comprehensive critique of power," including the reform government and Khatami himself.[101] The aftermath of Aghajari's death penalty, when the students disregarded the government's call for calm, revealed the increasing divergence of students from Khatami, who had been bogged down by his over-legalism. "Young people no longer take us seriously when we speak of *religious* democracy," admitted Bahzad Nabavi, a leading reformist.[102] Although the reformist camp in general remained committed to a peaceful campaign for political change, the nation's polity had been deeply polarized.

Given the enormous political battles between reformist and conservative rivals, how was social equilibrium maintained? What thwarted a political collapse lay in the emergence of a delicate balance between a patrimonial ruling elite and a mobilized public sphere, between the conservatives' vast state power but limited social support and the reformists' limited state power but vast social support. Opposite conservative control of the repressive state apparatus stood a society that had learned the art of resistance and mobilization in a more or less legal manner. The reformists were committed to the rule of law and peaceful methods as a matter of principle, hoping to bring about political change by expanding democratic enclaves that could circumvent conservative power. They wished to do so through legal means—ironically, the very channel through which the conservative judiciary undermined the reform project. The reformist strategy of "active calm" aimed to avert a conservative crackdown and to secure social peace, a condition considered vital for the reform project to proceed.

The more pragmatic conservatives, notably the supreme leader, wanted to turn reform into a "passive revolution"—to retain their power and privilege by appropriating the initiative for change, which involved conceding a few democratic enclaves at the top. In short, the Islamists' passive revolution was based on an idea of dual power within which they were to occupy the dominant position.[103] The conservatives needed Khatami's popular legitimacy to bind people to the Islamist system, hoping that in the long run such unequal power-sharing would eventually prevail. By accepting unequal dualism, they departed from Khomeini's unitarism (*wahdāt-i kalamih*) but fiercely resisted pluralism.

The conservative Islamists' ability to resist change lay partly in what may be termed the "resiliency of the indigenous," a capacity derived from relative autonomy from the outside world and facilitated by local skills and legitimacy produced by the "uniqueness" of an "indigenous" experience. Unlike the authoritarian regimes of the USSR, Greece, South Korea, or the Philippines, whose relative integration into the international community had made them vulnerable to outside pressure, Iran's Islamists remained relatively immune to such influences. By insisting on the originality and indigenous nature of their polity, Islamists could dismiss what the outside (Western) world thought of them. Whereas the "African socialism" of liberation movement regimes in Angola and Mozambique did not survive their economic dependence on the International Monetary Fund and World Bank, Iran's oil revenue and the Islamists' control of major sources of income sustained their political autonomy from the hostile West. Therefore, conservatives had to be challenged from within.

With its religious but also democratic idioms, the reform movement posed perhaps the most serious challenge to the conservative Islamists. It demolished their moral and political legitimacy. The discursive onslaught of post-Islamism was so devastating that, in the view of many Islamists, "the assaults that our sacred principles have endured [since Khatami] is far more than during the Pahlavies."[104] But was mere discursive victory sufficient to induce political change? Does the "power of the word" match the coercive force of "political power"? In Iran's experience, popular democratic sentiments and discourse articulated by the reform movement failed to dislodge the Islamists from the helm of political power. Popular sentiment was held hostage by relentless repression by the *pāsdārān*, Ansar-i Hizbullah, and the courts. These coercive bases of power needed to be neutralized, won over, or confronted, and the reformists seemed remarkably incapable of doing any of them. First, perhaps because of overconfidence, they failed to attract and incorporate segments of the conservative ranks with the ideals of reform; the lower- and middle-ranking segments of the Revolutionary Guards, for instance, might not have sided with their rightist leadership. Instead, similar to the rigid attitudes of their opponents, reformers at times unnecessarily antagonized centrist figures, such as Hashimi Rafsanjani, the former president, whom they pushed into the arms of the rightists while remaining reluctant to embrace secular democratic forces as genuine partners.

If the reform camp was unable to neutralize the conservative backlash, then they had to confront it by popular force via labor strikes, nonviolent civil disobedience, or peaceful disruptions. For, unlike the authoritarian states that rely on coercion, the power of a movement rests on the power of its social base, the collective strength of its grassroots. This social force, which is built and sustained through education, institutionalization, and mobilization, can not only pressure the state to reform and resist state repression; it can also ensure a movement's continuity.

Iran's reform movement failed to develop such a social base. It remained an entirely middle-class entity entangled in a modernist strategy that relied heavily on the transformation of the public sphere, advocating "rational dialogue," democratic values, tolerance, and rule of law. These were noble and necessary goals, but were not enough to overcome coercive force. Partly as a reaction to prevailing populist politics, post-Islamists did little to organize the popular classes, especially the poor and the working people, those who were interested in concrete and immediate issues. In fact, economics mattered little in post-Islamist literature. The deplorable state of the economy hit the poor and middle classes hardest, even though macroeconomic indicators, including a 7 percent growth rate, currency stabilization, and a smaller budget deficit, eventually showed some improvement. Given the worldwide post-Marxist ideological climate, the intellectual baggage of the reformist thinkers carried simply too much of Habermas and Foucault and not enough of Marx and Gramsci. While the Mushārikat Party possessed a fairly organized structure, its coalition partner Islamic Labor Party failed to mobilize the workers necessary to create strong support for the reform agenda at the base. Although factory councils and other labor organizations grew under Khatami's administration, neither the reformist Ministry of Labor nor the Islamic Labor Party paid much attention to the organization of syndicates and labor unions. Indeed, the number of Workers' Councils (*shura-yi kārgarān*), which had increased to 2,900 in the early years of reform, declined to no more than 1,300 by 2003.[105]

It is true that since the late 1980s, labor had experienced de-proletarianization and fragmentation, with the manufacturing sector shrinking in favor of the vast informal sector of dispersed activities; and despite voicing their economic demands, the working class remained largely on the political margin. However reformists did little to mobilize the massive collectives of state employees or white-collar workers, notably teachers. In addition, community organization, education, and mobilization remained feeble, even when the reformists took control of the local councils. Thus, as often is the case, the poor pursued their own localized strategy of "quiet encroachment" and paid little attention to national political struggles. With the grassroots absent from the reform project, the gradual indifference of the urban middle classes, students, youths, and women diminished the reformists' social power and allowed conservatives to finish off the reform project. Contributing notably to this process were the fragmentation of the reform camp and the lack of a common strategy among partners who held diverging visions about what kind of Iran they wanted.

Although it failed to dislodge the Islamists, the post-Islamist movement was able to fundamentally undermine the moral and political legitimacy of Islamism, which for over two decades had subjugated the majority of Iranians in the name of religion. It hegemonized the ideals of democracy and political (if not social) pluralism to heights never before reached in Iran or, Turkey aside, in the Muslim Middle East. Post-Islamism clearly demonstrated that one could be both Muslim and democrat, and that democratic ideals could take root in a Muslim society—not because of some essential affinity between Islam and democracy, but rather because of the struggles of ordinary citizens who compelled moral and intellectual leaders to articulate an inclusive religion and a democratic polity. A post-Islamist victory to reform the authoritarian state could spark a renaissance in religious, social, and political thought in Muslim societies. As it was, the reform movement startled the region's authoritarian regimes and religious movements, Egypt's included, and though it failed to dislocate the patrimonial state, it brought Iranian post-Islamism to precisely the same point as Egyptian Islamism: both were poised to turn their social power into state power. Would Egyptian Islamism succeed where Iran's post-Islamism had failed?

5 EGYPT'S "PASSIVE REVOLUTION"

The State and the Fragmentation of Islamism,
1992–2005

THE REVOLUTIONARY STRATEGY FOR CHANGE IN IRAN primarily targeted political power. Revolutionary leaders aimed in the first place to alter the political structure in the hope that doing so would spark change in society—in its institutions, value systems, and individuals. After they had won political power they needed to win social power, or to secure the consent of the populace in order to actualize their Islamist project. But popular mobilization for social change is often the work of grassroots social movements, not states. Social movements not only challenge authorities to enforce social change from the top; they also produce, practice, and popularize new ideas, institutions, and values at the bottom. Because in Iran there did not exist a strong movement to "Islamize" society, the Islamist project had to be augmented largely from the top after the revolution. The implication of this for political authority was enormous. The top-down method met formidable resistance, causing social conflict and ideological clashes, and eventually compelled many Islamist leaders to rethink their project by revising their perspective. The outcome was the "post-Islamist project" in which "reform" became the strategic goal to be achieved by pervasive social movements. The limits of "frontal attack," or insurrection, to produce social change forced leaders to adopt a different strategy, a "war of position," or a campaign for gradual social and political change in the hope of producing structural transformation and "religious democracy" in the long run.

A "war of position," or cumulative reform, was in essence what mainstream Egyptian Islamism undertook during the 1980s, and it produced some remarkable achievements. Perhaps the Egyptian method of working toward socioreligious reform by building a pervasive social movement through *da'wa* and associational work was what the Iranian post-Islamists needed to pursue. But where did this strategy take Egypt's social and political position? And what happened to its agent, Islamism?

At its height in the late 1980s, Egyptian Islamism represented a complex web of dispersed and heterogeneous organizations, activities, and sympathies around a distinct core embodied in the reformist Muslim Brotherhood, which aimed to Islamize the society at the grassroots, ultimately establishing an Islamic state, and in the revolutionary Islamists who combined social agitation and armed struggle. Challenged by these political Islamists, the institution of Azhar (the religious establishment sanctioned by the state) expanded its *da'wa* (call to "true" Islam), its institutional and social activities, contributing to the general spread of religiosity. Alongside the political core stood the vast sector of "civil Islam" with its large religious welfare and professional associations, Muslim youth and women's groups, and Islamic activism in universities, schools, and neighborhoods. Individual Muslim celebrities and media personalities, such as Mustafa Mahmood, Selim al-'Awa, Hasan Hanafi, and Muhammad Imara, carried out their own *da'wa*.

This broad movement caused significant change in society and posed the most serious challenge to the Egyptian regime. The Muslim Brothers' commitment to socioreligious change through *da'wa* and associational work wrested much of urban society from state control. Through independent mosques, schools, youth associations, women's groups, clinics, and publications, ordinary people negotiated alternative ways of being and doing that the Muslim Brotherhood's parliamentary activities aimed to turn into public policy.

The challenge of al-Jama'a al-Islamiyya militants seemed even more dramatic. During the 1980s, in addition to controlling university campuses, they moved into poor districts of Cairo and spread their influence in southern towns and villages. They agitated in the streets and mosques, resolved local disputes, and imposed moral discipline (*taghīr al-munkir*) by preventing "vice" such as drunkenness and mixing of the sexes. As the "organic intellectuals" of the humble social milieu of the *Sa'id* (southern Egypt), the militants also offered welfare services, literacy classes, clinics, transportation, income generation projects, and food for the poor.[1] By the early 1990s, they virtually ruled the southern towns and had established their "Islamic Republic of Imbaba" in the heart of the capital city. At this time of intense societal vigor, religion dominated the nation's political and cultural idioms, and the "Islamic solution" assumed an unprecedented currency. Islamic ethics found expression in language, behavior, physical appearance, dress codes, mosque attendance, radio and television programs, publications, and public spaces. It was also reflected in the spread of Islamic commodities, fashion, and leisure, which penetrated civil society, the military, and some state institutions. By the early 1990s, Egypt seemed to be going through an Islamic "revolution by stealth."

Things proved to be more complex, however. The "war of position," or cumulative reform project, reached its limits at the state's doorstep. The dilemma, which had also haunted Iran's political reform project, was a familiar one: How far could a reform movement march forward under a "weak" or nonhegemonic state threatened by social and economic forces and constrained by its own paternalistic attitudes toward sociopolitical change? The relative success of the movement in changing Egyptian society and in challenging the state was in part the cause of its own downturn. The "Islamic Republic of Egypt" or even "the impending crisis," which some had predicted, never arrived.[2] Instead, the Islamist movement experienced a process of simultaneous decline and fragmentation, as conservative religiosity, individualized piety, and the "secureligious state" converged. The net result was not a new ideological and doctrinal vision as in Iran. Rather, against the backdrop of contentious economic liberalization, social change, and cultural globalization, conservative Islamism merged with strong nativist sentiment while the state moved in to appropriate religious and moral authority.

This chapter delves into the process of Egypt's Islamic "passive revolution": socioreligious change initiated from below by the Islamist movement and subsequently appropriated by the target of that change, the state, which from then on attempted to contain and control its trajectory. Quite distinct from what happened in Iran, Egypt's "passive revolution" was the product of an Islamism without an Islamic state and a remarkable stagnation in religious and intellectual thought.

DECLINE OF THE CORE

Al-Jama'a militants' comparative advantage (in relation to other political groupings) grew out of their intimate connection to the territories they controlled. In a sense, they represented the "organic intellectuals," the disenfranchised but educated youth of the depressed towns and villages of the Sa'id, which, by virtue of northward migration, had been extended to such Cairo slums as 'Ayn al-Shams and Imbaba. Isolated from the modern north by mountains and desert, socioeconomic marginalization, and tribal social organization, the Saʿid had already become modern Egypt's internal other.[3] With the central state effectively absent, local tribal and kinship confederations governed people's daily lives. As Nasser's land reform program had gradually undermined this traditional social structure, al-Jamaʿa moved in to fill the void.[4] When the militants began to operate in such Cairo slum districts as Imbaba and ʿAyn al-Shams, they found familiar communities on the margins of the modern Egyptian state—squatter communities in no official municipality, with no effective police force, house numbers, or district maps, where a stranger could get lost in the labyrinth of endless alleys and back streets. Although the militants succeeded in penetrating ʿAyn al-Shams and Imbaba, they failed to make inroads into the more integrated districts of Jamaliyya, Bāb al-Sharqiyya, Sayida Zaynab, Dokki, Zamalek, or Maʿādi. Because the Jamaʿa was able to operate only where the state was effectively absent, the movement assumed a territorial or regional, and therefore local, character. In this sense, al-Jamaʿa reflected the image of the early Sicilian Mafia, an endemic premodern and territorial social movement that controlled local order by creating alternative codes of conduct.[5]

This territoriality, however, was as much an advantage as a limitation. Once the state reclaimed the Jamaʿa's territories, the displaced militants had to go on the run. They could neither defeat the state nor work within it; they could neither lead a revolution nor cause notable reform. Despite Abud al-Zumur's claim that the Jamaʿa aimed for a popular revolution in the image of Iran's, the group's vision of revolutionary change did not go beyond a military coup in which the populace had almost no role except to "defend the new regime" once it was established.[6] In their scheme of things, people possessed little agency.

At the same time, the militants did not know how (because they did not wish) to operate within the existing political arrangement. The Jamaʿa's daʿwa remained remarkably narrow and notoriously male. Focusing primarily on political and religious agitation, the militants failed to leave behind any novel ideas and practices, any institutional or discursive legacy through which to induce social change. There was little attempt, for instance, to hold free elections, practice local governance, establish NGOs, or supervise self-development projects. Al-Jamaʿa's welfare provisions assisted some of the poor but were essentially meant to make people dislike the regime and believe in Jamaʿa's "Islamic solution." Daʿwa focused primarily on people's moral obligations, on "forbidding wrongdoings" (*nahyi min al-munkir*), rather than on their rights and potential as agents of their own destiny. Thus the likes of Shaykh Jaber of Imbaba in Cairo and his gangs prowled neighborhoods, setting fire to video shops, closing down beauty salons, threatening to throw acid on unveiled women, preventing the sexes from mixing, and even condemning music at weddings,[7] the last utterly contrary to Egypt's festive culture. At the national level, militants attacked Coptic churches, gatherings, individuals, and property.[8] Violence against the Copts increased from fifty-two incidents during the 1970s to 111 during the 1980s and early 1990s, including forty-six murders from 1992 to 1994.[9] For Islamists, proselytizing by the Christian church hindered the establishment of an Islamic society and state. While their welfare provisions, dispute settlements, and campaigns against local bullies gained popularity, their severe moral order antagonized others, including powerful families.

What the Jama'a ultimately left behind was no more than a conservative religiosity and piety, one that was to be appropriated later by the establishment Islam. Consequently, when the Egyptian state reclaimed these territories using a twin strategy of arresting militants and establishing NGOs, the militants were rendered socially redundant and politically on the run, thus seeking refuge in underground cells, on sugar cane farms, in Europe, or in the safe haven of the Taliban's Afghanistan. Of course, exiled members continued their agitation from abroad, publishing *al-Murābitūn* in Denmark and *al-I'tisām* in Britain; and Yasser al-Serri established his Islamic Research Center in London. Those such as Rifa'i Ahmad Taha and Mustafa Hamza escaped to Afghanistan to gain and then give guerrilla training to new recruits before sending them back to Egypt via the Sudan and Libya to carry out military operations. The assassination of the speaker of Parliament in 1990 was the first such attack by these "returnees from Afghanistan." With its key "historical leadership" in custody[10] and the other leaders in exile, the Jama'a became further removed from the pulse of Egyptian society.

With the killing in October 1990 of the activist 'Ala' Muhidin and the subsequent siege of Imbaba in December 1992, the movement that had focused on *da'wa* and education was virtually transformed into a guerrilla military organization. Now, military leaders would issue fatwas and execute them without consulting the *da'wa* wing. In Asyut, beginning in 1992, military leaders became emirs and took charge of educational policies.[11] Both the target and the scale of its violence shifted from scattered incidents against civilians (nonconformists, secularists, and Copts) to widespread military attacks against the state. A semi–civil war seemed to be under way. The insurgents targeted policemen, top officials, foreign tourists, and Copts, opening fire on trains, vehicles, hotels, and banks. The four years from 1990 through 1993 were Egypt's bloodiest of the twentieth century. The death toll increased from 139 in 1991 to 207 in 1993 to 225 in 1994. Altogether, nearly 1,200 insurgents, policemen, civilians, and Copts perished between 1992 and 1996.[12]

Police and the military erected checkpoints at every corner in southern cities and villages, while nightly raids on militant hideouts continued ceaselessly. Thousands, including many innocents, were rounded up; many were tortured and detained without trial.[13] For those who were tried, the court sessions exhibited a feel of both misery and bravery. Early each morning, police trucks carrying anti-riot personnel were positioned outside courthouses in full gear, while dogs sniffed the premises for explosives. Defendants' relatives, veiled women in black attire and men in white *jalabiyya*s, filled noisy courtrooms and gazed anxiously at the accused, who, from inside iron cages, defiantly chanted religious verse and anti-government slogans.

Between 1992 and 2000, some 101 death sentences were handed down by security forces and military courts.[14] Mediation attempts by al-Jama'a's lawyer, Muntasir al-Zayat, a former member, were rebuffed by the government, and Interior Minister 'Abd al-Halim Musa was dismissed in 1993 for considering negotiations with the militants. As the insurgents became more hunted and desperate, their violent activity escalated. It reached its apex in the Luxor massacre of November 18, 1997, when insurgents brutally murdered and decapitated fifty-eight Western tourists and four Egyptians in the Temple of Hatshepsut.[15] The sheer savagery of the attack shocked the Egyptian public, disoriented the security apparatus, and crippled the country's most important foreign exchange earner, the tourist industry, for three years. In the hours after the attack, thousands of foreign tourists flocked to airports to exit the country en masse, leaving behind deserted luxury hotels, abandoned tourist sights, millions of redundant workers, and a nation caught between the brutality of the insurgents and the state.[16]

The massacre, however, heralded the impending demise of militant Islamism. For two days after the killings, the Jama'a did not utter a word. Then emerged a series of confused and contradictory statements. Exiled Egyptian "political leaders" in Europe expressed regret, imprisoned or "historic leaders" in Egypt condemned the operation, and "military leaders" based in Afghanistan claimed responsibility.[17] Muntasir al-Zayat, the Jama'a's lawyer, realized the organization and its "Islamic alternative" were in profound crisis and conveyed to the leadership the futility of a violent strategy that had deeply alienated the average Egyptian.[18] The crisis of a "frontal attack" then pushed al-Jama'a to pursue a fundamental shift in its strategy.

Even though their earlier ceasefire initiatives failed, by July 1997, imprisoned leaders were ready to enforce a unilateral halt to bloodshed and return to peaceful *da'wa*. Privately jubilant, the Interior Ministry, however, remained defiant, rejecting any hint of concession to or dialogue with the militants.[19] The exiled leadership's initial hostility to the ceasefire call subsided when Shaykh 'Umar 'Abd al-Rahman, Jama'a's spiritual leader (jailed in the United States for ordering the 1993 bombing of the World Trade Center) endorsed it.[20] Although internal disputes and sporadic attacks by splinter cells continued, Jama'a finally reaffirmed on March 25, 1999 its decision to renounce anti-government violence once and for all. Dismayed by the new strategy, Jihad leader Ayman al-Zawahiri, who until then had been virtually absent from the Egyptian scene, joined Osama bin Laden to establish the International Islamic Front to Fight the Jews and Crusaders (IIFFJC) in 1998. In response, al-Zayat proposed and 'Umar 'Abd al-Rahman endorsed an International Islamic Front to Defend Islam by Peaceful Means.[21] Although the latter remained merely an idea, it was followed by a number of initiatives for nonviolent activities. Former militants made formal requests to establish political parties within the existing system: Hizb al-Wasat, the Islamic Party of Reform (Hizb al-Islamiyya al-Islah),[22] and Hizb al-Shari'a. "Time has shown that violence and armed struggle have been harmful to all parties, to the country and Islam itself," militants concluded.[23] But the government turned down all the applications on the grounds that "religious parties" were not allowed.[24] This infuriated 'Abd al-Rahman and Ahmad Taha, who threatened to abandon peaceful means and mobilize "people led by the army, clerics, and university professors for a revolution."[25] However, in new political circumstances legal activism was too compelling to the imprisoned leaders to be thwarted by such threats.

Aggressive Israeli policy under Benjamin Netanyahu and Ariel Sharon, the crisis of the Algerian Islamist experience, the dramatic transformation of Iranian Islamism, and the ascendancy of post-Islamism under Khatami (which the Jama'a leader Ahmad Taha observed while residing in Iran) persuaded Jama'a's "historic leaders" to remain committed to their new nonviolent vision. Now, Jama'a's new primary target was not Egyptian "*jāhilī* rule" but the Jewish state, against which all groups in Egypt and the Muslim world should unite.[26] The historic leaders realized not only that they were incapable of defeating the Egyptian state, but also that their violent method had subverted their aim of "guiding people toward the path of God." They concluded that their violent strategy had in fact benefited the "enemies of Islam": Israel, the United States, the West, and secularists.[27] These political realities led the historic leaders to revisit their religious doctrine. To match their new political perspective they were compelled to craft new doctrinal arguments by reinterpreting the Islamic texts. In the end, militant Islamists found virtue in what the Muslim Brothers had been practicing for over six decades. But was the Muslim Brothers' strategy of societal transformation free from constraints?

THE MUSLIM BROTHERS IN ABEYANCE

In the early 1990s, the Muslim Brotherhood (MB), or Ikhwan al-Muslimin, was acting as though it was a shadow government. The MB controlled thousands of mosques, dominated the major national professional syndicates and the student unions in the north, ran various NGOs, influenced numerous schools, and constituted the most powerful opposition in Parliament. Foreign dignitaries from the U.S. ambassador to Yasser Arafat paid visits to the MB's downtown headquarters. The MB, in short, had captured a sizable space in civil society and was beginning to permeate state institutions, including the judiciary, universities, and al-Azhar. However, at its peak, the movement seemed to be looming at the state's backdoor, ready to pounce.

Primed by its clampdown on the Jama'a, startled by the 1995 assassination attempt on President Mubarak in Addis Ababa—feeling, in a word, threatened—the government set out to cripple the MB. An emergency law had already been deployed to bar public assemblies, and an anti-terrorism law passed in 1992 had made preventive detention legal and restricted the press. Against opposition outcry, the government marched on, weakening the Muslim Brothers' hold on universities and manipulating the election procedures of professional syndicates to exclude the MB. It shut down the lawyers' syndicate from 1996 to 2001, ignored dozens of court rulings against that action, and then did the same to the MB-dominated professional associations for three years beginning in 1996.[28] The Brotherhood's monthly, *Liwa' al-Islam*, published since 1945, was shut down, while the ruling National Democratic Party (NDP) continued to publish its own Islamic weekly with the almost identical title *al-Liwa' al-Islami*.

Then, beginning in June 1995, the government began in earnest, with a spate of arrests and military trials of leading Muslim Brothers. Detentions were typically carried out prior to national elections to prevent them from participating.[29] Prominent Islamist syndicate leaders such as 'Asam al-Eryan and Muhammad Sa'd (of the doctors' syndicate), Mukhtar Nawh and Khalid Badawi (of the lawyers' syndicate), and Muhammad 'Ali Bishr (of the engineering union) were jailed, and over 5,000 MB offices throughout the country, including its main headquarters in Cairo's Suq al-Tawfiqiyya, were shut down. The state took over some 60,000 mosques and forbade preachers from conducting sermons without clearance from the Ministry of Awqāf, depriving Islamists of a vital channel of da'wa.[30] By April 1997, sixty-one leading Muslim Brothers had been sentenced to up to five years in prison with hard labor. Finally, the suspension of the Islamic-oriented Labor Party, an MB ally, and its paper, al-Sha'b, was a further blow to the Muslim Brotherhood.

The Labor Party's support for Sudan's "Islamic project," its public protests against government corruption, and its pro-Iraq campaign had already angered state security forces. The last straw was al-Sha'b's fierce attack on the minister of culture for allowing the "blasphemous" novel A Banquet for Seaweed to be republished. For weeks, al-Sha'b urged Muslims "to join hands and avenge the insults which the Ministry of Culture directed against God and Islam."[31] As the al-Azhar students poured into the streets in protest, Egypt endured one of its deepest political crises. When the government consequently disbanded the Labor Party and its al-Sha'b, the Muslim Brothers' only channels of communication and legal means to act were those professional syndicates they still controlled.[32] Besides, Labor's internal power struggle between the Islamists led by 'Adel Husayn (who died in 2001) and the nationalists led by party president Ibrahim Shukri undermined the Islamist faction and its ally, the MB. It appeared as though the MB's role of diverting youth from joining violent Islamist groups had come to an end. The state no longer needed to tolerate the group.

With its offices closed down, publications disbanded, mosques controlled, leading activists jailed, and the organization under surveillance, the MB was pushed to the sidelines. "We don't do anything anymore," admitted the spokesman, Ma'mun al-Hudaybi, as early as March 1997.[33] Later, only the MB-dominated syndicates, notably the doctors' syndicate, could manage public activity, such as raising public awareness of atrocities committed against Muslims in the Balkans and Chechnya. Even this did not remain unpunished. The

MB was forced to limit its meetings to such occasions as Qur'an-reciting sessions, Ramadan *iftār* (feasts), and funerals, though organizers did not hesitate to turn these events into political rallies.[34] At the *iftār* party of January 1998 celebrating the movement's seventieth anniversary, some 700 guests, MB activists, and opposition groups declared their allegiance to Mustafa Mashhur, who had replaced Hamid Abu Nasr as the group's spiritual leader. Similarly, the 2000 funeral of Ibrahim Sharaf, the MB general secretary, drew hundreds of followers from across the country. Reportedly, tens of thousands attended the funeral of Mustafa Mashhur in November 2002. These scattered occasions notwithstanding, the apparent jubilance and Mashhur's claim that "the MB's state will be established" in thirty years could not conceal the group's profound state of crisis.[35]

Some members had already accepted that they "did not aim to rule or aspire to power" and simply wished to "continue making our *da'wa* toward God."[36] Younger leaders echoed this in their arguments for an Islamism without an Islamic state. In February 2000, 'Asam al-Eryan concluded that the Muslim Brotherhood's call for an Islamic republic was "a slogan that has passed its time. . . . The constitution already says that Egypt is an Islamic state and that Shari'a is the basis of legislation." Al-Eryan cited President Mubarak, who had insisted that the Personal Status Law be in line with Shari'a.[37] Thus the language of agitation shifted to a large degree from state power to public morality, virtues, and international issues. It was on such sensitive matters as "blasphemy," "insult to Islam," moral laxity, or oppression of Muslims in Palestine, Chechnya, or the Balkans that the group rallied to agitate the public. Islamism, it appeared, ceased to be primarily a political project and became simply an "Islamic phenomenon,"[38] a struggle against secular values in order to elevate personal piety, morality, Islamic identity, and ethos—a process I call cheap Islamization.

Al-Eryan's argument that the Egyptian state was already Islamic did hold some degree of truth. The constitution had clearly authorized Shari'a as the main source of law,[39] and the government often framed its policies in religious terms.[40] As I will show later, the state began to selectively appropriate the religious space left by the decline of political Islam. This demonstrated the complex dynamics of Islamism in Egypt. At one level, it reflected the hegemony of Islamism, which had imposed aspects of its frame, language, and institutions on the state. At the same time, however, the success of Islamism in changing certain social and cultural codes, institutions, and ethical moral structures deprived the core of the movement (al-Jama'a and the MB) of popular support for mobilization. For the reforms had passified large segments of the constituency by fulfilling some of their fundamental ethical and moral needs. These segments felt that their interests were already being served under the existing political system and felt no need to confront the state, especially when it would involve the risk of repression. In a sense, the constituency left the core ideological activists on their own, so when the state struck back at political Islamists there was little popular resistance or outcry. Thus, when al-Sha'b's Magdi Husayn and the Freedom Committee of the journalists' syndicate held a conference in 2000 to protest the detention of the MB's prominent members, few turned up, until "loads of youth cadres from the Labor Party were bused in to fill the empty seats."[41] But there was nothing like the public outcry in 1995, when many protested similar detentions of Muslim Brothers. Even the Brotherhood's surprise capture of seventeen seats in the 2000 parliamentary elections did not necessarily signal their comeback. The MB candidates ran as independents, on no group's electoral list, with no party platform or program, and with no campaign headquarters. Moreover, the candidates, mostly local activists, took advantage of "punitive votes" generated by the judiciary's decision to monitor the elections, preventing the electoral fraud that usually favored the ruling NDP.[42]

The Muslim Brothers survived the political shock wave, as they have done in their long history, thanks to their reliance on associational activism, kinship ties, and maneuvering between active presence and abeyance. However, the internal dynamics of Islamist movements, in addition to the dramatic domestic and international events at the turn of the century such as the September 11 attacks, have only reinforced the gradual change in the nature of Islamism from a political project challenging the state to one concerned with personal piety, ethical concerns, and global malaise. Political Islam in Egypt remained on the sidelines, while militant Islamism, despite its sensational media coverage, experienced a deep crisis. Perhaps nothing was more telling about the movement's destiny than the afflicted state of 'Umar 'Abd al-Rahman, serving a life sentence in a New Jersey prison. Forgotten and frail in a foreign jail, blind and lonely, with no access to anyone who spoke his language, the shaykh's only companion remained a few tapes of the Qur'an, recitation, and exegesis. Locked up in a prison cell, the spiritual leader almost faded from public memory. Egyptians could only hear his murmurs uttered through the lips of his son: "Why have Muslims abandoned me?"[43]

ISLAMIZATION WITHOUT AN ISLAMIC STATE

The decline of the Islamist core did not mean a waning of religious commitment and activism. On the contrary, many indications pointed to a growing, albeit fragmented, trend of conservative religiosity and piety. Of sixty-five societies included in the World Values Survey, Egyptians were found to be the most pious, with 98 percent declaring their religiosity, compared with 82 percent of Iranians and Americans, and 24 percent of Japanese, the least religious.[44] Comparative surveys of religiosity (in Egypt, Pakistan, Indonesia, Kazakhstan, Jordan, and Iran) confirmed that Egyptian Muslims revered devotional institutions and trusted the ulema and imams more than they did intellectuals, the army, the courts, and the universities.[45] Egyptian Muslims continued to flock to Friday prayer sermons, overflowing from mosques and into the streets. The middle class and professionals in particular showed a great commitment to Friday prayer rituals.[46]

As did women to the veil. By early 2000, the number of women wearing the *hijāb* surged again, with veiled women constituting a staggering majority of over 80 percent. In my survey of 466 women appearing in public at the Cairo Book Fair, 80 percent were veiled; the remainder included non-Muslims. Of the 374 who were veiled, 284 wore the *hijāb* (scarf), 75 the *khimar* (head and chest cover), and 15 the *niqāb* (face cover). A similar survey in a shopping mall in Zamalek, the most "westernized" Cairo neighborhood, showed that over 67 percent appeared in the veil.[47] This certainly was not the Cairo of 1969 when, as Janet Abu-Lughod observed, "One rarely sees *jalabiyyah*. . . . Almost no women are veiled."[48]

Even Egypt's most liberal institution, the American University in Cairo, saw a slow but steady growth of public piety among staff and students. While in the 1980s the headscarf was a rarity on campus, by early 2000 the *hijāb* had become common among students and staff, albeit with the fashion and sophistication that reflected their higher-class background. In 2003, ten students appeared with fully covered faces, causing considerable legal and security complications. The university's prayer halls, nonexistent in the 1980s, were now filled with religious students praying, in discussion, and forging new identities. Student activists of the Help Club held ceremonies to celebrate the entry of newly veiled women, born-again Muslims, to their midst. The *hijāb* assumed a momentum of its own. As more diverse women turned to veiling, they rendered the *hijāb* a hegemonic public symbol, conditioning, even pressuring, others to follow suit. With more and more women from the literate, intellectual, and affluent classes, including chic movie stars, wearing the *hijāb*, veiling ceased to be a sign of fanaticism, "*baladi*ness," or backwardness.

As Muslims became "more Muslim," Copts turned "more Christian." Manifested in rising church attendance, public display of Christian icons, and anxiety over political Islam, the largely middle-class Copts cemented a new religious awareness. "Welfare pluralism" or "NGOization," which offered opportunity on a sectarian basis, widened the communal divide.[49] Coptic Christians adhered to a religious conservatism (in scripturism, public morality, sexual conduct, family values, and gender politics) that could only be matched by their Muslim counterparts. Indeed, judged against Muslim women's modesty, lack of veiling among Coptic women often veiled their conservatism.

Perhaps nothing was more telling about the neoconservative social trend than the public's reaction to the Personal Status Law proposed in Parliament in 2000. The longstanding bill, which favored official recognition of '*urfi* marriage (a written contract concluded in front of two witnesses but not registered formally) and women's (conditional) right to initiate divorce and to travel abroad without a man's permission, caused profound public anxiety, notably among men. In an opinion poll in Cairo, half of the respondents (both men and women) said they were against women having the right to initiate divorce (*khul'*); 85 percent were against the inclusion of this right in a marriage contract (*isma*); and a staggering 90 percent opposed women traveling abroad without a man's permission.[50] Parliamentarians, by using Islamic language, forced a substantial revision of the bill. Even the traditionally liberal dailies such as *al-Wafd* did not spare commentaries and cartoons that reflected deep anxiety over the new law and the fear that it would subjugate men and disturb the harmony and stability of the family.[51] The daily attributed the rise of divorce to "misguided" claims of gender equality, which it argued went against the Qur'an and Shari'a.[52]

Art and music did not remain immune to the rise of pious passion. Nationalism, religiosity, and art converged in the profound moral outrage Arabs felt toward Israel's siege of Palestinian territories in 2002. Egypt's leading pop stars, among them 'Amr Diyab, Muhammad Munir, and Mustapha Qamar, produced bestselling albums with religious and nationalist lyrics, often performed in the style of melancholic religious recitation. Muhammad Munir's high-priced CD "al-Ard wa-Salaam, ya Madad ya Rasoul Allah" sold 100,000 copies. The most popular Egyptian singers, including 'Ali al-Hajar, Muhammad Tharwat, and Hani Shakir, joined voices to produce the religio-nationalistic album "al-Aqsa ya-Allah." Distinct from the traditional religious songs that were upbeat melodies praising the saints or the Prophet Muhammad, the new genre conveyed powerful spirituality, sorrow, and even tragedy. In passionate and sad lyrics, they pleaded with the creator to secure the nation from blunders and suffering.[53]

The new ethos found institutional and discursive expression in the vast, though fragmented, "Islamic sector," composed of Islamic media, publications, education, associations, business, *halaqāt* (religious gatherings), art, entertainment, tastes, and fashion. Business quickly capitalized on this growing market for Islamic commitment and commodities. The likes of Rajab al-Sueirki, a notorious polygamist who married nineteen times, ran his clothing store chain under the religious designation *al-Tawhīd wa al-Nūr*.[54] According to one drugstore owner, "Islamic names bring baraka, raise people's trust, and attract them to business."[55] Many private schools and clinics chose Islamic tags even though they differed little from non-Islamic institutions of the same type.[56]

These practices represented a new trend in religiosity. Thick on ritual and remarkably thin on dissent, they signified a shift from Islamism as a political project to one concerned primarily with personal salvation, ethical enhancement, and self-actualization. Mosques continued to pack people in for Friday prayers and informal sermons, but they were devoid of oppositional *da'wa*. In my experience of attending Friday prayer sermons for some six months of 1996 in Cairo's various mosques, from the poor Bulaq Abul-'Ala' to the rich al-Muhandisīn, from the traditionally militant Kubri-al-Jama'a and 'Amr ibn-Aas to the *ziwāyā* of old Cairo, I encountered few references to domestic politics. Because the Ministry of Awqāf controlled all mosques, only Azhari preachers were allowed to deliver sermons, and they focused overwhelmingly on conventional religious ethos and injunctions. The star preachers of the late 1990s and early 2000s were no longer the militant 'Umar 'Abd al-Rahman or Shaykh Kisk, or even the traditionalist Shaykh Sha'rawi. Rather, they were the likes of necktied and clean-shaven 'Umar 'Abd al-Kafi, Khalid al-Jindi, and 'Amr Khalid, whose sermons attracted massive crowds of youth and women from elite families.

Clearly, adherence to religious ethics and the search for spirituality were not new among Egyptian Muslims, including the rich and the powerful. In the course of sixteen years of interaction with various strata of Egyptian society, particularly the elite, I observed how the people revered the Book, the tradition, and the religious authorities in a more profound and widespread manner than Iranians did. But theirs was a passive religious attachment: as believers, they ordinarily and unquestioningly went along with carrying out their religious obligations. What appeared to be novel since the late 1990s, however, was that many lay Muslims, notably the young and women from affluent families, exhibited an *active piety*: not only did they practice their faith, they also preached it, wanting others to believe and behave like them. The adverse effect of this extraordinary quest for religious truth and identity became apparent before long. Unlike the passively pious, who remained indifferent about other people's religiosity, the actively pious began to judge others for what and how they believed. By privileging their own forms of devotion, they generated new lines of division and demarcation.

This kind of piety was largely the stuff of the comfortable and privileged classes. Indeed, there was little sign of religious transformation among the rural and urban poor, except perhaps for migrant laborers to the Arab Gulf states, many of whom returned to Egypt as pious petite bourgeoisie. Otherwise, the poor continued to practice folk piety, based on their own perceptions and social conditions. Most of them remained illiterate and thus "ignorant" about sacred texts and religious injunctions, upholding general conservative social mores (on gender, for instance). They felt blessed to live in an Islamic environment, but they constantly lamented "only a very few real Muslims were around." The harshness of their distressed lives often expressed itself in deep cynicism about fellow Muslims whose greed and betrayal had corrupted an imaginary moral community. "Since we are Muslims, then our society is surely an Islamic society," said Ramadan ʿAbd al-Futuh, an illiterate manual worker.[57] Many poor and rural families remained involved in Sufi orders of various kinds that had spread throughout the country, a faithline that centers on individual spirituality and universal love.[58] Others continued to construct new "saints" in the image of Shaykh Shaʿrawi[59] or hundreds of others from the *awliyâ* revered in villages of upper Egypt. The *mulid*s (birthdays) of the well-known saints, Sayyid Badawi, al-Husayn, Sayida Zaynab, ʿAysha, and Nafisa, continued to attract massive crowds from all over the country. Some estimated that as many as half of all Egyptians attended *mulid* festivals.[60] They came with food and family and passed days and nights in the streets and alleyways around the shrines of the saints. The participants blended mundane pleasures of picnicking and socializing with *żikr* (praising God) and experiencing spiritual ecstasy. In the evenings, children were left busy with the deafening noise of carnival games, while young adults marched up and down the streets, to see and be seen, attending to their faith and enjoying afford-able fun. The profane and festive mood of these sacred congregations made middle-class Islamists shun them as occasions that "have nothing to do with religion" "these people are simply try to have fun," they said.[61] More austere religious commentators charged them with playing with paganism.[62]

The middle layers and well-to-do classes, women in particular, but not the poor, experienced a new religious activism. While the middle- and lower-middle-class high achievers had already embraced political Islam during the 1980s (see Chapter Two), the elites and the new rich inclined toward a piety that could accommodate their privilege and power. Middle-class migrants to the Gulf (teachers, doctors, and other professionals) often returned home more pious: the women now wore the *hijāb* or *khimar*, while the men had grown facial hair, practices that made both groups feel "closer to God." Saudi reli-gious tradition socialized Muslim migrants to new religious experiences, such as strict prayer times in mosques, attending religious lessons, forced veiling, and abstaining from watching movies. Upon their return, many continued to practice such an ethos. Along with this ritualistic piety came strong ma-terialistic values and a hierarchical snobbery, expressed in the heavy-handed treatment of maids, drivers, and cooks.[63] The popularity of a new genre of lay preachers (shaykh and shaykha) reflected, and became a catalyst for, the growth of this new active religiosity.

PIETY AND PRIVILEGE: THE "PHENOMENON OF 'AMR KHALID"

In the late 1990s, 'Amr Khalid, an accountant-turned-preacher, had become a household name in Cairo. Khalid followed the leads of 'Umar 'Abd al-Kafi and Khalid al-Jindi but surpassed them in popularity among well-to-do youths and women. A gifted orator in the style of televangelists, he lectured in private homes and exclusive clubs but soon rose to stardom in the pulpit of al-Husari Mosque in the trendy al-Muhandisīn, before he was forced by the authorities to move to 6th of October City, a posh new community on Cairo's outskirts. His weekly lessons became a spiritual staple for thousands of young people who flocked from throughout the city's affluent districts to hear him. The crowd rushed hours in advance to get an ideal spot, filling the lecture hall and the surrounding sidewalks, often causing heavy traffic congestion. In 1999, 'Amr Khalid would deliver up to twenty-one lessons a week in socially promi-nent households, peaking at ninety-nine during Ramadan.[64] 'Amr Khalid's recorded sermons became an unparalleled bestseller at Cairo's massive Book

Fair in 2002[65] and traveled as far away as the markets of East Jerusalem, Beirut, Damascus, and the Arab Gulf states. The convergence of youth subculture, elitism, and a pietistic Islam produced this genre of *da'wa* against a backdrop of political Islam in crisis and a profound stagnation on Egypt's intellectual and political landscape.

The new preachers deliberately targeted the young and women of the elite classes, "the people with influence," because "they have the power to change things," according to Khalid al-Jindi.[66] Since elite families generally kept away from traditional mosques located in lower-class areas, young preachers brought their message to the comfort of their private homes, clubs, and the stylish mosques of posh neighborhoods. More important, in addition to face-to-face sermons to disseminate his message, 'Amr Khalid used a full range of media, including satellite television channels such as Dream TV, *Iqra'*, and Orbit, his state-of-the-art website, as well as audio- and videotapes—media that reached the upper-middle and more affluent classes in particular.[67] For some time, the popular state-sponsored magazines *al-Ahram al-Arabi* and *al-Ahram al-Riyadi* distributed his tapes as gifts to their readers. Khalid al-Jindi established a paid "Islamic Hotline" (*hātif al-Islāmi*) on which the public could seek advice from the shaykh.[68] Within a year, the number of daily calls increased from 250 to 1,000. For his part, 'Amr Khalid traveled with his message to the stylish Ajami and other upper-middle-class north coast resorts, and later went on speaking tours to Arab states, where his fame had already spread. By early 2000, Khalid was being treated like a pop star, with dignitaries such as Queen Ranya of Jordan attending his lectures. The colorful decor and a talk-show-like aura of his lecture halls, in contrast to the austere Azherite pulpits, reflected the taste of his main audience: the 12-to-35-year-old elite male and female who had never before been exposed to religious ideas in such an intense and direct manner.

Khalid resembled his audience. Young, clean-shaven, often wearing blue jeans and a polo shirt or a suit and tie, 'Amr Khalid embodied simultaneously the hipness (*rewish*) of 'Amr Diyab (Egypt's most revered pop star), the persuasive power of evangelist Billy Graham, and the unrefined therapy of American talk-show host Dr. Phil. For the young, Khalid was "the only preacher that embraced and tackled our spiritual needs," and someone who "makes us psychologically comfortable," who "treats us like adults, not children."[69] Unlike more orthodox preachers known for their joyless moralizing and austere methods, Khalid articulated a marriage of faith and fun. Speaking in sym-

pathetic, compassionate tones, and in colloquial Arabic, Khalid and his colleagues conveyed simple ethical messages about the moralities of everyday
life, discussing issues that ranged from relationships, appearance, and adul-
tery to posh restaurants, drunk driving, the *hijāb*, and the sins of summer
vacations in Marina.[70] In a sense, the new preachers functioned as "public
therapists" in a troubled society that showed little appreciation for professional psychotherapy. Emotional intensity, peace, and release (crying) often
imbued Khalid's sermons. "You should attend my lessons," Khalid alerted his
audience, "not to increase your knowledge, but to touch your heart."

From the likes of Khalid, young people heard the message that they could
be religious and still lead a normal life—work, study, have fun, and look like
anyone else in society. Khalid's words assured the audience that they could
be pious while maintaining their power and prestige. His message operated
within the consumer culture of Egypt's nouveau riche, where piety and privilege cohabit as enduring partners. Analogous to the Methodist Church of the
well-to-do in the American Bible Belt, where faith and fortune are happily
conjoined, Khalid's style made rich Egyptians feel good about themselves.

Khalid was not a scholar or an interpreter of the Qur'an and did not issue
fatwas. Rather he was devoted to correcting individuals' ethical values and
everyday behavior, fostering such values as humility, generosity, trust, loyalty,
and repentance. However, he was no liberal Muslim thinker. Some of his ideas
remained highly conservative and his methods manipulative. For instance,
Khalid based the "integrity of society . . . on the integrity of women," and the
latter on "her *hijāb*," because "one woman can easily entice one hundred men,
but one hundred men cannot entice a single woman." Since, according to this
logic, unveiled women are promoters of sin, a "complete, head to toe *hijāb* is an
obligation in Islam." Muslim women unconvinced of this were not really Muslim, he claimed, because Islam, in literal terms, simply means "submission" to
the word of God. "Even if you do not understand, you must obey him."

Armed with such logic and speaking with a tremendous force and conviction, the preachers were determined to make converts. They patiently provided
detailed and practical guidelines about how women should begin wearing the
hijāb, for example. Thus, before long, many of their listeners began to make
visible changes in their lives: veiling, wearing the *niqāb* (something Khalid
did not insist on), praying regularly in the mosques, and acquiring a pious
identity.[71] It was perhaps no exaggeration for Khalid al-Jindi to claim that
his efforts since 1999 had done more for the spread of Islam than his entire

twenty-year career.[72] He was especially successful in converting the rich and famous, including female movie stars.

Among his converts in 2001 was an elegant and affluent mother of two children living in an opulent gated community in Cairo, whose underdog public status as an average state employee hardly matched her economic elegance. Her ethical journey began on an ordinary day when she was invited by a friend to attend a private sermon delivered by al-Jindi, whom she had previously heard on a cable television program. In that sermon al-Jindi argued powerfully that wearing the *hijāb* in Islam was not a choice but an obligation, and women were not Muslims unless they wore the veil. "How can you refuse doing this simple duty to God when he has given you so much wealth, successful husbands, and healthy children in posh schools?" he challenged his audience. The women went home convinced by al-Jindi's irresistible contention, and all began wearing the *hijāb*. But the wealthy mother was torn between doubt and guilt. She pleaded with God to show her a sign if He wanted her to wear the veil. Before long, the sign came to her in a dream. With this, she became one of a multitude of well-to-do devout women who began to transform Egypt's urban public space.

Khalid advanced a religious discourse that contained passion, clarity, relevance, and humor, but lacked novelty, nuance, and vigor. While his style was highly imaginative, his theology remained deeply scriptural and lacked the perspective necessary to incorporate critical reason into his interpretations. This was not because he had never studied at al-Azhar. In fact, his doctrinal views hardly differed from those of orthodox Azharite shaykhs who dismissed him despite, or perhaps because of, his immense popularity. Rather, at that juncture in Egypt, when religious thought in general showed little sign of innovation, Khalid appeared to be an innovator, even though only in style. The mass appeal of the likes of Khalid was a byproduct of the crisis of Egypt's mass education, one that valorized memorizing, fragmenting knowledge, revering the printed word, and nurturing an authoritarian mentor. In comparison with the patronizing manner of a typical Azhari shaykh, the amiable and compassionate Khalid appeared to be a true democrat. For those who had learned to look for shortcuts to knowledge and were trained to be docile learners, Khalid emerged as a superior source of wisdom. And in this, he was not much different from the highly popular George Kurdahi, the slick presenter of the Arabic version of "Who Wants to be a Millionaire," from whom the audience felt it gained true knowledge. "He is easy to understand" was echoed by every young admirer of Khalid.

The lay preachers guided scores of well-off women down the path of active piety. However, women's drive for religiosity went beyond such catalysts as 'Amr Khalid. The *halaqāt*, the network of semi-private women's groups organized by Muslim women activists played a central role.

THE "SHAYKHAS" AND ACTIVE PIETY

The *halaqāt* became a phenomenon in Egypt's religious landscape in the mid-1990s. Small, fragmented groups of between ten and sixty women tapped into the vast urban female population to cultivate active piety.[73] Most were presided over by female preachers, or shaykhas, who gave religious lessons in local mosques or clubs and often in private homes. Shirin Fathi, an ex-physician and a renowned elite preacher at the al-Hilāl religious complex, attracted hundreds of women from affluent families.[74] The government stopped her lessons at Nasr mosque, close to the presidential palace, because they caused traffic jams and security concerns. Less well known shaykhas employed the simple language of *da'wa*, often framing their discourse in terms of their audience's socioeconomic desires, including "unlimited shopping in the hereafter."[75]

Women's quest for personal virtue compelled them not only to listen to preachers but also to conduct holy deeds through volunteer social services and charity work. They offered and collected donations, served in day-care centers, organized charity bazaars, taught in vocational and literary classes, and visited widows. They held initiation ceremonies to celebrate the rites of religious passage of born-again Muslims. In *hiflāt hijāb*, or "veiling parties," they blessed the donning of the *hijāb* by young and older females who were treated, ironically, as if they were in beauty pageants. Most activists came from middle-class and well-to-do families, including graduates of the American University in Cairo. Some used their private chauffeurs to visit homes, hospitals, and orphanages and reported back to their *halaqāt*.

Although the ethics espoused by female preachers largely converged with the conservative tenet of patriarchy (a central tenet in the discourse of conservative ulema) the ulema expressed strong opposition to female-led *da'wa*. Whereas they encouraged women to "act as caregivers in their homes and attend to their husbands," and pushed educated women to express ideas on women's matters, the ulema viewed female preaching as "degeneration."[76] The secular press and state media also denounced women *dā'iya* (preachers) as "inept" and "harmful."[77] Shaykh Tantawi warned against, and Azhar clerics flatly rejected, a woman's authority to issue fatwas. The Azhar was deeply concerned about the plurality of religious authority, which would undermine the Azhar's monopoly on moral prerogative and might engender chaos and confusion amongst believers. Nevertheless, male domination over the production, interpretation, and dissemination of religious knowledge was at the heart of opposition to women's religious authority.

It appears that Muslim women's participation as religious authorities implied a redefinition of gender roles, albeit in a rather paradoxical fashion. It empowered women and yet also reproduced patriarchal constraints. Did such activities consequently represent some kind of "Islamic feminism" or struggle for gender equality articulated within an Islamic paradigm?[78] Were Egyptian Muslim women, in this sense, comparable to their Iranian counterparts? Historically, female activists in the Middle East, secular or religious variants, such as 'Aysha Taymuriyya, Zaynab Fawwaz, Nazira Zayn al-Din, Malak Nasif, and Qadriyya Husayn, have always had to reinterpret Islamic precepts in order to further women's interests.[79] But "Islamic feminists" were distinct in that they saw an inherent privilege in religious discourse for Muslim women. Nevertheless, they all took women's rights as their fundamental point of departure and used religious language and practice to extend those rights.

Women active in the *halaqāt*, however, seemed to have different concerns. Theirs was primarily a preoccupation with self-perfection, to attain proximity to God and to seek Islamic ideals of piety, discipline, and self-enhancement.[80] Mundane acts of empowering women and serving others were simply steps along the path toward personal salvation. This renewal (*ihyā'*) could be achieved no longer by merely praying or fasting (*ibāda*); *da'wa*, making others equally pious, was now paramount. This could cause division by breeding competition and differentiation instead of solidarity. Women of identical religiosity would associate among themselves (*suhba*) and shun the "less pious," nonreligious, and non-Muslim. Although individual women enhanced their autonomy with this "turn to religion," by reproducing patriarchal constraints they in effect shut down possibilities for other women who did not share their ideology. Clearly, Egypt's Muslim activists were not, in contrast to their Iranian counterparts, involved in political contestation for women's rights; for them, Islamic activism provided "harmony and self-contentment through perfecting such qualities as patience (*sabr*), piety and discipline."[81] Their notion of self-enhancement differed from liberal feminists' embrace of autonomy, freedom, and equality. Instead of targeting patriarchy, they opposed Western feminists' emphasis on liberalism, individualism (as opposed to family), and tolerance (for instance, of homosexuality). Indeed, being "good women" and "doing housework" were considered acts of worship and fulfillment. "Each laborious task she undertakes," argued the preacher Shirin Fathi, "every stuffed vine leaf she meticulously rolls is not wasted, because in the end, it is an act of worship."[82] It was perhaps such patriarchal theology that informed the intimate relationship between Muna, a high-powered business-woman who wore a face cover, or *niqāb*, and her husband. "When it comes to my husband," she proudly declared, "I have to please him as religion says. I have to have sex with him whenever he wants and never refuse. It is exactly like praying and fasting."[83]

Even well-known activists such as Safinaz Qasim and Heba Rauf Ezzat, who spoke out about gender imbalance and were therefore labeled by some as "Islamic feminists," refuted the broader feminist paradigm.[84] They were primarily female Islamists for whom the liberation of women depended on establishing Shari'a. "Women's commitment to Shari'a," according to Safinaz Qasem, "is the highest degree of liberation a women can achieve."[85] Heba Rauf Ezzat denied the relevance of "Islamic feminism" altogether. For her, "patriarchy," notably "Islamic patriarchy," was "necessary in our societies . . . it upholds the family and takes care of women. . . . This is where old women find respect and honor."[86] Finally, the likes of scholar-activist Omaima Abu-Bakr questioned the adequacy of the concept of the "Islamic feminist" in the Egyptian context. She preferred the term "Muslim women scholars" to describe those who saw no necessary contradiction between being a devoted Muslim and a feminist. Islam's overarching egalitarian values, she suggested, could be an argument for gender equality.[87]

How can we explain this genre of religious attainment among Egypt's well-to-do women? If indeed the trend was rooted merely in an ethical desire for "self-enhancement," a longing for inner calm, or the need for community and solidarity,[88] then why did it spread mostly among the well-to-do, generally among women, and at that particular *historical juncture*? A prominent Egyptian observer finds it "striking how rare it is to find examples of religious fanaticism among the higher . . . social strata of the Egyptian population." This is so, he suggests, because "they are exempted from the feelings of inferiority experienced by the aspiring lower middle classes"[89]

There is indeed a recurring tendency to associate active religiosity with the lower class, the powerless, and the plebeian. Marx was famously concerned with the politics of religion, with how religion acted as the sigh of the oppressed.

Elites appeared on the analytical scene only as exploiters of mass religiosity. This perspective continued to inform the mainstream Marxist paradigm. Although such thinkers as Michael Lowy, observing the rise of religious activism, pointed accurately to religion's both conservative and radical potentials, they rarely addressed the religious attachment of the elites.[90] Weber, too, noted that the elites in general stayed away from religion. Exploring the religious orientations of nonprivileged classes, Weber suggested that the nobility's particular status, honor, was not compatible with such notions as sin, salvation, and religious humility.[91] These beliefs were too plebeian to be internalized by the elites. Privileged classes, for Weber, are rarely prone to the idea of salvation. They are concerned instead with "psychological reassurance of legitimacy."[92] Many of these interpretations had roots in the secular orientation of early social theorists, with the implicit assumption that the wealthy were modern and the modern rationalist and thus secular.[93] It is now clear that religion might serve also as the opium of the rich, as a source of tranquillity to ward off their moral and spiritual (as opposed to material) helplessness; to offer the elites a meaning for what they cannot control, say, the mysteries of pain and death. Even a "feeling of inferiority," so often cited as causing "religious fanaticism," can be found among the "upper strata" of society, particularly among its women.

Elite Muslim women in general might be more prone to piety than other social groups because the space of sin for them is far broader than for others. Affluent Muslim women, in comparison with men, the poor, and non-Muslims, showed a greater inclination to piety, because their class position and lifestyle were more closely associated with "sin" and therefore caused guilt. As members of a privileged class, they are likely to attend nightclubs, bars, or drinking parties, go dancing, date, or appear "half-naked" on beaches. If they are unable to justify and reconcile such conducts with their Muslimness, then they are likely to feel moral anxiety and regret. Although affluent men enjoy a similar lifestyle, they are not subject to the same standards of sin and guilt as women. The centrality of the woman's body in moral judgments, together with gender determinants of "sin," subjects her to potentially "sinful" acts. While both Muslim men and women might appear half-naked on beaches, only the women would be considered immoral. Only a woman's uncovered hair, not a man's, provokes moral pressure. In in-depth interviews, "born-again" Muslim women invariably talked about the agony of feeling guilty.[94] Sumaya, a 38-year-old interior designer wearing a face cover, related that in her 30s she "stayed out late at night, drinking and dancing." At those parties, "a man can laugh with you, touch you, and you cannot stop any of these acts." And "these violations always made me feel guilty." Hana, in her 20s, went through a profound "psychological instability," as she put it, following years of "leftist intellectualism," not praying but drinking, dating, and doubting. Even though she never doubted God, Hana asked for guidance from a pious old woman. Her advice was: "There is nothing to read. Just obey God, and the rest will follow." The "real breakthrough in my religious awakening," said Hana, "was when I watched my grandmother die," after which Hana left her graduate studies, got married, and began to teach in an Islamic primary school.[95]

An intense state of uncertainly seemed to spark women's turn to active piety. This class of women may have been particularly susceptible to uncertainty because they were exposed to more "truths" than they were able to handle; they could afford to access diverse, often extremely different, lifestyles, ideas, and options, the truth of which they were unable to determine. For some, even the plurality of fatwas by different shaykhs became the source of confusion and concern. In such a state of "existential anxiety," to use Giddens's term, the available mediums of practicing piety—listening to lay preachers like 'Amr Khalid, attending the halaqāt, watching religious satellite channels such as Iqra'—played a decisive role in turning individuals' confusion into comfort, their anxiety into peace. They offered women an authoritative life in a world of multiple options.[96]

There was still a social factor. Gender bias had created a class of well-to-do women who dressed well, attended exclusive clubs, and shopped in Western boutiques, but, unlike their male counterparts, they remained socially invisible. In other words, women's "symbolic capital" did not match their economic standing, and this in a society that was intensely obsessed with the merit of social status. While their male counterparts were publicly and successfully engaged in business or bureaucracy, women either reluctantly undertook low-status "women's jobs" or preferred the isolation of housework to the humiliation of such lowly public positions. Perhaps Shirin Fathi's valorization of "housework as worship" offered meaning and a sense of purpose to rich women who found little worth and pleasure in the monotony and solitude of housework, though most was carried out by their maids. Thus they had little opportunity for social attainment—public presence, prestige, and social assertiveness. These social-psychological gaps in women's lives were filled by the structure of piety with its attendant components—identity, institutions, rituals—and by feeling more content and certain that they were doing something useful.

But why did religiosity, and not something else, fill that gap? Women's informal networks of clubs, private parties, and associations failed to provide alternative social roles because they had already been turned into a structure through which the new preachers spread their evangelical messages among women, activating their passive piety. Indeed, the hegemony of conservative sensibilities had drastically marginalized, even suppressed, alternative modes of reasoning. It was within these informal gatherings, in addition to those in mosques and clubs, that preachers like 'Amr Khalid, Khalid al-Jindi, and female *dā'iya* delivered religious sermons and held celebrations. Ordinary women were often exposed to them casually by tagging along with friends, as a way of passing time or satisfying simple curiosities. However, once in the sessions, most of them encountered powerful words and penetrating arguments that they had neither the intellectual ability nor the moral courage to ignore. The result was a tormenting sense of guilt and self-blame over their "immodest" past: not covering their hair, mingling with the opposite sex, appearing half-naked on beaches. To regain calm and tranquility, they needed to repent and abide by the injunctions, often by joining a group or community of faith. They needed to immerse themselves in a structure of piety, which conditioned members with a prepackaged set of ideas, behaviors, and moral fixity that created a new identity that separated members from their past activities and associations. The structure of piety provided a mechanism within which women could express their selfhood in a collective way, fulfill their longing for change and individuality, and yet remain committed to social norms. "I have killed my femininity by wearing the *niqāb* in order to go to paradise"[97] represents the kind of self-actualization that Muslim women could get away with without their disgruntled husbands, fathers, or mothers being able to do anything about it. Such assertion of individuality-within-constraints had become the game of the day, a legitimate social norm. Indeed, the more normalized pious behavior became, the easier it was for newcomers to join in, radically detaching these women from their mothers' generation, which had lived a life with less pious passions.

In other words, the women of the "old rich," who had also endured gender imbalance, responded differently. The segmenting of the occupational structure had effectively excluded affluent women from comparable public positions held by men. Nevertheless, older elite women did not stay at home.

They set out to generate their own public positions in the volunteer sector, by setting up and managing charity associations that they saw as contributing to national development. Volunteerism made them publicly visible, meaningful, and confident, providing high-status social roles on a par with those of their male associates.[98] Many of today's traditional NGO leaders are these same educated women of charity and charm.[99]

The Egyptian nouveaux riche of the 1980s and 1990s, however, displayed little interest in volunteer work. They were imbued with the general ethics of their class—hoarding wealth, pretending the games of high culture, disdaining civic responsibility, valuing education so far as it brought status, or going after Western passports. They showed little regard for national loyalty and developmentalist ideals. This class embodied Egypt's post-*infitāh* mentality, where "possessive individualism" stood at the heart of its free-market ethics.[100] The nationalism of the nouveaux riche was confined to cultural populism, a sort of narrow-minded nativism that, ironically, juxtaposed the snobbery of the dispossessed with cosmopolitan connection and consumerism. Helping the poor for the sake of the poor meant little. Their disdain of volunteerism derived not only from an absence of social responsibility, but also from an unsubtle dislike of associating with the poor. Only when the women of this class turned actively pious did they begin showing concern for charity work, making charitable donations, helping orphans, and visiting widows—not necessarily out of inherent concern but rather as a religious obligation, one that remained deeply orthodox.

THE YOUNG AND RELIGIOSITY

What about the religiosity of youth? Did the habitus of the young—particularly of the globalized segments—affect religious thought in Egypt in the way that the behavior of Iranian youths influenced doctrinal matters there? These cosmopolitan youth in Egypt espoused a flexible piety that could accommodate their youthful habitus, and in so doing further pluralized their religion. However, failing to develop political clout, the young and their eclectic and inclusive religiosity remained marginal to and defensive before the orthodoxy. During the 1980s, young Egyptians were seen as Islamists waging a guerrilla war, militants penetrating college campuses, or devotees memorizing the Qur'an in the backstreet *ziwāyā*, small mosques, of sprawling slums. Mainstream youths were expected to be pious and adhere strictly to Islamic moral discipline. Yet in their daily lives they defied their constructed image.

"The youth of this country are rebelling against the old traditions," a defiant 20-year-old female student stated in Cairo; "we are breaking away from your chains; we are not willing to live the lives of the older generations. Women smoking shisha is the least shocking form of rebellion going on."[101]

The media explosion of "satanic youth" in January 1997 demonstrated a prevailing moral panic about the vulnerability of the young to Western culture and about the emerging self-assertion of modern Egyptian youths. Every Thursday night, hundreds of well-to-do youngsters gathered in a large abandoned building to socialize, have fun, and dance to heavy metal music. Although six weeks of sensational media coverage and the arrest of dozens accused of "satanism" (who were released later for lack of evidence) put an end to the gatherings, they proved the existence of underground subcultures that few adults had noticed. The music-based subculture, however, did not die out after the "satanist" affair. It later reappeared in the form of raving, beginning with small gatherings that grew rapidly after 1998. Raves encompassed music genres from around the world, including Egyptian pop, but catered to elite youths, those with "glamour, high fashion, and lifestyle."[102] The Egyptian rave was largely sex-free, but it did involve alcohol and (unofficially) drugs (ecstasy pills). Indeed, studies indicated that experimentation with alcohol was not confined to the children of the well-to-do; one out of every three students in the cities had drunk alcohol (mainly beer).[103] Although only just over 5 percent admitted experimenting with drugs (mostly cannabis), by the early 1990s the problem had become more severe. Law enforcement professionals warned that the use of ecstasy in particular was on the rise.[104]

While in general a "culture of silence" prevailed with regard to sexuality,[105] premarital sex seemed to be significant among Muslim youths, despite normative and religious sanctions. Approximate but indicative surveys of female high school and college students in Cairo showed 45 percent had had some kind of sexual experience. Over 70 percent of male students said they would not mind having premarital sex, but would not marry their partners.[106] Most used pornography and masturbated regularly even though they considered doing so religiously and physically wrong.[107] A more comprehensive study found "substantial rates of premarital sex among university students."[108] The phenomenon was confirmed by medical and health professionals who expressed surprise at the extent of youngsters' knowledge about specific sexual practices.[109]

Aside from the influence of satellite television and illicit videos, the changing structure of Egyptian households also seemed to play a role. Divorce, desertion, and migration had made one out of three Egyptian families fatherless. When mothers went out, the young had a place for romance.[110] In general, while elite couples sought romantic encounters in dim discos, at raves, or in holiday resorts, lower-class youths resorted to such affordable fun as strolling along the Nile or meeting on the benches of inconspicuous Metro stations, enjoying a discreet privacy ensured paradoxically by the safety of its publicness. There romantically involved couples could sit and talk while pretending to wait for trains.[111]

These young people who struggled to inscribe their youthfulness through such manners were deeply religious. They often prayed, fasted, and expressed fear of God. Many heavy metal "satanists" whom I interviewed were devout Muslims, but they also enjoyed rock music, drinking, and romance. The mainstream young combined prayer, partying, pornography, faith, and fun, even though their activities might make them feel remorse and regret. Here is how a lower-class young man working in Dahab, a tourist resort visited by many foreign women, attempted to reconcile God, sex, and power in pursuit of both mundane and spiritual needs: "I used to pray before I came to Dahab. My relationship to God was very strong and very spiritual. Now, my relationship to God is very strange. I always ask him to provide me with a woman, and when I have a partner, I ask him to protect me from the police."[112]

This might sound like a contradiction, but it actually represents consolation and accommodation. The young enjoyed dancing, raving, illicit relationships and having fun, but found solace and comfort in their prayers and faith. "I do both good and bad things, not just bad things; the good things erase the bad things," according to a law student in Cairo.[113] A religious man who drank alcohol and "tried everything" also prayed regularly hoping that God would forgive his ongoing misdeeds. Many young girls saw themselves as committed Muslims but still uncovered their hair or wore the veil only during Ramadan or only during fasting hours. Many of those who enjoyed showing their hair found consolation in deciding to cover it after marriage, when their youthful phase was over. As a student stated, "during adolescence, all the young do the same; there is no haram or halal [wrong or right] at such age."[114]

In this state of liminality, through such creative inbetweenness, the young attempted to reimagine their religion in order to reconcile their youthful desires for individuality with the existing moral order. Their eclectic mannerisms exemplified what I call an "accommodating innovation," a process whereby the young utilized prevailing moral codes and institutions to assert their youthful claims; they did not radically depart from these codes and institutions, but made them work in their interest. The growing practice of 'urfi marriage (an informal oral contract requiring two witnesses) among the young, which officials described as a "danger" to "national security,"[115] reflected young people's use of this traditional practice to get around moral constraints on dating and economic constraints on formal marriage.[116] Yet this and other accommodating innovations occurred, not against or outside the boundaries of the dominant moral order and religious thinking, but within them. The Egyptian young never articulated their innovations as legitimate alternative visions, but remained remorseful, apologetic, and subservient to orthodoxy. Unlike their Iranian counterparts, they were free to listen to their music, follow fashion, pursue dating games, and enjoy affordable fun, so long as they recognized their limits. Failing to forge a youth movement, a political force, young Egyptians held little power to cause a breakthrough in religious thought.

Indeed the appeal of 'Amr Khalid among the young may be seen in the context of such "accommodating innovation," in the sense that it was a reinvented religious style but entrenched in conservative discourse. Cosmopolitan Egyptian youths fostered a new religious subculture expressed in a distinctly novel style, taste, and language. These globalizing youth displayed many seemingly contradictory behaviors: they were religious believers but distrusted political Islam, if they knew anything about it at all; they swung back and forth from 'Amr Diyab to 'Amr Khalid, from partying to prayers, and yet they felt the burden of social control exerted by elders, teachers, and neighbors. As young Egyptians were socialized in a cultural condition and educational tradition that often restrained individuality and novelty, they were compelled to assert them in "social way," through "fashion." Thus the religious subculture that galvanized around the "phenomenon of 'Amr Khalid" was partly an expression of "fashion" in the Simmelian sense, in the sense of an outlet that accommodates contradictory human tendencies: change and adaptation, difference and similarity, individuality and social norms. Resorting to this type of piety permitted the elite young to assert their individuality and undertake change, and yet remain committed to collective norms and social equalization.

SHARING ISLAM AND THE NATION

The pious sentiments of the late 1990s represented only one, albeit a major, aspect of Egypt's socioreligious change over the past two decades. Concurrent with this was another set of societal trends: conspicuous consumption, glitzy shopping malls and gated communities, Western-style vacations, cable television, X-rated movies, and alternative lifestyles. While lower-class youth sought pleasure in backstreet teahouses, *mulid* festivals, or *shamal nasīm* (ancient spring holiday) excursions, the affluent socialized in standard global discotheques, shopping malls, and the resort paradises of Marina or al-Guna. Rich youngsters formed a subculture of dating, illicit sex, heavy metal music, and "satanic" parties, while the lower class resorted to *'urfi* marriage and underground campus romances. In this midst, elite parents stood caught in the ongoing tension between seeking gratification from the abundance of global cultural products and deep anxiety over their "corrupting" influence on their vulnerable children.[117]

This social cleavage, unseen in Egypt's post-colonial history, expressed itself most glaringly in its spatial dimension. The poor and the struggling middle classes were pushed into the sprawling urban slums and *'ashwa'iyyat*, the overcrowded informal cities, while the rich began a historic exodus to opulent gated communities on the fringes of the capital whose mere names—Dream Land, Utopia, Beverly Hills—spoke of a new cultural anomaly. There in those "dreamlands," away from the daily anguish of plebeian life—poverty, pollution, filth, and "street bums"—the super-rich lived a fantasy life. They inhabited, worked, played, studied, and clubbed in urban enclaves that allowed little contact with ordinary Egyptians. Even their native maids were replaced by imported houseworkers from the Philippines, Thailand, and Bangladesh.[118]

By the late 1990s, it was as if the vast discrepancy in consumption had fractured Egypt's social and urban fabric, splitting the nation into disparate cultural universes. Yet the diverse Muslim fragments—rich and the poor, old and new, local and cosmopolitan—all astonishingly shared two crucial discursive components: religion and nativism. Religious loyalty did not replace nationalist sentiment, principally because Israeli and U.S. regional dominance had caused an impassioned national uproar. Instead, Islamic sentiment eroded nationalism's secular expression. In short, the "Islamic phenomenon" and nativist sentiment seemed to engulf the entire Muslim population, including the globalized upper class. Thus it was not uncommon for elite families to mix their California holidays with Haj or 'Umra, or to hire private shaykhs to tutor their children in the teachings of Islam in the security of their luxurious habitat.

Some might call this a "hybrid reality," a mixing of "modernity" and "tradition." There is, however, little novelty or merit in such a characterization.

For hybridity is not limited to the sociocultural practices of Egypt's new elites. Indeed, all cultures are more or less "hybrid." The impoverished middle classes in Egypt were not excluded. Ibtihal's family represented perhaps a typical middle-class "hybrid." In March 2000, my family and I visited Ibtihal for a late lunch on the occasion of 'Id al-Adha, the Islamic New Year. Ibtihal was a low-income veil-wearing teacher in a private Islamic school. Assertive and active in two Islamic associations and charity work, she was married to an articulate and opinionated man. As a retired state employee, he earned extra cash through freelance acting. He read daily papers and followed the news. He praised Nasser as a leader for standing up to Israel and the United States and despised radical Islamists, who, he believed, were "terrorists supported by foreign powers such as the United States, Iran, or Afghanistan." Their son, a slick, well-groomed teenager, studied engineering in a provincial university. He proudly showed us his brand new computer and Internet connection, which the family valued for its importance in this age of information. Their soft-spoken 17-year-old daughter greeted us in a modest dress and head scarf, though she removed the hijāb once she felt comfortable with us. Ibtihal's family lived in a poor neighborhood of old Ma'adi, in a very small flat of three tiny rooms packed with furniture, an extremely small kitchen, and walls adorned with Qur'anic calligraphy. Everyone in the family was both religious and nationalist. They all agreed that "America has neither politics nor religion" and that the Arabs had many problems, but those were manufactured outside the region. "The solution to the problems is for the Arabs to get together and fight Israel," they concluded.[119]

This blend of religiosity and nationalism, one that most Egyptians remarkably shared, was precisely what the Egyptian state both cherished and championed. In some ways, this societal tendency was reflected in and contributed to an "Islamization" of the secular state. At its height, the Islamist movement had not only captured a large part of civil society, but also significantly influenced the state, conditioning it to share and further appropriate religious discourse. It socialized the state to the society's prevailing sensibilities, and by penetrating the state apparatus helped create a kind of "secularreligious" state.

RELIGIOSITY OF THE SECULAR STATE

In 1992 Interior Minister Muhammad 'Ali Mahjub publicly announced that all laws in Egypt were based on Islamic Shari'a and that the "Egyptian government would never allow the establishment of a secular state."[120] Similarly, the mufti of al-Azhar, Shaykh Tantawi, said, "Egypt has an Islamic state," even though "we do not have a religious party or a political religion."[121] Even an Islamist opposition leader, 'Asam al-Eryan, of the Muslim Brothers, could publicly acknowledge in 2000 that "Egypt was an Islamic state." This remarkable convergence indicated the state's ideological direction. The constitution had already stipulated, since the presidency of Anwar Sadat, that Islam was the religion of the state and Shari'a the principal source of legislation. This meant that the state, according to Shaykh Tantawi, "does not accept the separation of religion from politics."[122]

Since the late 1970s, Egyptian governments have simultaneously campaigned against political Islam while taking every opportunity to publicly display themselves as the guardian of religious values and morality. The political elites' embrace of Islam did not simply aim to secure political legitimacy; it also reflected their genuine belief in the religious supervision of society. The official outcries in recent years about the "Shi'ite conspiracy," "satanism," "anti-religious" literature, and homosexuality exemplified not only a real anxiety over moral disintegration, but also efforts to project the state in a religious frame. The October 1996 discovery of an underground Shi'ite group allegedly led by preacher Shaykh Hasan Muhammad Shahata triggered extensive official media coverage of a "danger" that was "dividing our Islamic nation."[123] The campaign projected an image of the state as guardian of the people's religion, Sunni Islam, against corrupting alien thought.[124] During weeks of public clamor, the media characterized Shi'ites as those who "pray without *wudū'* (washing),"[125] were "worse than *khawārij*," "fanatics" who "promote homosexuality"[126] and display "anti-Islamic" behavior.[127] Shi'ism was described as the "AIDS of Islam,"[128] reinforcing public misperceptions. Parliament called for deploying "religious caravans" to combat Shi'i thought, and al-Azhar ordered the confiscation of Shi'i literature.[129] And no one publicly questioned these representations, which in effect denied Shi'ism as legitimate doctrine in Islam.

The arrest in May 2001 of fifty-two Egyptians accused of practicing sodomy on the tourist ship *Queen Boat* reaffirmed that "contempt of religion" was a matter of state security.[130] The extensive publicity given to the *Queen Boat* case evoked the 1997 national revulsion over the penetration of "satanism" among the young. Hundreds of articles, books, and interviews lamented what was in fact no more than youngsters listening to heavy metal music.

This "alien phenomenon" was seen as an outcome of unfettered globalization that threatened "our religious values." Later, the government established Internet crime units in the Ministry of the Interior to monitor moral crimes. Three vice squads monitored Internet users twenty-four hours a day; by July 2003 some 150 arrests had been documented.[131] Extending the Islamic holiday of 'Id al-Adha, the Islamic New Year, and broadcasting prayer calls in Cairo's Metro in 2002 were some of the more recent state-sponsored religious manifestations.

This Islamic association inevitably pushed the government closer to official religious establishments: al-Azhar, the Ministry of Awqāf, and the Supreme Council for Islamic Affairs. As early as 1981, following the assassination of Anwar Sadat by al- Jama'a, President Mubarak had recognized Azhar's principal "mission": to rid "Egypt of the extremist and deviationist minority" and "to educate youth and give them a correct religious upbringing."[132] The mission proved to be paramount later, when opposition Islamists launched their political onslaught. In turn, Shaykh Tantawi praised Mubarak's twenty-year presidency, which he and "establishment Islam" had helped him to achieve, because the president "observed the commandments of Islam" and under him Azhar's institutions grew from 3,000 to 6,000.[133] Between 1986 and 1996, 'Abd al-Sabur Shahin (the Islamist who charged Nasr Abu Zayd with apostasy) was President Mubarak's key advisor on Islam and the chairman of the ruling NDP's Religious Committee.[134] The weekly Sawt al-Azhar (published in 1999) joined the NDP's Islamic publication al-Liwa' al-Islami and 'Aqidati in offering an alternative vision of Islam, filling the void created by the decline of political Islam. This was to be an Islam that was "not only a religion, but also a way of life."[135] Leaders of the main official religious establishments were members of the ruling NDP, which continued to reaffirm its commitment to Shari'a as the main source of law, to emphasize religious education and upbringing, to call on Islamic media to fight against "immoral cultural imports," and to focus on the moral guidance of the young.[136]

The government's attempts to reclaim religious space and to share moral authority earned it some legitimacy, but it also gave free rein to state religious authorities to aggressively pursue their Islamization project from the top. Rather than being subordinate to the government, the Azhar followed its own mission of "safeguarding religiosity," which, although it partially served the state, often clashed with the regime's secular imperatives and certain interests of the society. Shaykh Tantawi's fatwa in 1999, which barred people from obtaining loans for purposes other than direct investment (for example, building a house), was bound to disrupt Parliament's plans to introduce laws governing mortgages, even though he was forced by the media to retract it.[137] Two years later, al-Azhar agreed to allow bank interest on the condition that the parties agreed on a fixed rate.[138] When he was the grand shaykh of al-Azhar, Shaykh Jād al-Haqq had reportedly gone as far as "trying to build an independent fiefdom, a theocratic authority like the Vatican."[139] In addition, al-Azhar did not hesitate to side with the public's denunciation in 2000 of the republication of the novel *A Banquet for the Seaweeds*. The rector of al-Azhar University urged the Ministry of Culture to burn the novel.[140] It was the Azhar's Islamic Research Institute that held the prerogative of banning any publication that it deemed "harmful to Islam."[141]

These opportunities offered the official religious establishment, and by extension opposition Islamists, substantial power to influence cultural politics and public morality. Al-Azhar scrutinized scores of books, films, plays, and people.[142] The Cairo Book Fair, which had previously enjoyed relative freedom as a site of intellectual debates, came under state security. Dozens of books on state and religion were barred from discussion or removed altogether. Prominent secular judge and commentator on Islam Sa'id al-'Ashmawi was himself banned,[143] while Maxim Rodinson's *Muhammad* and Muhammad Shukri's *al-Khubz al-Hafi* were stricken from classrooms at the American University in Cairo following a concerted Islamist campaign. Subsequently, all books ordered by the university for library or instructional use had to be approved by an official censor.[144] During the same year, Azhar censored as many as 250 religious and literary works. Among these, the publication of the novel *A Banquet for the Seaweeds* caused an unparalleled uproar. The Islamist Labor Party printed provocative extracts from the novel to incite the public to unite in order to "save Islam." Ensuing confrontations in the streets and within government brought Egypt to the brink of an intense political crisis. Parallel to the steps taken by al-Azhar, the Ministry of Awqāf had begun in 1996 to monitor Islamic *da'wa* by taking control of all 71,000 governmental and nongovernmental mosques and *ziwāyā*.[145] In late 2001 the ministry began to oversee the construction of new mosques and the selection of preachers; it screened out "undesirable" preachers, though conservative Wahabi shaykhs still managed to get around the screening process.[146]

Such political climate fanned the smoldering embers of the virtually dead Front of al-Azhar Ulema (Jibhat al-Ulema al-Azhar), reviving it to become the most outspoken conservative group in the religious establishment. Founded in 1946 as a professional association for al-Azhar employees, by the late 1990s the Ulema Front had become the mouthpiece of fundamentalist ulema who wished to eliminate all secular tendencies in the state and society. As part of its crusade, it charged the liberal minister of culture with staging a coup against Egypt's Islamic constitution.[147] The Ulema Front's leader, Yahya Isma'il, called on "the entire Islamic nation" to rise against Hasan Hanafi, a prominent Muslim philosopher, because he "aims at destroying everything holy and undermining all ethics."[148] The Ulema Front did not even spare the moderate Azhar Shaykh Tantawi; they attacked his school reform initiative, which would have required pupils to memorize less of the Qur'an and omitted from the curriculum the study of *hadīth* or Shari'a elements that were politically subversive, such as jihad, *hudūd* and *jināyat*.[149] It also denounced Tantawi's views on the legality of banking interest and organ transplants, and condemned his hosting of a rabbi at al-Azhar Mosque. Although the impatient Tantawi pushed for the dissolution of the Ulema Front in 1999 and the detention of Yahya Isma'il in 2002,[150] the group continued to hunt the establishment.

The Ulema Front represented the type of institution that lay on the faultline between civil society and the state, from which social movements might influence state machinery. In Egypt, schooling provided a critical medium through which Islamists quietly encroached on the state domain, creating opportunities for advancement. Since the 1980s, Islamist instructors had dominated a large number of higher education faculties, including engineering, science, and, most critical, the Teacher Training College (Dar al-'Ulum). All Arabic-language professors were reportedly members of the Muslim Brotherhood.[151] They trained future schoolteachers, who then carried Islamization into the classrooms through basic education. What partially contributed to this trend was the Ministry of Education under Ahmad Fathi Sorur (1987–91), who promoted greater religiosity in schools as a way to bolster the state's religious legitimacy. He introduced a revised curriculum with greater Islamic content and called for the teaching of religious ethics.

Thus the 1990s witnessed significant cases of indoctrination by teachers who turned schools into what Kamal Baha'idin, the new minister of education, worriedly called "factories of terrorism."[152] A ministry report to Parliament in 1993 revealed that at least ninety schools and 300 teachers had links to Islamist groups.[153] To the ministry, such infiltration was tantamount to a "threat to national secularity," but the general growth of religious culture in schools, independent of political Islam, was more significant. Despite the arrest between 1993 and 1995 of more than 1,000 Islamist teachers, religious sentiments and ideas continued to dominate the schools. A 1997 study of 354 "basic education" teachers confirmed that 86 percent adhered to a fundamental Islamist dictum: "religious legacy has answers to all of the problems that Egyptian society is facing."[154]

Classes on religion and Arabic literature often turned into sessions of religious and moral indoctrination. Teachers introduced extracurricular activities and broadcast religious sermons in class, sometimes including horrifying details about *kufr* (apostasy) and hell. Even private foreign schools committed to liberal education did not escape influence; my own two children were subject to blatant religious preaching often mixed with moral blackmail. "If you or your mother does not wear the *hijāb*, you might end up in hell," they were told. By early 2000 one could hardly find anyone without a headscarf in schools, while some even wore the *niqāb*. The moderate Islamic modesty that the political authorities sought to inculcate in the young had exceeded its limits. The government began to regulate school uniforms, banning the *niqāb* but leaving headscarves to parental discretion. Many students, however, successfully challenged the government's actions in court.

The courts' sympathy attested to a lurking but systematic Islamist encroachment, through judges, attorneys, and thought, on the judiciary. Faruq 'Abd al-'Alim, the fundamentalist judge who had convicted Nasr Abu Zayd, appeared in court not in judicial robes but in traditional *jalabiyya*. He decried Egyptian law because it was not, in his view, in conformity with Shari'a.[155] Such judges and attorneys used their position not only to alter the judiciary system, but also to spread Islamism to the rest of society and other official institutions. They invoked the legal principle of *hisba* to justify the fight against secular thought. Derived from the Islamic injunction "encourage good and forbid wrong,"[156] *hisba* entitled any Muslim to take legal action against anything or anyone he considered harmful to Islam. Since Abu Zayd's conviction in 1995, *hisba* contributed to what Egyptian anthropologist Reem Saad described in 1997 as the "privatization of repression," at times with tacit state backing. It allowed courts to put ideas and beliefs on trial. Fundamentalist lawyers such as Nabih al-Wahsh and Yusif al-Badri, known as *shaykh al-takfir* or "blasphemy shaykhs," filed lawsuits against writers, professors, artists, and journalists whom they saw as "insulting" Islam, creating havoc in intellectual circles. In 1995 alone, fifty-four *hisba* cases were filed against leading cultural figures such as Najib Mahfuz, actress Yusra, and poet Hijazi;[157] another eighty were filed between 1996 and 1998.[158]

Yusif Shahin's acclaimed film *al-Muhājir* was banned for portraying biblical prophets. And in April 2000 the state security prosecutor convicted writer Salahidin Muhsin for suggesting in his books that progress would come from science and not religion.[159] Feminist Nawal al-Saʿdawi was put on trial for calling the veil "nonobligatory," the Hajj "paganism," and Muslim scholars "obsessed with sex." Shaykh Nasr Farid Wasil, the first mufti of the republic, described her as a heretic, thus "ousting her from Islam."[160] In an ironic twist, the fundamentalist ʿAbd al-Sabur Shahin, who had accused Nasr Abu Zayd of apostasy, came under the same charge by his former associate Yusif al-Badri for including in his new book *Abi Adām* (*Adam, My Father*) an analysis of the story of man's creation described in the Qur'an. Al-Badri publicly called on Shahin to renounce the book, demanding he either repent or face the charge.[161] In 1998, observing this explosion of lawsuits, the government amended the *hisba* law by restricting the right to file such suits to the state.

The role of the media in the dissemination of orthodox religiosity was crucial. Both mainstream print and electronic media were influenced by Islamization. Since the 1950s, and more so since Sadat's presidency, the mostly state-owned press shifted toward conservative religiosity and self-censorship.[162] The secular liberal content of the 1950s and 1960s became increasingly conservative. By the 1990s, it was rare for the media to feature women wearing bathing suits (except to condemn the practice), criticize conservative morals, or pose such questions as "What is the shape of God, where does he stay?" or "Is war *haram* or *halal*?"[163]

The moral tone and anti-secular message of official religious publications like *al-Liwa' al-Islami* and the pro-government *ʿAqidati* became almost indistinguishable from their opposition Islamist counterparts. In the mid-1990s *al-Liwa' al-Islami* carried articles urging women to abide by Shariʿa, to refrain from wearing makeup, and to obey their husbands on matters of travel,[164] and forbidding workers from employment in places where liquor was consumed or sold.[165] The publication went beyond presenting the *hijāb* as "tantamount to the liberation of women," advocating *niqāb* as "a virtue for women who wish to pave the path of perfection."[166]

In the same spirit, *ʿAqidati* attacked secular intellectuals and the Egyptian cinema for their moral corruption, for movies created by the "Jewish mind"

and "American money," cinema that threatened "our values, norms and traditions."[167] In joint projects with 'Aqidati, the Ministry of Youth organized
"religious caravans," dispatching al-Azhar preachers to the provinces to teach
the young "correct Islam," which was centered on religious obligations and
rituals (for example, acceptable forms of the veil and where not to pray) in a
highly orthodox fashion and with little critical discussion or debate.[168] Such
state-sponsored weeklies often served as forums for conservative Islamists
such as Shaykh Nasr Farid Wasil, Yusif al-Qardawi, or Shaykh 'Abd al-Sabur
Shahin. More important, radio and television promoted religious sensibil-
ity by increasing Islamic programs that provided hardliners such as 'Abd al-
Sabur Shahin a weekly platform.[169]

The religiosity of Egypt's secular state resulted as much from its authorities' deliberate policy as from the Islamist movement's *socialization of the state*
toward religious sensibilities. This "forward linkage" effect of social movement activism shows how Islamist mobilization conditioned the state to take
account of the society's religious mode. The political elites were compelled
to adopt religious discourse in order to regain moral mastery over society
and secure political legitimacy, but in this process they were conditioned to
think and act religiously. Consequently, the state assumed a schizophrenic
"secularreligious" disposition: it adopted laws with roots in both religious and
secular values, based its authority on both discourses, and committed itself
to both local religious and global secular standards and expectations. The
post–September 11 global climate intensified this dual character. It was no
surprise that while the government expressed loyalty to the legal and ethical
codes of Islam, it refused to abide by rules set by Islamist groups.[170] This dual
character of the Egyptian state distinguished it from Iran's Islamic Republic,
which ignored global secular standards and expectations.

The advent of "globalization," with its technological wonders, marketiza-
tion, and flow of tourism, fascinated the Egyptian state. But its social costs
and the widening of class divisions bred social unrest, and cultural imports
threatened the "moral character" of children, causing panic among elders.
Egyptian dailies decried Internet sites (some 1.6 million in 2003) for their ability to debase "our moral values" and corrupt the young.[171] The late 1990s saw
an "alarming" rise in violence among the young in a culture that cherished
nonviolence. A 2000 report by the Childhood Studies Center showed a 60 percent increase in the incidence of violence among school students, a 40 percent
rise in felonies, and a 70 percent surge in gang-related crimes. In this new

"culture of violence," "everything around you—traffic, video games, computer games—all provoke violence among people."[172]

How could these social rifts, alienation, and cultural anomie be mended?
What sort of ideological frame could be deployed? Secular alternatives—technological advancement, democracy, and pluralism—which some officials
claimed to offer the young, failed to materialize.[173] Income disparities and a
deteriorating public education system meant that technological competence
was largely the province of the elite,[174] while the pluralist vision fell victim to a
growing "political deliberalization" and cultural repression.[175]

Facing political turmoil from within and a moral-cultural onslaught from
without, under a regime determined to pursue costly economic restructur-
ing, the state saw a combination of religion and cultural nationalism as the
only effective recourse for safeguarding social integration and morality.[176] It
was as though morals were invoked to secure the market and religion to ensure rule. Safeguarding morals and the market—this farcical return to the
function of the traditional *muhtasib* might be ironic. But it reflected Egypt's
religious "passive revolution," characterized by the fusion of piety and power,
the "statization" of religion, and the religiosity of the state, with far-reaching
consequences for religious and intellectual thought, democratic practice, and
political change.

STAGNATION IN SOCIORELIGIOUS THOUGHT

What did the evolution of Islamism (the decline of organized political Islam,
the increase in individualized piety, and the religiosity of the state) mean for
religious thought and intellectual practice? Did these experiments lead to any
novel perspectives on Islamic politics, or on the social role of religion? What
did they mean for political change and democratic challenge?

The Islamist movement in Egypt did undergo some rethinking of its strategy, theoretical vision, and pragmatic dimensions. Al-Jama'a al-Islamiyya's
decision to renounce violence, opting instead to pursue its goals through
peaceful and legal political action was, as some described, a "monumental
strategic change." In a twelve-volume reexamination of their project (*Silsilat
Tashih al-Mafāhim*, 2002), al-Jama'a's imprisoned leaders based their strategic
shift on religious doctrine.[177] Drawing on the Qur'an, sunna, and Shari'a, they
argued that the violent method, jihad, should not be allowed when peaceful
da'wa was possible, when opponents changed their adversarial position, and
when there was a possibility of reconciliation.[178] They decided, in addition,

that Islam prohibited fighting against "people of the Book," and especially prohibited killing women, children, the elderly, and the innocent, which Islam considers immoral acts. Murdering innocent tourists was described as particularly evil since, as *musta'menin* (those needing protection), they were assured of safety by the natives.[179] Violence also tarnished the image of Islam and harmed the nation, they concluded. But a fundamental reason for al-Jama'a's revised strategy was the failure of armed struggle to achieve its objective. In effect, al-Jama'a came to the conclusion that, when you see that you can't win, you should stop fighting.[180] Although the Egyptian government continued to deny the right of ex-militants to establish political parties (as it prevented Hizb al-Wasat, Hizb al-Islamiyya al-Islah, and Hizb al-Shari'a from doing in 1999), al-Jama'a persisted in calling on its members to pursue only a peaceful *da'wa*.[181] The group's altered outlook brought it closer to the Muslim Brothers, who were also undergoing transformation.

For the first time, in 1997, Mustafa Mashhur, the leader of the Muslim Brotherhood, spoke of "pluralism," emphasizing that his organization was not a Muslim party (*Jama'a al-Muslimin*) but a party with Muslim membership (*Jama'a min al-Muslimin*).[182] The "younger" leaders such as 'Asam al-Eryan went so far as to attribute the global idioms of democracy, civil society, transparency, and accountability to the thoughts of Hasan al-Banna.[183] Al-Eryan appeared to favor Muhammad Khatami's concept of "Islamic democracy," describing it as "blending democracy with the spirit of Islam, with our culture and civilization."[184] Some even spoke of women's and minority rights, which they thought could be accommodated within an Islamic polity. Undoubtedly these modern concepts were a step forward from the MB's earlier adherence to "shura," a vague notion postulating that an authoritarian but just ruler (who is vested with both temporal and spiritual authority) should be subjected to the principle of consultation.

The perspective that informed the young al-Wasat Party went beyond the new discourse of the Muslim Brotherhood. Indeed, the formation of al-Wasat represented a significant shift in Egyptian Islamist politics, signaling the emergence of a "post-Islamist" polity. Established in 1996 by young defectors from the MB (such as Abul-'Ala Mādi, a former student and engineering syndicate leader), al-Wasat denounced the authoritarian disposition of the MB, its underground activities, and Islamist politics in general. Al-Wasat privileged modern democracy over Islamic "shura," embraced pluralism in religion, and welcomed gender mixing and ideological tendencies. Not only were Copts admitted to the party; the main ideologue of the group, Rafiq Habib, was a Christian. In al-Wasat's view, women should play a role equal to men, serving in the army and acting as judges.[185] Al-Wasat, therefore, was "not a religious party, but a civil party with an Islamic background," according to its leader.[186] It saw Egyptian Islam not simply as a religion but as a civilizational and Arab cultural frame encompassing both Muslims and Christians.[187] In al-Wasat's vision, the umma, as the ultimate source of power, should be revived to restrain the expansionist role of the state through which elites had taken control of polity and culture.[188] To this end, Rafiq Habib proposed a new interpretation of *ahliyya* to mean strengthening local, formal, and informal social groupings as the basis for a new nation-building; it also meant promoting social movements such as Islamism to revive the Islamic legacy of Egyptian civilization.[189] But, Habib emphasized, both Christian and Islamic establishments, notably al-Azhar, should stand independent from the state. Shari'a, which the constitution considered the main source of law, should be subject to modern interpretations, or *ijtihād*, and should not apply to non-Muslims if it conflicted with their beliefs.[190] Although the government refused to recognize al-Wasat (to the delight of the Muslim Brothers), the party's activists succeeded in 2000 in establishing the Egyptian Society for Culture and Dialogue, an NGO that aimed to legally pursue some of the party's objectives.[191]

These changes certainly represented a new turn in Egypt's Islamist politics. However, they remained only marginal to conservative orthodoxy in religious thinking. Although a certain pragmatism evolved in political strategy, religious thought in general (and therefore political vision) experienced little innovation. Stagnation (*jumūd*) in *fiqh* (religious jurisprudence) was confirmed by Islamic thinkers ranging from Yusif al-Qardawi and Selim al-Awa to activists like 'Asam al-Eryan.[192] The theology expressed by the Islamists remained profoundly scriptural, with too narrow a perspective to historicize or bring critical reason to interpretations. The likes of Khalid 'Abd al-Karim, Sa'id al-'Ashmawi, and Nasr Abu Zayd, who attempted innovation, faced censorship, threats, and charges of apostasy. Sa'id al-'Ashmawi was pushed to the sidelines; Khalid 'Abd al-Karim (known as the "red shaykh") was accused (by the state and al-Azhar) of blasphemy for arguing that the message of the Qur'an must be taken in the context of society at the time of prophet.[193] And Nasr Abu Zayd, charged with apostasy, was compelled to seek exile instead of having to divorce his wife. Even moderate Muslim writers like Jamal al-Banna (the bother of Hasan al-Banna), whose three-volume *Nahw Fiqh Jadid* suggested tossing aside much of pre-twentieth century *ahādīth* (because they were fabricated) and who argued that wearing the *hijāb* was not a religious obligation, were not tolerated.[194]

While the Jamaʿa's renunciation of violence was a great stride strategically, it did not change the doctrinal foundation of its politics: strict adherence to Shariʿa. In every new step and political position the "prison leaders" took, they defensively referred to the sunna and Shariʿa as if politics beyond the boundaries of the scriptures did not exist; as though religion still held solutions to all human problems.[195] Their retreat from Ibn Taymiyya's notion of "rebellion against an infidel ruler" was justified not on a critique of such fatwas in essence, but on the grounds that the Egyptian state had ceased to be an "infidel" because it had indeed accepted Shariʿa.[196] Otherwise, for these Jamaʿa leaders, overthrowing a secular state was still permissible. The Jamaʿa's ideologues made it clear that the group had not surrendered its demand for a state ruled by Islam. What it had changed was the way to achieve this objective. They continued to revere the spirit of Ibn Taymiyya—his absolute belief in the supremacy of sacred text and the indissoluble link between religion and the state, the very injunctions that had already inflicted enduring scars on religious thought and politics in Egypt.[197] The "new" Jamaʿa did not cease to uphold *hisba* as the legal guardian of religion—when the state proves unable to enforce religious obligations in society, they still believed, then the *hisba* law should.[198]

Like the new peaceful al-Jamaʿa, the Muslim Brothers' use of modern political vocabularies had serious limitations. Democracy was acceptable as long as "it did not contradict the scriptures, the Qur'an and sunna."[199] For the Muslim Brothers, the value of democratic principles lay in procedures, primarily in serving to implement Shariʿa rather than in expressing the will of the populace to govern themselves. "What if in a Muslim society citizens decide to follow secular laws?" I asked ʿAsam al-Eryan. "Good true Muslims cannot and will not ignore Shariʿa," he presumed. The Muslim Brothers assumed religious authority would safeguard society over people's own judgment of themselves. In fact, none of the existing Islamic factions, including al-Wasat, could tolerate a Muslim exiting his religion, the penalty for which is death. All favored a state crackdown on what they described as "immoral" lifestyles and artistic expression, and were impatient with nonreligious behavior.[200]

The only modernist voice came from a handful of "Islamic liberals" such as Muhammad Selim al-Awa, Muhammad Imara, Tariq al-Bishri, and Ahmad Kamal Abul-Majd, all of whom appeared to speak the language of *tanwīr* (enlightenment) integrating notions of democracy, civil society, and human rights into their doctrines.[201] Although some critics argued that these intellectuals used such modern concepts to counter secularists with their own idioms and to secure "recognition for the Islamic camp,"[202] the social impact of these religious intellectuals remained negligible. Neither their small follow-ing nor their "modernist" project made significant inroads into society. Far from turning into an intellectual basis for a religious reformation movement, the idea of *tanwīr* progressively retreated, giving way to the fundamentalist-scripturist onslaught. The dominant voice remained that of the Salafis, the *ahl al-hadīth*, who projected the Islam of early *sahāba* (the Prophet's compan-ions) as simultaneously the "religion, the state, the prayer, and rule" to fight innovation (*bid'a*), historicism, and pluralism. Their core institution, the semiofficial Jama'iyya Ansar al-Sunna al-Muhammadiyya, controlling 500 mosques and scores of schools and welfare associations, carried the banner of preserving a puritan Islam that "applied to all times and places."[203]

Thus there was little in Egypt's religious thought to match the critical edge of Iran's post-Islamism or the innovation and vigor of its Turkish counter-part.[204] In the Egypt of the late 1990s, the dominant religious thought had in effect receded a century to before the time of Rifa' al-Tahtawi, Muhammad 'Abduh, and Rashid Reda, the modernist protagonists who had carried the banner of religious reformation. *Al-Manar al-Jadid* of the late 1990s, seem-ingly the most innovative publication of religious thought, barely matched its predecessor, *al-Manar* (1896–1936), in scope and perspective,[205] and was much more limited in its circulation.[206] The *tanwīr* of the 1930s had lost to the textu-alist dogma of a revived Ibn Taymiyya.[207]

The degeneration in religious thought resonated in what was a deep stagna-tion in Egypt's intellectual life. Scores of Arab critics, including Edward Said, Muhammad Sid-Ahmed, Sabri Hafez, Samia Mehrez, Bashir Nafi, and Hazem Saghiya, deplored with great anguish the degeneration of intellectual qual-ity in scholarship, journalism, artistic expression, political writing, and social criticism. "Egypt was once the *qibla* [center] of progress and enlightenment in the Arab World," "a safe haven for all kinds of Arab and Muslim intellectuals and political activists,"[208] one lamented. "It has now become one of the reasons for its cultural deterioration."[209] The cosmopolitan communities and culture and the flourishing intellectual and artistic life of the 1930s had declined to narrow-minded outlooks coupled with consumer culture.[210] In 1997 only 375 books were published in Egypt, compared with thousands of books and some

200 newspapers and journals at the beginning of the Liberal Age in the 1930s.[211] Ironically, in this age of high piety, bestsellers consisted overwhelmingly of sleaze literature.[212] Egyptian journalism, the oldest among Middle Eastern countries, regressed to "the profession of those without a profession," according to Saʿid ʿAbdal-Khaliq of al-Wafd.[213] Its oldest daily, al-Ahram, deteriorated to the extent that, according to Muhammad Sid-Ahmed, intellectuals read it "mainly to see who died."[214] Egypt had produced better and freer cinema in the 1930s than it did in the late 1990s.[215] The nation's cultural production was relegated to the inelegant singer Shaʿban ʿAbd al-Rahim, "Shaʿbula," whose immense popularity and vulgarity compelled the Majlis al-Shura to debate this "phenomenon."[216] No wonder the veteran journalist Jamal Badawi mourned the "death of Egypt's enlightenment" in this "age of Shaʿbula."[217]

In what Sabry Hafez described as "these bleak conditions,"[218] the average Egyptian intellectual was imbued with a deep-seated "nativism," an outlook that fostered insularity, a particularistic mindset, and intolerance.[219] He established a binary opposition between an "authentic" national self and the alien cultural "West," with an epistemological implication summed up in the dictum "taʿaruf al-ashyaʾ bi azdhadiha" (things are known by their opposites). Thus ideas and individuals were valued not on their own merits but for their imagined geographic origins. The nativist intellectual remained oblivious to the fact that the "indigenous" and "alien" were in constant interaction and modification, and that so many of his own cultural traits (dress code, food, entertainment) had originally been "alien" before they became "indigenized."

Uncritical exaltation of an imagined "golden age" and "indigenous" culture often blinded the nativist intelligentsia to domestic failures and shortcomings, causing them to seek justification outside the national self. Consequently, conspiracy theory, this antipode of critical inquiry, virtually turned into a paradigm to explain misfortunes. "Whoever follows the position of most of Egypt's intellectuals, journalists, and politicians," an Arab columnist put it sarcastically, "begins to think that the world wakes up every morning, rubs its eyes, and exclaims: 'Oh my goodness, it's seven. I am late, I have to start immediately to conspire against Egypt.'"[220] The domineering regional policies of Israel and the United States made them the prime source of conspiratorial imaginations. The brutality of Israeli occupation was found not only in subjugating the Palestinian people but also in entangling the mainstream Arab intelligentsia in an unrefined and black-and-white view of the world. Thus a spate of elaborate stories emerged in the print media and in public discourse about how, according to al-*Ahram al-Arabi* and *Rawz al-Yusif*, for instance, the Israeli Mossad and the CIA were behind the Luxor massacre.[221] An Islamist member of Parliament went so far as to claim in 2002 that the sanitary towels the Ministry of Education provided for girls in schools were funded by a Jewish-owned U.S. company and could make Egyptian girls infertile.[222] Most Egyptian intellectuals withheld support from the convicted sociologist Saad Eddin Ibrahim because he had accepted research funds from abroad, had friends in the West, and favored normalization with Israel. When the Bush administration, in August 2002, criticized the Egyptian government for its prosecution of Ibrahim, the nationalist anti-American outcries virtually stifled the voices of human rights victims at home. The Egyptian intelligentsia failed to develop a position to oppose U.S. foreign policy in the Middle East and, at the same time, to campaign for human rights and democratic freedoms at home. Thus the humiliating surveillance of Israeli-U.S. allies in the region drove generations of Arab intellectuals into a narrow-minded nativism and cultural nationalism that largely benefited authoritarian Arab states. The struggle to work toward democracy at home lost out to the fervent desire to regain dignity abroad.[223]

There was still the problem of confidence. A critique of the self demands self-confidence. One needs to be intellectually secure enough to publicly utter "I do not know," or to acknowledge one's own shortcomings and one's opponents' achievements. Poverty of perspective and the shortage of intellectual courage make the nativist intelligentsia further inward-looking, defensive, and demagogic, often reluctant to engage, exchange, and modify ideas. The more insular one becomes, the less one learns about the complexities of the "other" culture, so that imagination becomes a substitute for inquiry.[224]

As much as they ignored or attacked the "culture" of "the other," nativists cherished anything they considered "authentic," religion being the most important. As an element of *turāth* (heritage), Islam became a fundamental ingredient in intellectuals' worldview, with serious implications for cultural production in Egypt. By sharing the languages of religiosity and cultural nationalism, nativist intellectuals, the religious establishment, and the state formed a tacit discursive block to the detriment of genuine *tanwīr* and critical thought. Indeed, the institutional structure for this shared discourse had already been established since at least the time of Nasser, who incorporated both religious elites and the intelligentsia (editors of newspapers, magazines, writers, artists, managers of cultural institutions) into the state structure, making them state employees. In this tense cohabitation, the "cultural actor" maneuvered between the "religious" and the "political," cultivating support on one side when threatened from the other. Thus the mainstream intelligentsia often sought protection instead of independence; "rather than spearhead criticism, they have demonstrated compliance."[225] The ultimate casualties of this state of affairs were critical voices, independent minds, and innovative thinking. The ill-fated blend of authoritarian polity, religious morality, and nativist sensibilities progressively constricted the room to entertain democratic ideals, alternative thought, and self-criticism. It was within this paltry intellectual atmosphere that the likes of 'Amr Khalid rose to stardom and moral authority unintentionally cementing Egypt's path toward an Islamic passive revolution.

FROM THE "PASSIVE REVOLUTION" INTO A NEW DAWN?

The tidal wave of Islamism that seemed poised to wash away the Egyptian state actually left it intact and subsided by the late 1990s. In fact, the state skillfully surfed the wave, weathered its initial crash ashore, and rode its smooth sprawl into society. But along the way society, state, and movement all went through significant change. The Islamist movement rendered the state more religious (as it moved to rob Islamism of its moral authority), more nationalist and nativist (as the state moved to assert its cultural Arab-Islamic authenticity), and more repressive, since the liquidation of radical Islamists offered the opportunity to control other forms of dissent. The "secularreligious" state both controlled and connected with conservative social forces, hindering the rise of innovative intellectual and political initiatives.

Egypt's religious thought remained stagnant not because Sunni Islam had an intrinsic limitation that stifled innovation; after all, Turkish post-Islamists also came from a Sunni tradition. Rather, the rigidity of religious thought in Egypt owed a great deal to the absence of effective societal pressure or pervasive social movements, that would have compelled religious authority to rethink its orthodoxy, transcend strict adherence to scriptures, and open up to a republican theology. Even intellectual leadership remained largely complicit. Neither the state nor societal forces questioned the prevailing "fundamentalist" reading of Islam. Those who did so fell victim to Islamist fury, since no effective popular outcry came to their rescue.[226]

Civil society dominated by Islamist sensitivities served the nation's authoritarian ethos and the state's undemocratic character. By its ability to maneuver between religion, nation, and repression, the ruling elite managed to dodge the popular anger unleashed by the volatile post–September 11 years. Israel's violence against the Palestinians and the U.S. "war on terror" fueled nationalist-religious sentiment that the elite deftly redirected toward external adversaries. Entrenched in "old-fashioned pan-Arab nationalism," and lured by the language of religiosity and moral politics, the political class failed to forge a movement to rectify authoritarian rule at home.

The trajectory of Egyptian religious politics in the 1990s, then, radically departed from that of Iran. Out of the anomalies of Iran's Islamic Republic had emerged social movements (formed by Muslim women, youths, the intelligentsia, and other grassroots clusters) that aspired to undo Islamism altogether, deploying a perception of Islam that could embrace democratic ideals and individual liberties. Struggle for democracy had been placed at the top of society's agenda; the challenge, however, was how to impose this demand on the state. Social movements with similar democratic aims were lacking in Egypt. It is true that the U.S. "call for democracy" in the region had already instigated a few policy initiatives from above, such as some alterations in textbooks, a moderate tone of official religious discourse, and some "political reforms" by the NDP in dialogue with legal opposition parties.[227] However, Egypt's "reform initiative," prompted from abroad and above, proved no more than a "false spring" and got bogged down in reluctance and procrastination.[228] If anything, U.S. pressure, instead of enhancing democracy, delegitimized the initiative, for it had been proposed by an "occupying power."

Egypt needed broad societal pressure to compel both the traditional political forces (political parties and the Islamist movement) and the regime to push for intellectual change and democratic reform. Only as late as 2004 did signs of an embryonic and fragmented movement seem to surface. Described as a "new dawn" in the nation's political life, it was reflected in the simultaneous constellation of several social developments. A number of new independent dailies, notably *al-Misr al-Yowm*, *Nahdit Misr*, *al-Dustur*, and an energized *al-'Arabi*, brought fresh air to the morbid body of Egyptian press, so that even the government publications began to raise more critical voices. Within the ruling NDP emerged a new trend calling for the democratization of the party, while the newly established Ghad Party seriously contested the Mubarak regime. More important was the formation of the nascent Egyptian Movement for Change (*Kifaya*, meaning "enough"), which placed democratic transformation at the top of its agenda. The novelty of this movement was that it chose to work with "popular forces" rather than traditional opposition parties, it brought the campaign into the streets instead of broadcasting it from headquarters, and it concentrated primarily on domestic concerns rather than nationalistic demands. Resting broadly on the campaign of intellectuals, rights activists, NGOs, women's groups, Muslims and Coptic Christians alike, Kifaya embraced activists from multiple ideological orientations, including Nasserists (notably its new *Karāma* group), nationalists, communists, liberals, and those with an Islamist orientation.

Significantly, these developments converged against the background of an escalating spirit of protest in Egyptian society. After years of political intimidation and fear, Egyptians began to express their grievances in the streets more daringly and loudly. Kifaya and then Muslim Brotherhood supporters broke the taboo of unlawful street marches by staging numerous demonstrations and rallies in urban squares. Protesters chanted political slogans calling for an end to Emergency Law, the release of political prisoners, and no more torture, and they urged President Mubarak to step down. Judges, journalists, students, workers, and college professors formed new institutions (the Popular Campaign for Change, the National Coalition for Democratic Transformation, the National Alliance for Reform and Change, Youths for Change, College Faculty for Change, The Street Is Ours, and others) and organized rallies around explicitly political demands. A new political climate, a "Cairo spring" imbued with a sense of optimism and hope had been created, one that reminded one of the Iran of the late 1990s.

How and why did such a mood and movement come to life suddenly after years of stagnation and nativist politics? It had a precursor, largely rooted in the sentiments and activities that surrounded the Egyptian Popular Committee for Solidarity with the Palestinian Intifada (EPCSPI). Set up in October 2000 to protest the Israeli siege of the Palestinian territories in 2000 and then the U.S.-led occupation of Iraq, the EPCSPI had brought together representatives from Egypt's various political trends, including leftists, nationalists, Islamists, women's activists, and human rights groups. It spearheaded a new style of communication, organizational flexibility, and mobilization. It set up a website, developed a mailing list, initiated charity drives, organized boycotts of American and Israeli products, revived street actions, and collected 200,000 signatures on petitions to close down the Israeli embassy in Cairo. The Egyptian Anti-Globalization Group and the National Campaign Against the War on Iraq, the Committee for the Defense of Workers' Rights, and some human rights NGOs, adopted similar styles of activism.[229] Thousands of young Egyptian volunteers and hundreds of companies and organizations collected food and medicine for Palestinians, and boycotts of American and Israeli products drew in many more. Alternative news websites fostered networks of critical and informed constituencies. Satellite TV rapidly spread in the Arab world, helping to bring unusual information to break the hold of the barren domestic news channels.

Kifaya, whose leaders had already been active in EPCSPI, built on this experience to foreground Egypt's nascent "democracy movement"; it did so within a global and national setting that had been deeply transformed. Having emerged out of new international conditions in which the language of democracy had been central, and triggered by the prospect of President Mubarak seeking a fifth term in office, Kifaya placed electoral reform at the center of its campaign. On the other hand, glaring inequality and declining purchasing power had already rendered lower- and middle-class Egyptians weary of a regime that had extended its repressive measures beyond the Islamist insurgents onto ordinary citizens.[230] Egyptians could feel, for instance, how in the aftermath of the terrorist bombing in Taba in 2005, security forces had rounded up and held some 2,400 people without charges.[231] At the same time, President Mubarak had begun to lose the raison d'etre of anti-Israeli rhetoric, which had long galvanized nationalist sentiment. With a prospect of declining tension in Palestinian-Israeli conflicts following the death of Yasser Arafat, the presidency of Mahmud 'Abbas, and the prospect of Israeli withdrawal from Gaza, Mubarak became increasingly close to Ariel Sharon. His new trade deal with the United States, which required the inclusion of Israel as a third party, exploded in the Egyptian media as the "second Camp David." Consequently, with international pressure mounting on Egypt, the regime became increasingly vulnerable and defensive, and political activists found a space to be extraordinarily daring in their protest and mobilization.

In this midst, the language of reform uttered by a "modernizing'" faction of the ruling elite, led by Jamal Mubarak, supplied a political opportunity for activists to raise their voices in the street and in print. In conditions where Kifaya appeared as the new effective player on Egypt's political stage, the Muslim Brotherhood surfaced once again in a state of nervousness and yet determination. Maneuvering between cooperating with Kifaya in a united front and acting as the sole opposition to the regime, the MB began to mobilize in earnest—in the streets, in organizations, and on college campuses.

As usual, they used the occasions of Ramadan *iftār* and funerals to assemble; while their student organizations came from underground, attempting along with the socialist and Nasserist student groups to form an activist alliance of college students.

It was the collective sentiment around such a rudimentary "democracy movement" that galvanized international support and compelled the Egyptian government in May 2005 to amend the constitution to allow for competitive presidential elections. Beyond influencing the behavior of the regime, the unfolding movement also enforced a slight shift in religio-political language. Pushed by the rising popularity of democratic demands, mindful of not falling behind the new popular dissent and being in tune with the international discourse on democracy, the Muslim Brothers' younger leadership conceded to some aspects of democratic discourse. The MB seemed to move away from the idea of establishing an Islamic caliphate based on Qur'anic *shura* (consultation) toward acknowledging the rights of the Coptic minority, behaving like a political party, and speaking the language of citizenship and political equality. Even though adopting such ideas fell far short of a post-Islamist turn, it was a significant development in Egyptian politics.

It is premature to pronounce this fragile movement a harbinger of a democratic Egypt. The balance of power remains disproportionately in favor of the ruling elites, and the rigid political structure continues to rein in the nation. Even the amended constitution continues to exclude many from participating in multicandidate presidential elections. Although the opposition Muslim Brotherhood captured a record eighty-eight seats in the legislative elections of 2005, the Parliament remained in full control of the ruling NDP. With its two-thirds majority, the NDP can in theory pass any law deemed necessary to consolidate its position. But the NDP's parliamentary majority was achieved through blatant manipulation, fraud, and violence. At polling places in the marginal constituencies, the police either ignored or sided with thuggish elements who physically prevented voters from entering the polling stations, making sure the MB candidates would not win. Scenes of men and women climbing over the fences of polling stations to cast their votes, or lying down on roads to block the NDP convoys bringing supporters from other constituencies, were indeed remarkable. Such acts of resistance, reminiscent of the anti-fascist struggles of Italian peasants in Bertolucci's *1900*, however, were too sporadic to break the structure of power. Indeed, the "democracy movement" remained the preoccupation of limited activists. Kifaya's calls to boycott the referendum did not resonate among ordinary Egyptians, who for the most part stayed uninformed and aloof.

On the other hand, the Muslim Brotherhood's new language of democracy remained acutely uncertain and ambivalent, reflecting both experimentation and a growing generational struggle within the movement. Alongside the idioms of "pluralism" and "popular will," the leadership still spoke of the supremacy of Shari'a, the age-old dictum *"Islām huwa al-hall"* (Islam is the solution), and Islam as both religion and state.[232] Without undertaking a comprehensive internal debate and deliberation, and engulfed by generational rift, the group seemed to be carried by events. Chiefly pushed by international and domestic events, the leadership did adopt new vocabularies without, however, discarding the old ones. The MB's "reform initiatives" of 2004 were too slim either to place them "very close" to principles propounded by al-Wasat, or for that matter to reflect a "post-Islamist" turn.[233] The rising fortune of the Muslim Brothers in the legislative elections had as much to do with their power of mobilization as the people's mistrust of the ruling NDP's corruption, thuggery, and violence.[234]

By 2005, Egyptian politics had taken a new turn, marked by a new hope, energy, and outlook. Yet the drive for meaningful democratic reform encountered formidable structural impediments. Even if such societal energy develops into a robust democracy movement like Iran's reform movement, it still has to overcome the challenge of incumbent powerholders who may once again resort to religion, nation, and coercion to preserve the status quo. The question of political power is yet to be settled.

6 THE POLITICS OF PRESENCE
Imagining a Post-Islamist Democracy

IF ONE OBVIOUS CONCLUSION can be drawn from the preceding chapters, it is that Islam is the subject of intense conflict between diverse segments of the faithful. Women, youths, the middle classes, the poor and the powerful, the "modern" and the "traditional," clerics and laymen are all engaged in redefining the truth of their creed through either ordinary daily practice or deliberate campaigns. In doing so, they render religion a plural reality with multiple meanings.

As the foregoing discussions demonstrated, some groups vehemently opposed democratic principles on the grounds that sovereignty belonged to God, not to the people. For them, democracy meant the "dictatorship of capital" and the supremacy of consumerism, and they feared its practice would strip them of their position and power. In contrast, many Muslims fought for democratic ideals, citizen participation, individual rights, pluralism, and tolerance, and they did so at the risk of persecution and prison. For many, Islam was not only compatible with democracy; their association was "inevitable." And then there were those, the extremely poor, whose preoccupation with daily subsistence rendered them unavailable to show interest in such quarrels.

Therefore, congruence between Islam and democracy is not simply a philosophical issue, as it is widely assumed, but a political one.[1] It is a matter of struggle. The pertinent question is not whether Islam and democracy are compatible (least of all because of the contested meanings attached to both Islam and democracy), but rather how and under what conditions Muslims can *make* their religion compatible with desired notions of democracy; how they can legitimize and popularize an inclusive reading of their doctrine in the same way that democrats have been struggling to broaden narrow (white, male, propertied, and merely liberal) notions of democracy. I am aware of no Muslim who expresses this vision more vividly than Mustafa Tajzadeh, a reformist interior vice-minister in the Islamic Republic of Iran. Commenting on the ambiguity of Iran's constitution regarding democracy and theocracy, he argues: "even if a text was despotic, our national, regional and global conditions would call upon us to come up with a democratic interpretation; because our independence, territorial integrity, our security and national interest are tied to such deduction. When you can turn English monarchy into democracy, or develop a democratic Marxism, why not democratize the Islamic Republic?"[2] In other words, we humans define the truth of sacred texts. "We can question all and every religious injunction . . . if they do not lead us to justice," the cleric Ahmad Qabil stated, endorsing democracy in Iran.[3]

But the mere individual's ambition to present alternative understanding may not go very far. Nasr Abu Zayd's endeavor to offer an unorthodox approach to interpreting the Qur'an earned him the wrath of the conservative religious establishment in Egypt, leading to his banishment from his homeland and its religious scene. Engaging in social and intellectual mobilization, building networks of activism, and providing education must be accomplished on a massive scale. There is no escape from mobilizing consensus around a libratory interpretation of religion whenever and wherever religion becomes a key element in popular ethos. Indeed, concurrent with the spread of religious conservatism in the Muslim world, and of anti-Islamic sentiment in the West following the September 11 attacks, various networks and organizations began to convey the message that Islam is in principle a democratic religion, and that those who think otherwise are misguided.[4] These networks and groups have emerged largely in Western nations, mostly in cyberspace, and are aimed primarily at educating—often in a defensive tone—non-Muslims. However, the major challenge is to forge intellectual and social mobilization in nations with a Muslim majority in order to challenge both the authoritarian (religious or secular) regimes and the "fundamentalist" opposition. Such movements would inevitably democratize religious discourse and the authoritarian states that often benefit from the orthodox presentation of religion.

Indeed, some hopeful signs can already be observed. Since the late 1990s, against the backdrop of intensifying religious sentiment in the Muslim world, a nascent post-Islamist trend has begun to accommodate aspects of democratization, pluralism, women's rights, youth concerns, and social development with adherence to religion. Hizbullah transcended its exclusivist Islamist platform by adapting to the pluralistic political reality of Lebanon. In Egypt, Hizb al-Wasat dissociated itself from both the violent strategy of al-Jama'a and the authoritarian disposition of its Muslim Brotherhood predecessors. Even in Saudi Arabia, a post-Wahabi trend attempted to incorporate notions of "liberal Islam" seeking a compromise with democracy.[5] While the Islamist Hizb Tahrir held its ground in Tajikistan, the Islamic Renaissance Party (IRP) was integrated into that country's secular political process.[6] The Jama'at-i Islami of India has experienced a qualitative shift from a movement resting on an organic, complete, and exclusivist Islam—one that rejected democracy and was intolerant of other faithlines—into a movement that embraces ambiguity and interpretation in its foundational thoughts, values democracy and pluralism, and cooperates with ideological "others."[7] Leaders of the current Moroccan religious movement, *al-'Adl wa al-Ihsān* (justice and benevolence), discard an exclusive understanding of Islam, rely on interpretation and historicizing, and acknowledge flexibility and ambiguity; they reject imposing Shari'a laws or the wearing of the *hijāb* and endorse human rights, pluralism, democracy, and separation of powers.[8] And notwithstanding an initial unease in the West about growing religious revivalism, Turkey has barely experienced typical Islamist politics; instead, its major religious parties (the Welfare Party, the Virtue Party, and particularly the Justice and Development Party) have espoused a largely post-Islamist disposition, advocating a pious society in a secular democratic state. However, except for Turkey, which already had a multiparty democracy, none of these movements have assumed governmental power to consider how and to what extent they would be willing or able to forge a democratic governance. How then can we examine the sociopolitical environment that allows one to envision a post-Islamist democracy?

CONTRASTING TRAJECTORIES

In narrating the histories of socioreligious movements in Iran and Egypt in the past three decades, I have attempted to demonstrate in detail how and under what conditions Muslim social forces may, or may not, be able to get Islam to embrace a democratic ethos. The paradoxes of Iran's Islamic Republic generated oppositional, post-Islamist movements that espoused and popularized ideas of secular democratic polity, gender equality, and inclusive religiosity.

In the aftermath of a revolution in which they had participated massively, Iranian women faced an authoritarian Islamic regime that imposed forced veiling, gender segregation, and widespread surveillance and revoked the prerevolutionary laws that favored women. Women responded by deploying their "power of presence" in the public sphere and through deliberate campaigns articulated largely in religious idioms. By their daily resistance and struggles, women conveyed a reading of Islam that promoted gender equality and egalitarian ethics, denouncing the Islamization of the state that interfered in private lives. Piety was to be a choice rather than an obligation. In contrast, Egyptian middle-class and well-to-do women followed a new conservative religiosity, or active piety, which accompanied widespread veiling, indifference to gender hierarchy, and values that reinforced patriarchal relations. Unlike many Iranian women who embraced feminism, Muslim women activists in Egypt showed little interest in gender issues. Theirs was a concern for individual self-enhancement through religious devotion and pietistic behavior. In a sense, Iranian women were exiting from what Egyptian women aspired to.

Facing similar social control, the young in Iran took up parallel social and political aspirations. In fact young people in both countries tended to reimagine Islam in ways that suited their youthful sensibilities, a practice that inevitably fragmented religious perceptions and defied religious authority's narrow and exclusive interpretations. But in Iran, where moral and political authority converged, draconian social control gave rise to a unique youth identity and collective defiance. Young people both became central to and were further mobilized by the post-Islamist reform movement. The assertion of youthful aspirations, the defense of their habitus, lay at the heart of their conflict with moral and political authority. With the state as the target of their struggles, Iranian youths engendered one of the most remarkable youth movements in the Muslim world. The struggle to reclaim youthfulness melded with the effort to attain democratic ideals. In contrast, Egyptian youth, operating under the constraints of "passive revolution," opted for the strategy of "accommodating innovation," attempting to lodge their youthful claims within the existing political, economic, and moral conditions. In the process, they redefined dominant norms and institutions, merged divine and diversion, and adopted more inclusive religious mores. Yet this subculture took shape within, not against or outside, the existing regime of moral and political power; Egyptian youth did not form a movement of their own or develop political clout. They never confidently articulated their unorthodox practice of Islam as a credible perspective, but instead expressed remorse and apologized for what they considered their "wrongdoings."

The post-Islamist intellectuals in Iran went beyond systematically enunciating what Muslim youths and women voiced in daily life. To secure both the sanctity of religion and the rationality of the state, they called for a secular democratic polity, challenging orthodox religious interpretations through hermeneutic and historical methods, which opened the way for a significant rethinking of sacred texts. Post-Islamist intellectuals transcended revolutionary and nationalist ideologies, consciously embraced modernity, pluralism, and human rights, while also cherishing faith and spirituality. Their "postcolonial" position in rejecting the dichotomy of a "national" self versus the "Western" other further distanced them from Egypt's intellectual class, who were imbued with nationalism and moral politics. Engulfed by the pervasive "Islamic mode," the Egyptian intelligentsia converged with the major actors in society, including the new rich, ruling elites, and al-Azhar, to share the language of nativism and conservative moral ethos to the detriment of critical voices, innovative religious thought, and effective calls for democratic change.

Only the urban poor exhibited a remarkably similar politics in the two countries; they tended to practice their folk religion and pursue pragmatic relations with both Islamist and post-Islamist movements. Their tactical support, whether of the opposition or the state, depended on their perceived immediate gains. Otherwise, the poor ordinarily remained preoccupied with the everyday struggle for survival and self-development. This confirmed the fact that the poor could not afford to be ideological; their precarious life compels them to adhere to meaningful and manageable strategies that yield a direct outcome. Such pragmatic politics challenged the assumption that viewed the urban poor as harbingers of populist anti-democratic sentiment in the Muslim world, even though, rather than spearheading the struggle for democracy, the poor left that fight to the political class, the middle layers, the intelligentsia, and the students.

But why did these two Muslim nations experience two different types of socioreligious movements—one inclined toward democratic politics and a secular state, and the other toward nationalist-religious dogma and a moralist polity? Rather than reducing the explanation to differences in Sunni and Shi'a doctrines or in political cultures, the logic should be sought in the consequences of "revolution" versus "social movement"—the fact that Iran experienced an Islamic revolution without an Islamic movement, while Egypt developed an Islamist movement without a revolution.

Revolutions signify extraordinary change par excellence, rare moments of utopian visions and extreme measures, followed by contestation and compromise to merge utopian ideals with hard realities, thus leading to surging dissent from both the revolutionary ranks and opponents. The Islamic revolution involved particular incongruities: its distinctly religious ideology and moralist regime that, paradoxically, ruled a modern citizenry through a modern state. Although the Islamic revolution caused divergence and dissent at home, it inspired Islamist movements around the Muslim world, including Egypt. The paradoxes of the Iranian revolution and the Islamic state gave birth, within two decades, to wide-ranging post-Islamist movements that aimed to undo Islamism as a political project. In contrast, in Egypt, where an Islamic revolution failed to materialize, Islamism grew in the form of a social movement to spark fundamental changes in society through *da'wa* and associational work. With a conservative moral vision, populist language, patriarchal disposition, and adherence to scripture, the movement continued to struggle for the Islamization of both society and the state. In short, Egyptian Islamists aspired to what Iranian post-Islamists were struggling to leave behind.

Of course, the states did not remain aloof from these complex processes and struggles. While social struggles in Iran deepened the divide between the rising post-Islamist and eroding Islamist trends, Egyptian Islamism intensified the tension between religious and secular sensibilities, leading in the end to a hybrid entity embodied in a "seculareligious" state. At the same time, tensions between the "regimes" and the "states" also increased. Regimes represented the ideology, structure, and governing mode of the political elites, who ruled through the "states"—the institutions that organize, supervise, and regulate national societies. The logic and imperatives that governed the states came to clash with those of the regimes. Indeed, notable opposition to the Islamic regime in Iran came from the state institutions (the bureaucracy, central bank, planning apparatus, and the like) whose functionaries wished to assert their secular, rational, and modernist logic, even though the discrepancies between the two began to crumble later. In somewhat similar fashion, a few institutions of the Egyptian state such as al-Azhar, the judiciary, and the legislature, clashed with Mubarak's regime, which was committed to international secular standards and expectations.

The outcome of these conflicts and negotiations was an ironic convergence between the states in Iran and Egypt. While Egypt's secular regime made overtures with Islamic sensibilities, Iran's Islamic state moved toward secular pursuits. Yet both retained their overall authoritarian political control. In Iran, conservative Islamists coercively halted reformist advances while making piecemeal concessions. And the Egyptian state, by appropriating aspects of conservative religiosity and nationalist sentiment underwent an Islamic "passive revolution," a sort of managed religious restoration in which the state, in reality the target of change, succeeded in staying in charge. Even though the fragile Kifaya movement pointed to some change in the political climate and religious discourse, political structure in Egypt remained authoritarian, religious thought largely stagnant and exclusive, and the political class nativist. Little in Egypt resembled Iran's Post-Islamist trajectory.

Iran's pioneering post-Islamism was remarkably pervasive in perspective and far-reaching in outcome. It emerged in a nation that had experienced the first Islamic state in the modern times. The movement made great strides in popularizing the ideals of pluralism, nonviolence and a democratic polity; it transformed religious thought and ascended to governmental power by taking over the executive and legislative branches. Yet despite its decade-long presence in civil society and the state, Iran's post-Islamist movement was forced into retreat by the conservative Islamist faction. The reformists' Parliament was made powerless, their press smothered, their activists arrested, and their president helpless. Out of three phases of democratic reform envisaged by the post-Islamists (i.e., bringing in line the nonelected institutions of the state; establishing a democratic interpretation of the constitution; and finally changing the constitution in favor of a full-fledged democratic polity), the reform government got bogged down in the first.[9] Many native observers attributed the source of the conflict to a clash between "tradition" (represented by conservative Islamists) and "modernity" (spearheaded by post-Islamist reformers), as if holding onto power in the name of "religious values" played little role.

Just as Iran's post-Islamism failed to democratize and fully secularize the Islamic state, Egypt's Islamist movement failed to fully "Islamize" the Egyptian state. Both movements encountered serious obstacles in transforming the polity, notwithstanding their strong social power. The regime in Egypt managed to crush the radical Islamists and curb the gradualist Muslim Brotherhood (MB), while attempting to project itself as a state committed to religious sensibilities. The Islamist movement failed to alter the polity not because Egypt's Islamism itself was undemocratic, which it was, but rather because the state did not tolerate any formidable opposition, whether democratic or undemocratic, Islamist or secular. In other words, the political impasse in both of these countries was less a function of religion than of structural impediments and the longtime vested interests of ruling elites.

SOCIAL MOVEMENTS AND POLITICAL CHANGE

To what extent then can social movements in the Middle East alter the political status quo without resorting to violent revolutions? The debate over social movements in general swirls intensely around the modalities of social mobilization, around how the movements are made. Few analyses of the relationship between social movements and sociopolitical change venture beyond what protest actions may entail in either repression or reform.[10] More significantly, little attention is paid to the interplay of social movement activism and state power.[11] The "Westo-centric" orientation of social movement theory, rooted in the democratic structures of Western societies, treats social movements as merely the stuff of civil society, where collective protests, lobbying, and pressure are used to force legal change. For the most part, the state and its coercive power matter little. At the same time, the "decentered" understanding of power, notwithstanding its merits, has drastically undercut our attention to state power as a key medium of social and political transformation. For such thinkers as Alberto Melucci and Manuel Castells, for instance, the new social movements (feminist or environmentalist) are not against the dominant power but rather against "dominant codes," principally because no one knows where power lies, or because it is entirely diffused.[12] Foucault, among others, is right in insisting that altering the state's power might not necessarily lead to transformations in other areas of social life such as the family, the workplace, or gender relations,[13] but this should not downplay the debilitating role of the state against a social movement's forward march. At the same time, both the liberal and (orthodox) Marxian perspectives offer little help, since they regard the state either as a neutral and coherent institution that represents the public interest (a liberal view), or as the "executive organ of the ruling class" that cannot be won over without a violent revolution (an orthodox Marxian view). Joel Migdal's instructive point that the states' actual "practices" are different from, indeed more limited than, their apparent coherent and controlling "image" says, unfortunately, little about what this means to struggles that aim to change the polity.[14]

Perhaps Gramsci's perception of the state as the unity of consent and coercion, his rejection of the separation of civil society and the state, and his notions of "war of position" and "passive revolution" might signal a way out. "War of position" describes a strategy of the subaltern to establish societal hegemony—that is, to win over the hearts and minds of the majority by painstakingly working to capture trenches within civil society with the aim of encircling the state. "Passive revolution" is the political elites' strategy to avert social movements by appropriating their aims, so that the state, the original target of change, takes charge of the process. Although it unleashes some degree of reform, "passive revolution" ultimately aims to demobilize social actors. Gramsci's perspective can help us explore how societal processes, social movements as well as activism in everyday life, can contribute to refashioning state institutions and norms.

Drawing on the experience of Iran and Egypt, I suggest that multipurpose movements, such as Islamism and post-Islamism, generate change in four domains. The most common work of social movements is to pressure opponents or authorities to meet social demands.[15] This is carried out through mobilization, threatening disruption, or raising uncertainty.[16] For instance, the Islamist campaign in Egypt compelled the government to restrict many liberal publications, persecute authors, and prohibit films. Second, even if social movements are not engaged in a political campaign, they may still be involved in what Melucci calls "cultural production."[17] The very operation of a social movement is in itself a change, since it involves creating new social formations, groups, networks, and relationships. Its "animating effects," by enforcing and unfolding such alternative relations and institutions, enhance the cultural production of different value systems, norms, behavior, symbols, and discourse. This process of building "hegemony" is expressed in producing alternative ways of being and doing things. Islamism displays a most vivid example of such a moral and intellectual conquest of civil society, albeit in a conservative direction, through Islamic business, education, morality, fashions, weddings, welfare associations, and a "development model."

Third, social movements may also induce change by discretely operating on the faultline between the state and civil society—in educational, judicial, media, and other institutions. In the early 1990s, Egyptian Islamists succeeded in penetrating the state education system, influencing policy-makers, teachers, and above all a generation of students through their activities at teacher training colleges. Islamist judges, at times appearing in traditional garb, or *jalabiya*s, enforced Islamic law, punishing secular individuals while supporting Islamic-oriented legal suits. Even police and the military were not immune. Finally, social movements, if they are tolerated by the incumbent regimes, may be able to capture segments of governmental power through routine electoral means. The cases of Turkey's ruling Rifah Party and Iran's reform government are only two recent examples. Both movements managed to form legitimate governments.

However, the ability of social movements to effectively share political power depends on maintaining their popular support. Unlike the authoritarian states, which rest primarily on coercive force, social movements depend only on their capacity to mobilize their social basis; without this, movements cease to exist. The greatest challenge of a social movement is how to retain its movement character and at the same time exert governmental power. While sharing state power may enable social movements to turn some of their ideas into public policy, failure to do so, even though due to opponents' sabotage, would undermine their support base, thus rendering them powerless. First and foremost, it seems, social movements need to weave their institutional foundation into the fabric of society—something that Iran's reform movement failed to do, but Egypt's MB succeeded in doing. For not only can a solid social base compel opponents and states to undertake political reform, it can also protect movements from repression and ensure revival and continuity even after a period of downturn. Democracy movements must pay close attention to the economic dimension if they are to sustain popular support. People might prefer a populist dictator who brings them immediate prosperity over the promise of a democratic future. A UN survey of Latin America, which found that "a majority would choose a dictator over an elected leader if that provided economic benefits," indicates how real the possibility of "escape from freedom" can be.[18]

Still, crucial questions remain: To what extent can social movement mobilization enforce intended political and structural change? How far can states accommodate the radical projects of their social movement adversaries? And how far can a movement's conquest of civil society and encroachment into the political apparatus proceed? Political scientists have spoken of the possibility of a political pact in which a segment of ruling elites and the opposition come to an agreement to form a new regime. In Chile and Spain, the transition from military dictatorship to democracy took place through such a pact. On the other hand, political reform can occur when ruling groups, enveloped by popular and elite pressure (and possibly by international demand or economic crisis), see compromise as their only option. Such radical reform, or "refolution," as Kis put it, characterized Polish and Hungarian transitions to democracy.[19] In Mexico, the democracy movement (composed of students, peasants, and workers' organizations) managed a prolonged campaign that compelled the state to undertake a democratic transition in the 1990s.[20]

MIDDLE EASTERN SAGA

The Middle East experience has been quite different. Regimes have been too resistant to political change and democracy movements too feeble to force it. It is not that popular dissent has been absent or that the people are inherently indifferent to democracy. Looking back at recent history, one is struck by the extent to which popular movements arose in Syria, Iraq, Jordan, and Lebanon during the late 1950s, after Nasser nationalized the Suez Canal.[21]

The unsuccessful tripartite aggression by Britain, France, and Israel, in October 1956, to reclaim control of the canal caused an outpouring of popular protest from Arab countries in support of Egypt. Although 1956 was probably the last major pan-Arab solidarity movement until the 2002 wave of pro-Palestinian support, social protests by workers, artisans, women, and students for domestic social development, citizens' rights, and political participation have been quite significant. Labor movements in Lebanon, Syria, Egypt, Yemen, and Morocco have carried out strikes and street protests over both economic and political issues. Since the 1980s, during the era of IMF-recommended structural adjustment programs, Arab labor unions have tried to resist cancellations of consumer commodity subsidies, price rises, pay cuts, and layoffs. Despite no-strike deals and repression of activists, strike-induced work stoppages have occurred. Fear of popular resistance has often forced governments, such as those of Egypt, Jordan, and Morocco, to delay structural adjustment programs or retain certain social policies. Ordinary people have responded radically to the violation of traditional social contracts. Massive protests in Morocco, Tunis, the Sudan, Lebanon, Algeria, and Egypt during the 1980s sent strong messages to authoritarian regimes. Even though structural changes since the 1980s, such as de-peasantization, the growth of the informal sector, the fragmentation of labor, and the proliferation of NGOs, have significantly diminished class-based mobilization, street protests have flourished when opportunity has allowed. Indeed, since early 2000, popular mobilization in support of Palestinian and Iraqi people has been remarkable. In 2002, hundreds of thousands of protestors marched in Yemen, Iraq, Khartoum, Rabat, Bahrain, and Damascus against the impending U.S. attack on Iraq. For a short while, it seemed, states lost their tight control over "the street," where new, publicly vocal opposition groups multiplied.

Yet these remarkable struggles, carried out largely by the political classes, were directed primarily against outside adversaries (Israel and the United States) with the tacit but cautious endorsement of the states where they occurred, rather than against the repressive rule of those states. If anything, campaigns against authoritarian regimes have been subsumed by powerful nationalist-nativist sentiment, the kind of mass politics that can easily lend itself to enigmatic demagogues or authoritarian populists.[22] Virtue lies not in opaque mass politics but in protracted social movements that have the potential to force systematic change, and whose members are motivated not by emotional impulses or ideological devotion but by their common interests and their leaders' actions.

In Iran and Egypt, social movements succeeded in winning the hearts and minds of the majority and even threatened their governments by forcing them to change some policies, but they ultimately failed to effectively reform their states. Iran's post-Islamist reform movement penetrated the state, only to face the classic dilemma of a parallel power structure in which Islamist opponents, through their control of coercive institutions and economic networks, managed to intercept its progress. And the ruling elite in Egypt continued to neutralize the forward march of Islamism through repression, violence, and a "passive revolution." Even though they left their mark, both movements were forced into retreat. Egypt's secular state tilted toward religion while Iran's religious state became more secular, but in both cases the structures of authoritarian rule remained intact. It was as if the authoritarian "secularreligious" state had become the destined manifestation of "passive revolution" in the Muslim-majority nations of the Middle East.

Precisely because of this exasperating impasse, some social actors have opted for foreign intervention as the only possible way to remove ossified autocratic regimes and "install democracy." The "removal" of the Taliban in Afghanistan and the rapid Anglo-U.S. overthrow of the Ba'athist regime in Iraq hoped those efforts would jumpstart democratization in the Middle East. They often made reference to the democratizing experiences of Germany and Japan following their defeat in World War II, even though those countries' social structures, economies, and experience of war differed from those of the Middle East. Even more comparable "imposed democracies," such as the Philippines and Korea, had plunged into dictatorship by the 1970s. They had to wait until the 1980s and 1990s for their domestic social movements to push for homegrown democratic rules.[23]

If anything, foreign intervention in the Middle East has historically worked against, and not for, democratic governance. Most autocratic kingdoms, such as the Hashemite Kingdom of Jordan and those of the Persian Gulf, were created by Britain, which also supported Colonel Qaddafi and King Idris in Libya, both of whom went on to establish autocratic rule. The United States and Britain actively backed the Shah's dictatorship in Iran after helping to overthrow the democratic rule of Muhammad Musaddiq in the 1950s. Iraq's Ba'athist regime enjoyed U.S. and British support, as do most of the region's current authoritarian regimes: Saudi Arabia and the oil shaykhdoms, Jordan, the Turkish generals, Morocco's king, and Egypt's Mubarak. Even the Taliban once had U.S. backing, when UNOCAL wanted to build a gas pipeline through Afghanistan.

This is not to dismiss, a priori, any possible international intervention, solidarity, and support (whether from states or civil society organizations) for the project of political change.[24] The point rather is to explore how to manage foreign support. No doubt "democracy by conquest" is different from international multilateral pressure on repressive states, when it is initiated in association with endogenous pro-democracy movements in the region and draws on international consensus. It may take the form of international institutions or foreign states basing their diplomatic and economic relations on, for instance, respect for human rights. The case of apartheid in South Africa is an obvious example. Democratic Europe's political and economic pressure on its southern dictatorships (Greece, Portugal, and Spain) played a positive role. Even Turkey under Recep Tayyip Erdogan's "Islamic government" "has pulled Turkey further toward democracy than it had moved in the previous quarter century."[25] It has passed laws that have abolished the death penalty, put an end to army dominated security courts, removed curbs on free speech, brought the military budget under civilian control, authorized Kurdish-language broadcasting, and eased tension between Turkey and Greece.[26] These developments are at least partly a response to European Union demands in exchange for considering Turkey's membership.

In contrast, military occupation and war, even if launched in the name of "liberation," are not only immoral (because they presuppose domination, victimize innocent people, inflict destruction, and violate international consensus); they are also unlikely to succeed. The idea of "regime change" is rooted in the false assumption that installing "democracy" as the most noble value justifies drastic consequences and violations. The experience of Iraq confirms the point. Within the first year alone, the Anglo-U.S. occupation reportedly cost Iraq 100,000 dead, colossal material loss, and infrastructural destruction. Many people question whether "regime change" was worth the idea. Besides, at least in the Middle East, even though people long for democratic governance and participation,[27] they are unlikely to embrace it if it comes at the cost of their dignity. The march of American soldiers up and down Arab streets, even in the name of "freedom," violates Arab national dignity. It often turns people toward nativism or makes them susceptible to the demagogic manipulations of xenophobic populists who wail against democratic ideals and cosmopolitan association. Indeed, Israel's continuous occupation of Palestinian lands has already played a destructive, anti-democratic role in the Arab world. The U.S. invasion of Iraq is likely to reinforce this unfortunate legacy. Already signs are that the future of Iraq will be marred by either sectarian conflict or a centralized authoritarian state, unless a nationwide citizen movement for democracy emerges from below. Even a senior advisor to the occupation authority in Baghdad has conceded that the coalition occupation has greatly worsened the long-term prospects for democracy in Iraq.[28]

POLITICS OF PRESENCE

The region's Muslim majority, it appears, is caught between, on the one hand, authoritarian regimes and Islamist opposition, both of which tend to impose severe social control in the name of nation and religion; and on the other, flagrant foreign intervention and occupation in the name of democratization. If "democracy by conquest" is not an option, and if authoritarian states resist the democratic quest of organized movements, then what strategy can ordinary citizens pursue? Does the answer, as some might propose, lie in a rapid and violent popular revolution to depose authoritarian states?

The proposition is not as simple as it appears. First, it is doubtful that revolutions can ever be planned. Even though revolutionaries do engage in plotting and preparing, revolutions do not necessarily result from prior schemes. Rather they often follow their own mysterious logic, subject to a highly complex mix of structural, international, coincidental, and psychological factors. We often analyze revolutions in retrospect, rarely engage in ones that are expected or desired. For revolutions are never predictable. Second, most people do not particularly wish to be involved in violent revolutionary strategies.

Individuals often express cynicism about engaging in revolutions whose outcome they cannot foresee. At most, they wish to remain "free-riders," wanting *others* to carry them out on their behalf. Third, are revolutions necessarily desirable? Those who have experienced them usually identify violent revolution with massive disruption, destruction, and uncertainty. Besides, nothing guarantees that a democratic order will follow from a revolutionary change. Finally, supposing that revolutions are desirable and *can* be planned, what are people under authoritarian rule to do in the meantime? What options do they have in tackling their own repressive institutions and arrangements if they wish to avoid violent strategies?

Some might choose complicity or "loyalty" by joining mainstream currents. Others, while not approving of the status quo, might well disengage, surrendering their voice and exiting the political stage altogether in the hope that things will someday, somehow, change. Still others may choose to express their contention loudly and clearly, even if it means remaining at the margins of society—being vocal but marginal, or worse, irrelevant. It is, however, extremely challenging to be heavily *present* at the heart of society, and yet not to deviate from the objective, to be both effective and ethical. More precisely, I am referring to that delicate *art of presence* in harsh circumstances, the ability to create social space within which those individuals who refuse to exit can advance the cause of human rights, equality, and justice, and do so even under adverse political conditions. It is this difficult strategy, one that demands sharp vision, veracity, and above all endurance, that holds the most promise. Meaningful change in the Muslim Middle East may eventually benefit from such a protracted strategy.

The public life and activism of Iranian Muslim women, such as Nobel Laureate Shirin Ebadi, may illustrate that art of persistent presence. Ebadi became the first female Muslim judge in Iran; she held the presidency of Tehran's city court until the Islamic revolution, when she was forced to resign on the grounds that Islam did not allow women to be judges. Yet she and a host of women activists (religious and nonreligious) who had been demoted by the revolutionary regime refused to remain silent; they waged a relentless campaign by writing, reasoning, reinterpreting the Islamic texts, engaging in public debate, and lobbying to reverse the unjust ruling until women were once more able to serve as judges in the Islamic Republic. But such a struggle, this double strategy of no-silence and no-violence, could not have gone very far without broad societal support for change.

The idea that Muslim women should be allowed to serve as judges, only one example of the struggles taking place for gender equality in Islam, had already gained a great deal of public legitimacy through the grassroots campaigns of rights activists and ordinary men and women. Its appeal was further rooted in the yearning of Iranian women in general to assert their public presence in society, not necessarily by undertaking extraordinary activities, such as involvement in contentious politics, but through the practices of everyday life, such as working outside the home, pursuing higher education, engaging in sports, performing art and music, traveling, and executing banking transactions in place of their husbands. And these very ordinary practices, once normalized among the general public, were able to undermine gender hierarchy in society while imposing their logic on the state's political, legal, and economic institutions.

Understandably, reform of authoritarian states requires distinct and arduous struggles, the significance and difficulties of which I have already addressed. However, democratic societal change remains indispensable to meaningful and sustained democratic reform of the state. Change in society's sensibilities is the precondition for far-reaching democratic transformation. While social change might occur partly as the unintended outcome of structural processes, such as migration, urbanization, demographic shifts, or a rise in literacy, it is also partly the result of global factors and the exchange of ideas, information, and models. But the most crucial element for democratic reform is an active citizenry: a sustained presence of individuals, groups, and movements in every available social space, whether institutional or informal, collective or individual, where they assert their rights and fulfill their responsibilities. For it is precisely in such spaces that alternative ideas, practices, and politics are produced. The art of presence is ultimately about asserting collective will in spite of all odds, circumventing constraints, utilizing what is possible, and discovering new spaces within which to make oneself heard, seen, and felt. Authoritarian regimes may be able to suppress organized movements or silence collectives. But they are limited when it comes to stifling an entire society, the mass of ordinary citizens in their daily lives.

I envision a strategy whereby every social group generates change in society through active citizenship in their immediate domains: children at home and in schools, students in colleges, teachers in classrooms, workers on shop floors, athletes in stadiums, artists through their art, intellectuals through the media, women at home and in public. Not only are they to voice their claims, broadcast violations done unto them, and make themselves heard, but also to take responsibility for excelling at what they do. An authoritarian regime should not be a reason for not producing brilliant novels, intricate handicrafts, math champions, world-class athletes, dedicated teachers, or a global film industry. Excellence is power; it is identity. Through the art of presence, I imagine the way in which a society, through the practices of daily life, may regenerate itself by affirming the values that deject the authoritarian personality, gets ahead of its elites, and becomes capable of enforcing its collective sensibilities on the state and its henchmen. Citizens equipped with the art of presence would subvert authoritarian rule, since the state usually rules not as an externality to society, but by weaving its logic—through norms and institutions as well as coercion—into the fabric of society. Challenges to those norms, institutions, and the logic of power are likely to subvert a state's "governmentality," its ability to govern. In this regard, women's struggle to resist patriarchy in their day-to-day interactions becomes particularly critical, precisely because patriarchy is embedded in the perception and practice of religious authoritarian polity. Even though patriarchy may subordinate women's public presence (e.g., by bringing gender inequality into the public sphere), it cannot escape from the incrementally egalitarian effect of women's public role. When girls outnumber boys in colleges, women are more likely to become professionals whose authority men are compelled to accept, if not internalize. This alone would point to a significant shift in society's balance of power.

By the art of presence, or an active citizenry, I do not necessarily mean pervasive social movements or collective mobilization for political transformation; nor do I intend to privilege individual active citizenry over contentious movements; in fact, a citizenry of motivated individuals is likely to embrace and facilitate organized collective action. Yet I also recognize that authoritarian rule routinely impedes contentious collective actions and organized movements, and that it is unrealistic to expect a civil society to be in a constant state of vigor, vitality, and collective struggle. Society, after all, is made up of ordinary people who get tired, demoralized, and disheartened. Activism, the *extraordinary* practices that produce social change, is the stuff of *activists*, who may energize collective sentiment when the opportunity allows. The point is not to reiterate the political significance of contentious movements in causing political change, or to downplay the need to undercut the coercive power of the states. The point rather is to discover and recognize societal spaces in which lay citizens, through the ordinary practices of everyday life, through the art of presence, may recondition the established political elites and refashion state institutions into their sensibilities.

Such a refashioning of the state may result not only from an active citizenry, individual initiative, and education, but more pervasively from the long-term impact of social movement activism. Through their cultural production—establishing new social facts on the ground, new lifestyles, new modes of thinking, behaving, being, and doing—movements can acclimatize states to new societal trends. For instance, to gain legitimacy, the Egyptian government had to abide by the many, albeit conservative, codes, conducts, and institutions that Egyptian Islamism hegemonized in society. In a different setting, the Islamic Republic began to recognize the popular desire for secularization, democratic polity, and civil liberties, which Iran's social movements had helped to articulate. I call this laborious process of society influencing the state *socialization of the state*. It means conditioning the state and its henchmen to societal sensibilities, ideals, and expectations. Socialization of the state is in effect "governmentality" in reverse.[29]

It would be naive to romanticize "society" at the expense of demonizing the state. Just as states may be oppressive, societies can be divided, individualized, authoritarian, and exploitive. Feminists have long taken issue with "society" for its patriarchal disposition in the organization of the household and family life, in private relations, in science and technology, and in everyday language. We saw how Egyptian society in the 1990s pushed the state not in a democratic but in a conservative direction. In general, an effective state is indispensable in preventing not only societal abuses,[30] but also social collapse and disintegration. In short, socializing the polity (the state) to democratic values may not succeed without politicizing society in a democratic direction. Otherwise, an active citizenry can easily recede into co-optation, conservatism, orientation to market attractions, selfish individualism, or conventional globalized networks that transform it into a citizenry devoid of collective sensitivity and aspiration. It is thus crucial for an active citizenry to think and act politically, even within its own immediate sphere, even though its aim might not be revolution or regime change; but it must be concerned with solidarity, social justice, and an inclusive social order.[31]

An active citizenry of this sort cannot remain parochial, introverted, and nativist; it is compelled to join a cosmopolitan humanity, to link up with global civil activism, and to work for solidarity. Those actively present in the

Muslim Middle East cannot expect global camaraderie if they remain ignorant or indifferent to the plight of people like themselves in other corners of
the world—in Chiapas, in Darfur, or in the inner cities of the West. Nor can
they afford any longer to treat the West as though it were a unitary category,
without recognizing its internal divisions and struggles; they cannot afford
to discount the sympathy of Western humanists for the struggles of Muslims within their own societies. In turn, global recognition and solidarity
are crucial in encouraging and energizing those in the Muslim world who
endure the plight of presence. I stress recognition and solidarity rather than
acts of dismissing, stereotyping, or patronizing. But this requires a deep sensitivity to and understanding of the complex texture, multilayered dispositions, and seemingly contradictory directions of popular struggles in this
part of the world.

REFERENCE MATTER

PERSIAN AND ARABIC JOURNALS CITED

1. Persian-language periodicals published in Iran

Aftab-i Yazd, reformist daily
Bahar, reformist daily
Baztab, conservative website
Dowran-e Imruz, reformist daily
Farzānih, women's magazine
Haftih Namih-i Subh, extremist Islamist weekly
Hambastigi, reformist daily
Harim, extremist monthly
Hayat-i Naw, reformist daily
Huviyyat-i Khish, Islamist student weekly
Iran, moderate daily
Iran-i Farda, liberal Islamic monthly
Iran-i Imruz, international Persian website
Itila'at, moderate daily
Jumhūri-i Islāmi, conservative daily
Kayhan, hard-line conservative daily
Khurdad, reformist daily
Kiyan, post-Islamist monthly
Lithārāt, extremist Islamist weekly
Mashriq, extremist Islamist monthly
Mushārikat, reformist daily
Nuruz, reformist daily
Partaw-i Suhkan, conservative monthly
Payam-i Danishju, radical student magazine

Payam-i Hajar, Islamic women's magazine
Payam-i Imruz, pro-reform news monthly
Quds, conservative daily
Rah-e Now, reformist weekly.
Risālat, conservative daily
Ruydad, reformist website
Salam, reformist daily
Shalamchih, extremist Islamist weekly
Sharq, reformist daily
Womeniniran.com, feminist website
Yas-i Naw, reformist daily
Zanan, feminist monthly

2. Arabic-language periodicals published in Egypt

al-Ahram, official daily
al-Aharar, pro-government national daily
al-Ahrar al-Hilwan, local weekly
al-Ahrar al-Saʻid, regional weekly
al-Azhar, al-Azhar Institute's monthly
al-Haqiqa, social and political weekly
al-Hayat, daily Arabic international
al-Liwa' al-Islami, official Islamic weekly
al-Manar al-Jadid, analytical Islamic monthly
al-Mukhtar al-Islami, Muslim Brothers' monthly
al-Muslimun, international daily
al-Muslim al-Muʻasir, international daily
al-Muslim al-Saqir, Islamic children's magazine
al-Nur, Liberal Party/Muslim Brotherhood publication
al-Qahira, literary and social weekly
al-Shaʻb, Islamic Labor Party
al-Tasawwuf al-Islami, publication of the Sufi Council
al-Usrat al-ʻArabi, family news weekly
al-Wafd, liberal nationalist daily
ʻAqidati, pro-government Islamic weekly
Liwa' al-Islam, Muslim Brotherhood weekly magazine
Minbar al-Islam, Islamic monthly of al-Azhar
Minbar al-Sharq, political monthly of the Islamic Labor Party
Sawt al-Azhar, Islamic weekly of al-Azhar

NOTES

Notes to Chapter 1

1. Said, *Orientalism*; Rodinson, *Europe and the Mystique of Islam*.

2. See Bayat, "The Use and Abuse of 'Muslim Societies,'" p. 5.

3. Lewis, "The Roots of Muslim Rage."

4. These are the words of Israel's foremost "revisionist historian," Benny Morris, quoted in Beinin, "No More Tears," p. 40. A number of influential academics in the United States, such as Eliot Cohen of Johns Hopkins University and Kenneth Adelman of the Defense Department's Defense Policy Board have suggested that Islam is essentially intolerant, expansionist, and violent. Some evangelical Protestants have declared Islam an "evil" religion (quoted by William Pfaff in the *Herald Tribune*, December 5, 2002). In some ways such projections can be a self-defeating teleology, for if Islam is essentially alien to democratic ideals, then what can one do about it? The solution for democratization (in the sense of change of government with free elections, plus an independent judiciary, freedom of speech, rule of law, and minority rights) seems to be either to secularize Muslims or to convert them to a different "democratic" religion. This task, assuming it is desirable, would logically be far more formidable than encouraging "moderate Islam."

5. This camp includes such authors as John Voll, John Esposito, and Khaled Abou El Fadl, among others, as well as institutions such as the Center for the Study of Islam and Democracy (United States), the Center for Muslim Democrats (France), and many websites. See note 4 in Chapter 6.

6. Interview with Rashed al-Ghannoushi, *al-Ahram Weekly*, December 24–30, 1998, p. 9.

7. See, for instance, Bahrul Uloom, "Islam, Democracy, and the Future of Iraq."

8. Indeed many questions surround the concept of democracy. Is it equal to

Robert Dahl's "polyarchy"—a consensual government by competing elites representing different social interests in a pluralist framework? (Dahl, *Democracy and Its Critics*). If so, where do the other domains of public life, economy, society, and culture stand? How do we account for individualism: is it a prerequisite for democracy or its antithesis? Is capitalism, with its corporate power and mighty manufacturing of consent, not undemocratic? These questions are as old as democracy itself. They have been raised by a host of movements and critics that have sought to make "democracy" democratic. Marxism has highlighted the conflict of economic liberalism and democratic ideals; social democracy and associationalism have emphasized citizenship and equality (for an excellent discussion see Held, *Models of Democracy*). And feminists have long taken issue with democratic theory for dismissing structural inequality, patriarchy, and the separation of the public domain (of government, where all are to be equal) and the private domain (the sphere of family and interpersonal relationships, which are exploitative) (see Pateman, *The Sexual Contract*). For a very useful discussion of how economic freedom can undermine civil and political freedoms, see Chan, *Liberalism, Democracy and Development*.

9. Beckford, *Social Theory and Religion*, p. 2.

10. For the plurality of Christian interpretations and practices, see Peterson, Vasquez, and Williams, *Christianity, Social Change, and Globalization*.

11. Influential thinkers remembering World Wars I and II concluded for some time that Catholicism and democracy were not compatible; see S. Lipset, K. Seong, and J. C. Torres, "Social Requisites of Democracy," *International Social Science Journal*, vol. 13, no. 6 (May 1993): 29.

12. Quoted in Bainton, *Here I Stand*, pp. 184–85.

13. Martin Luther's tract *On the Jews and Their Lies* is said to be a principal inspiration for Hitler's *Mein Kampf*. For some, European fascism was the fruit of a Christian culture; see Paul, "The Great Scandal." For similar views see also Scholder, *The Churches and the Third Reich*; and Griech-Polelle, *Bishop von Galen*.

14. See www.hom.net/angels/democracy.html.

15. *International Herald Tribune*, Sept. 7, 2000, p. 6.

16. The most conspicuous manifestation of what Michael Lowy calls the "war of Gods" in the 1970s was in Latin American Catholicism, where Christians were deeply divided over their support for (or opposition to) democracy. See Lowy, *The War of Gods*.

17. Nasr Abu Zayd has advocated that Muslims should go beyond hermeneutically interpreting the scriptures with which they are bound to disagree. Disagreement, multiple meanings, and ambiguity, he argues, are embedded in the Qur'an itself. Similarly, Khalid Mas'ud, a scholar of *fiqh* (jurisprudence), suggests that the ambiguity in and conflicting *aḥādīth* (the Prophet's saying and doings) indicate the plurality of views on many religious matters at the time of the Prophet; see Abu Zayd, *Rethinking*

the Quran. Professor Khalid Mas'ud's statement is based on my personal communication with him. My contention is that, irrespective of the truth of their arguments, Abu Zayd's and Mas'ud's scholarly interventions account for an aspect of the struggle to see Islamic texts in different lights.

18. UNESCO, *Statistical Yearbook*, 2003.

19. A survey of political opinions in five Arab countries (Algeria, Morocco, Palestine, Lebanon, and Jordan) gives "freedom from occupation" a higher score than free elections, transparency, free media, unions, or accountable governments. See *Arab Human Development Report*, 2004.

20. The preceding discussion and conclusions regarding liberation theology in Latin America draw on the following: Smith, *The Emergence of Liberation Theology*; Gutierrez, *A Theology of Liberation*; Boff and Boff, *Salvation and Liberation*; Lowy, *The War of Gods*; Kovel, "The Vatican Strikes Back"; Bonine, "The Sociohistorical Meaning of Liberation Theology; and Nepstad, "Popular Religion, Protest, and Revolt";

21. See Bayat, "The 'Street' and the Politics of Dissent."

22. See Bayat, "The Coming of a Post-Islamist Society.

23. Roy's "Le Post-Islamisme" is an introduction to a number of essays that Roy considers to speak of a post-Islamist trend. Reinhard Schulze uses "post-Islamism" to describe a "post-modern Islamism" as an increasingly fragmented and "ethnized" worldview due to growing reinterpretations and localization of Islamism; see Schulze, "The Ethnization of Islamic Cultures." For Gilles Kepel in *Jihad* (p. 368), the term describes the new orientation of some Islamists who, in the name of democracy and human rights, have departed from radical, *jihādi*, and *salafi* doctrines. Others fall short of conceptualizing the term altogether. One exception is Farhad Khosrokhavar's treatment of the term in assessing the views of some "post-Islamist intellectuals in Iran" such as 'Abd al-Karim Surush; see Khosrokhavar, "The Islamic Revolution in Iran."

24. For instance, see Rashwan, "Wishful Thinking."

25. See Roussillon, "Decline of Islamism?"

26. See, for instance, Ismail, "The Paradox of Islamist Politics." See also Burgat, *Face to Face with Political Islam*, pp. 180–81. Olivier Roy has defined post-Islamism as the "privatization of re-Islamization." It refers to individualized "neo-fundamentalism." See Roy, *Globalised Islam*, p. 97. I use the term in a fundamentally different fashion.

27. See interviews with Rashed al-Ghannoushi in *al-Ahram Weekly*, October 1–9, 1998; and *al-Ahram Weekly*, December 24–30, 1998, p. 9.

28. See Ahmad, "From Islamism to Post-Islamism."

29. For an analysis of Saudi Arabia's "Islamo-liberal" trend or reform movement, see Lacroix, "A New Element in the Saudi Political-Intellectual Field."

30. See Aras and Caha, "Fethullah Gulen"; see also Dagi, "Rethinking Human Rights."

Notes to Chapter 2

1. In 1978 the per capita income in Iran was $2,400; but in Egypt in 1988 it was still only $660. During the 1970s, some 15 percent of Tehran's population lived in the squatter areas (and about 15 percent in slums); for Cairo in the early 1990s this figure was 50 percent.

2. Hamid Dabashi, *Theology of Discontent*, p. 110. For instance, Said A. Arjomand states: "in 1961–78 . . . the religious institutions came under relentless attack by the Pahlavi state and had to court the masses more assiduously in order to mobilize them in its defense"; see Arjomand, "Shi'ite Islam and the Revolution in Iran," p. 302.

3. Moaddel, *Class, Politics and Ideology in the Iranian Revolution*; and Moaddel, "The Significance of Discourse in the Iranian Revolution. See also an interesting critique of Moaddel by John Foran in "The Iranian Revolution and the Study of Discourses."

4. Keddie, *Roots of Revolution*; Keddie, "Islamic Revival in the Middle East."

5. Parsons, "The Iranian Revoluiton," p. 3.

6. Keddie, *Roots of Revolution*, p. 72.

7. Arjomand, *The Turban for the Crown*, pp. 106, 197–200.

8. Ibid., p. 6.

9. Abrahamian, *Iran between Two Revolutions*; Halliday, *Iran*; Milani, *The Making of the Islamic Revolution in Iran*; Keddie, *Iran and the Muslim World*.

10. Parsa, *Social Origins of the Iranian Revolution*.

11. Munson, *Islam and Revolution in the Middle East*.

12. Snow and Marshall, "Cultural Imperialism, Social Movements."

13. Burgat and Dowell, *The Islamic Movement in North Africa*.

14. Ibrahim, "Anatomy of Egypt's Militant Islamic Groups"; Kepel, *Muslim Extremism in Egypt*.

15. See, for instance, Skocpol, *States and Social Revolutions*.

16. Davies, "Toward a Theory of Revolution," p. 6.

17. Gurr, *Why Men Rebel*.

18. Tilly, *From Mobilization to Revolution*.

19. Kim, "Disjunctive Justice."

20. More precisely, a revolution is, in Huntington's words, "a rapid, fundamental, and violent domestic change in the dominant values and myths of a society, in its political institutions, social structure, leadership, and government activity and politics"; see Huntington, "Modernization and Revolution," p. 22.

21. Staniszkis, *Poland's Self-Limiting Revolution*, p. 17.

22. Kuczynski and Nowak, "The Solidarity Movement."

23. See Bayat, "Workless Revolutionaries: The Movement of the Unemployed in Iran, 1979."

24. Roth, *The Social Democrats in Imperial Germany*, p. 170.

25. Bendix, *Nation-Building*, pp. 86–89; Lipset, *Political Man*, pp. 70–73.

26. Gramsci, *Prison Notebooks*, pp. 106–14; 206–8.

27. Ibid., p. 207.

28. Femia, *Gramsci's Political Thought*, p. 192.

29. See Abrahamian, *Iran between Two Revolutions*; Keddie, *Roots of Revolution*; Milani, *The Making of the Islamic Revolution in Iran*; Halliday, *Iran*.

30. On the anti-democratic nature of the Shah's regime and its political implications see Halliday, *Iran* (on SAVAK activities); Lajevardi, *Labor Unions*; Katouzian, *The Political Economy of Modern Iran*.

31. On guerrilla activities in Iran see Halliday, *Iran*; Abrahamian, *Iran between Two Revolutions*.

32. Keddie, *Religion and Rebellion in Iran*; Alghar, *Religion and State in Iran*; Arjomand, "The Ulama's Traditionalist Opposition."

33. See Arjomand, "The Ulama's Traditionalist Opposition," p. 186. Unlike Arjomand, Ervand Abrahamian, a historian of Iran, believes that most of the clergy remained supportive of constitutionalism (personal communication).

34. Abrahamian, *Iran between Two Revolutions*, pp. 111–12.

35. For more detail see Akhavi, *Religion and Politics in Contemporary Iran*, pp. 99–105.

36. Abrahamian, *Iran between Two Revolutions*, p. 140.

37. Calculated from data provided by Abrahamian, *Iran between Two Revolutions*, pp. 144–45.

38. See Mottahedeh, *The Mantle of the Prophet*, p. 316.

39. Interestingly, after the Islamic Revolution, the mayor of Tehran, Karbaschi, was attached by the conservative "student" weekly *Payam-i Danishju*, because he had created hundreds of public parks and green spots in the city where men and women could mingle in public.

40. See Mu'meni, "Islam-i Mowjud," p. 74. See also Behnam, "Zan, Khanivadih va Tajaddud," p. 234.

41. See Akhavi, *Religion and Politics*, Appendixes.

42. Ashraf, "Zaminih-i Ijtima'i-yi Sunnatgari va Tajaddudkhahi,"p. 177.

43. According to Ayatollah Muhammad Taqi Misbah Yazdi, a leading conservative cleric in postrevolution Iran; reported by the Islamic Republic News Agency, 26 Khordad 1376/1997, cited on the *Iran-i Imruz* website.

44. Abrahamian, *Iran between Two Revolutions*, p. 321.

45. Halliday, *Iran*.

46. Katouzian, *The Political Economy of Modern Iran*, p. 276.

47. Bayat, *Workers and Revolution in Iran*, p. 25.

48. Arman, "Naqsh-i Javanan dar Inqilab," p. 95.

49. On these see Milani, *The Making of the Iranian Islamic Revolution*, pp. 115–19.

50. Ibid., p. 116.

51. The generally modern or foreign nature of merchandise in the Tehran bazaar is obvious in comparison with the merchandise in bazaars of Cairo or Istanbul.

52. Personal communication with Tahereh Qaderi, whose 1985 Ph.D dissertation on bazaars in Iran in the 1970s is available at the University of Kent, Canterbury, England. The political reflection of this division was revealed only one year after the revolution, when different segments of the bazaar exhibited support for different political leaders. They were notably divided between supporters of President Bani Sadr and Ayatollah Beheshti.

53. Akhavi, *Religion and Politics*, pp. 134–35.

54. Ibid., p. 129.

55. This concern seemed to continue even up to the eve of the revolution. During the famous lectures at the Quba Mosque organized by modernist clergy in the fall of 1977, I observed that most of the preaching, in particular that of Ayatollah Mutahhari and Mehdi Bazargan, centered on attacking rival secular, materialist, and Marxist ideas. On the final evening, which was devoted to participants' questions and comments, I presented a critical review of Bazargan's lecture. The angry response of Ayatollah Mutahhari to my comments pointed to a sense of insecurity of Islamists at the time.

56. Mutahhari, "Rahbar-i Nasl-i Javan."

57. Ashtiani, "Ihya'-yi Fikr-i Dini va Sarkardigi-yi Islam-i Siyasi dar Inqilab-i Iran"; see also Mirsepassi-Ashtiani, "The Crisis of Secularism."

58. See Afshari, "A Critique of Dabashi's Reconstruction of Islamic Ideology," This contention is confirmed by the cleric Abdullah Nuri, who argued that before the revolution "there was little discussion about the *vilāyat-i faqīh*"; see his *Shukaran-i Islah*, p. 51.

59. This assumption is made by Akhavi, *Religion and Politics*, p. 101; Arjomand, *The Turban for the Crown*; Mottahedeh, *The Mantle of the Prophet*; and Kazemi, *Poverty and Revolution*.

60. See Khomeini, *Sahifih-yi Nur*. Interestingly, the term *mustaż'afin* appeared in his language only during the height of the revolution (Aban 1357) when he used it merely to repudiate the leftists by attempting to offer an alternative conceptualization of the poor. For a more detailed discussion see Bayat, *Street Politics*.

61. See Anonymous, *Bahthi dar Bāreyi Marja'iyyat va Ruhaniyyat*.

62. Shari'ati, *Jahatgiri-i Tabaqati-yi Islam*.

63. Arjomand, "Shi'it Islam and the Revolution in Iran," pp. 311–13.

64. The number of books can be verified from UNESCO statistical sources. However, on the number of Islamic associations, only those formal titles, numbering 1,800, are reliable. It is impossible to verify the other categories.

65. See also Mirsepassi-Ashtiani, "The Crisis of Secularism," p. 77; Mottahedeh, *The Mantle of the Prophet*; Dabashi, *Theology of Discontent*.

66. Akhavi, *Religion and Politics*, p. 160. It is important to note that at the time Iran had one of the strictest censorship policies in the world. About censorship in the popular press, see also Millard, "Popular Press in Iran."

67. See Tehranian, *Socio-Economic and Communication Indicators*, p. 63.

68. On these figures see ibid., pp. 56–57. The total number of registered periodicals jumped from 104 in 1975 to 227 in 1980, one year after the revolution. However, a crackdown on oppositional publications and organizations reduced the number to a mere 66. In other words, some 161 periodicals, almost all secular, were banned from publication. For figures, see Markaz-i Amar-i Iran, *Iran dar A'inih-i Amar*.

69. See Akhavi, *Religion and Politics*, pp. 161–62.

70. Ibid., p. 138.

71. The phrase is Arjomand's; see his "Shi'ite Islam and the Revolution in Iran," p. 312.

72. My own school, Tahiri-i Islami, with both primary and secondary levels, was part of the Islamic conglomerate *Jami'ih-i Ta'limat-i Islami*.

73. See, for instance, Kazemi, *Poverty and Revolution*; Mottahedeh, *The Mantle of the Prophet*.

74. Interview, in Banuazizi, "Alounaknishinan-e Khiaban-e Professor Brown," p. 59.

75. It is important to note that, unlike attending mosques, shrines, or *hay'at*, these were commodities that ordinary and middle-income people had to pay for. I exclude those leisure items and activities that only the rich could afford to consume, such as frequenting cabarets and taking European holidays (as opposed to attending Hajj).

76. For these figures see UNESCO, *Statistical Yearbook*, various years.

77. Quoted in Nafici, "Iranian Cinema," p. 548.

78. In Afshari, "A Critique," p. 80.

79. Khomeini, *Hukumat-i Islami*, p. 160.

80. On the Mujahidin see Abrahamian, *Radical Islam*.

81. In S. E. Ibrahim, "The Changing Face of Egypt's Islamic Activism," p. 7.

82. Data obtained from the Egyptian Ministry of Culture, November 1995.

83. Personal communication with Professor Mustafa El-Sayyed of Cairo University, 1996.

84. The newspapers included *al-Sha'b* of the Islamic Labor Party, *al-Nur* of the Liberal Party/Muslim Brotherhood. *Al-Muslimun* and *al-Muslim al-Mu'asir* are international dailies. In addition, *al-Liwa' al-Islam*, of the National Democratic Party; *Aqitati*, an Al-Azhar–sanctioned journal; and *Liwa' al-Islam* are published weekly. Periodicals include: *al-Mukhtar al-Islami* (MB), *Minbar al-Sharq* (Labor Party), *al-Tasawuf al-Islami* (the Sufi Council), *Minbar al-Islam* and *al-Azhar* (Al-Azhar

Institute), *al-Muslim al-Saqir* (Islamic children). In addition, a number of dailies and weeklies are published by the leading Islamic political organizations and parties. They include: *al-Ahrar* (daily), *al-Aharar* (weekly), *al-Haqiqa* (weekly), *al-Nur* (weekly), *al-Usrat al-'Arabi* (weekly), plus over thirty specialized and regional publications such as *al-Uruba, Shabab al-Aharar, Ahrar al-Sa'id,* and *Ahrar al-Hilwan.* Despite this some Islamists decry the "crisis" of religious publications in contemporary Egypt. See, for instance, articles in *Liwa al-Islam,* vol. 50, no. 2 (Oct. 1995): 11–15; *al-Wasat,* no. 195, Oct. 10, 1995, pp. 32–34.

85. See UNESCO publications; also Brindle, "Egypt's Film Industry," which describes a steady reduction in the production of domestic movies.

86. See al-Fawal, *al-Barnamaj al-Diniyya fi al-Teliviziyun al-Misri,*Data for religious programs on television in 1990 extracted from the above source; for 1975, they were obtained from a sample of daily television programs printed in the daily paper *al-Ahram.*

87. *Al-Ahram,* December 17, 1988.

88. S. E. Ibrahim, "The Changing Face," p. 4.

89. Ibid., p. 4.

90. See Guenena, "The Changing Face of Egypt's Islamic Activism," pp. 7–8.

91. Indeed, some evidence suggests that the spread of militants in the slums of Cairo began in the 1970s when, following the dismantling of al-Takfir wa al-Hijra, escapee militants from upper Egypt sought refuge in the overcrowded and "invisible" informal communities, *'ashwā'iyyāt.* See Issawi, *al-Ashwa'iyyat wa Tagarub al-Tanmiyyah.*

92. See Abdul-Fattah, "The Story of the Decade," p. 7.

93. Quoted in Saad, "Islamists Take Control of Liberal Syndicate," p. 2.

94. The social profile of militant Islamists is discussed in S. E. Ibrahim, "Anatomy of Egypt's Militant Islamic Groups"; Kepel, *Muslim Extremism,*pp. 210–18; and Guenena, "The Jihad." Although Akhwan got support from different social layers, nevertheless the new (educated, professional, and *muwazifin*) middle class was the major player. No detailed study has been published on the social profile of the al-Ikhwan. However, their clear influence in the professional associations points to their largely urban-middle-class constituency.

95. I am grateful to Professor Saad Eddin Ibrahim for bringing these historical facts to my attention.

96. For a fine discussion on this matter see Hamid Enayat, "The Concept of *Vilāyat-i Faqīh* in Imam Khomeini," *Kiyan,* vol. 6, no. 34 (January–February 1997) (in Persian). Published in English in Piscatori, *Islam in the Political Process.*

97. In his memoir, Bani Sadr, the first president of the Islamic Republic and one of the closest aides to Ayatollah Khomeini in Paris, says: "In Paris, Khomeini did not believe that the Shah would fall. Two or three times a week I would reassure him that

the Shah would reliquish power. . . . Reporters would ask him 'what is your frame of reference, your model? What is an Islamic state?' We weighed our anwers carefully. To what period of our history could we refer? The Abbasid dynasty? The Umayyads? Or the period of first caliphs? *We had to formulate an ideology worthy of a revolution.*" Quoted in *al-Ahram Weekly*, October 26, 1995, p. 5 (my emphasis).

98. See Lapidus, *A History of Islamic Societies*, pp. 617–20.

99. On clergy-bazaar relations, see Ashraf, "Bazaar-Mosque Alliance."

100. Mitchell, *The Society of Muslim Brothers*, pp. 328–30.

101. The following few paragraphs rely heavily on Kepel, *Muslim Extremism*; Guenena, *Jihad*; and Naquib, "The Political Ideology of the Jihad Movement."

102. On radical Islamic groups, see Kepel, *Muslim Extremism*; S. E. Ibrahim, "Anatomy of Egypt's Militant Islamic Groups"; Ansari, "Islamic Militants"; Kupfer-schmidt, "Reformist and Militant Islam." See also various issues of *Civil Society*, Ibn Khaldun Center for Developmental Studies, Cairo.

103. This section relies heavily on Mubarak, *al-Irhabiyun Qadimun*. I have also utilized an interview with Hamdi 'Abd al-Rahman, the amir of Suhag in *al-Musawwar*, no. 4041, March 22, 2002, pp. 26–29.

104. Both trends continued to use the original name, al-Jama'a al-Islamiyya, causing confusion for some time until the radical trend evolved into a violent political organization carrying the name Jama'iyya al-Islamiyya.

105. It is not clear on what basis Fuad Ajami asserts that the militants who killed Sadat had no ideas and no takeover plan given the known plan of a revolutionary takeover by the Jama'a to kill Sadat, take over Cairo's TV station, and attack the police headquarters; see Ajami, *The Dream Palace of the Arabs*.

106. Mubarak, *Al-Irhabiyoun Qadimoun*, p. 170.

107. Ibid., pp. 264–65.

108. See Reuters news agency report from Cairo.

109. Rif'at Sid-Ahmad calls this coalition "Cambative Islam"; see "Ightiyal al-Sadat," in *al-Hayat*, December 12, 1997, p. 18.

110. On the Labor Party and its development, I have relied on Singer, "The Socialist Labor Party."

111. Marsot, *Egypt's Liberal Experiment*; Lapidus, *A History of Islamic Societies*.

112. See Lapidus, *A History of Islamic Societies*, p. 627.

113. In Egypt, one can see this in the day-to-day behavior of upper- and upper-middle-class families. While young people get married in fancy hotels like Marriott or Hilton, I have not observed alcohol being served in such occasions. Young girls and boys from "Westernized" classes mostly fast during Ramadan; many regularly pray and express respect to Islam and the clergy. In contrast, in Iran in the late 1960s and 1970s, modern classes in general expressed a great laxity in observing religion

114. It was only very recently, in January 1997, when a group of clergy formed the

Ulema Front, distinct from official al-Azhar, that the government began encroaching on their prerogatives, including requiring them to ask for permssion to preach in the mosques, and bringing private mosques under the control of of the Ministry of Awqāf. See *al-Hayat*, January 25, 1997, p. 7.

115. Quoted in Zubaida, *Islam, the People, and the State*, p. 48.

116. Interview in *al-Ahram Weekly*, November 16–22, 1995, p. 2.

117. I observed this interaction in a mosque in Cairo in October 1996.

118. See Denoeux, *Urban Unrest in the Middle East*.

119. Al-Ahram Strategic Studies Center, *Taqrir Halat al-Diniyya fi Misr*, pp. 236–37.

120. See S. E. Ibrahim, "Egyptian Law 32," p. 38.

121. Ibid., pp. 34–35.

122. See Sullivan, *Private Voluntary Organizations in Egypt*, pp. 65–68.

123. Qandil and Ben-Nafisah, *al-Jama'iyyat al-Ahliyya fi Misr*, pp. 282–83.

124. Ibid., p. 282.

125. See Qandil, "Taqdim Ada' al-Islamiyin fi Niqabat al-Mahniyya."

126. Ibid. Also based on my interview with a member of the Doctors Syndicate, Cairo, 1990.

127. Law 100/1993 said that for a syndicate election to be legitimate at least 50 percent of the total membership must vote. Seventeen syndicates rejected this law, leading to major confrontations with the government.

128. See *al-Liwa' al-Islami*, September 28, 1995, p. 15.

129. MacLeod, *Accommodating Protest*.

130. See Sullivan, *Private Voluntary Associations*, p. 73.

131. Qandil, "Taqdim Ada' al-Islamiyin."

132. On Egyptian Islamic schools, I have relied on studies by Linda Herrera, 1995–96.

133. *Al-Liwa' al-Islami*, December 5, 1996, p. 14.

134. Ibid.

135. See *al-Liwa' al-Islami*, September 28, 1995, p. 15.

136. Statement made by Ahmed 'Umar Hashim, the president of al-Azhar University, in *'Aqidati*, Novemebr 7, 1995, p. 3.

137. *Al-Liwa' al-Islami*, with a respectable circulation, supported the fundamentalist critiques of Professor Abu-Zayd and sided with conservative views at the Beijing Women's Conference.

138. See Heba Rauf in *Sha'b*, January 3, 1997, p. 9. See also interview with the author in March 1997.

139. Of course, unity can be built by political coalitions, but this requires a hegemonic element to enforce consensus on other dissenting parties. In Egypt this was lacking. An indignant and well-organized clergy might have played that role, as they did in Iran; but in Egypt, the ulema were not in political opposition. Nevertheless, if

the situation changes, al-Azhar and its ulema are likely to join the bandwagon, even becoming major actors in an "Islamic order." Indeed, even today there are signs that this state institution may be used by militant young Muslims, Egyptians and foreign alike, to acquire Islamic knowledge while taking a critical stand against the conciliatory politics of al-Azhar. Unrest at al-Azhar University during October 1995, when many students protested the government arrests and military trials of Muslim Brothers, point to the political potential of this institution. For details see *al-Ahram Weekly* and *'Aqidati* during the last two weeks of October and the first week of November 1995. For this discussion I have also relied on personal communication with Malika Zighal, a Ph.D. student at Princeton University, in spring 1994.

Notes to Chapter 3

1. For an interesting treatment of Foucault and the Iranian revolution, see Afary and Anderson, *Foucault and the Iranian Revolution.*

2. For a fine spatial analysis of postrevolution urban space see, Amir Ibrahimi, "Public and Private."

3. See Ehsani, "Municipal Matters"; see also his "The Nation and Its Periphery," showing that these spatial changes occurred also in small provincial towns. I am indebted to him for discussing these matters with me.

4. For a good analysis of the economics of the Iranian Islamists, see Behdad, "A Disputed Utopia."

5. See Schirazi, *The Constitution of Iran.*

6. See Ehsani, "Municipal Matters."

7. For an interesting report on these cultural centers and their social implications see Amir Ibrahimi, "The Impact of the Bahman Cultural Complex"; see also her "Integration of South Tehran."

8. *Itila'at*, 31/2/1377 (1999).

9. These figures were provided by one of the engineers of the project. For the report see McAllister, "Tehran's Grand Mosque."

10. See, for example, *Haftih Namih-i Subh*, 12 Dey 1374 (1995); *Jumhuri-i Islami*, 10 Bahman 1374 (1995).

11. *Farhang-i Âfarinesh*, 26 Day 1374 (1995).

12. This analysis of youngsters' behavior and thought is based on my personal observations and conversations with a spectrum of youth in north and south Tehran and in rural areas of Shahriar at various times from 1979to 1981 and from 1995 to 2002.

13. Of 646 people killed in Tehran in street clashes during the revolution (from August 23, 1977, to February 19, 1978), the largest group after artisans and shopkeepers (189) were students (149). See Bayat, *Street Politics*, p. 39.

14. This is according to a national survey reported in *Aftab*, July 30, 2001, p. 9.

15. Zahra Rahnavard, in *Bahar*, 29 Khurdad 1379, p. 2. A one-day symposium was organized to discuss why the youth showed such a disinterest in religious lessons.

16. Cited in *http://daily*news.yahoo.com [July 25, 2000].

17. See Qutbi, "Causeless Rebellion."

18. According to a July 2000 report by Muhammad Ali Zam, director of cultural and artistic affairs for Tehran, the average age of prostitutes declined from 27 to 20.See Muhammad Ali Zam, *Bahar*, 15 Tir 1379 (2000), p. 13. The document became a highly controversial survey as the conservatives disputed its authenticity and negative impact on their image.

19. Official interviews with youngsters cited in Yaghmaiyan, *Social Change in Iran*, pp. 65–71. In fact Iranian youths had created a wealth of slang that a linguist compiled into a dictionary of youth slang and secret language; see Sama'i, *Farhang-i Lughat-i Zaban-i Makhfi* [Dictionary of secret language].

20. Reported by the Sina News Agency, June 17, 2004, cited on the *Iran-i Imruz* website; and in *Aftab*, January 16, 2003, p. 9; see a report by IRNA, August 5, 2001.

21. A study conducted by psychologist Dawood Jeshan on 120 runaway girls in Tehran, reported by the Sina News Agency, cited on the *Iran-I Imruz* website [June 17, 2004].

22. My fieldwork in Tehran, 1995 and 1998.

23. Reported by Professor Mahmoud Golzari, paper presented at the workshop "Young Girls and the Challenges of Life," May 2004, cited in ISNA News agency, 22 Urdibahasht 1383 (2004), womeniniran.com.

24. In an interview with *Siyasat-i Ruz*, quoted in Farahi, "You Cannot Resolve Sexual Misconduct by Exhortation." Although public information did not exist, researchers and medical professionals were alarmed by the extent of unwanted pregnancies. Doctors said unofficially that not a week passed without at least two or three young girls coming in for an abortion. Reportedly some 60 percent of those requesting abortions were unmarried young girls. UNFPA officials in Tehran referred to a survey on "morality" (meaning sexuality) among young people. But the results were so "terrible" that they had to be destroyed. Attention to physical appearance, clothing, and fashion, not to mention plastic surgery on the nose, became a widespread trend among young females; interview with a medical anthropologist working on the subject, spring 2001.

25. See *Salam*, 27 Shahrivar 1375 (1996).

26. See Jalil 'Irfan-Manash, *Iran*, 19 Aban 1375 (1996).

27. Muhammad Hadi Taskhiri of the Organization of Islamic Culture and Communication in the Second International Seminar on Hijab, 28 Aban 1376, reported in *Zanan*, no. 26, Mahr/Aban 1376, pp. 8–9.

28. A survey of the Supreme Council of Youth, cited by Golzari at the Second International Seminar on Hijab, reported in ibid., p. 9.

29. This finding was reported by the National Radio and TV, Organization of

Islamic Propaganda, and the Organization of Friday Prayers (Setad-i Namaz), cited by ʿImad al-Din Bāqi, *Payam-i Imruz*, no. 39, Urdibahasht 1379, p. 14.

30. Report by the head of Tehran's cultural and artistic affairs, www.nandotimes. com [July 5, 2000].

31. See Serajzadeh, "Non-attending Believers"; and a survey conducted by the National Organization of Youth, reported in *Aftab*, 8 Urdibahasht 1380 (2001). In fact, contrary to general expectations, theocracy in Iran has not led to the erosion of religiosity. A comprehensive and nationwide survey showed that between 1975 and 2001 people's religious beliefs remained unaltered. Theocracy, however, changed the features of their religiosity to more faith than practice, more individualized than institutional religion, and more selective than wholesale adherence. See Kazemipur and Rezaei, "Religious Life under Theocracy."

32. Interview with Azam, an anonymous participant, June 2002.

33. See *Nuruz*, 1 Aban 1380, p. 3.

34. See Murtaza Nabavi in *Risālat*, October 27, 2001, p. 2.

35. See Jean-Michel Cadiot, AP Report, IranMania.com [August 20, 2001].

36. Charles Recknaged and Azam Gorgin, "Iran: New Morality Police," on the website of Radio Free Europe July 26, 2000.

37. See *Nuruz*, 20 and 21 Murdad 1380 (2001).

38. *Nuruz*, 29 Mahr 1380 (2001).

39. See "Leisure Time and Amusement" in *Aftab-e Yaz*, April 3, 2001, p. 9; "Shad Zistan-e Zanan," *Dowran-i Imruz*, 20 Bahman 1379 (1990), p. 2.

40. "Approaches to the Concept of Living," cited in *Aftab-e Yazd*, January 9, 2001, p. 7; and January 11, 2001, p. 7.

41. See "Khandidan Aslan Zisht Nist," in *Iran*, March 18, 2001, p. 4.

42. For a discussion of fun, Islam, and politics, see Bayat, "Islamism and the Politics of Fun."

43. See, for instance, Fitzgerald, *The Great Gatsby*.

44. Massey, "The Spatial Construction of Youth Cultures," p. 122.

45. These changes seemed to be confirmed by a large-scale survey; see Kian-Thiebaut, "Political Impacts."

46. On the number of NGOs in Iran, see *Hayat-i Naw*, 10 Urdibahasht 1380 (2001), p. 11; *Nuruz*, 15 Murdad 1380 (2001), p. 9; and *Iran-i Imruz*, August 11, 2003.

47. Mahdi, "The Student Movement," p. 10.

48. See interview with student leader Hashmatullah Tabarzadi, *Iran-i Farda*, no. 38, p. 17. See also interviews with Majid Toulaʾi and Morad Saghafi in the same issue.

49. Muhammadi, *Darāmadi bar Raftar-Shināsi*, pp. 93–95.

50. Statement by Muhammad Jawad Larijani, *Risālat*, 9-10-1373 (1994).

51. Tāhiripur and Anjam-Shuʿa, "Gustarish-i Amuzish-i ʿAli va Tawsʿih Jamiʿat-i Danishjuyi."

52. Muhammadi, *Darāmadi bar Raftar-Shināsi*, p. 86.

53. Much of the information on college life is based on my own observations and interviews with anonymous students at Tehran University and Azad University branches in Tehran, Qazvin, and Garmsar, Summer 2002.

54. See Mahdi, "The Student Movement," p. 16.

55. For a perceptive analysis see Muhammadi, *Darāmadi bar Raftar-Shināsi.*

56. See Rahimpur, "Madhiyāt-i Junbish-i Danishjuyih."

57. This figure is based on *Kiyan*'s own survey of its readers; see *Kiyan*, vol. 5, no. 26, August–September 1995.

58. Student leader Hashmatullah Tabarzadi, interview in *Huviyyat-i Khish*, May 1, 1999, p. 8.

59. Asgharzadeh's interview with the *New York Times*, November 5, 2002.

60. See *The Manifesto of the DTV* on 16 Azar 1376 (1997).

61. Reported in an interview with Mustafa Mu'in, the minister of science, research, and technology, in *Nuruz*, 11 Tir 1380 (2001), p. 10.

62. See Ardalan, "Zanan az Sazmanha-yi Siyasi-yi Danishjuyi Gurizanand, Chira?"

63. See Paydar, *Women and Political Process.*

64. See Karimi, "Sahm-i Zanan dar Bazar-i Kar-i Iran."

65. For leftist groups' position on women's issues, see Shahidian, "The Iranian Left." See also Tohidi, "Mas'alih Zanan va Rawshanfikran Tay-yi Tahavvulat-i Dahi-yi Akhir."

66. See, for instance, a speech by Golnar Dastgheib, an Islamist female parliamentarian, at the Havana Inter-Parliamentary Union, printed in Tabari and Yeganeh, *Under the Shadow of Islam.* See also Tabari, "Islam and the Struggle," p. 17.

67. See *Payam-i Hajar*, no. 1, Shahrivar 19, 1359 (1980), p. 2.

68. Statement by the Iranian Women's Delegation to the UN Decade of Women Conference, July 1980.

69. See, for instance, statements by two conservative Islamist women members of the Fifth Majlis, Munirih Nubakhat and Marziyih Wahid Dastjerdi, quoted in *Zanan*, no. 42, Farvardin-Urdibahasht 1377 (1998), p. 3.

70. Quoted in *Zanan*, no. 26, p. 3.

71. Maryam Behruzi, quoted in *Itila'at*, 3 Esfand 1361 (1982), p. 6.

72. Tabataba'i, "Understanding Islam in Its Totality," p. 174.

73. Quoted in *Risālat*, 26 Farvardin 1375.

74. President Rafsanjani, quoted in *Zanan*, no. 26, p. 5.

75. Maryam Behruzi, a member of Parliament in the 4th Majlis, quoted in Kian-Thiebaut, "Women and Politics," p. 44.

76. Quoted in Kian-Thiebaut, "Women and Politics," p. 39.

77. See *Iran-i Farda*, no. 36, Shahrivar 1376 (19997), p. 12; *Zanan*, no. 27, Azar-Day 1374 (1995), p. 6.

78. Moghadam, "Women's Employment Issues."

79. Khatam, "Sakhtar-i Ishtighal-i Zanan-i Shahri." Karimi, "Sahm-e Zanan dar bazaar-e Kar-e Iran."

80. *Zanan*, no. 27, p. 42.

81. Observation by Masarat Amir Ibrahimi, interview in *Bad Jins*, 6th ed., December 2002, online.

82. Mina, "Women's Mobility in Tehran."

83. For an excellent report see Hoodfar, *Volunteer Health Workers in Iran*.

84. Between 1990 and 1995, the population growth rate had dropped to an annual average of 2 percent. For all the growth rate figures see *Yearbook of the United Nations* (New York: United Nations, various years).

85. Iranian women competed in sports with women from Pakistan, Syria, Libya, and Cameroon. On women's sports, see special issue of *Zanan*, no. 30; see also *Zanan*, no. 9, Bahman 1371 (1991).

86. Womeniniran.com [June 6, 2003].

87. See *Zanan*, no. 42, Urdibahasht 1998, p. 61; see also womeniniran.com for reports on women's soccer teams [June 2003].

88. For an excellent discussion of how the new cultural centers in South Tehran have become "safe" places for lower-class women to be active in the public sphere in south Tehran, see Amir Ibrahimi, "Ta'sir Farhangsara-yi Bahman bar Zandigi-yi Ijtima'i va Farhangi-yi Zanan va Javanan-i Tahran."

89. *Itila'at*, 15 Aban 1369 (6 November 1990).

90. In a 1994 survey, Iranian women were asked if they would wear a veil, and if so what type, if they were not required to do so. About 20 percent preferred no veil, 10 percent a light headcover, 40 percent a scarf and manteau or shawl, and 25 percent a full *chador*; see 'Abdi and Gudarzi, *Tahavvulat-i Farhangiyyih dar Iran*, p. 148.

91. A woman's letter to *Zanan*, no. 35, Tir 1376, p. 26.

92. Parliament member Reja'i, quoted in *Itila'at*, 15 Bahman 1367 (1988).

93. Post-Islamist women activists were especially encouraged by the collaborative approach of some secular feminists. For a discussion and attempts to build an alliance of post-Islamist and secular feminists, see Tohidi, *Feminism*. See also her "Islamic Feminism."

94. For a fine exposition of *Zanan*'s views and vision, see Najmabadi, "Feminism in an Islamic Republic."

95. See *Zanan*'s own survey of its readership in *Zanan*, no. 52, Murdad-Shahrivar 1374 (1995), pp. 54–58.

96. Tabari, "Islam and the Struggle," p. 17.

97. If Eve was "weaker," the feminists argued, then she was less guilty than Adam

in causing his fall. They went on to suggest that woman (Eve) was more noble than man (Adam), because man was created from earth and woman from man. Indeed woman was considered superior because only she, not man, gives birth, or "increases the world." See Lerner, *The Creation of Feminist Consciousness*, pp. 138–66. On instances of feminist theology in Christianity and Judaism, see Bayes and Tohidi *Globalization, Gender and Religion*, chap. 2.

98. *Zanan*, no. 9, p. 34.

99. Attention to children is emphasized in such verses as "*al-māl wa bunūn*" (the wealth and children)(Kahf: 46), and the *ahādīth*: "Children are the butterflies of heaven," or "no sin is bigger than ignoring children" exemplify the centrality of caring for children. See *Zanan*, no. 38, Aban 1376, pp. 2–5.

100. See Sa'idzadih, "Kalbud shikafi-yi Tarh-i Intiqal-i Umur-i Idari," p. 15.

101. According to *The Qur'an*, translated by Abdullah Yusuf Ali (Beirut: Dar al-Arabia, n.d.).

102. See interview with Mustafa Malakian in *Zanan*, no. 64, pp. 32–35.

103. Shukri and Labriz, "Mard: Sharik ya Ra'īs?," *Zanan*, no. 2, March 1992, pp. 26–32.

104. *Zanan*, no. 23, Farvardin-Urdibahasht 1374 (1995), pp. 46–57.

105. See, for instance, *Kar*, "Musharikat-i Siyasi-yi Zanan."

106. *Zanan*, no. 35, Tir 1376, p. 6.

107. Clerics Ayatollah Bojnordi of Qum Seminary stated: "*Fiqh* [which contains some discriminatory rulings] is nothing but the particular perceptions of *fuqahā* (jurists); and it can be changed"; see *Farzānih*, no. 8.

108. Quoted in *Māhnāmih-i Guzarish*, no. 148, Tir 1382.

109. *Jumhūri-i Islāmi*, 12 Mahr 1376 (1997).

110. *Zanan*, no. 43, Khurdad 1377 (1998).

111. *Zanan*, no. 38, Abab 1379 (2000), p. 59.

112. Reported in *Zanan*, no. 42, Farvardin-Urdibahasht 1377 (1998), p. 3.

113. *Haftih Namih-i Subh*, no. 32, Aban 1375 (1996), and 28 Farvardin 1375 (1996).

114. See the report of the magazine's trial in *Zanan*, no. 43, Khurdad 1377 (1998), p. 4.

115. For a fine analysis of the gender debates among the Iranian Shi'i clerics, see Mir-Hosseini, *Islam and Gender*.

116. This is compared to 283,253 permanent or normal marriages during the same period. See *Hayat-i Naw*, 11 Aban 1381 (2002), p. 11. It has to be noted that *mut'a* marriage is not always registered. Therefore its real frequency might be higher.

117. For the complete list, see *Zanan*, no. 28, Farvardin 1375 (1996), p. 3.

118. *Zanan*, no. 38, Aban 1376 (1997), p. 38.

119. But women's share of seats in the Parliament, 6 percent, was still far short of the world average of 11.6 percent; the average in Arab countries was 4.3 percent; see *Zanan*, no. 33, p. 76.

120. Cited in Mostaghimi, "Rights—Iran." Over 80 percent of divorces in 2000 were initiated by women. For the report, see Shadi Sadr in *Yas-i Naw*, cited on the website of *Zanan-i Iran* [May 4, 2003].

121. *Zanan*, no. 34, Urdibahasht 1376 (1997), p. 4; and no. 37, Shahrivar-Mahr 1376 (1997), p. 8. A study by Uzra Shalbaf confirmed that women (wives) with higher education had more extensive decision-making power in families, although their domestic responsibilities had changed only modestly. M.A. thesis, Faculty of Social Sciences, Sociology, University of Tehran, 2001, womeniniran.com [May 21, 2003].

122. See *Zanan*, no. 41.

123. See Azadih, "Junbish-i Ijtima'i-yi Zananih," *Zanan-e Iran* website [November 11, 2003].

124. Mahdi, *Iran-i Imruz* website [July 2002]; Moghadam, "Feminism in Iran and Algeria"; Hoodfar, "The Women's Movement in Iran"; Azadeh, "Jonbesh-e Ejtemai-ye 'Zananeh'," www.womeniniran.com.

125. Jala'ipur, "Mas'alih-i Ijtima'i, Na Junbish-i Ijtima'i"; see also his "Tahlil-i az Puyish-i Zanan-i Iran."

126. Reported in *Zanan*, no. 26, p. 5.

127. Between 1990 and 1997 some thirteen new women's magazines were published (*Nada, Rahruvan-i Sumayih, Burish, Pigāh, Mi'raj, Jalvih, Payam-i Zan, Zanan, Takāpū, Farzānih, Rayhanih, Tūbā*, and *Bānū*. Between Khatami's election and 2002, there emerged twenty-three new women's publications: *Zan va Pazhūhish, Zan* (a newspaper), *Irshād-i Niswān, Hamsar, Mahtab, Kitāb-i Zanān, Pūshish, Qarn-i 21, Zanān-i Junūb, Zān-i Imrūz, al-Zahra, Banu, Nūr-i Barān, Shamīmi Nargis, Surūsh-Bānuvān, Tarh va Mūd, Yās, Irāndukht, Mutali'āt-i Zān, Malinih, 'Arūs, Zanān-i Farda, Zan-i Sharqi, Kawkab*. As of 2000, five of these journals had been shut down by the authorities. See *Yas-i Naw*, May 23, 1382 (2003).

128. For a critical survey of the Women's Studies programs see Jalali-Na'ini, "Ta'sīs-i Rishtih-i Mutal'āt-i Zanān dar Irān."

129. For an elaboration of the concept of the "passive network" see Bayat, *Street Politics*, chap. 1.

130. Sexual tension was at the center of Ayatollah Javadi Āmuli's argument against women being able to act as *qādis* or *faqīh*; see *Zanan*, no. 9, p. 30.

131. Quoted in *Zanan*, no. 37, Shahrivar-Mahr 1376 (1998), p. 56. In some sense this process resembles the strategy of "quiet encroachment," which I have elaborated elsewhere to conceptualize the politics of ordinary people, the urban marginals in developing countries. It describes the nonconfrontational politics of redistributing social goods, public space, land, collective consumption, and business opportunities by means of prolonged, quiet, and discrete direct actions. Like the movement by the urban poor, the women's movement in Iran was a discrete, protracted, and incremental process of capturing gains, a process closely tied to the practices of everyday life. However,

whereas the urban marginals operate on the periphery of, and therefore can get around, both the normative and (modern) legal structures, women actors needed to function at the center of, and thus challenge the constraining codes of such structures.

132. Dawani, *Nahzat-i Ruhāniyān-i Irān*, p. 67.

133. *Guzidihhayyih az Maqalat-i Payam-i Hajar*, no. 1, Tehran: Women's Association of the Islamic Revolution, July 12, 1980.

134. Quoted in *Zanan*, no. 9, p. 30.

135. A study on sexuality and social outlook ("Jinsiyat va Nigarish-i Ijtimā'i") sponsored by the Ministry of Culture revealed a high discrepancy between the views of men and women on "contentment in life," with women expecting much more than men. Reported by IRNA News agency, 11 Khurdad 1383 (2004), cited on the *Iran-i Imruz* website.

136. For a good study of the Reformation, see Cameron, *The European Reformation*.

137. Khatami, *Bim-i Mawj*, p. 139.

138. Ibid., pp. 198–205.

139. Ibid.; see also Surush, speech at Imperial College, London, 1996, reported in *Kiyan*, vol. 6, no. 30, June 1996, p. 43.

140. A leading religious philosopher, Mustafa Malakian, disputed the accuracy of the term "religious intellectuals" since, he argued, the term "intellectual" in the European tradition has been associated with reason and rationality, and "religion" with irrationality and superstition. But Iranian intellectuals were religious people even though they believed in "Islam 1" (Qur'an and Sunna [the way the prophet lived]) rather than "Islam 2" (laws and interpretations) or "Islam 3" (popular Islam). Malakian proposed instead "new religious thinkers" (*naw andish-i dīni*). See his interview with Akbar Ganji, in *Rah-i Naw*, no. 13, Tir 1377 (1998), pp. 21–22.

141. See for instance, Jala'ipur, several articles in his collection *Pas az Duvvum-i Khurdad*, especially pp. 24–25, 286–90; Ganji, *Talaqqi-yi Fashisti az Din va Hukumat*; Hajjariyan, *Az Shahid-i Qudsi ta Shahid-i Bazari*; and Ashkivary, *Naw Girā'-i Dīni*

142. Khatami in the early years was emphatic about building such self-confidence. See his speech to the youth in Mas'ud La'li, *Khatami az Chih Miguyad*.

143. Interview with Hajjariyan in Baqi, *Barayi-i Tarikh*.

144. See Jala'ipur, *Pas az Duvvum-i Khurdad*.

145. Jala'ipur expressed it this way to David Hirst in *Guardian Weekly*, posted on wolfie.guardian.co.uk [December 4, 1998].

146. Shamsulva'izin saw a continuity between the current "religious intellectuals" and those of the prerevolution, viewing the 1990s period as one of 'revisioning' (*baznegari*) (see editorial, "Religious Intellectuals and the Third Republic," *Kiyan*, no. 37, vol. 7, June 1997). But in this book I argue that there was a distinct break.

147. Surush, "Religion and the Contemporary World," lecture presented in Los Angeles, 1997, cited in *Kiyan*, no. 36, April–May 1997, p. 56.

148. Its despotic past is highlighted prominently in Zibakalam, *Ma Chira Chinin Shudim?*

149. See Jala'ipur, *Pas az Duvvum-i Khurdad*, pp. 76–78.

150. See Ganji, *Tarik-khanih-i Ashbāh*, pp. 106–7; also Surush, "Idioluji va Din-i Dunyayi," *Kiyan*, no. 31, Tir/Murdad 1375 (1996), pp. 2–11.

151. Ganji, *Tarik-khanih-i Ashbāh*, p. 11.

152. Secular intellectuals, despite some initial hesitation, came to acknowledge that there was "such a thing as "religious intellectual" and that they had "some serious things to say"; see Daryush Ashuri, interview in *Farhang-i Tawsi'ih*, no. 31, cited in *Iran-i Farda*, no. 41, Farvardin 1377 (1998), p. 37.

153. "Post-colonial intellectuals" have been articulate and represented by such writers as Edward Said, Homi Bhaba, and many in the Subaltern Studies Group in India.

154. *Kiyan*, no. 26, p. 9.

155. Jala'ipur, *Pas az Duvvum-i Khurdad*, p. 194, 200.

156. Ibid., p. 194.

157. Muhammad Khatami, lecture presented to German intellectuals, reported in IRNA, 22 Tir, 1379 (2000).

158. Ibid.

159. Khatami, *Bim-i Mawj*, p. 193. Similarly, the cleric Muhammad Mujtahid Shabastari also proposes that Islamist thought leaders should establish a dialogue with modern Western thinkers, instead of being defensive. See *Kiyan*, no. 32, September–October 1996, p. 59, for a report on his lecture in Berlin, September 7, 1996.

160. See Kadivar, *Baha-yi Azadi*, pp. 153–54.

161. Sadiq Zibakalam, a professor of political science and a post-Islamist who served on the Committee of Cultural Revolution in the early 1980s, has stated, "Those days I would think that there were two kinds of social science and humanities, Islamic and un-Islamic. Now I realize that there is nothing more absurd than this view in the scientific realm" (quoted in *Iran-i Farda*, no. 49, Aban-Azar 1377 (1998). Similarly, Akbar Ganji has said that "there is no ground for the existence of such a thing as religious social science" (see Ganji, *Talaqqi-yi Fashisti*, p. 94). For Surush's position see his "Social Science in the University System," pp. 195–200.

162. Nuri, *Shukaran-i Islah*, p. 256.

163. Surush, in an interview with Roger Hardi, BBC World Service Program on Islam and Democracy.

164. See research paper by the cleric Muhsin Kadivar, "Freedom of Thought and Religion in Islam," presented at the International Congress of Human Rights and the Dialogue of Civilizations, Tehran, May 2001. See also his statement in *Hambastigi*, January 4, 2001, p. 3.

165. Surush elaborates on this in *Teori-i ghabz va bast Shariat* and in his article "Hurriyat va Rawhaniyat."

166. See, for instance, Surush, "Hurriyat va Rawhaniyat"; Aghajari, "Islamic Protestantism"; and Aghajari, *Hukumat-i Dini va Hukumat-i Dimukratik.*

167. Kadivar, *Iran-i Imruz* website [September 5, 2001].

168. Aghajari, "Islamic Protestantism."

169. Nuri, *Shukaran-i Islah*, p. 238. This idea is shared by many other clerics, including Muhammad Javad Akbariyan of the Qum Seminary who wrote in the daily *Khurdad* "Let us believe that we do not know the whole truth. . . . Only then can we come to think of freedom as a God-given right."

170. Ibid., p. 242.

171. Ibid., p. 243.

172. See, for instance, Kadivar, *Nazarihha-yi dawlat dar fiqh-i Shi'i.*

173. Surush, "Hasanat va Khadamat-i Din"; and Surush, "Tahlil-i Mafhum-i Hukumat-i Dini."

174. Surush in an interview with Roger Hardi of BBC; Jala'ipur with David Hirst of the *Guardian Weekly.* Kadivar expressed similar views in a lecture at the MESA Annual Meeting, November 25, 2002, Washington, D.C.

175. Surush, "Concepts of the Religious State," speech, University of Quebec, Montreal, July 17, 1996.

176. Interview with Muhsin Kadivar, in *Zanan*, no. 87, pp. 34–37.

177. Surush, "Hasanat va Khadamat-i Din."

178. Kadivar, lecture at MESA Annual Meeting, 2002.

179. My interview with Mujtahid Shabastari, Berlin, October 7, 2003.

180. Interview with Mustafa Malakian, a teacher in the Qum Seminary, in *Rah-i Naw*, no. 13, Tir 1377 (1998).

181. See, for instance, Plantinga, *Christianity and Plurality*; Wentz, *The Culture of Religious Pluralism.*

182. The initial audience for these ideas, according to a survey carried out by the monthly *Kiyan*, the major publication of religious intellectuals, was overwhelmingly male and roughly 30 years old. About half were married, some one-third were students, and the rest were employees of the state sector. About 80 percent were practicing Muslims, 20 percent secular. See *Kiyan*, vol. 5, no. 26, August–September 1995, pp. 46–49.

183. Muhammad Mujtahid Shabastari, lecture in Berlin, 1997; also my interview with Shabastari in Berlin, November 2003.

184. According to Mashallah Shamsulva'izin, the editor of *Kiyan*, interview in Tehran, January 4, 2004.

185. In 1989 and 1990, some ninety-one new publications appeared, and by 1993, seventy-eight others. See Farhang, "Karnamih-i Panjsalih-i Gushayish-i Tazih-i Matbu'ati."

186. They included Mujtahid Shabastari, Alireza Alavitabar, Muhsin Kadivar, and Said Hajjarian. Interview with Shamsulva'izin, 2004.

187. Jala'ipur, *Pas az Duvvum-i Khurdad*, pp. 44–45. Also interview with participants in these groups, August 2006.

188. In 1994 the flourishing debate in society compelled the Qum Bureau of the Assembly of Experts (*Majlis-i Khibrigān*) to begin its own research and discussion circles. A number of projects such as "*Marja'iyyat* and Leadership" (*Marja'iyyat va Rahbari*) and "Electing or Appointing" (*Intikhāb ya Intisāb*) unearthed the idea of the *vilāyat-i faqīh*. Here the post-Islamist Muhsin Kadivar confronted conservative clerics such as Ayatollah Meshkini, Misbah Yazdi, and Muhsin Kharazi on whether the government in Islam was to represent (*vakil*) the people or rule (*vali*) them. Some debates lasted up to eight hours; interview with Muhsin Kadivar, Amman, March 6, 2004.

189. Muhsin Kadivar's intellectual activities here entailed a three volume important book on Shi'ite political thought (*Nazarihaā-yi Dawlat*) in which he traced the origin of the idea of *vilāyat-i faqīh*, concluding that it was a recent (late nineteenth-century) innovation. Interview with Muhsin Kadivar, 2004.

190. Interview with Tajzadeh, in *Payam-i Imruz*, no. 41, Mahr 1379 (2000), pp. 42–43. See also interview with Sa'id Hajjariyan, in *Waqā'i-i Itifāqiyyih*, 27 Tir 1383 (2004). Although many ex-revolutionaries had, after the war, returned to college or learned foreign languages to pursue social and political studies, their intellectual development was owed partially to the prolific Husayn Bashiriyyih, a professor of politics, for writing and translating major surveys of political theory, including the work of Hobbs, Marx, Habermas, Foucault, Martin Luther, Darwin, and Churchill.

191. For these narratives see Baqi's interview with Hajjariyan in Baqi, *Barayi-i Tarikh*.

192. As discussed by Przeworski, "The Role of Theory in Comparative Politics," p. 1049.

193. Hajjariyan, in Baqi, *Barayi-i Tarikh*, pp. 45–46.

194. Nuri, *Shukarān*, p. 262.

195. Ibid., p. 255.

196. Expressed by Nuri, Surush, Jala'ipur, and others. See also Ashkivary, interviewed in *Shahrvand*, no. 491, June 20, 2000 (www.shahrvand.com).

197. Nuri, *Shukarān*, p. 226. See also Jala'ipur, interviewed by David Hirst, "Modernists' Take on Iran's Mullas," www.wolfie.guardian.co.uk [December 4, 1998].

198. Ganji, *Talaqqi-yi Fashisti*, p. 100. In fact, the concept of *vilāyat-i faqīh* was absent in the first draft of the constitution, which had been approved by both the Revolutionary Council and Ayatollah Khomeini. It was only on the insistence of some clerics that it was eventually inserted in the final draft (This is according to former president Hashemi Rafsanjani, who also was a member of the Revolutionary Council formed during the revolution.)

199. See Jala'ipur, *Pas az Duvvum-i Khurdad*, p. 191. Ganji, *Rah-i Naw*, no. 20, 14 Shahrivar 1377 (1998). Some of these views are also stressed by other ayatollahs such as

Hashemi Rafsanjani and especially Ayatollah JavadiĀmuli; see *Majallih-i Hukumat-i Islami*, no. 8, Summer 1377 (1998), pp. 28–29.

200. Ganji, *Islahgari-yi Mi'maranih*, p. 54.

201. *Bahar*, 2 Khurdad, 1379 (2000), p. 2.

202. Abdullah Nuri, for example, argued in his trial that we should consider Khomeini's approach to the United States, the Middle East peace process, and Israel in historical terms. In short, times have changed, and we should reconsider our attitudes toward these issues. See Nuri, *Shukaran-i Islah*, pp. 128, 139, 145, 149.

203. This was acknowledged by Yusifi Ashkivary, who has argued that we need to find answers to the question of the relationship between religion and the state. "Does Islam propose a particular form for the state? Are religious laws eternal? Would the state have a particular obligation toward religion?" See his interview in *Shahrvand*, no. 491, June 20, 2000.

204. See, for instance, Hashim Aghajari, a leader of OMIR and member of Parliament, in *Iran*, 5 Urdibahasht 1379 (2000).

205. Jala'ipur, in an interview with David Hirst, www.wolfie.guardian.co.uk [December 4, 1998].

206. Mujtahid Shabastari, *Naqdi bar Qira'at-i Rasmi az Din*, p. 144.

207. See Hamidreza Jala'ipur, untitled article on the website of *Ruyadad*, 15 Mahr 1381 (2002). For the sources of other views on religious democracy see Mujtahid Shabastari, "Dimukrasi-yi Dini"; 'Alavitabar, "Questions about Religious Democracy."

208. Hajjariyan, a letter to Roya Monfared, a dissident sociologist living abroad; published on the website of *Iran-i Imruz*, 15 Shahrivar 1380.

209. The statement was made by a veteran secular journalist, Mas'ud Bahnud, in an interview with *Iran*, 15 Tir 1379 (2000).

210. These included Ayatollah 'Abd al-Qasim Musavi Khu'i (d. 1992 in Najaf), Ayatollah Kazim Shari'atmadari (d. 1983), Ayatollah Muhammad Reza Golpaīgani, Ayatollah Araki, and Ayatollah Muntazari (who sees only a supervisory role for *vali-i faqīh*). Also, Ayatollah Shirazi, leader of the Bahraini Shi'is, and Shaykh Muhammad Fadhlullah (the Lebanese Shi'i leader) did not support Khomeini's *vilāyat-i faqīh*; my interview, December 2005, Beirut.

211. See Muntazari, *Khatirat-i Ayatullah Husayn Muntazari*, which is undated, but appeared in 2001 in the United States; Bazargan, *Shast Sal Khidmat va Muqawimat*; see also various reports by Amnesty International covering the 1980s.

212. For an excellent elaboration on Islamic economics in Iran see Behdad, "A Disputed Utopia."

213. See Karbasian, "The Process of Income Distribution in Iran," p. 44. See also Behdad, "Winners and Losers."

214. This figure is cited by Muhsin Reza'i, the former commander of the Revolutionary Guards, in *Iran-i Farda*, no. 44, Tir 1377(1998), p. 16.

215. On the urban riots of 1990s see Bayat, *Street Politics*, pp. 106–08.

216. Reported by the President of Tehran University during the Cultural Revolution, Muhammad Malaki; see Malaki, "The Students and the Cultural Revolution," p. 18.

217. For a good discussion, see Turbat, "Farar-i Maghzha az Iran bih Amrika.

218. According to an official, about 80 percent of the winners of scientific competitions from Iran left for Western universities; *Jumhūri-i Islāmi*, 15 Shahrivar 1379 (1990). According to the minister of science and technology, some 22,000 leading academics and industrialists left Iran during 2000 alone; cited in IRNA, May 2001.

219. See Turbat, "Farar-i Maghzha az Iran bih Amrika, p. 78; see also the daily *Iran*, February 19, 2002, p. 2.

220. Interview with Tabarzadi, a hard-line Islamist student leader, in *Huviyyat-i Khish*, May 1, 1999, p. 8. It is translated by and quoted in Yaghmaian, "Student Movement," p. 35.

221. Interview with Tabarzadi.

222. See Kadivar, *Baha-yi Azadi*, p. 146.

223. *Itila'at*, 15 Farvardin 1377 (1998), quoted in *Iran-i Farda*, no. 42, Urdibahasht 1377 (1998), p. 34.

224. Report by Hujjat al-Islam Muhammad 'Ali Zam, head of the Cultural and Artistic Department of Tehran Municipality, cited in *Bahār*, 15 Tir 1379 (2000), p. 13.

225. See Nuruzi, "Nigāhi bi Amār-i Huqūqi."

226. *Hambastigi*, 30 Aban 1379 (2000), p. 7.

227. A self-reflection by Hashmatullah Tabarzadi in *Huviyyat-i Khish*, May 1, 1999, p. 8; quoted in Yaghmaian, "Student Movement," p. 35. Tabarzadi's recollections are revealing and worth quoting at length: "Like Marxism that has a utopia, a utopia was shaped in the minds of Moslem and revolutionary forces [at the beginning of the Revolution]. Our utopia was to establish a world Islamic government. In our models at that time, the leader had a special and superior position. He was viewed and propagated as a charismatic and sacred person. Revolutionary forces . . . were judged by the degree of their closeness to the ideas of the Leader. . . . The legitimacy of each person or group was determined by the degree of subordination and closeness to the leader and the first person. . . . Now this is contrary to a civil society where . . . power is distributed according to people's votes. The pyramid of power is bottom up. . . . The system of *vilāyat-i faqīh* showed its limitations in the political, economic, and administrative system especially after [signing] the [UN] resolution [ending the war between Iran and Iraq]. It became clear that despite many of the slogans . . . like justice and the defense of toilers and the deprived . . . the country, instead of approaching its utopia of more justice and equality, was being pushed back. . . . It was due to these that the first sparks of self-examination surfaced, and intellectual debates found their space in society." See also Irani, "Society and the Religious Intellectuals."

228. *Kiyan*, editorial, no. 12, vol. 3, Khurdad 1372 (1993).

229. For the actual wording of Khomeini's letter to then President Khamenei, see Khomeini, *Sahifih-yi Nur*, vol. 20, p. 170. Some went even further, arguing that the "*vali-i faqīh* could suspend the principle of *tawhīd*."

230. Khomeini, *Shu'un va Khiyarat-i Vali-yi Faqīh*, p. 57.

231. It contradicts the principle that sovereignty in the Islamic Republic belongs to the people, and that the *faqīh* is elected, can be dismissed by, and is accountable to the Assembly of Experts. The latter is elected by the people.

232. Initially, the constitution authorized the *faqīh* to be elected directly by the people from among the grand clergy, *marja'*. And the *marja'* have traditionally been selected by their peers in a long process without a precise institutional procedure (see Mallat, *The Renewal of Islamic Law*, p. 44). The constitution was amended after Khomeini's death. It was no longer necessary for the *faqīh* or the religious leadership of the Shi'a community, to be from the *marja'*. In addition, he was to be elected not directly by the people but by the Assembly of Experts. This angered a number of the grand clergy.

233. It is this logic that convinced many post-Islamists, such as Sa'id Hajjariyan and Akbar Ganji, that the "secular state is the unintended consequence of *vilāyat-i mutlaqih-i faqīh*." Ganji, *Talaqqi-yi Fashisti*, p. 97. Hajjariyan, "The Process of the Secularization."

234. Kadivar, *Baha-yi Azadi*, p. 156.

235. Hujjat al-Islam Muhammad 'Ali Rahmani, cited in *Nuruz*, 7 Murdad 1380, p. 2.

236. Thus "the fundamental task of the religious intellectual [was] to struggle against the abuse of religion" (Surush's lecture at the Islamic Center in Oakland, Calif., March 4, 1997). Post-Islamists have made numerous arguments for separating religion from the state, advocating a healthy formula of both a "minimalist state" and "minimalist religion." Surush and 'Abdullah Nuri, for instance, argue that a maximalist Catholic Church led to secularism and eventually undermined religion altogether. See Nuri, *Shukaran-i Islah*, p. 13; Surush, "Development and Fundamental Questions," lecture delivered at Essex University, UK, October 12, 1996.

237. See, for instance, 'Abdullah Nuri's defense of such concepts during his trial, *Shukaran-i Islah*, pp. 265–68.

238. Reported in Muhammadi, *Darāmadi bar Raftar-Shināsi*, p. 102, n.21.

239. Behdad and Nomani, "Involution and De-involution."

240. Hooglund, "Change in Rural Patterns."

241. Reported on the website of *Baztab* [January 7, 2003].

242. Reza'i, "Nime-yi Pur-i Livan," p. 118.

243. In a survey of the city of Isfahan in 2003, 30 percent of families were reported to be "matriarchal" and another 40 percent "child-centered"; cited in Adib, "Exiled Opposition and Neo-Liberalism" (in Persian), on the website of *Akhbār-i Rūz* [April 8, 2004].

244. See, for example, a study sponsored by the Ministry of Culture and National Guidance, "Jinsiyat va Nigarish-i Ijtimāʿi," which concluded that Iranian women had acquired a new "autonomous identity," the nuclear family was consolidated, and women were much less satisfied with their lives than their male counterparts; reported by IRNA, 11 Khurdad 1383 (2004).

245. Only half of Iranian youths considered "making their parents happy" to be a main goal, compared to 80 percent of the young in Egypt and 86 percent in Jordan. Moaddel, "The Worldviews of Islamic Politics."

246. See Behdad and Nomani, "Workers, Peasants, and Peddlers."

247. Reja'i, "Poverty and Political Developments."

248. For a discussion of the economics of this "educated" middle class see, ʿAzimi, "Chenin Shive-yi Gām Bardashtan beh Sou-yi Buhran Ast," p. 41.

Notes to Chapter 4

1. See special report in *Payam-i Imruz*, no. 45, Isfand 1380 (2001), pp. 19–23; see also Piran, "Se Sath-i Tahlili-yi Vaqiʿiyih," p. 21.

2. According to Mustafa Muʿin, the minister of science and technology, in *Nuruz*, 11 Tir 1380 (2001), p. 10.

3. See interview by the Iranian Students News Agency (ISNA) with Reza Dalbari, the leader of the Islamic Association at Amir Kabir University, which appeared on the website of *Iran-i Imruz* [January 20, 2003].

4. For a theoretical discussion of "social movement animation," see my "Islamism and Social Movement Theory."

5. Between 1997 and 2003, the number of women's NGOs grew more than fourfold, women publishers by 56 percent, women authors by 265 percent, and professional female athletes twelvefold. Report by Zahra Shujaʿi, vice president for women's affairs, cited on the website of Muhammad ʿAli Abtahi, 24 Isfand 1382 (2003).

6. *Iran Briefing*, December 1997, vol. 7, no. 4.

7. Reported in *Kiyan*, no. 40, Feb.–March 1997.

8. *Al-Hayat*, March 10, 1998.

9. Saʿid Hajjariyan, interview, on the Persian website of *Ruydad*, 10 Aban 1381 [November 21, 2002].

10. Reported in *Aftab-i Yazd*, December 14, 2000, p. 5.

11. *Hayat-i Naw*, August 29, 2000.

12. Interview with ʿAlireza Mahjoub, general secretary of Labor House, and Hasan Sadiqi, the head of the Central Islamic Work Councils, reported in *Hambastigi*, June 23, 2001, p. 5.

13. Reported in the daily *Nuruz*, 4 Tir 1380 (2001), p. 9.

14. Reported in the daily *Iran*, April 27, 2002. On women's NGOs see Hamidreza

Jala'ipur, *Jami'a Shinasi-i Junbishhā-yi Ijtima'i*, Table 4. Also see the website of Muhammad 'Ali Abtahi, 24 Isfand 1382 (2003).

15. See *al-Hayat*, April 23, 1998.

16. It is estimated that in Iran each daily newspaper is read by an average of four people. According to Issa Saharkhiz, editor of *Aftab* monthly; lecture in Amsterdam, 25 June 2004.

17. Reported in *Kiyan*, November–January 1999, p. 57.

18. *Yas-i Naw*, "Nashriyat-i Zanan az Ruz-i Sifr ta Imruz," 23 Day 1382 (2003), p. 11.

19. The circulation of the main conservative dailies in 2000 were as follows: *Kayhan* 200,000, *Jumhuri-i Islami* 70,000, *Quds* 56,000, and *Risālat* 36,000; see *Hayat-i Naw*, September 3, 2000.

20. Issa Saharkhiz, lecture in Amsterdam, June 24, 2004.

21. See 'Ali Bahrampur, "Qualitative Development of the Press after the Duvvum-i Khurdad," *Aftab*, no. 10, Azar 1380 (2001), pp. 48–53.

22. Reported in *al-Hayat*, February 19 and March 2, 1999.

23. I base this on the findings of Kian Tajbakhsh about the workings of city councils on Birjand and Sanandaj, two provincial cities. See his "Political Decentralization."

24. *Al-Hayat*, September 26, 1998.

25. Ibid.

26. For a discussion of the influence of Iran on the Middle East, see Bayat and Baktiari, "Revolutionary Iran and Egypt."

27. See the statement by OMIR (Organization of the Mujahedin of the Islamic Revolution) in *Bahar*, 2 Khurdad 1379 (2000), p. 2.

28. Reported in *Kiyan*, no. 30, June 1996, p. 43.

29. Reported in *Azād*, 11 Mahr 1378 (1999).

30. Cited in *Hayat-i Naw*, September 30, 2000, p. 3.

31. Cited in *Khurdad*, 5 Mahr 1378 (1999).

32. Cited in *Khurdad*, 27 Shahrivar 1378 (1999).

33. See *Azād*, 11 Mahr 1378 (1999).

34. *Salam*, 4 Aban 1374 (1995).

35. Cited in *Kiyan*, no. 48, August–September 1999.

36. Cited in *Iran-i Farda*, no. 36, Shahrivar 1376 (1998), p. 10; *Iran-i Farda*, no, 40, Bahman 1376 (1997), p. 27.

37. Ayatollah Misbah Yazdi , cited in *Hambastigi*, March 12, 2001, p. 2.

38. In *Lithārāt*, cited in *Iran-i Farda*, no. 41, Farvardin 1377 (1998), p. 37.

39. Stated by the cleric Wa'iz Tabasi, the custodian of Imam Reza Shrine in Mashad, see *Quds*, 17 Aban 1376 (1997); cited also in *Iran-i Farda*, Day 1376 (1997).

40. *Mashriq*, no. 5, Murdad 1374 (1995), p. 6.

41. Hujjat al-Islam Sazgar, director of the Political-Ideological Department of the Army in Kirman; see the weekly *Shalamchih*, no. 33.

42. Islamist monthly *Subh*, no. 74.

43. Stated by Mullah Hasani, Friday prayer leader (appointee of the supreme *faqīh*) in Urumiyih, cited in *Iran-i Farda*, no. 36, p. 13.

44. An interview with Islamist intellectual Dr. Muhammad Madadpur, in *Abrar*, July 18, 2000, p. 6.

45. Interview with an Iranian conservative cleric on British television, channel 4, February 28, 2001.

46. See *Bahar*, May 29, 2000, p. 2; and *Iran*, May 7, 2000.

47. Speech by Husayn Shari'atmadari, reported on the *Iran-i Imruz* website [July 13, 2000].

48. Ayatollah 'Ali Khamenei, reported in *Ham-Mihan*, 24 Urdibahasht 1379 (2000).

49. See speech by Ayatollah 'Ali Khamenei, reported in *Iran*, May 13, 2000, p. 4.

50. See Gramsci, *Prison Notebooks*.

51. Speech by Ayatollah Khamenei, reported on the *Iran-i Imruz* website, 6 Murdad 1381 (2002). The moderate conservative daily *Risālat*, while recognizing the necessity of "new religious thought," followed a formulation similar to that of the supreme leader, advocating "justice-seeking reforms," which in essence meant to ignore reforming the political system; see *Risālat*, January 2, 2002, p. 3.

52. See the monthly *Partaw Sukhan*, 14 Day 1379 (2000). This publication was supervised by Ayatollah Mizbah Yazdi, an outspoken conservative cleric.

53. In *Shalamchih*, cited in *Iran-i Farda*, no. 45, Murdad 1377 (1998), p. 24.

54. Based on the "confessions" of Amir Farshad Ibrahimi, a member of such a group, cited in *Payam-i Imruz*, no. 40, Tir-Murdad 1379 (2000), pp. 28–29.

55. For the text of Amir Farshad Ibrahimi's confessions, see *Payam-i Imruz*, no. 40, Tir-Murdad 1379 (2000), pp. 14–34. The magazine includes interviews with many of those who were implicated by these "confessions" and who disputed Ibrahimi's claims. A report on the backgrounds of seventy-two members of Ansar-i Hizbullah who were arrested on charges of violence (and immediately released) gives some idea of their social composition: of those seventy-two, there were some fifty theology students in Qum and Isfahan, four Revolutionary Guards, three sons of war victims, four brothers of war victims, twelve *basīj* members, and a few shopkeepers; in *Lithārāt*, cited in *Iran-i Farda*, no. 41, Farvardin 1377 (1998), p. 37.

56. According to the intelligence minister, 'Ali Yunasi, in *Itila'at*, 6 Shahrivar 1378 (1999).

57. *Al-Hayat*, December 22, 1998, and January 25, 1999.

58. Bahzad Nabavi, in a statement on the website of *Ruydad* [November 10, 2002].

59. Reported in *Kiyan*, December 1997–January 1998.

60. A veteran journalist who was among the delegation on the bus related this astonishing story.

61. The exiled publication *Inqilāb-i Islāmi*, published by former president Bani

Sadr, printed the names of 107 people it claimed had been murdered by such elements. See *Inqilāb-i Islāmi*, no. 477, December 1999.

62. Mushārikat, 6 Urdibahasht 1379 (2000), p. 2; see also Moaveni, "Ballot Blowing in the Wind."

63. *Yas-i Naw*, August 9, 2003, *Imruz* website [August 10, 2003].

64. See the biographies of Hajjariyan's assassins published by the Ministry of Intelligence, reported on the website of *Iran-i Imruz* [April 4, 2000].

65. Reported by Jim Muir, BBC, July 7, 2002.

66. Before he went to prison, Ganji reminded the public that one official had warned him to stop talking about the serial murders, "otherwise I would get seven to fifteen years jail"; see *Bayān*, 10 Urdibahasht 2000. He added that whatever might happen to him in prison (i.e., murder) the Islamic Republic would be responsible.

67. See, for instance, Nuri's *Shukaran-i Islah*; Baqi's *Tirajidi-i Dimukrasi dar Iran*; Kadivar's *Baha-yi Azadi*. Muhsin Mirdamadi published a three-volume book of his defense in the Press Court in January 2003 when his daily, *Nuruz*, was banned. Muhajirani's account of his impeachment was reprinted six times within twenty days of its publication.

68. For *basiji* activities see Darabi, "Tarh-i Basij va Ahdaf-i Ān."

69. See Bayat, "Iran's Brave New World," also published in *Middle East International*, July 1999 (London).

70. Reported on the website of *Imruz* [January 2, 2002].

71. Representatives of many exiled groups attended the conference "Civil Society, Rule of Law and Its Relevance to People's Rule in Iran," held in Copenhagen, November 1998; reported in Gulf2000 e-mail, November 17, 1998 (www.Gulf2000project. columbia.edu).

72. *Financial Times*, December 26, 2001.

73. *Nuruz*, 8 Day 1380 (2001), p. 11.

74. Stated by a member of the Council of Guardians, cited in *Iran*, 15 Tir 1381 (2002).

75. Some important groups affiliated with the SCC included the Islamic Association of Doctors, the Islamic Society of Workers, the Islamic Society of Academics, the Islamic Society of College Students, the Islamic Society of Teachers, the Society of Tehran Preachers, and the Islamic Center of Alumni of the Indian Subcontinent. See Hujjat Murtaji, *Jinahayih Siyāsi dar Irān-i Imrūz*, p. 14.

76. *Aftab-i Yazd*, January 3, 2001, p. 2.

77. Personal communication with Mujtaba Sadriya, who has conducted a study of the political and economic elites that ruled the Islamic Republic, January 2005.

78. When in January 2003, the Islamic Association of the Guilds and the Bazaar, linked to the conservative Jam'iyyat-i Mu'talifih, called for a strike in the bazaar to protest the printing in the reformist daily *Hayat-i Naw* of an allegedly offending car-

toon, only a handful of bazaaries responded. And no more than 300 people turned out for the association's rally. See the website of *Ruydad*, January 13, 2003. The declining political significance of the bazaar for the clerical class is emphasized in a detailed study by Keshavarzian, "A Bazaar and Two Regimes."

79. Reported in Akhavipur and Azdanloo, "Economic Basis of Political Factions in Iran."

80. See a useful report in *Oxford Analytica*, reprinted in *Payam-i Imruz*, issue 32, Murdad 1378 (1999), pp. 44–45.

81. These included the Qum Seminary, Daftar-i Tablīqāt-i Islāmi, Shurā-i Hamāhangi-i Tablīqāt-i Islāmi, Majmāʿ-i Islāmi-i Ahl-i Bayt, Sāzmān-i Tablīgāt-i Islāmi, Markaz-i Jahān-i Islāmi, and others; see *Aftab-i Yazd*, December 13, 2000, p. 2.

82. Muhammadi, *Darāmadi bar Raftar-Shināsi*, pp. 95–96.

83. See an interesting report by Arash Hasan-nia, "Nikukarani kih Nizarat ra Dust Nadarand," *Sharq*, 25 Shahrivar 1383/September 15, 2004.

84. See, for instance, the statements by Ayatollah Shahrudi, the head of the judiciary, on how "religious democracy" was in conflict with democracy as such; cited on the *Iran-i Imruz* Persian website [December 24, 2002].

85. See an interesting report by de Bellaigue, "Who Rules Iran?"; see also Fathi, "Political Fervor of Iranian Clerics."

86. *Aftab-i Yazd*, 1 Isfand 1379 (February 19, 2001), p. 2.

87. See, for instance, *Jumhuri-i Islami*, May 1, 2000.

88. Even Ayatollah Shahrudi, the head the judiciary, publicly said that the words of Rahbar had special—that is, extralegal—executive value (*Iran*, April 25, 2000). When Khamenei vetoed the Parliament's decision on the press law, the reformist speaker of the Majlis justified his interference by referring to his absolute power, the *vilāyat-i mutlaqih-i faqīh*.

89. *Harīm*, 13 Aban 1381 (2002).

90. *Iran-i Imruz* website [November 7, 2002].

91. See the website of *Ruydad* [November 11, 2002].

92. See lead article in *Abrar*, November 17, 2002, p. 1.

93. See *Imruz* website [November 17, 2002].

94. Newark (N.J.) *Star-Ledger*, November 14, 2002.

95. *Newsweek* website [December 7, 2002].

96. On the eleventh day of the sit-ins, days after deputies' "political fast," the editorial of the reformist daily *Yas-i Naw* was still wondering where the masses, students, teachers and workers were.

97. Based upon *Yas-i Naw* and *Sharq*, January 9 through January 30, 2004.

98. A perceptive analysis may be found in Saghafi, "The Reform Nobody Wants Anymore."

99. Ali-Reza ʿAlavitabar, a reformist intellectual, called on the student movement

to pursue the tactic of "two steps forward, one step back"; see *Subh-i Imrūz*, 15 Azar 1378 (1999). See also *Mushārikat*, 7 Urdibahasht 1379 (2000). According to the Tehran University Student Association, "The strategy of the student movement at present is to assist the implementation of reform. . . . Protection of human dignity, justice, eradicating despotism, institutionalizing freedom and rights in the light of religiosity and spirituality constitute the major themes of the reform objectives"; manifesto of the Islamic Association of Tehran University Students, cited by ISNA (Iranian Students News Agency), 17 Tir 1379 (2000).

100. *Bahar*, 16 Khurdad 1379 (2000), p. 3.

101. *Hayat-i Naw*, 24 Murdad 1379 (2000).

102. See interview with Bahzad Nabavi in *Sharq*, May 9, 2004.

103. See, for instance, Muhibbian, "Towsiyiha-i bih Jibhih-i Musharikat."

104. Cited in Khurdad, 7 Aban 1378 (1999).

105. Cited by ʿAlireza Mahjub, the general secretary of Labor House (Khānih-i Kārgar) in an interview with ISNA, April 6, 2004.

Notes to Chapter 5

1. Mubarak, *al-Irhabiyun Qadimun*.

2. Sivan, "The Islamic Republic of Egypt"; Cassandra, "The Impending Crisis in Egypt."

3. Over 82 percent of people in villages in the south and 74 percent in the city of Asyut were poor.

4. In fact scholars such as Mamoun Fandy, a political scientist from the Saʿid, characterized the Jamaʿa as essentially a "regional movement" from the south struggling against the privileged north. See Fandy, "Egypt's Islamic Group."

5. See Hobsbawm, *Primitive Rebels*.

6. Mubarak, *al-Irhabiyun Qadimun*, pp. 181–82.

7. Ibid., pp. 264–65.

8. Hamdi al-Basir, "Al-Unf fil-Mahaliyyat" (Violence in localities: a study of the village of Sanbu in Dayrut [Asyut governorate] (in Arabic), paper presented at the Second Annual Conference of Political Studies, "Politics and Localities in Egypt," Cairo University, December 3–5, 1994.

9. Mubarak, *al-Irhabiyun Qadimun*, p. 378.

10. The main figures in the first generation of leaders included ʿAbud al-Zumur, Karam Zuhdi, Najih Ibrahim, Tariq al-Zumur, Farid al-Dawalibi, and Hamdi ʿAbd al-Rahman.

11. *Al-Hayat*, January 13, 1999, p. 8; interview with ʿAbd al-Hasan Salih, a local leader and the head of the local city council in Asyut.

12. The Egyptian Organization for Human Rights, *Annual Reports*, 1991, 1992, 1993, 1994, 1995, 1996, 1997, Cairo.

13. Arbitrary arrests by the security forces were protested not only by the human rights organizations, but also by members of Parliament and the Egyptian opposition press. See Gamal Essam el-Din, "Parliament Scrutinizes Policing Policies," *al-Ahram Weekly*, December 11–17, 1997, p. 2; see also *al-Wafd*, December 11, 1997, p. 3.

14. Khaled Dawoud, "Jama'a Militant Sentenced to Death," *al-Ahram Weekly*, April 20–26, 2000.

15. *Cairo Times*, December 27, 1997, p. 5.

16. According to Egypt's central bank, earnings from foreign tourism during 1999–2000 amounted to EL17 billion (about US$4 billion). This accounts for 25 to 30 percent of foreign earnings. At the time, some 2.3 million Egyptians were employed in tourism. Cited in al-Sharbini, "Azmat al-Siyaha al-Masriya wa Imkaniyat al-Ta'wid," p. 151.

17. See details in *Ahram Weekly*, December 4–10, 1997, p. 3; *al-Ahram Weekly*, December 11–17, 1997, p. 2; while exiled leaders in Europe (Usama Rushdi and Yasir Sirri) regretted the incident, Ayman al-Zawahiri's al-Jihad group based in Afghanistan welcomed the massacre but said future attacks should be focused on the Americans and Israelis; see *al-Ahram Weekly*, November 27–December 3, 1997, p. 3. Imprisoned leaders in Egypt said that the attack was carried out "by young members . . . acting on their own"; *al-Ahram Weekly*, December 11–17, 1997, p.2.

18. See a profile of Muntasir al-Zayat in the *Cairo Times*, January 22–February 4, 1998, p. 10.

19. *Al-Ahram Weekly*, August 28–September 3, 1997, p. 3; *al-Ahram Weekly*, September 11–17, 1997, p. 2.

20. *Al-Hayat*, August 31, 1997, p. 4.

21. *Al-Hayat*, October 22 and 24, 1998.

22. The initiators included Salih Hashim (a founder of al-Jama'a and member of the "historical leadership"), Jamal Sultan (a former member of al-Takfir wa al-Hijra, and editor-in-chief of *al-Manar al-Jadid*, who also contributed articles in *al-Sh'ab*, and Kamal Habib, an ex-Jihadi and a journalist for *al-Sh'ab*.

23. *Cairo Times*, January 21–February 3, 1999, p. 5.

24. Religious parties, said Interior Minister al-Alfi, "would threaten social stability and national unity," *al-Ahram Weekly*, September 11–17, 1997, p. 2.

25. *Al-Ahram Weekly*, June 22–28, 2000, p. 4.

26. See interviews with the historic leaders of al-Jama'a in Torrah Prison by *al-Musawwar*'s editor-in-chief, in *al-Musawwar*, no. 4054, June 21, 2002; see also *al-Hayat*, October 11, 2000.

27. Al-Jama'a explained its strategic political change in a multi-volume series discussed and written in the prison and outside after they were released. The most important volume is Hafiz and al-Majid Muhammad, *Mubadirat Waqf al-'Unf*.

28. See the *Cairo Times*, February 3–9, 2000, p. 11. For instance, just weeks before

the parliamentary elections of 2000, the government detained some 1,000 MB activists, including a number of electoral candidates.

29. *Cairo Times*, April 3–16, 1997, p. 6; *al-Hayat*, October 17, 1999. Desperate to indict the MB's members, the state security resorted at times to dubious evidence, turning the courthouses into a laughing stock. On one such occasion the prosecutor presented evidence, a videotape of an alleged "secret meeting" of MB leaders in a private house in Cairo. However the videotape showed only the backs of some people entering a house, some with T-shirts printed with Nike logos. It became clear that the secret police had videotaped the wrong building (*Cairo Times*, February 3–9, 2000, p. 11).

30. According to Law 238-1996, no preacher could deliver sermons without clearance from the Ministry of Awqāf. This, according to Minister Mahmud Zaqzuq, was to cut off the access of unqualified and extremist preachers. Between 1996 and 2001, nevertheless, some 30,000 permits were issued; see Zaqzuq, "Hawl Shurut Bina' al-Masajid," p. 9.

31. Cited in Dawoud, "Closing the Circle."

32. The main MB periodical legally published was *al-Mukhtar al-Islami*, which, similar to the Islamist Labor Party's monthly *Minbar al-Sharq*, devoted itself to broad political, international, and religious topics. However, beginning in 2000, *al-Sha'b* began publishing online at alshaab.com, albeit in a far more limited format and circulation.

33. Quoted in Negus, "Down but Not Out," p. 7.

34. See *al-Halat al-Diniyya fi Misr*, pp. 210–11. As early as 1997, Mustafa Mashur admitted, "We can no longer celebrate Ramadan. If we meet, it must be in secret." "Only when one of us dies we all get together at funerals," said a member. *Cairo Times*, April 3–16, 1997, p. 6.

35. *Al-Ahram Weekly*, October 5–11, 2000. The state of crisis was clear from explicit discussions of 'Asam al-Eryan, the MB's prominent leader and the general secretary of the doctors' syndicate, whom I interviewed on November 17, 2001, in Cairo. He acknowledged that they do not do much work. "There is no newspaper, no magazine, no meeting, there is nothing!" He went on to suggest that this state had caused ideological and doctrinal stagnation in the MB.

36. *Al-Hayat*, January 12, 1998, p. 1.

37. *Cairo Times*, February 10–16, 2000, p. 10. It is important to note that, contrary to what al-Eryan stated, the constitution suggests that the Shari'a is a *main* (not *the only*) source of law in Egypt.

38. Interview with Dr. 'Asam al-Eryan; Cairo, November 17, 2001.

39. So, the state could not charge the MB with failing to apply Islamic law, but with "conspiracy to overthrow the system."

40. Thus in 1996, before the professional syndicate elections, Mustafa Mashhur wrote in *al-Sh'ab*, "We will fight these elections. We are aiming to get into the government through this way. We want to use this platform to mobilize people to call for the necessity of applying Shari'a. Because this is the solution to all of the problems that

people are suffering from, be they economic, social, political, moral, or whatever."
Al-Sh'ab, May 20, 1996.

41. Reported in *Cairo Times*, February 3–9, 2000, p. 11.

42. The Muslim Brothers' parliamentary seats began to decline. In 1984, the MB and Wafd Party coalition won fifty-eight seats with the majority going to the MB. Their slogan was "Islam is the Solution." In 1987 the coalition of MB and Labor and Liberal Parties, won seventy-eight seats, with thirty-six seats going to the MB. In 1995 the Muslim Brothers ran independently but with a clear MB identity, and won only one seat.

43. Interview with 'Abd al-Rahman's son, *Cairo Times*, August 2–8, 2001.

44. Cited in Moaddel, "Religion, Gender, and Politics," p. 5.

45. The most trusted institutions after the ulema and imams of mosques were intellectuals, the army, the courts, universities, and schools. Other institutions included in the survey were elders, television, major companies, the press, the civil service, Parliament, and finally political parties (the least trusted). The survey was conducted by Riaz Hassan, professor of sociology at Flinders University, Australia. The Egyptian sample of 788 was taken from various governorates. A preliminary results of the survey was reported in Hassan, "Faithlines." See also Moaddel, "Religion, Gender, and politics."

46. Survey of the professional middle class, carried out by my students at the American University in Cairo, Caroline Wahba, Christine Emil Wahba, Sherine Greiss, and Dana Sajdi, Department of Sociology and Anthropology, unpublished papers, 1980, 1990.

47. The Cairo Book Fair survey was based on a random sampling of women lined up to enter the fair on January 26, 2002, Cairo. The Zamalek survey of 157 women was carried out in July 2003 at the entrance to a shopping mall. Of the total, fifty-eight were unveiled. I have subtracted approximately 25 percent from the latter on the assumption that they were Egyptian Christians and foreign expatriates. I am grateful for Wesam Younis for helping to carry out this later survey.

48. Abu-Lughod, *Cairo*, p. 239.

49. See Tadros, "NGO-State Relations in Egypt."

50. Some 83 percent were against *'urfi* marriage. The poll was conducted by *al-Ahram Weekly* among 1,500 citizens in February 2001. The results were reported in Hassan, "The Meaning of Emancipation."

51. *Al-Wafd*, January 27, 28, 30, 2000.

52. *Al-Wafd*, March 13, 2003, p. 14.

53. The most popular albums included: Muhammad Rahim's "Al-Rahman" singing without music; Mustafa Qamar's "al-Quds"; 'Amr Diyab's "ya Rasul Allah ya Muhammad" and "Akhir kilam 'andina . . . al-Haqq haqq-i rabbina"; Angham's three albums with a Gulf state company; Samira Sa'id's "Khāliq al-'Ażīm" and "Allāh Akbar"; Muhammad Fu'ad's "al-Haqq" as well as a nationalist album called "Janīn"; Iman al-Bahr Darwish's "Izn yā Bilāl" with ten songs; and Muhammad al-Hellow's

"al-Quds Tasrakh" with religious and nationalist songs. See Fuad, "The Season of Religious Songs," *al-Qahira*, no. 10, May 21, 2002, p. 11.

54. *Cairo Times*, August 30–September 5, 2001, p. 8.

55. Quoted in *Sawt al-Azhar*, February 25, 2000, p. 2.

56. See a report by Abir 'Abd al-'Azim, *Sawt al-Azhar*, February 25, 2000, p. 2.

57. These observations are based on in-depth interviews with thirteen low-skilled workers (working in a cast iron foundry, an auto-mechanic workshop, a small factory, and a plumbing workshop) conducted by Basma al-Dajani, a student at the American University in Cairo, Fall 1990.

58. For a fine discussion of Sufi orders in Egypt, see Gilsenan, *Saint and Sufi*. For the Sufi basis of "popular religion" in Egypt, see Fahmi, "al-Din al-Sha'bi fi Misr."

59. See Schielke, "Habitus of the Authentic."

60. See Diyab, "al-Din al-Sha'bi."

61. Dr. 'Asam al-Eryan, a prominent leader of the Muslim Brotherhood, interview, Cairo, November 2001.

62. Schielke, "Pious Fun at Saints' Festivals," p. 23; see also Schielke, "Habitus of the Authentic."

63. Based on interviews with twelve middle-class migrant families who had returned to Egypt after spending years in Saudi Arabia; conducted by Menna al-Sheiby, "The Social Impact of Labor Migration: A Closer Look at Migration to the Gulf (Saudi Arabia)," Third World Development course, AUC, spring 2002.

64. Mostafa, "In Layman's Terms."

65. Elbendary, "Books? What Books . . . ," p. 14.

66. Quoted in Mostafa, "In Layman's Terms," p. 83.

67. For this information I am indebted to my student Dalia Ahmed Mustafa and her term paper "Modern *Da'wa* and E-Piety: An Investigation of 'Amr Khalid and His Populist Islamic Micromobilization," fall 2001.

68. *Hatif al-Islami* was advertised in the weekly *'Aqidati*, March 5, 2002, p. 5. Callers could record their questions and expect to receive an answer within twenty-four hours. The advice fee was one pound per minute.

69. These quotes are from my interviews with 'Amr Khalid's fans, Cairo, May 2002, and those conducted by Dalia Mustafa presented in "Modern *Da'wa*."

70. Marina is a popular upper-middle-class resort on the Mediterranean coast.

71. The first AUC student who decided to put on the *niqab*, or face cover, had attended 'Amr Khalid's lectures.

72. Mostafa, "In Layman's Terms," p. 83.

73. There is no precise figure on the number of women's *halaqat*, but anecdotal evidence suggests that there were a large number, with most people saying there were such groups in their neighborhoods.

74. See Hafez, "Terms of Empowerment."

75. In one such sermon in Cairo, a shaykha informed her audience that in the hereafter God would reward devout women with "unlimited access to shopping." "You can shop for whatever you desire and in whatever quantity you wish," she promised. Although pious men in the shaykha's view were to be rewarded by their access to virgin women, virtuous wives would have the advantage of being these men's favored sexual partners. Reported by Haniya Shulkami, conversation with the author, Cairo, December 2001.

76. Hafez, "Terms of Empowerment," pp. 85–86.

77. *Rawz al-Yusif*, a secular nationalist monthly, special issue on new preachers, no. 3751, 2000 p. 29.

78. As formulated by Badran, "Islamic Feminism," p. 18. For an elaboration of Islamic feminism see Cook, *Women Claim Islam*.

79. For historical accounts see Ahmad, *Women and Gender in Islam*. Badran, *Feminism, Islam and Nation*.

80. Hafez, "Terms of Empowerment". By drawing on the *halaqāt*, Saba Mahmood provides a theoretically sophisticated critique of liberal feminist theory. See Mahmood, *Politics of Piety*.

81. Hafez, "Terms of Empowerment," p. 59.

82. Preacher Shirin Fathi, cited in ibid., p. 92.

83. Interview with Muna conducted by Noha Abu-Ghazzia, Cairo, spring 2003.

84. Azza Karam identifies these women as "Islamic feminists"; see her *Women, Islamists and the State*.

85. Quoted in ibid., p. 219. For a personal and political profile of Safinaz Kazem, see Howeidy, "Born to Be Wild," p. 19.

86. Cited in Hafez, "Terms of Empowerment," p. 130.

87. My interview with Omaima Abu-Bakr and Huda Sadda, Cairo, January 7, 2002. See also Abu-Bakr, "Islamic Feminism."

88. Duval, "New Veils and New Voices."

89. Amin, *Whatever Happened to the Egyptians?*, pp. 37–38.

90. Lowy, *War of Gods*.

91. See Weber, *Sociology of Religion*, p. 85.

92. Ibid., p. 107.

93. See Aldridge, *Religion in the Contemporary World*.

94. Interestingly, women expressed that their moment of *hidāyā*, guidance, would begin by taking a shower to wash off their sins—something quite similar to the ritual of born-again Christians.

95. My interview with Hana, Cairo, spring 1995.

96. Giddens's discussion of existential anxiety in late modernity is instructive, although the context of his analysis is different from that of these women. See Giddens, *Modernity and Self-Identity*.

97. Interviews with middle-aged elite women, conducted by Noha Abu-Ghazia, spring 2003, Cairo.

98. Such women's activities are relatively well documented. See, for instance, Thompson, *Colonial Citizens.*

99. This observation is based on my research into a number of NGOs that specialize in social development. See Bayat, "Activism and Social Development."

100. For a critical analysis of post-*infitāh* ideals and ethics, see Ibrahim, *New Arab Social Order.*

101. Huda's statement in response to my question, "What is it like to be young in today's Egyptian society?", spring 2003, Cairo, Egypt.

102. Ticket prices ranged from LE75 to 150, with alcoholic drinks available for LE20 and water LE10. See Matar, "Glows Ticks and Grooves," p. 16.

103. The figure for the country was 22 percent, based on a survey of 14,656 male high school students in 1990; see Soueif et al., "Use of Psychoactive Substances," pp. 71–72.

104. Reportedly, the quantity seized by the police jumped from 2,276 units in 2000 to 7,008 units in 2001, *Cairo Times*, March 14–20, 2002, p. 16.

105. See Population Council, *Transitions to Adulthood.*

106. See Khalifa, "The Withering Youth of Egypt."

107. Ibid. This is confirmed by interviews with youngsters conducted by Rime Naguib, sociology student, AUC, spring 2002.

108. See Fatma el-Zanaty, "Behavioral Research among Egyptian University Students," reported in Ibrahim and Wassef, "Caught between Two Worlds: Youth in the Egyptian Hinterland," p. 163.

109. *Cairo Times*, May 15–28, 1997, p. 12. Sexual activity among youth was also confirmed by Mona al-Dabbaqh, in interviews with a number of "deviant" adolescents in a hospital in Cairo in the late 1990s. Mona al-Dabbaqh, "Addiction among the Egyptian Upper Class" (M.A. thesis, AUC, 1996).

110. Shahida al-Baz, cited in *Cairo Times*, May 15–28, 1997, p. 12.

111. Ironically, the partially segregated trains made the traditional young women more mobile. Parents would not mind if their daughters took trains (as opposed to taxies or buses) since segregated trains were thought to protect their daughters from male harassment. Nasrawi, "An Ethnography of Cairo's Metro."

112. Cited in 'Abd al-Rahman, "Sex: Urfi Marriage as Survival Strategy in Dahab," AUC term paper, fall 2001, p. 18.

113. Quoted in Rime Naguib, "Egyptian Youth: A Tentative Study," AUC term paper, spring 2002.

114. Ibid.

115. *Al-Wafd*, May 4, 2000; *al-Ahram*, May 6, 2000, p. 13.

116. CAPMAS reported that more than 5 million young men and 3.4 million young women created an uproar over the moral implications of so many unmarried

individuals. Indeed the age of marriage reached 30–40 for men and 20–30 for women; see *al-Wafd*, January 1, 2002, p. 3.

117. The public expression of such anxiety spread in the media and academic conferences on the "ethics of the era of globalization." In May 2002, a large national conference organized by the Center for Educational Studies discussed the deteriorating morality of Egyptians. It recommended a national project focused on "moral development"; reported in *al-Wafd*, May 23, 2002, p. 15.

118. Based on my own personal observations in the late 1990s. Much of the discussion draws on Bayat and Dennis, "Egypt." For a political economy analysis see Mitchell, "Dreamland," in *Rule of Experts.*

119. Home visit in Cairo, Old Ma'adi, March 18, 2000.

120. *Al-Ahram* (daily), September 1, 1992.

121. Quoted in *Sawt al-Azhar*, December 7, 2001, p. 4.

122. Ibid.

123. A government statement, quoted in Halawi, "Police Clampdown on Shi'i Group."

124. For some reports see *al-Hayat*, October 22, 1996; and October 27, 1996.

125. According to Dr. Suhayr al-Fil, professor of Islamic studies, al-Azhar University, in an interview with *al-Liwa' al-Islami*, November 14, 1996, p. 14.

126. According to Shaykh Dr. 'Abd al-Munim al-Barri in an interview in *'Aqidati*, November 5, 1996, p. 11.

127. *Al-Liwa' al-Islami*, October 31, 1996, p. 14.

128. According to Dr. 'Abd al-Masih Jad, the dean of the faculty of *Da'wa* in Azhar, in *'Aqidati*, October 29, 1996, p. 10.

129. Reported in *'Aqidati*, October 29, 1996, p. 1.

130. See Said, "Homosexuality and Human Rights in Egypt."

131. Reported by Hisham Bahjat, a human rights advocate, July 14, 2003, lecture at the American University in Cairo.

132. *Al-Ahram* (daily), October 22, 1981.

133. Reported in *Rawz al-Yusif*, October 6, 2001. See also *al-Hayat*, January 15, 1999.

134. See Weaver, "Revolution by Stealth," p. 46.

135. According to Jamal Badawi, the editor-in-chief, reported in *al-Ahram Weekly*, October 14–20, 1999, p. 3. It is interesting to note that Jamal Badawi was previously the editor of the "secular" opposition daily *al-Wafd.*

136. For documentation of NDP's Islamic discourse see 'Awda, "al-Hizb al-Watani wa Tatwir al-Khitab al-Dini."

137. Reported in Sara El-Khalili, "Now You Say It . . . ," p. 10.

138. Reported in *Sawt al-Azhar*, December 6, 2002, p. 1.

139. According to al-Asma'wi, an ex-judge and a secular Islamic writer, cited in Weaver, "Revolution by Stealth," p. 45.

140. *Al-Ahram Weekly*, June 8–14, 2000.

141. See Napoli, "Egyptian Sleight of Hand."

142. See various reports by the Egyptian Organization of Human Rights. For instance, Hamid Abu-Ahmad's translation of *Who Killed Palomino Molero* by Mario Vargas Llosa was found to offend public morality, and 'Ala'Hamid was sentenced to eight years and a fine in 1991 for his *Distance in a Man's Mind* because it was seen as subversive to Islam. The Azhar found Faraj Fuda's *To Be or Not to Be* anti-Islamic, and Fuda was murdered by the al-Jama'a al-Islamiyya for his "blasphemy" in 1992; see Napoli, "Egyptian Sleight of Hand." In 1997, Azhar's Islamic Research Academy found that Sayad al-Qowimi's book *Rabb al-Zaman* denigrated both Joseph and the Bible and the companions of the Prophet Muhammad. The court, however, revoked the book's confiscation; see *al-Ahram Weekly*, September 18–24, 1997, p. 3.

143. Reported in Sarwish, "The Hydra Grows Another Head," p. 27.

144. Over 40 percent of the seventy-seven books reviewed by the censor in December 1999 were either banned or confined to "restricted use" in the library.

145. Reported in *al-Liwa' al-Islami*, January 10, 2002, pp. 4–5. Of course, the nationalization of mosques goes back to the Nasser era. Indeed, before the new ruling in 1996, Law 157/1960 granted the supervision of all mosques in the country to the Ministry of Awqāf. The 1996 ruling simply began to enforce that law.

146. According to a cabinet decision in November 2001, the building of new mosques was to be subject to some conditions that were, according to Selim al-'Awa, "unprecedented in the history of Islam"; see Selim al-'Awa, "Hadyat al-Hukuma fi Ramadan," p. 9. Building mosques without authorization or within 500 meters of each other was disallowed. Construction of *ziwāyā*, small mosques usually constructed on the ground floor of residential buildings, was totally forbidden; reported in *al-Wafd*, November 23, 2001.

147. *Al-Hayat*, June 3, 2000, p. 5.

148. Cited in *Cairo Times*, May 15–28, 1997, p. 6.

149. *Al-Hayat*, December 3, 1997, p. 7.

150. *Cairo Times*, May 14–27, 1998. See also Muna al-Nahhas, "Defying al-Azhar," *al-Ahram Weekly*, August 29–December 4, 2002, p. 2.

151. Reported in Weaver, "Revolution by Stealth," p. 47.

152. See Herrera, "The Islamization of Education in Egypt."

153. Reported in *Rawz al-Yusif*, May 10, 1993, pp. 26–28.

154. See Nuwir, *al-Mu'alimun wa al-Siyasa fi Misr*, pp. 157–58.

155. Weaver, "Revolution by Stealth."

156. *Hisba* was originally the name of the office of the *muhtasib* or inspector of the markets. The institution had come into Islam from Byzantine times, being Islamized by the Abbasids. For a discussion of this concept and for the details of Abu Zayd's case, see Najjar, "Islamic Fundamentalism and the Intellectuals."

157. See Cooperman, "First Bombs, Now Law-Suits," pp. 38–40.

158. Reported in Weaver, "Revolution by Stealth."

159. Reported in Halawi, "Detained for Deriding Islam."

160. Dawoud, "Off with Her Head," *al-Ahram Weekly*, April 12–18, 2000; see also *Cairo Times*, August 2–8, 2001, p. 6.

161. See *al-Ahram Weekly*, January 21–27, 1999.

162. This is based on a survey of mostly state-owned media between the 1950s and 1990s; see Hartounian, "Impact of the Relation between Government and Religion."

163. Ibid., p. 83.

164. *Al-Liwa' al-Islami*, October 7, 1999.

165. *Al-Liwa' al-Islami*, October 28, 1999.

166. *Al-Liwa' al-Islami*, January 10, 2002, pp. 16–17.

167. *'Aqidati*, March 5, 2002, p. 19.

168. Ibid., p. 21.

169. Hartounian, Impact of the Relation between Government and Religion," pp. 103–11.

170. Whereas after September 11 Mubarak emphasized the Shari'a as the basis for democracy and human rights, his government would rebuff Azhar's fatwa to ban Ahmad Shihawi's book *Wasiya fi 'Ishq al-Nisa'* (*Commandments in Love for Women*) for denigrating Islam; report in *Cairo Times*, November 13–19, 2003.

171. In early 2003 there were seventeen Internet cafes in Cairo being used by young people between ages 20 and 28; *al-Wafd*, March 2, 2003, p. 3.

172. Reported in Shahin, "Dangerous Minds," p. 17.

173. Expressed by the minister of youth, 'Ali al-Din Hilal Desouqui. My interviews, Cairo, November 3, 2001.

174. For the contour of social policies in Egypt, see Bayat, "The Political Economy of Social Policy in Egypt."

175. For a fine analysis of economic reform and political constraints, see Kienle, *Grand Delusion*.

176. The role of religion, especially Islam, in national integration and moral supervision has been emphasized clearly in the rationale behind the introduction of "teaching religion" in Egyptian schools. See Daba'a, "Ta'lim al-Din al-Islami fi Misr."

177. During my research on the subject, four initial volumes had been published. The volumes prepared by the Jama'a "historic leaders" in prison published under the series name *Silsilat Tashih al-Mafahim* included Hafiz and al-Majid Muhammad, *Mubadirat Waqf al-'Unf*; Ibrahim and Sharif, *Hurmat al-Ghuluw fi Din wa Takfir al-Muslimin*; Abdul-Azim and Ibrahim 'Abdullah, *Taslit al-Adwa' 'ala Ma Waqi'a fi al-Jihad min Ikhta'*; Sharif and Hafiz, *al-Nas wa al-Tabi'in fi Tashih Mafahim al-Muhtasibin*. Because the books did not refer to state violence, Muntassir al-Zayat senses a "smell of state intervention" in the production of these books; see al-Zayat,

"Recognizing the Religious Flow," p. 15. By 2006, volume 16 of the series had been published.

178. 'Usama Hafiz and al-Majid Muhammad, *Mubadirat Waqf al-'Unf.*

179. Abdul-Azim and Abdullah, *Taslit al-Adwa' 'ala Ma Wāqi'a fi al-Jihad min Ikhta'.*

180. Hafiz and al-Majid Muhammad, *Mubadirat Waqf al-'Unf.*

181. See a very interesting interview of imprisoned leaders in *al-Musawwar*, no. 4054, June 21, 2002, pp. 4–22.

182. Cited in Negus, "Down but Not Out," p. 7.

183. My interview with 'Asam al-Eryan, November 17, 2001, Cairo.

184. Ibid.

185. My interview with Abul-'Ala Mādi, March 2001, Cairo. See also an interview with Abul-'Ala Mādi, the leader of the al-Wasat Party in the *Cairo Times*, August 2–8 2001, p. 19.

186. My interview with Abul-'Ala Mādi, an al-Wasat leader, March 2000, Cairo.

187. The history and philosophy behind al-Wasat is documented in Hizb al-Wasat, *Awraq Hizb al-Wasat.*

188. For the program of the al-Wasat Party see Hizb al-Wasat, *Awraq Hizb al-Wasat al-Misri.*

189. See Habib, *al-Umma wa al-Dawla.*

190. See Hizb al-Wasat, *Awraq Hizb al-Wasat al-Misry*, pp. 19–20.

191. See *al-Ahram Weekly*, April 20–26, 2000; *Cairo Times*, April 13–19, 2000.

192. Al-Qaradawi believed that *fiqh*, among other things, was suffering from *jumūd*, or stagnation; see *al-Mukhtar al-Islami*, no. 226, September 2001, p. 74. Others expressed similar thoughts in my interviews with them.

193. So, on the recommendation of al-Azhar's Islamic Research Academy, state security confiscated 'Abd al-Karim's books, including *The Society of Yathrib*; reported in the *Cairo Times*, February 5–18, 1998.

194. See Negus, "Brothers' Brother," on the profile of Jamal al-Banna, *Cairo Times*, September 30 –October 13, 1999, p. 16; also Jamal al-Banna, *Nahw Fiqh Jadid.*

195. See, for instance, Jama'a leader Hamdi 'Abd al-Rahman (amir of Suhag) in an interview with *al-Musawwar*, no. 4041, March 22, 2002, pp. 26–29.

196. Interviews with Jama'a's leaders in Torrah Prison, *al-Musawwar*, June 21, 2002, pp. 4–22.

197. On Ibn Taymiyya, see Laoust, "Ibn Taimiyya."

198. See *al-Musawwar*, June 21, 2002, pp. 26–29.

199. According to 'Asam al-Eryan; my interview, Cairo, October 2001.

200. According to Abul-'Ala Mādi, my interview.

201. Baker's *Islam without Fear* focuses on a small number of religious intellectuals who have little influence on Egyptian religious discourse. Baker's otherwise inter-

esting book overestimates a more sophisticated but marginal trend in the Egyptian intellectual landscape.

202. See Abaza, "Tanwir and Islamization," p. 92.

203. For the Salafi influence on Egypt's religious thought see, 'Awda, "al-Salafi-yyun fi Misr." In the 1930s, recalls a veteran Egyptian intellectual, an author could publish "Why I Am an Atheist," "something no one would dare do now," and an al-Azhar shaykh would respond by writing "Why I Am a Muslim." See "Kadry Hefny: A Psychology of Hope," *al-Ahram Weekly*, July 8–14, 2004, p. 27.

204. On Turkey, see Meeker, "The New Muslim Intellectuals."

205. On Rashid Reda, the publisher of *al-Manar*, see Shahin, *Through Muslim Eyes*.

206. According to 'Asam al-Eryan, in an interview, Cairo, October 2001.

207. In May–June 2002, on the occasion of a celebration of the life and work of 'Abd al-Rahman al-Kawakibi at the international conference "Muslim Reform and Its Future in the Arab World," Aleppo, Syria, aimed precisely to revive the century-old thought of these Islamic reformers to counter the tide of religious rigidity and dogma that had dominated the Arab world.

208. According to Bashir Nafi, professor of modern Islamic history, interview in *al-Ahram Weekly*, January 14–20, 1999, p. 4. See also Edward Said, "Enemies of the State."

209. Saghiya, "Problem of Egypt's Political Culture."

210. The cosmopolitanism of Cairo and Alexandria in pre-revolution Egypt is discussed in Zubaida, "Cosmopolitanism in the Arab World."

211. Weaver, "Revolution by Stealth," p. 42.

212. The 1996 bestsellers included: *Secret Negotiations* by Muhammad Hasnein Heikal (200,000 copies sold); *The Age of Fifi Abdou* by Emad Nassef (150,000); *A Journey to Paradise and Hell* by Mustafa Mahmoud (100,000); *Women from Hell* by Emad Nassef (100,000); *Girls for Export* by Emad Nassef (90,000); *The Red File* by Emad Nassef (70,000); *The War of the Whores* by Emad Nassef (70,000); *A Scandal Called Saida Sultana* by Muhammad al-Ghity (60,000), and *How Egyptians Joke about Their Leaders* by Adel Hamouda (60,000); see *Cairo Times*, April 17–30, p. 18.

213. Quoted in *al-Ahram Weekly*, January 6–12, 2000, p. 3.

214. Quoted in Weaver, "Revolution by Stealth," p. 41.

215. Ibid., p. 42.

216. *Al-Wafd*, December 31, 2001.

217. Jamal Badawi, "The Age of Sha'bula," *al-Wafd*, October 2002.

218. Hafez, "The Novel, Politics and Islam," p. 141.

219. For an interesting discussion of nativism, see Boroujerdi, *Iranian Intellectuals and the West*.

220. Saghiya, "Problems of Egypt's Political Culture." For a discussion of conspiracies and conspiracy theories, see Bayat, "Conspiracies and Theories."

221. See report in the *Cairo Times*, November 27–December 10, 1997, p. 5.

222. Reported in *Egyptian Mail*, May 25, 2002, p. 1.

223. According to a poll conducted by the American Zogby Institute one year before Ariel Sharon came to power, 79 percent of Egyptians said that the Palestinian issue was for them personally the most important and pressing political issue; cited in *Rawz al-Yusif*, July 28, 2001.

224. In the early 1990s, the major outcry against anthropologist Reem Saad's documentary "Marriage Egyptian Style" came from Egyptian intellectuals. In a meeting to discuss the issue with the Ministry of Culture, it was the Egyptian intellectuals who asked the ministry to ban the film in Egypt because it "had tarnished the image of Egypt abroad." And it was Abu-Shadi, a liberal ministry's official, who argued, "This is a free country. . . . Others who feel differently should make different films"; personal communication with Khaled Fahmi, who was present at that meeting, August 2004, Cairo.

225. See Mehreaz, "Take Them out of the Ball Game." "Instead of working to eliminate the very idea of appointed custodians of religion and morality," writes Egyptian literary critic Sabry Hafez, "they seek to show that they are [as] pious as any fundamentalist, and twist their own works to prove their credentials"; see Hafez, "The Novel, Politics and Islam," p. 141.

226. Thus the front page of *Sawt al-Azhar* would not spare a Nile Television presenter, who had said that wearing the *hijāb* was a preference rather than an obligation, by calling on the Ministry of Information to shut down the program. See Habib, "al-Qawl al-Tayib," p. 1. In a different case, in October 2002, a statement about masturbation in Dream cable TV caused a national media uproar over the "moral degradation'" of society, with the religious leaders demanding revenge; see *al-Wafd*, October 26, 2002.

227. The policy items included a decision to change primary education textbooks to include lessons in "tolerance," "education for peace," "extremism," and the like; al-Azhar called on its preachers to present a more tolerant message of Islam. The NDP's "political reform," included diminishing state security courts, abolishing hard labor, and creating a national council for human rights. In addition, earlier, the first woman judge (Tahani al-Jibali) was appointed to the Supreme Constitutional Court, and Coptic Christmas was declared a national holiday. See the details in *al-Ahram Weekly*, May 1–7, 2003; and *al-Hayat*, January 16, 2003, p. 17.

228. See Salama, "'Change' and Real Change."

229. These passages draw on Bayat, "The 'Street' and the Politics of Dissent."

230. Ghobashi, "Egypt Looks Ahead."

231. Beinin, "Popular Social Movements."

232. See, for instance, the speech by Mahmud Ghazlan, a member of Maktab al-Irshad, published on the website of *Afaq 'Arabiyya*, [December 1, 2005].

233. As claimed, for instance, by Utvik, "Hizb al-Wasat and the Potential for Change," p. 33. On the MB see Tamam, *Tahawulat al-Akhwan al-Muslimun*.

234. See *al-Ahram Weekly,* November 24–30, 2005, several reports. In one of these reports, ʿAsam al-Eryan, a Muslim Brotherhood leader, acknowledged that up to 20 percent of the votes for Muslim Brothers were protest votes against the ruling NDP.

Notes to Chapter 6

1. Critical views are expressed by, for instance, the Christian right in the United States as well as mainstream media and intellectuals such as Daniel Pipes. For sympathetic views see Esposito, "Islam and Democracy"; Aboul-Fadl, *Islam and the Challenge of Democracy.*

2. Tajzadih, "Matn ya Vahn?"

3. "Secular Democracy, Religious Democracy," a debate in Tehran, July 21, 2004, reported on the website of *Iran-i Imruz* [July 25, 2004].

4. The Center for the Study of Islam and Democracy in Washington, D.C., is one such organization; others include Dialogues: Islamic World-U.S.-The West (New York); the Council of Muslim Democrats (France); and the Islamic Society of North America; see also the websites www.Islamonline.com and www.muslimwakeup.com.

5. See Lacroix, "Between Islamists and Liberals."

6. See Olimova, "Social Protests and the Islamic Movement in Central Eurasia"; and Akcali, "Secularism under Threat."

7. See Ahmad, "From Islamism to Post-Islamism: The Transformation of the Jamaʿat-i Islami in North India." Ph.D. thesis, University of Amsterdam, 2005.

8. Based on discussions with two young leaders of the movement, Rabat, Morocco, January 30, 2006.

9. The three phases of democratic transition in Iran were formulated by ʿAlavitabar, "Guzar bi Mardum-salari dar Seh Gam."

10. See, for instance, Tarrow, *Power in Movement.* See also Giugni, "Was It Worth the Effort?"; Giugni, MacAdam, and Tilly, *From Contention to Democracy.*

11. Only as recently as 2003 did a book-length treatment of the subject appear. See Goldstone, *States, Parties and Social Movements.* Tarrow, *Power in Movements,* and Della Porta and Diani, *Social Movements,* do take up the issue, but the discussions do not go far beyond invoking notions of co-optation or repression.

12. See Melucci, "A Strange Kind of Newness," and his *Challenging Codes.* See also Castells, *The Power of Identity,* pp. 359–60.

13. Foucault, *Knowledge/Power,* pp. 55–62.

14. Migdal, *State in Society.*

15. This is what Polish sociologist Piotr Sztompka calls "manifest change"; see Sztompka, *Sociology of Social Change,* pp. 274–96.

16. Tarrow, *Power in Movement.*

17. Melucci, *Nomads of the Present,* p. 60. Melucci's "cultural production" is roughly what Sztompka calls "latent change"; see Sztompka, *Sociology of Social Change.*

18. Forero, "Latin America Graft and Poverty."

19. Kis, "Between Reform and Revolution."

20. Cadena-Roa, "State Pacts, Elites."

21. These passages heavily draw on Bayat, "The 'Street' and the Politics of Dissent."

22. This does not imply that "civil society" is missing in the Muslim Middle East, or that people have been passive in light of the new structural changes. I have described the alternative mode of mobilization in the Arab world in ibid.

23. Grugel, *Democratization*, pp. 42–43.

24. Mahmood Mamdani's otherwise fine book, *Good Muslims, Bad Muslims*, rejects any kind of foreign intervention.

25. Kinzer, "Will Turkey Make It?"

26. Ibid.

27. The World Value Survey (WVS) carried out between 1999 and 2002 in Algeria, Egypt, Jordan, and Morocco found that over 90 percent of respondents believed that, despite its problems, democracy is still the best form of government; cited in Tessler and Gao, "Gauging Arab Support for Democracy."

28. See Diamond, "What Went Wrong in Iraq."

29. Foucault describes "governmentality" in terms of the state devising mechanisms, methods, and ideas through which citizens govern themselves in accordance with the interests of those who govern. See Foucault, *Power*.

30. These range from Hobbes through the Marxists. See Held, *States and Societies*.

31. I am grateful to Kaveh Ehsani for bringing these important points to my attention. For a discussion, see Mamdani, *Citizens and Subjects*.

BIBLIOGRAPHY

Abaza, Mona. "Tanwir and Islamization: Rethinking the Struggle over Intellectual Inclusion in Egypt." *Cairo Papers in Social Science*, vol. 22, no. 4 (Winter 1999).

'Abdi, 'Abbas, and Muhsin Gudarzi. *Tahavvulat-i Farhangi dar Iran*. Tehran: Intesharat-i Ravish, 1999.

Abdul-Fattah, Nabil. "The Story of the Decade." *Al-Ahram Weekly*, September 17–23, 1992.

Aboul-Fadl, Khaled. *Islam and the Challenge of Democracy*. Princeton, N.J.: Princeton University Press, 2004.

Abrahamian, Ervand, *Iran between Two Revolutions*. Princeton, N.J.: Princeton University Press, 1982.

———. *Radical Islam: The Iranian Mojahedin*. London: Tauris, 1989.

Abu-Bakr, Omaima. "Islamic Feminism: What's in a Name? Preliminary Reflections." *Middle East Women's Studies*, vol. XV, no. 4 (Winter/Spring 2001): 1–4.

Abu-Lughod, Janet. *Cairo: The City Victorious*. Princeton, N.J.: Princeton University Press, 1971.

Abu Zayd, Nasr. *Rethinking the Quran: Towards a Humanistic Hermeneutics*. Utrecht: Humanistics University Press, 2004.

Abdul-Azim, Hamdi 'Abd al-Rahman, and Najih Ibrahim. *Taslit al-Adwa' 'ala Ma Wāqi'a fi al-Jihad min Ikhta'*. Cairo: Maktaba al-Turath al-Islami, January 2002.

Afary, Janet, and Kevin Anderson. *Foucault and the Iranian Revolution*. Chicago: University of Chicago Press, 2005.

Afshari, Reza. "A Critique of Dabashi's Reconstruction of Islamic Ideology as a Prerequisite for the Iranian Revolution." *Critique: Journal of Critical Studies of the Middle East*, no. 5 (Fall 1994).

Aghajari, Hashim. "Islamic Protestantism." Lecture in Teachers Hall, Hamadan, 29 Khurdad 1381 (2002).

———. *Hukumat-i Dini va Hukumat-i Dimukratik.* Tehran: Mu'asasi-yi Nashr va Tahqiqat-i Zikr, 2002.

Ahmad, Irfan. "From Islamism to Post-Islamism: The Transformation of the Jamaat-e-Islami in North India." Ph.D. dissertation, University of Amsterdam, November 2005.

Ahmad, Leila. *Women and Gender in Islam.* Cairo: American University in Cairo Press, 1998.

Ajami, Fuad. *The Dream Palace of the Arabs.* New York: Pantheon, 1998.

Akcali, Pinar. "Secularism under Threat: Radical Islam in Central Asia." Paper presented in the workshop "Towards Social Stability and Democratic Governance in Central Eurasia: Challenges to Regional Security." Leiden, the Netherlands, September 8–11, 2004.

Akhavi, Shahroukh. *Religion and Politics in Contemporary Iran.* Albany, N.Y.: SUNY Press, 1980.

Akhavipur, Hossein, and Heidar Azdanloo. "Economic Basis of Political Factions in Iran." *Critique: Journal for the Critical Studies of the Middle East* (Fall 1998): 76–77.

Al-Ahram Strategic Studies Center. *Taqrir Halat al-Diniyya fi Misr.* Cairo: 1996 and 1998.

'Alavitabar, 'Alireza. "Guzar bi Mardum-salari dar Seh Gam." *Aftab,* no. 19, Mahr 1381 (2002): 4–5.

———. "Questions about Religious Democracy." *Aftab,* no. 9, Aban 1380 (2001).

Al-Banna, Jamal. *Nahw Fiqh Jadid.* Cairo: 1995, 1997, 1999.

Al-Bashir, Hamdi. "Al-'Unf fi al-Mahaliyyat." Paper presented at the Second Annual Conference of Political Studies, "Politics and Localities in Egypt." Cairo University, December 3–5, 1994.

Aldridge, Alan. *Religion in the Contemporary World: A Sociological Introduction.* Cambridge, UK: Polity Press, 2000.

Al-Fawal, Najwa. *Al-Barnamaj al-Diniyya fi al-Televiziyun al-Misri.* Cairo: National Center for Sociological and Criminological Studies, 1994.

Alghar, Hamid. *Religion and State in Iran, 1785–1906.* Berkeley: University of California Press, 1969.

Al-Sharbini, Ahmad. "Azmat al-Siyah al-Misriyya wa Imkaniyyat al-Ta'wid." *Ahwal a-Masriya,* vol. 4, no. 15 (Winter 2002).

Al-Zayat, Montassir. "Recognizing the Religious Flow Helps Loosen the Political and Public Stress in the Arab World." *Al-Hayat,* Mat 13, 2002.

Amin, Galal. *Whatever Happened to the Egyptians? Changes in Egyptian Society from 1950 to the Present.* Cairo: American University in Cairo Press, 2001.

Amir Ibrahimi, Masarat. "The Impact of the Bahman Cultural Complex on the Social and Cultural Life of Tehran's Women and Youth," *Guftugu* (Fall 1995).

———. "Public and Private." *Pages* (Rotterdam, Witte de Wit), no. 1 (February 2004).

———. "Integration of South Tehran and the Emergence of a New Urban Citizenship." Unpublished paper, Tehran, 1999.

———. "Ta'sir Farhangsara-yi Bahman bar Zandigui-yi Ijtima'i va Farhangui-yi Zanan va Javanan-i Tahran." *Guftugu*, no. 9 (Fall 1995): 17–25.

Anonymous, ed. *Bahthi dar Bārayi Marj'iyyat va Ruhaniyyat*. Publisher unknown, undated (in Persian).

Ansari, Hamid. "The Islamic Militants in Egyptian Politics." *International Journal of Middle East Studies*, vol. 16, no. 1 (March 1984).

Arab Human Development Report. Vol. 3. New York: United Nations Development Program, 2004.

———. New York: United Nations Development Program, 2002.

Aras, Bulent, and Omer Caha. "Fethullah Gulen and His Liberal 'Turkish Islam' Movement." *Middle East Review of International Affairs*, vol. 4, no. 4 (December 2000).

Ardalan, Parvin. "Zanan az Sazmanha-yi Siyasi-yi Danishjuy Gurizanand, Chira?" *Zanan*, no. 49, Azar 1377 (1998).

Arjomand, S. A. "The Ulama's Traditionalist Opposition to Parliamentarism: 1907-1909." *Middle Eastern Studies*, vol. 17, no. 2 (1981).

———. "Shi'ite Islam and the Revolution in Iran." *Government and Opposition*, vol. 16, no. 3 (1981): 311–13.

———. *The Turban for the Crown*. Oxford, UK: Oxford University Press, 1988.

Arman, Mahrdad. "Naqsh-i Javanan dar Inqilab." *Kankash: A Persian Journal of History and Politics*, no. 5 (Fall 1988).

Ashkivari, Hasan Yusifi, ed. *Naw Girā'-i Dīni*. Tehran: Qasidih, 1998.

Ashraf, Ahmad. "Zaminih-i Ijtima'i-yi Sunnatgari va Tajaddudkhahi." *Iran-Namih*, vol. 11, no. 2 (Spring 1993).

———. "Bazaar-Mosque Alliance: The Social Roots of Revolts and Revolutions." *Politics, Culture, and Society*, vol. 1, no. 4 (Summer 1988).

Ashtiani, 'Ali. "Ihya'-yi Fikr-i Dini va Sarkardigi-yi Islam-i Siyasi dar Inqilab-i Iran." *Kankash: A Persian Journal of History and Politics*, no. 6 (Fall 1989).

'Awda, Jihad. "Al-Hizb al-Watani wa Tatwir al-Khitab al-Dini." *Al-Dimuqratiya*, no. 9 (January 2003): 9–22.

———. "Al-Salafiyyun fi Misr." *Ahwal Misriyya*, no. 23 (Winter 2004): 8–24.

Azadih, Nasrin. "Junbish-i Ijtima'i-yi Zananih." *Zanan-e Iran* website [November 11, 2003].

'Azimi, Husayn. "Chenin Shive-yi Gam Bardashtan beh Sou-ye Bohran Ast." *Payam-i Imruz*, no. 42, Day 1379 (2000).

Badran, Margot. "Islamic Feminism: What's in a Name?" *Al-Ahram Weekly*, January 2002.

———. *Feminism, Islam and Nation*. Princeton, N.J.: Princeton University Press, 1995.

Bahrampur, 'Ali. "Tahavvulat-i Kayfi-yi Matbu't pas az Duvvum-i Khurdad." *Aftab*, no. 10, Azar 1380 (2001): 48–53.

Bahrul Uloom, Syed Mohammad. "Islam, Democracy, and the Future of Iraq." In Richard Bulliet, ed., *Under Siege: Islam and Democracy*. Occasional Paper no. 1, Middle East Institute, Columbia University, 1994.

Bainton, Roland. *Here I Stand: A Life of Martin Luther*. New York: Mentor, 1977.

Baker, Raymond. *Islam without Fear: Egypt and the New Islamists*. Cambridge, Mass.: Harvard University Press, 2003.

Banu'azizi, 'Ali. "Alounaknishinan-i Khiaban-i Professor Brown." *Alifba*, vol. 2, no. 3 (Summer 1983).

Baqi, Imdadeddin. *Barayi-i Tarikh*. Tehran: Nashr-e Ney, 2000.

———. *Tirajidi-i Dimukrasi dar Iran*. Tehran: Nashr-e Ney, 2001.

Bayat, Asef. "Activism and Social Development in the Middle East." *International Journal of Middle East Studies*, vol. 34, no. 1 (February 2002).

———. "The Coming of a Post-Islamist Society." *Critique: Critical Middle East Studies*, no. 9 (Fall 1996): 43–52.

———. "Conspiracies and Conspiracy Theories." *ISIM Review*, no. 18 (Fall 2006).

———. "Iran's Brave New World." *Al-Ahram Weekly*, July 22–26, 1999.

———. "Islamism and Social Movement Theory." *Third World Quarterly*, vol. 26, no. 6 (July 2005): 891–908.

———. "The Political Economy of Social Policy in Egypt." In Masoud Karshenas and Val Moghadam, eds., *Social Policy and Development in the Middle East and North Africa*. London: Palgrave, 2006.

———. "The 'Street' and the Politics of Dissent in the Arab World." *Middle East Report*, no. 226 (March 2003): 10–17.

———. *Street Politics: Poor People's Movements in Iran*. New York: Columbia University Press, 1997.

———. "The Use and Abuse of 'Muslim Societies.'" *ISIM Newsletter* no. 13, December 2003.

———. *Workers and Revolution in Iran*. London: Zed Books, 1987.

———. "Workless Revolutionaries: The Movement of the Unemployed in Iran, 1979." *International Review of Social History*, vol. 42, no. 2 (Summer 1997).

Bayat, Asef, and Bahman Baktiari. "Revolutionary Iran and Egypt: Exporting Inspirations and Anxieties." In Nikki Keddie and Rudi Matthee, eds., *Iran and the Surrounding World*, pp. 305–26. Seattle: University of Washington Press, 2002.

Bayat, Asef, and Eric Dennis. "Egypt: Twenty Years of Urban Transformation." Urban Change Working Paper no. 5, London: International Institute of Environment and Development, 2002.

Bayes, Jane H., and Nayereh Tohidi, eds. *Globalization, Gender, and Religion: The Politics of Women's Rights in Catholic and Muslim Contexts*. New York: Palgrave, 2001.

Bazargan, Mehdi. *Shast Saal Khedmat va Moghavemat*. Tehran: Rasa Press, n.d.

Beckford, James. *Social Theory and Religion*. Cambridge, UK: Cambridge University Press, 2003.

Behdad, Sohrab. "A Disputed Utopia: Islamic Economics in Revolutionary Iran." *Comparative Studies in Society and History*, vol. 36, no. 4 (October 1994).

———. "Winers and Losers of the Iranian Revolution: A Study in Income Distribution." *International Journal of Middle East Studies*, vol. 21 (1989), pp. 327–58.

Behdad, Sohrab, and Farhad Nomani. "Involution and De-involution: Changes in the Iranian Labor Force, 1976–1996." Paper presented at the conference, "20th Century Iran: History from Below," Amsterdam, May 25–27, 2001.

———. "Workers, Peasants, and Peddlers: A Study of Labor Stratification in the Post-Revolutionary Iran." *International Journal of Middle East Studies*, vol. 34, no. 4 (November 2002).

Behnam, Vida. "Zan, Khanivadih va Tajaddud." *Iran Namih*, vol. XI, no. 2 (Spring 1993).

Beinin, Joel. "No More Tears: Benny Morris and the Road from Liberal Zionism." *Middle East Report*, no. 230 (Spring 2004).

———. "Popular Social Movements and the Future of Egyptian Politics." *Middle East Report Online*, March 10, 2005.

Bendix, R. *Nation-Building and Citizenship*. New York: Wiley, 1964.

Boff, L., and C. Boff. *Salvation and Liberation*. New York: Orbis, 1984.

Bonine, Enrique Dussel. "The Sociohistorical Meaning of Liberation Theology: Reflections about Its Origin and World Context." In Dwight Hopkins et al., eds., *Religions/Globalizations*, pp. 33–45. Durham, N.C.: Duke University Press, 2001.

Boroujerdi, Mehrzad. *Iranian Intellectuals and the West: The Tormented Triumph of Nativism*. Syracuse, N.Y.: Syracuse University Press, 1996.

Brindle, Simon. "Egypt's Film Industry." *Business Monthly: Journal of the American Chamber of Commerce in Egypt*, vol. 11, no. 6 (July 1995).

Burgat, Francois. *Face to Face with Political Islam*. London: I. B. Tauris, 2003.

Burgat, Francois, and William Dowell. *The Islamic Movement in North Africa*. Austin: University of Texas Press, 1993.

Cadena-Roa, Jorge. "State Pacts, Elites, and Social Movement in Mexico's Transition to Democracy." In Jack Goldstone, ed. *States, Parties, and Social Movements*, pp. 107–43. Cambridge, UK: Cambridge University Press, 2003.

Cameron, Euan. *The European Reformation*. Oxford, UK: Clarendon Press, 1991.

Cassandra. "The Impending Crisis in Egypt." *Middle East Journal*, vol. 49, no. 1 (Winter 1995): 9–27.

Castells, Manuel. *The Power of Identity*. Oxford, UK: Blackwell, 1997.

Chan, Sylvia. *Liberalism, Democracy and Development*. Cambridge, UK: Cambridge University Press, 2002.

Cook, Mariam. *Women Claim Islam: Creating Islamic Feminism through Literature.* New York: Routledge, 2001.

Cooperman, Alan. "First Bombs, Now Law-Suits." *U.S. News and World Report,* vol. 121, no. 25 (1996).

Daba'a, Mahmud. "Ta'lim al-Din al-Islami fi Misr." An expert presentation on curriculum-building for Egyptian schools in the workshop "Religious Education and Education of Religion in Egypt and Sweden." Alexandria, September 19–21, 2002.

Dabashi, Hamid. *Theology of Discontent: The Ideological Foundation of the Islamic Revolution in Iran.* New York: New York University Press, 1993.

Dagi, Ihsan. "Rethinking Human Rights, Democracy and the West: Post-Islamist Intellectuals in Turkey." *Critique: Critical Studies of the Middle East,* vol. 13, no. 2 (Summer 2004): 135–52.

Dahl, Robert A. *Democracy and Its Critics.* New Haven, Conn.: Yale University Press, 1989.

Darabi, Ghulam Husayn. "Tarh-i Basij va Ahdaf-i An." *Iran-i Farda,* no. 49, Aban-Azar 1377 (1998): 113–15.

Davies, James. "Toward a Theory of Revolution." *American Sociological Review,* vol. 27, no. 1 (February 1962).

Dawani, Ali. *Nahzat-i Ruhāniyān-i Irān.* Vol. 3. Tehran: Imam Reza Cultural Foundation, 1999.

Dawoud, Khaled. "Closing the Circle." *Al-Ahram Weekly,* October 5–11, 2000.

———. "Gama'a Militant Sentenced to Death." *Al-Ahram Weekly,* April 20–26, 2000.

———. "Off with Her Head." *Al-Ahram Weekly,* April 12–18, 2000.

de Bellaigue, Christopher. "Who Rules Iran?" *New York Review of Books,* June 27, 2002.

Della Porta, Donatella, and Mario Diani. *Social Movements: An Introduction.* Oxford, UK: Blackwell, 1999.

Denoeux, Guilain. *Urban Unrest in the Middle East: A Comparative Study of Informal Networks in Egypt, Iran, and Lebanon.* Albany: State University of New York Press, 1993.

Diyab, Muhammad Hafiz. "Al-Din al-Sha'bi, al-Zakira wa Mu'sh." *Sutuh,* no. 30, pp. 16–18.

Diamond, Larry. "What Went Wrong in Iraq." *Foreign Affairs* (Sept.–Oct. 2004): 34–56.

Duval, S. "New Veils and New Voices: Islamist Women's Groups in Egypt." In Karin Ask and Marit Tjornsland, eds., *Women and Islamization,* pp. 45–73. Oxford, UK: Berg, 1998.

Egyptian Organization for Human Rights. *Annual Report,* 1991, 1992, 1993, 1994, 1995, 1996, 1997. Cairo.

Ehsani, Kaveh. "Municipal Matters: The Urbanization of Consciousness and Political Change in Tehran." *Middle East Report* (Fall 1999): 22–27.

————. "The Nation and Its Periphery." Unpublished paper presented in Leiden, April 2005.

Elbendary, Amina. "Books? What Books . . . " *Al-Ahram Weekly*, January 31–February 6, 2002.

El-Khalili, Sara. "Now You Say It . . . " *Cairo Times*, November 11–24, 1999.

Enayat, Hamid. "Mafhum-i Nazarih-i Vilāyat-i Faqīh: Didgah-i Imam Khomeini." *Kiyan*, vol. 6, no. 34 (January–February 1997).

Esposito, John. *Islam and Democracy*. Oxford, UK: Oxford University Press, 1996.

Essam el-Din, Gamal. "Parliament Scrutinizes Policing Policies." *Al-Ahram Weekly*, December 11–17, 1997.

Fahmi, 'Ali. "Al-Din al-Sha'bi fi Misr." *Al-Dimuqratiyya*, no. 12 (October 2003): 49–51.

Fandy, Mamoun. "Egypt's Islamic Group: Regional Revenge?" *Middle East Journal*, vol. 48, no. 4 (1994): 607–25.

Farahi, Muzhgan. "You Cannot Resolve Sexual Misconduct by Exhortation." *Guzarish*, no. 148, Tir 1382 (2003).

Farhang, Umid. "Karnamih-i Panjsalih-i Gushayish-i Tazih-i Matbu'ati." *Guftugu*, no. 4 (1994).

Fathi, Nazila. "Political Fervor of Iranian Clerics Begins to Ebb." *New York Times*, January 17, 2003.

Femia, Joseph. *Gramsci's Political Thought*. Oxford, UK: Clarendon Press, 1981.

Fitzgerald, F. Scott. *The Great Gatsby*, Cambridge: Cambridge University Press [1925].

Foran, John. "The Iranian Revolution and the Study of Discourses: A Comment on Moaddel." *Critique: Journal for Critical Studies of the Middle East* (Spring 1994): 51–63.

Forero, Juan. "Latin America Graft and Poverty Trying Patience with Democracy." *New York Times*, June 24, 2004.

Foucault, M. *Knowledge/Power*. New York: Pantheon Books, 1972.

————. *Power*, New York: New Press, 1994.

Fu'ad, Khalid. "Al-Fasl al-Aghani Diniyya." *Al-Qahira*, May 21, 2002.

Ganji, Akbar. *Islahgari-yi Mi'maranih*. Tehran: Tarh-i Naw, 2000.

————. *Talaqqi-yi fashisti az din va hukumat*. Tehran: Tarh-i Naw, 1999.

————. *Tarik-khanih-i Ashbah*. Tehran: Tarh-i Naw, 1999.

Ghobashi, Mona. "Egypt Looks Ahead to Portentous Year." *Middle East Report Online*, February 2, 2005.

Giddens, Anthony. *Modernity and Self-Identity: Self and Society in the Late Modern Age*. Stanford, Calif.: Stanford University Press, 1991.

Gilsenan, Michael. *Saint and Sufi in Modern Egypt: An Essay in the Sociology of Religion*. Oxford: Clarendon Press, 1973.

Giugni, Marco. "Was It Worth the Effort? The Outcome and Consequences of Social Movements." *American Review of Sociology*, vol. 24: 341–93.

Giugni, Marco, Doug MacAdam, and Charles Tilly, eds. *From Contention to Democracy.* Lanham, Md.: Rowman and Littlefield, 1998.

Goldstone, Jack, ed. *States, Parties and Social Movements.* Cambridge, UK: Cambridge University Press, 2003.

Gramsci, Antonio. *Prison Notebooks.* New York: International Publishers, 1971.

Griech-Polelle, Beth. *Bishop von Galen: German Catholicism and National Socialism.* New Haven, Conn.: Yale University Press, 2002.

Grugel, Jean. *Democratization: A Critical Introduction.* London: Palgrave, 2002.

Guenena, Ni'mat. "The Changing Face of Egypt's Islamic Activism: 1974–1995." Unpublished paper, Ibn Khaldun Center for Developmental Studies, Cairo, September 1995.

———. "The Jihad: An Islamic Alternative in Egypt." *Cairo Papers in Social Science,* vol. 9. no. 1 (1986).

Gurr, Ted. *Why Men Rebel.* Princeton, N.J.: Princeton University Press, 1970.

Gutierrez, G. *A Theology of Liberation.* New York: Orbis Books, 1988.

Habib, Muhammad. "Al-Qawl al-Tayib." *Sawt al-Azhar,* December 6, 2002.

Habib, Rafiq. *Al-Umma wa al-Dawla: Bayan Tahrir al-Umma.* Cairo: Dar al-Shuruq, 2001.

Hafez, Sabry. "The Novel, Politics and Islam." *New Left Review,* no. 5 (2nd ser.) (September–October 2000).

Hafez, Sherine. "The Terms of Empowerment: Islamic Women Activists in Egypt." M.A. thesis, American University in Cairo, 2001.

Hafiz, 'Usama Ibrahim, and 'Asam 'Abd al-Majid Muhammad. *Mubadirat Waqf al-'Unf.* Cairo: Maktaba al-Turath al-Islami, 2002.

Hajjariyan, Sa'id. "The Process of the Secularization of Shi'i Faqh." *Kiyan,* vol. 5, no. 24 (April–May 1995).

———. *Az Shahid-i Qudsi ta Shahid-i Bazari.* Tehran: Tarh-i Naw, 2001.

Halawi, Jailan. "Detained for Deriding Islam." *Al-Ahram Weekly,* April 13–19, 2000.

———. "Police Clampdown on Shi'i Group." *Al-Ahram Weekly,* October 24–30, 1996.

Halliday, Fred. *Iran: Dictatorship and Development.* London: Penguin, 1978.

Hartounian, Mourad Ruben. *Impact of the Relation between Government and Religion on Egyptian Media Content: 1950–1995.* M.A. thesis, Department of Mass Communication, American University in Cairo, 1997.

Hasan-nia, Arash. "Nikukarani kih Nizarat ra Dust Nadarand." *Sharq,* 25 Shahrivar 1383/15, September 2004.

Hassan, Fayza. "The Meaning of Emancipation." *Al-Ahram Weekly,* March 1–7, 2001.

Hassan, Riaz. "Faithlines: Social Structure and Religiosity in Muslim Societies: An Empirical Study." Unpublished paper, April 1998.

Held, David. *Models of Democracy.* Cambridge, UK: Polity Press, 1996.

———. *States and Societies.* Oxford, UK: Martin Robertson, 1983.

Herrera, Linda. "The Islamization of Education in Egypt: Between Politics, Culture, and the Market." In John Esposito and F. Burgat, eds., *Modernizing Islam.* New Brunswick, N.J.: Rutgers University Press, 2002.

Hizb al-Wasat. *Awraq Hizb al-Wasat.* Introduction by Rafiq Habib. Cairo: Hizb al-Wasat, 1996.

———. *Awraq Hizb al-Wasat al-Misri.* Introduction by Salih 'Abd al-Karim. Cairo: Hizb al-Wasat, 1998.

Hobsbawm, Eric. *Primitive Rebels.* New York: Norton, 1959.

Hoodfar, Homa. "Devices and Desires: Population Policy and Gender Roles in the Islamic Republic." *Middle East Report,* vol. 24, no. 190 (1994).

———. "The Women's Movement in Iran: Women at the Crossroads of Secularization and Islamization." *Women Living under Muslim Law* (Paris), pamphlet no. 1, Winter 1999.

———. *Volunteer Health Workers in Iran as Social Activists: Can Governmental NGOs Be Agents of Democratization?* Women Living under Muslim Law (Paris), Occasional paper no. 10, December 1998.

Hooglund, Eric. "Change in Rural Patterns." Paper presented in the workshop "Twentieth Century Iran: History from Below." Amsterdam, May 24–26, 2001.

Howeidy, Amira. "Born to Be Wild." *Al-Ahram Weekly,* December 23–29, 1999.

Huntington, Samuel. "Modernization and Revolution." In Claude E. Welch and M. B. Taintor, eds., *Revolution and Political Change.* North Scituate, Mass.: Duxbury Press, 1972.

Ibrahim, Barbara, and Hind Wassef. "Caught between Two Worlds: Youth in the Egyptian Hinterland." In Roel Meijer, ed., *Alienation or Integration of Arab Youth.* London: Curzon Press, 2000.

Ibrahim, Najih, and 'Ali Muhamma 'Ali Sharif. *Hurmat al-Ghuluw fi Din wa Takfir al-Muslimin.* Cairo: Maktaba al-Turath al-Islami, 2002.

Ibrahim, Saad Eddin. "Anatomy of Egypt's Militant Islamic Groups: Methodological Note and Preliminary Findings." *International Journal of Middle East Studies,* vol. 12 (1980): 423–53.

———. "Egyptian Law 32 On Egypt's Private Sector Organizations: A Critical Assessment." Working Paper no. 3. Cairo: Ibn Khaldoun Center for Development Studies, November 1996..

———. "The Changing Face of Egypt's Islamic Activism: How Much of a Threat?" Working Paper. Cairo: Ibn Khaldoun Center, May 1995.

———. *The New Arab Social Order.* Boulder, Colo.: Westview Press, 1985.

Irani, Naser. "Society and the Religious Intellectuals." In introduction to 'Alireza Jalaipur, *Pas az Duvvum-i Khurdad.*

Ismail, Salwa. "The Paradox of Islamist Politics." *Middle East Report,* no. 221 (Winter 2001): 34–39.

Issawi, 'Ali. *Al-Ashwa'iyyat wa Tagarub al-Tanmiyyah*. Cairo: Cairo University, 1995.

Jala'ipur, Hamidreza. *Jami'a Shinasi-i Junbashhā-yi Ijtima'i*. Tehran: Tarh-i Naw, 2003.

———. "Mas'alih-i Ijtima'i, Na Junbish-i Ijtima'i." *Yas-i Naw*, 10 Aban (2003).

———. *Pas Az Dovvom-e Khordad*. Tehran: Kavir, 1999.

———. "Tahlil-i az Puyish-i Zanan-i Iran," Iran-i Imruz website, 12 Aban 1382 (2003).

Jalali-Na'ini, Ziba. "Ta'sīs-i Rishtih-i Mutal'āt-i Zanān dar Irān." *Guftugu*, no. 38, Azar 1382: 7–23.

Kadivar, Muhsin. *Baha-yi Azadi*. Tehran: Nashr-e Ney, 1999.

———. "Freedom of Thought and Religion in Islam." Presented at the International Congress of Human Rights and the Dialogue of Civilizations, Tehran, May 2001.

———. *Nazarihha-yi dawlat dar fiqh-i Shi'i*. Tehran: Nashr Nay, 1997.

Kar, Mihrangiz. "*Mushārikat*-i Siyasi-yi Zanan: Vaqa'iyat va Khiyāl." *Zanan*, no. 47: 12–13.

Karam, Azza. *Women, Islamists and the State*. London: Macmillan, 1998.

Karbasian, 'Ali Akbar. "The Process of Income Distribution in Iran" (in Persian). *Iran-i Farda*, no. 17, Ordibehesi 1374 (1995).

Karimi, Zahra. "Sahm-i Zanan dar Bazar-i Kar-i Iran." *Itila'at-i Siyasi Iqtisadi*, nos. 179–180, Murdad-Shahrivar 1381 (2002): 208–19.

Katouzian, Homa. *The Political Economy of Modern Iran*. London: Macmillan, 1982.

Kazemi, Farhad. *Poverty and Revolution in Iran*. New York: New York University Press, 1981.

Kazemipur, A., and A. Rezaei. "Religious Life under Theocracy: The Case of Iran." *Journal for the Scientific Study of Religion*, vol. 42, no. 3 (September 2003): 347–61.

Keddie, Nikki. *Iran and the Muslim World*. New York: New York University Press, 1995.

———. "Islamic Revival in the Middle East: A Comparison of Iran and Egypt." In Samih Farsoun, ed., *Arab Society: Continuity and Change*. London: Croom Helm, 1985.

———. *Religion and Rebellion in Iran: The Tobacco Protest of 1891–92*. London: Frank Cass, 1966.

———. *Roots of Revolution: An Interpretive History of Modern Iran*. New Haven, Conn.: Yale University Press, 1981.

Kepel, Gilles. *Muslim Extremism in Egypt*, Berkeley: University of California Press, 1986.

———. *Jihad: The Trial of Political Islam*, London: I. B. Tauris, 2002.

Keshavarzian, Arang. *A Bazaar and Two Regimes: Governance and Mobilization in Tehran's Marketplace, from 1963–the Present*. Ph.D. dissertation, Princeton University, 2003.

Khalifa, Ayman. "The Withering Youth of Egypt." *Ru'ya*, no. 7 (Sring 1995): 6–10.

Khatam, A'zam. "Sakhtar-i Ishtighal-i Zanan-i Shahri: Qabl va Ba'd az Inqilab." *Guftugu*, no. 28 (Summer 2000): 129–39.

Khatami, Muhammad. *Bim-i Mawj.* Tehran: Sima-yi Javan, 1993.

Khomeini, Ruhollah. *Hukumat-i Islami: Islam Din-i Siyasat Ast.* Publisher unknown, 1970 (Arabic year 1392).

———. *Sahifih-yi Nur.* Collected works compiled and edited by the Ministry of National Guidance, Tehran, 1982.

———. *Shu'un va Khiyarat-i Vali-yi Faqih.* Tehran: Ministry of Culture and Islamic Guidance, 1999.

Khosrokhavar, Farhad. "The Islamic Revolution in Iran: Retrospect after a Quarter of a Century." *Thesis Eleven*, vol. 76, no. 1 (2004): 70–84.

Kian-Thiebaut, Azadeh. "Political Impacts of Iranian Youth's Individuation: How Family Matters." Unpublished paper presented at the annual meeting of the Middle East Studies Association (MESA), Washington D.C., November 24, 2002.

———. "Women and Politics in Post-Islamist Iran." *Women Living under Muslim Law* (Paris), Dossier 21 (September 1998): 44.

Kienle, Eberhard. *The Grand Delusion: Democracy and Economic Reform in Egypt.* London: I. B. Tauris, 2001.

Kim, Quee-Young. "Disjunctive Justice and Revolutionary Movement: The 4.19 (Sa-il-gu) Upheaval and the Fall of the Syngman Rhee Regime in South Korea." In Quee-Young Kim, ed., *Revolutions in the Third World*, pp. 56–70. Leiden, the Netherlands: E. J. Brill, 1991.

Kinzer, Stephen. "Will Turkey Make It?" *New York Review of Books*, July 15, 2004.

Kis, Jonus. "Between Reform and Revolution: Three Hypotheses about the Nature of Regime Change," *Constellations*, vol. 1, no. 3: 399–421.

Kovel, Joel. "The Vatican Strikes Back." *Monthly Review*, vol. 36, no. 1 (April 1985).

Kuczynski, P., and K. Nowak. "The Solidarity Movement in Relation to Society and the State." In L. Kriesberg et al., eds., *Research in Social Movement, Conflicts and Change*, vol. 10. Greenwich, Conn.: Jai Press, 1988.

Kupferschmidt, Uri. "Reformist and Militant Islam in Urban and Rural Egypt." *Middle Eastern Studies*, vol. 23 (October 1987): 403–18.

La'li, Mas'ud, ed. *Khatami az Chih Miguyad.* Tehran: Nashr Ikhlas, 1999.

Lacroix, Stéphane. "Between Islamists and Liberals: Saudi Arabia's New 'Islamo-Liberal' Reformists." *Middle East Journal*, vol. 58, no. 3 (Summer 2004): 345–65.

———. A New Element in the Saudi Political-Intellectual Field: The Emergence of an Islamo-Liberal Reformist Trend." Paper presented in the workshop "Saudi Futures: Trends and Challenges in the Post-9/11 and Post-Iraq-War World." Leiden, the Netherlands, February 20–21, 2004.

Lajevardi, Habib. *Labor Unions and Autocracy in Iran.* Syracuse, N.Y.: Syracuse University Press, 1985.

Laoust, H. "Ibn Taimiyya." *The Encyclopedia of Islam.* Leiden, the Netherlands: Brill, 1986.

Lapidus, Ira. *A History of Islamic Societies.* Cambridge, UK: Cambridge University Press, 1988.

Lerner, Gerda. *The Creation of Feminist Consciousness.* Oxford, UK: Oxford University Press, 1993.

Lewis, Bernard. "The Roots of Muslim Rage." *Foreign Policy,* vol. 17, no. 4 (Summer 2001/2002).

Lipset, S. M. *Political Man: The Social Bases of Politics.* Garden City, N.Y.: Doubleday, 1959.

Lowy, Michael. *The War of Gods: Religion and Politics in Latin America.* London: Verso, 1996.

MacLeod, Arlene. *Accommodating Protest: Working Women, the New Veiling, and Change in Cairo.* New York: Columbia University Press, 1991.

Mahdi, Ali Akbar. "The Student Movement in the Islamic Republic of Iran." *Journal of Iranian Research and Analysis,* vol. 15, no. 2 (November 1999).

Mahmood, Saba. *Politics of Piety.* Princeton, N.J.: Princeton University Press, 2005.

Malaki, Muhammad. "The Students and the Cultural Revolution." *Andīshih-i Jām'iyih,* 25/26/27, Shahrivar/Mahr/Aban 1381 (2002).

Malakian, Mustafa. "Interview." *Rah-i Naw,* no. 13, Tir 1377 (1998).

Mallat, Chibli. *The Renewal of Islamic Law.* London: Cambridge University Press, 1993.

Mamdani, Mahmood. *Citizens and Subjects.* Princeton, N.J.: Princeton University Press, 1996.

———. *Good Muslims, Bad Muslims.* New York: Pantheon, 2004.

Markaz-i Amar-i Iran. *Iran dar A'inihi Amar,* no. 4, Tehran, 1363.

Marsot, Afaf Lutfi El-Sayyid. *Egypt's Liberal Experiment.* Cambridge, UK: Cambridge University Press, 1977.

Massey, Doreen. "The Spatial Construction of Youth Cultures." In Tracy Skelton, ed., *Cool Places.* London: Routledge, 1998.

Matar, Nadia. "Glows Ticks and Grooves." *Cairo Times,* March 14–20, 2002.

McAllister, Matthew. "Tehran's Grand Mosque a Symbol of Prayer, Pride, and Waste." *Newsday,* April 25, 2001.

Meeker, Michael. "The New Muslim Intellectuals in the Republic of Turkey." In Richard Tapper, ed., *Islam in Modern Turkey.* London: I. B. Tauris, 1991.

Mehreaz, Samia. "Take Them out of the Ball Game: Egypt's Cultural Players in Crisis." *Middle East Report,* no. 219 (Summer 2001): 10–15.

Melucci, Alberto. *Challenging Codes: Collective Action in the Information Age.* Cambridge, UK: Cambridge University Press, 1996.

———. *Nomads of the Present.* Cambridge, UK: Cambridge University Press, 1989.

———. "A Strange Kind of Newness: What's New about the 'New' Social Movements." In E. Larana et al., eds., *New Social Movements: From Ideology to Identity*. Philadelphia: Temple University Press, 1994.

Migdal, Joel. *State in Society*. Cambridge, UK: Cambridge University Press, 2001.

Milani, Mohsen. *The Making of the Islamic Revolution in Iran*. Boulder, Colo.: Westview Press, 1994.

Millard, William. "Popular Press in Iran." *Guftugu*, no. 4, Tehran, 1994 (in Persian).

Mina, D. "Women's Mobility in Tehran." A presentation in the seminar 'Women and the City," Tehran, College of Social Sciences, University of Tehran, December 30, 2003.

Mir-Hosseini, Ziba. *Islam and Gender: The Religious Debate in Contemporary Iran*. Princeton, N.J.: Princeton University Press, 1999.

Mirsepassi-Ashtiani, Ali. "The Crisis of Secularism and Political Islam in Iran." *Social Text*, vol. 12, no. 3 (Spring 1994): 51–84.

Mitchell, Richard. *The Society of Muslim Brothers*. Oxford, UK: Oxford University Press, 1969.

Mitchell, Timothy. *Rule of Experts*. Berkeley: University of California Press, 2002.

Moaddel, Mansour. *Class, Politics and Ideology in the Iranian Revolution*. New York: Columbia University Press, 1993.

———. "Religion, Gender, and Politics in Egypt, Jordan and Iran: Findings of Comparative National Surveys." Unpublished report, 2002.

———. "The Significance of Discourse in the Iranian Revolution: A Reply to Foran." *Critique: Journal for Critical Studies of the Middle East*, no. 4 (Spring 1994).

———. "The Worldviews of Islamic Publics: The Cases of Egypt, Iran, and Jordan." *Comparative Sociology*, vol. 1, nos. 3–4 (2002), pp. 299–319.

Moaveni, Azadeh. "Ballot Blowing in the Wind." *Al-Ahram Weekly*, May 4, 2000.

Moghadam, Val. "Feminism in Iran and Algeria: Two Models of Collective Action for Women's Rights." *Journal of Iranian Research and Analysis*, vol. 19, no. 1 (April 2003): 18–31.

———. "Women's Employment Issues in Contemporary Iran: Problems and Prospects in the 1990s." *Iranian Studies*, vol. 28 (1995): 175–200.

Mo'meni, Baghir. "Islam-i Mowjud, Islam-i Mow'oud." *Nuqtih*, vol. 1, no. 1 (1995) (in Persian).

Mostafa, Hadia. "In Layman's Terms." *Egypt Today*, vol. 21, issue 9 (September 2000): 81–83.

Mostaqimi, Ramin. "Rights—Iran: Women Carve Out Spaces within Islamic Society." *Interpress News Agency*, June 25, 2003.

Mottahedeh, Roy. *The Mantle of the Prophet*. New York: Pantheon, 1985.

Mubarak, Hisham. *Al-Irhabiyun Qadimun*. Cairo: Kitab al-Mahrusa, 1995.

Muhammadi, Majid. *Darāmadi bar Raftar-Shināsi-yi Siyasi-yi Danishjuyan dar Iran-i Ibruz*. Tehran: Intisharat-i Kavir, 1998.

Muhibbian, Amir. "Towsiyiha-i bih Jibhih-i Mushārikat." *Dariche* website, www. dariche.org [December 22, 2002].

Mujtahid Shabastari, Muhammad. "Dimukrasi-yi Dini." *Aftab*, no. 7, Shahrivar 1380 (2001): 4–5.

———. *Naqdi bar Qira'at-i Rasmi az Din*. Tehran: Tarh-i Naw, 2000.

Munson, Henry. *Islam and Revolution in the Middle East*. New Haven, Conn.: Yale University Press, 1988.

Muntazari, Ayatollah Husayn 'Ali. *Khatirat-i Ayatullah Husayn Muntazari*. Place of publication and publisher unknown, 2001.

Murtaji, Hujjat. *Jinahayih Siyāsi dar Irān-i Imrūz*. Tehran: Naqsh-o-Negar, 1998.

Mutahhari, Murtaza. "Rahbar-i Nasl-i Javan." *Guftar-i Mah*, no. 3: 46–48.

Nafici, Hamid. "Iranian Cinema under the Islamic Republic." *American Anthropologist*, vol. 97, no. 3 (September 1995).

Najjar, Fauzi. "Islamic Fundamentalism and the Intellectuals: The Case of Nasr Hamid Abu-Zeid." *British Journal of Middle East Studies*, vol. 27, no. 2 (November 2000): 177–200.

Najmabadi, Afsaneh. "Feminism in an Islamic Republic: Years of Hardship, Years of Growth." In Yvonne Haddad and John Esposito, eds., *Islam, Gender and Social Change*, pp. 59–84. Oxford: Oxford University Press, 1998.

Napoli, James. "Egyptian Sleight of Hand." *Index on Censorship*, vol. 21, no. 2 (1992): 23–25.

Naquib, Sameh. "The Political Ideology of the Jihad Movement." M.A. thesis, Sociology Department, American University in Cairo, 1993.

Nasrawi, Seif. "An Ethnography of Cairo's Metro." Term paper for Urban Sociology class, Fall 2002, American University in Cairo.

Negus, Sana. "Brothers' Brother" (on the Profile of Jamal al-Banna). *Cairo Times*, September 30–October 13, 1999.

Negus, Steve. "Down but Not Out." *Cairo Times*, April 3–16, 1997.

Nepstad, Sharon, E. "Popular Religion, Protest, and Revolt: The Emergence of Political Insurgency in the Nicaraguan and Salvadoran Churches of the 1960s–1980s." In Christian Smith, ed., *Disruptive Religion: The Force of Faith in Social-Movement Activism*, pp. 105–24. London: Routledge, 1996.

Nuri, 'Abdullah. *Shukaran-i Islah*. Tehran: Tarh-i Naw, 1999.

Nuruzi, Kambiz. "Nigāhi bi Amār-i Huqūqi." *Rah-i Naw*, no. 1, 5 Urdibahasht 1377.

Nuwir, 'Abd al-Salam. *Al-Mu'alimun wa al-Siyasa fi Misr*. Cairo, al-Ahram Center for Strategic and political Studies, 2001.

Olimova, Saodat. "Social Protests and the Islamic Movement in Central Eurasia." Paper presented in the workshop "Towards Social Stability and Democratic Governance in Central Eurasia: Challenges to Regional Security." Leiden, the Netherlands, September 8–11, 2004.

Parsa, Misagh. *Social Origins of the Iranian Revolution*. New Brunswick, N.J.: Rutgers University Press, 1989.

Parsons, Anthony. "The Iranian Revolution." *Middle East Review* (Spring 1998).

Pateman, C. *The Sexual Contract*. Cambridge, UK: Polity Press, 1988.

Paul, Gregory. "The Great Scandal: Christianity's Role in the Rise of the Nazis." *Free Inquiry Magazine*, vol. 23, no. 4.

Paydar, Parvin. *Women and Political Process in Iran*. Cambridge, UK: Cambridge University Press, 1995.

Peterson, Anna, M. Vasquez, and P. Williams, eds. *Christianity, Social Change, and Globalization in the Americas*. New Brunswick, N.J.: Rutgers University Press, 2001.

Piran, Parviz. "Se Sath-i Tahlili-yi Vaqi'iyih." In 'Ali Riza'i, ed., *Intikhab-i Naw*. Tehran: Tarh-i Naw, 1998.

Piscatori, James, ed. *Islam in the Political Process*. Cambridge, UK: Cambridge University Press, 1983.

Plantinga, Richard, ed. *Christianity and Plurality*. Oxford, UK: Blackwell, 1999.

Population Council. *Transitions to Adulthood: A National Survey of Egyptian Adolescents*. Cairo: Population Council, March 1999.

Przeworski, Adam. "The Role of Theory in Comparative Politics." *World Politics*, vol. 48, no. 1 (1996).

Qandil, Amani. "Taqdim Ada' al-Islamiyin fi Niqabat al-Mahniyya." Cairo: CEDEJ/ Cairo University, 1993.

Qandil, Amani, and Sarah Ben-Nafisah. *Al-Jama'iyyat al-Ahliyya fi Misr*. Cairo: Al-Ahram Center for Strategic Studies, 1995.

Qutbi, Mansur. "Causeless Rebellion in the Land of Iran." *Iran Javan*, no. 166, Mahr 1379 (2000).

Rahimpur, Jawad. "Mahiyat-i Junbish-i Danishjuyi: Practik va Istratijik." *Iran-i Farda*, no. 49, Aban-Azar 1377 (1998).

Rashwan, Diaa. "Wishful Thinking, Present and Future." *Al-Ahram Weekly*, February 7–13, 2002.

Reja'i, Alireza. "Poverty and Political Developments in Iran." In F. Raiis-dana, Z. Shadi-talab, and P. Piran, eds., *Poverty in Iran*. Tehran, School of Bahzīsti va Tavānbakhshi, 1379 (2000).

Reza'i, Abdulali. "Nime-yi Pur-i Livan." In A. Reza'I and A. Abdi, eds. *Intikhab-i Naw*. Tehran: Tarh-i Naw, 1997.

Rodinson, Maxime. *Europe and the Mystique of Islam*. Seattle: University of Washington Press, 1987.

Roth, Guenther. *The Social Democrats in Imperial Germany: A Study of Working Class Isolation and National Integration*. Totowa, N.J.: Bedminster Press, 1963.

Roussillon, Alain. "Decline of Islamism or the Failure of Neo-Orientalism?" (in Persian). *Guftugu*, no. 29 (Fall 2000): 163–85.

Roy, Olivier. *Globalised Islam: The Search for a New Ummah*. London: Hurst, 2004.

———. "Le Post-Islamisme." *Revue du Monde Musulmans et de la Méditerannée* 85–86 (1999).

Saad, Rania. "Islamists Take Control of Liberal Syndicate." *Al-Ahram Weekly*, September 17–23, 1992.

Saghafi, Morad. "The Reform Nobody Wants Anymore," *ISIM Review*, no. 15 (Winter 2005).

Saghiya, Hazem. "Problem of Egypt's Political Culture." *Al-Hayat*, July 29, 2001.

Said, Atef Shahat. "Homosexuality and Human Rights in Egypt." *ISIM Newsletter*, no. 9, January 2002.

Said, Edward. "Enemies of the State." *Al-Ahram Weekly*, June 21–27, 2001.

———. *Orientalism*. New York: Vintage, 1979.

Sa'idzadih, Sayyid Muhsin. "Kalbud-shikafi-yi Tarh-i Intiqal-i Umur-i Idari." *Zanan*, no. 43.

Salama, Salama A. "'Change' and Real Change." *Al-Ahram Weekly*, June 10–16, 2004.

Selim al-'Awa, Muhammad. "Hadyat al-Hukuma fi Ramadan." *Al-Wafd*, December 4, 2001.

Sama'i, Mahdi, ed. *Farhang-i Lughat-i Zaban-i Makhfi*. Tehran: Nashr Markaz, 2003.

Sarwish, Adel. "The Hydra Grows Another Head: The Fundamentalist Arab Governments in the Gulf Are Buying Out Journalists and Writers in Egypt." *Index on Censorship*, vol. 12, no. 6 (June 1992).

Schielke, Samuli. "Habitus of the Authentic, Order of the Rational: Contesting Saints' Festivals in Contemporary Egypt." *Critique: Critical Middle Eastern Studies*, vol. 12, no. 2 (Fall 2003): 155–175.

———. "Pious Fun at Saints' Festivals in Modern Egypt." *ISIM Newsletter*, no. 7, 2001.

Schirazi, Asghar. *The Constitution of Iran: Politics and the State in the Islamic Republic*. London: I. B. Tauris, 1997.

Scholder, Klaus. *The Churches and the Third Reich*. Vols. 1 and 2. Philadelphia: Fortress Press, 1988.

Schultze, Reinhard. "The Ethnization of Islamic Cultures in the Late 20th Century or From Political Islam to Post-Islamism." In George Stauth, ed., *Islam: Motor or Challenge of Modernity. Yearbook of the Sociology of Islam*, no. 1 (1998): 187–98.

Serajzadeh, Seyed Hossein. "Non-attending Believers: Religiosity of Iranian Youth and Its Implications for Secularization Theory." A paper presented at the World Congress of Sociology, Montreal, 1999.

Shahidian, Hamid. "The Iranian Left and the "Woman Question" in the Revolution of 1978–1979." *International Journal of Middle East Studies*, vol. 26 (May 1994): 223–47.

Shahin, Alaa. "Dangerous Minds." *Al-Ahram Weekly*, September 13–19, 2001.

Shahin, Emad Eldin. *Through Muslim Eyes: A. Rashid Reda and the West*. Herndon, Va.: International Institute of Islamic Thought, 1993.

Shamsulva'izin, M. "Rawshanfikran-i Dini va Jumhari-yi Sevvum," *Kiyan*, no. 37, vol. 7 (June 1997).

Shari'ati, 'Ali. *Jahatgiri-i Tabaqati-yi Islam*. Tehran: publisher unknown, 1980.

Sharif, 'Ali Muhammad 'Ali, and 'Usama Ibrahim Hafiz. *Al-Nas wa al-Tabi'in fi Tashih Mafahim al-Muhtasibin*. Cairo: Maktaba al-Turath al-Islami, January 2002.

Shukri, Shukufih, and Sahirih Labriz. "Mard: Shrik ya Ra'is?" *Zanan*, no. 2 (March 1992): 26–32.

Sid Ahmad, Rif'at. "Ightilal al-Sadat." *Al-Hayat*, December 12, 1997.

Singer, Hanna F. "The Socialist Labor Party: A Case Study of a Contemporary Egyptian Opposition Party." In *Cairo Papers in Social Science*, vol. 16, monograph 1 (Spring 1993).

Sivan, E. "The Islamic Republic of Egypt." *Orbis*, vol. 31, no. 1 (Spring 1987): 43–54.

Skocpol, Theda. *States and Social Revolutions*. Cambridge, UK: Cambridge University Press, 1979.

Smith, Christian. *The Emergence of Liberation Theology*. Chicago: University of Chicago Press, 1991.

Snow, David, and Susan Marshall. "Cultural Imperialism, Social Movements, and the Islamic Revival." *Research in Social Movements, Conflict, and Change*, vol. 7 (1984): 131–52.

Soueif, M. I., et al. "Use of Psychoactive Substances among Male Secondary School Pupils in Egypt: A Study of a Nationwide Representative Sample." *Drug and Alcohol Dependence*, vol. 26 (1990): 63–79.

Staniszkis, Jadwiga. *Poland's Self-Limiting Revolution*. Princeton, N.J.: Princeton University Press, 1984.

Sullivan, Denis. *Private Voluntary Organizations in Egypt*. Miami: University Press of Florida, 1994.

Surush, A. "Concepts of Religious State." Speech, University of Quebec, Montreal, July 17, 1996.

———. "Development and Fundamental Questions." Lecture delivered at Essex University, UK, October 12, 1996.

———. "Hasanat va Khadamat-i Din." *Kiyan*, no. 27, Mahr-Aban 1374 (1995): 12–13.

———. "Hurriyat va Rawhaniyat." *Kiyan*, no. 24, Farvardin-Urdibahasht 1374 (1995).

———. "Idioluji va Din-i Dunyayi." *Kiyan*, no. 31, Tir/Murdad 1375 (1996): 2–11.

———. "Tahlil-i Mafhum-i Hukumat-i Dini." *Kiyan*, no. 32, Shahrivar-Mahr 1375 (1996).

———. *Teori-i ghabz va bast Shariat*. Tehran: Sirat Cultural Center, 1994.

Sztompka, Piotr. *The Sociology of Social Change*. Oxford, UK: Blackwells 1999.

Tabari, Azar. "Islam and the Struggle for Emancipation of Iranian Women." In A. Tabari and N. Yeganeh, ed., *Under the Shadow of Islam*. London: Zed Books, 1982.

Tabari, A., and N. Yeganeh, eds. *Under the Shadow of Islam.* London: Zed Books, 1982.

Tabatabaii, Shahin. "Understanding Islam in Its Totality Is the Only Way to Understand Women's Role," In A. Tabari and N. Yeganeh, eds., *Under the Shadow of Islam.* London: Zed Books, 1982.

Tadros, Mariz. "NGO-State Relations in Egypt: Welfare Assistance in a Poor Urban Community of Cairo." D. Phil. dissertation, University of Oxford, June 2004.

Tāhiripur, Farzad, and Mas'ud Anjam-Shu'a. "Gustarish-i Amuzish-i 'Āli va Taws'ih Jami'at-i Danishjuyi." *Barnamih va Taws'ih*, vol. 2, no. 5, Spring 1372 (1993).

Tajbakhsh, Kian. "Political Decentralization and the Creation of Local Government in Iran." *Social Research*, vol. 67, no. 2 (September 2000): 377–404.

Tajzadih, Mustafa. "Matn ya Vahn?" *Imruz*, 03/16/1383 (2004).

Tamam, Husam. *Tahawulat al-Akhwan al-Muslimun.* Cairo: Madbuli, 2006.

Tarrow, Sidney. *Power in Movement: Collective Action, Social Movements and Politics.* Cambridge, UK: Cambridge University Press, 1994.

Tehranian, Majid. *Socio-Economic and Communication Indicators in Development Planning: A Case Study of Iran.* Paris: UNESCO, 1980.

Tessler, Mark, and Eleanor Gao. "Gauging Arab Support for Democracy." *Journal of Democracy*, vol. 16, no. 3 (July 2005): 86–87.

Thompson, Elizabeth. *Colonial Citizens: Republican Rights, Paternal Privilege, and Gender in French Syria and Lebanon.* New York: Columbia University Press, 2000.

Tilly, Charles. *From Mobilization to Revolution.* Reading, Mass.: Addison-Wesley, 1978.

Tohidi, Nayehreh. "Islamic Feminism: Women Negotiating Modernity and Patriarchy in Iran." In Ibrahim Abu-Rabi, ed., *Blackwell Companion to Contemporary Islamic Thought.* Oxford, UK: Blackwell, 2006.

———. "Mas'alih Zanan va Rawshanfikran Tay-yi Tahavvulat-i Dahi-yi Akhir." *Nime-yi Digar*, no. 10, Winter 1368 (1989): 51–95.

———. *Feminism, Islamgaraii va Dimukrasi.* Los Angeles: Kitābsarih, 1996.

Turbat, Akbar. "Farar-i Maghzha az Iran bih Amrika." *Aftab*, no. 32, Day/Bahman 1382 (2003): 70–79.

UNESCO. *Statistical Yearbook.* Paris, various years.

Utvik, Bjorn Olav. "Hizb al-Wasat and the Potential for Change in Egyptian Islamism." *Critique: Critical Studies of the Middle East*, vol. 14, no. 3 (Fall 2005).

Weaver, Mary Anne. "Revolution by Stealth." *New Yorker*, June 8, 1998.

Weber, Max. *The Sociology of Religion.* Boston: Beacon Press, 1964.

Wentz, Richard. *The Culture of Religious Pluralism.* Boulder, Colo.: Westview Press, 1998.

Yaghmaian, Behzad. *Social Change in Iran.* Albany: SUNY Press, 2002.

———. "Student Movements in the Islamic Republic of Iran." *Journal of Iranian Research and Analysis*, vol. 15, no. 2 (November 1999).

Zaqzuq, Mahmud. "Hawl Shurut Bina' al-Masajid." *Al-Wafd*, December 10, 2001.

Zubaida, Sami. "Cosmopolitanism in the Arab World." Unpublished paper, 2004.

———. *Islam, the People, and the State*. London: Routledge, 1989.

INDEX

'Abbas, Mahmud, 184
'Abd al-Futuh, Ramadan, 150
'Abd al-Ghani, Safwat, 39
'Abd al-Kafi, 'Umar, 149, 151
'Abd al-Karim, Khalid, 176, 250n193
'Abdal-Khaliq, Sa'id, 179
'Abd al-Majid Muhammad, 'Asam, 241n27,
    249n177
'Abd al-Rahim, Sha'ban, 179
'Abd al-Rahman, Hamdi, 219n103, 240n10,
    249n177, 250n195
'Abd al-Rahman, Shaykh 'Umar, 32, 39, 142,
    146, 149
'Abdi, 'Abbas, 66, 70, 86, 93, 94, 121, 128
'Abduh, Muhammad, 37, 86, 178
Abdul-Azim, Hamdi 'Abd al-Rahman. See
    'Abd al-Rahman, Hamdi
Abou El Fadl, Khaled, 211n5
Abrahamian, Ervand, 17, 215n33
Abu-Ahmad, Hamid, 248n142
Abu-Bakr, Omaima, 157, 245n87
Abul-Majd, Ahmad Kamal, 177–78
Abu-Lughod, Janet, 147
Abu Nasr, Hamid, 145
Abu Zayd, Nasr, 92; charged with apostasy,
    168, 171, 172, 176, 188, 220n137, 248n156; on
    interpretation of scripture, 5, 212n17
ACC. See Association of Combatant Clergy
Adelman, Kenneth, 211n4
Afghanistan: Mujahidin resistance to
    Soviet Union, 39; relations with United
    States, 9, 123, 198, 199; Taliban, 40, 140,
    198, 199

Afshari, 'Ali, 120, 122
Afshari, Reza, 29
Aghajari, Hashem, 70, 86, 89, 94; trial of, 120,
    121, 122, 128–29, 132
Aghasi, 32
Ahmad, Jalal Al-i: "Westoxication," 86
Ahwaz, 129
Ajami, Fuad, 219n105
Akbariyan, Muhammad Javad, 230n169
Akhavi, Shahroukh, 216n59
Al-Afghani, 37, 86
'Alavitabar, 'Alireza, 90, 93, 94, 96, 112, 230n186,
    239n99, 253n9
alcohol: banning of, 9, 137; use of, 31, 33, 162,
    172, 246n103
Algeria, 213n19; attitudes toward democracy
    in, 254n27; authoritarian rule in, 197;
    Islamism in, 9, 29, 142
'Ali, Muhammad, 37
Al-Qa'ida, 36, 39, 40, 142
American University (Cairo), 147, 155, 169,
    243n46, 244n71
Amir Kabir University, 108
Amr Bih Ma'ruf, 75
Amuli, Ayatollah Javadi, 227n130, 231n199
Angham, 243n53
Angola, 133
anti-Semitism, 5, 212n13
Arafat, Yasser, 184
Arak, 98
Araki, Ayatollah, 232n210
Aramin, Muhsin, 94
Ardabili, Ayatollah Musavi, 99

Arjomand, Sa'id Amir, 17, 20, 214n2, 215n33, 216n59
Arkoun, Muhammad, 92, 123
art of presence, 15, 201–5
Asgharzadih, Ibrahim, 66, 70, 86
Ashkevari, Hasan Yusifi-, 101, 121, 232n203
'Ashmawi, Sa'id al-, 169, 176
Ashuri, Daryush, 229n152
Association for the Defense of a Free Press (Iran), 109
Association of Combatant Clergy (ACC), 67, 112, 132
Association of Islamic Scholars (Iran), 126
Ataturk, Kemal, 25
Austria, 20
'Awa, Muhammad Selim al-, 137, 176, 177–78
'Awa, Selim al-, 248n146
A'wani, Ghulamreza, 91
Ayandih, 128
Ayoub, Muhammad, 123
Azad University, 68, 125, 224n53
al-Azhar University, 169, 220n136, 221n139

Badawi, Jamal, 179, 247n135
Badawi, Khalid, 144
bād jins, 81
Badri, Yusif al-, 171, 172
Baha'idin, Kamal, 170
Bahnud, Mas'ud, 120, 232n209
Bahrain, 197–98, 232n210; Islamism in, 9
Baker, Raymond: Islam without Fear, 250n201
Balkans, the, 145
Bam: earthquakes in, 130
Bani-Sadr, Abul-Hasan, 28, 53, 98, 216n52, 218n97, 237n61
Banna, Ahmad Sayyif al-Islam Hasan al-, 35
Banna, Hasan al-, 35, 37–38, 42, 175, 176
Banna, Jamal al-: Nahw Fiqh Jadid, 176–77
Banquet for the Seaweeds, A, 144, 169
Baqi, Imdad al-Din, 120, 238n67
Barri, Shaykh Dr. 'Abd al-Munim al-, 247n126
Bashiriyyih, Husayn, 87, 231n190
Bayat, Asadullah, 121
bazaar merchants, 27, 53, 109, 216n51; and Iranian clergy, 26, 28, 37, 56, 124, 125, 216n52, 238n78
Bazargan, Mehdi, 29, 86, 87, 98, 216n55
Beauvoir, Simone de, 77
Beckford, James, 5
Beheshti, Ayatollah Muhammad, 29, 216n52
Behruzi, Maryam, 72–73
Bendix, Reinhard, 20

bin Laden, Osama, 5, 39, 40, 142
Birjand, 236n23
Bishr, Muhammad 'Ali, 144
Bishri, Tariq al-, 177–78
Bitaraf, Habibullah, 66, 97
blood money, 80, 83
Bojnordi, Ayatollah, 226n107
Bonine, Enrique Dussel, 213n20
Borujerdi, Ayatollah Sayyed Husayn, 26, 28
Būnyād-i Jānbāzān, 125
Burgat, François, 18
Burqani, Ahmad, 93, 97, 109
Bush, George W., 180; on Iran as part of "axis of evil," 111

Cairo: American University, 147, 155, 169, 243n46, 244n71; 'Ayn al-Shams, 39, 138–39; Book Fair, 169, 243n47; Cairo university, 39; earthquakes of 1992, 34, 44; gated communities in, 165; Imbaba, 39–40, 44, 137, 138–39, 140, 218n91; internet cafes in, 249n171; Islamic Community Development Association in, 43; al-Jama'a al-Islamiyya in, 39–40, 137, 138–39, 140; Jamaliyya, 39; poverty in, 214n1; 6th of October City, 151; Suq al-Tawfiqiyya, 144; Zamalek, 39, 147, 243n47
Camp David Accords, 35, 39, 184
capitalism, 6, 7, 27, 187, 212n8. See also globalization and Muslim societies
Carter, Jimmy: human rights policy, 23
Castells, Manuel, 194
censorship: in Egypt, 169, 176–77, 248n142, 250n193, 252n226; in Iran, 30, 33, 46, 79, 93, 217nn66,68, 227n127
Center for Muslim Democrats (France), 211n5
Center for Strategic Studies (CSS), 94–95
Center for the Study of Islam and Democracy (United States), 211n5
Chan, Sylvia, 212n8
Chechnya, 145
Chile, 196
Christianity: and anti-Semitism, 5; Catholicism, 5, 84–85, 121, 212nn11,16, 234n236; Copts, 140, 141, 148, 175–76, 183, 185, 252n227; evangelicals, 211n4, 245n94; and feminism, 77; liberation theology, 4, 8; Lutheranism, 5, 89, 114, 129; Protestant Reformation, 5, 84–85, 89, 114, 129; relationship to democracy, 5, 212nn11,13,16
Churchill, Winston, 231n190

class, socioeconomic: bazaaries, 26, 27,
28, 37, 53, 56, 109, 124, 125, 216nn51,52,
238n78; feudal class, 27, 28; and Iranian
revolution, 17; social mobility, 7, 8, 27;
upper class, 12, 22, 56, 57, 124–25, 149–50,
151–52, 153–61, 163, 165–66, 190, 219n113;
working class, 22, 27, 82, 98, 109, 134–35, 150,
244n57. See also intelligentsia, Egyptian;
middle class; poor, the/lower class;
professionals; religious intellectual,
Iranian
clergy, Egyptian: al-Azhar, 12, 33, 37, 42, 45,
46, 137, 143, 144, 147, 149, 154, 155–56, 167,
168–70, 173, 176, 191, 192, 217n84, 219n114,
220n139, 243n45, 248n142, 249n170, 250n193,
252n227; Front of al-Azhar Ulema (Jibhat
al-Ulema al-Azhar), 169–70, 219n114; vs.
Iranian clergy, 21, 36–37, 41–42, 47
clergy, Iranian, 13, 17, 27, 46, 243n45;
Association of Combatant Clergy (ACC),
67, 112, 132; and bazaaries, 26, 28, 37, 56, 124,
125, 216n52, 238n78; and Constitutional
Revolution of 1905–1906, 24, 215n33; and
coup of 1953, 26; and education, 25; vs.
Egyptian clergy, 21, 36–37, 41–42, 47;
Friday prayer leaders, 79, 106, 107, 113, 115,
118, 124, 128, 129, 237n43; hierarchy of, 23,
47; income of, 25, 28, 31, 37, 101; influence
of post-Islamism on, 91, 92, 94, 101, 102,
126; as interpreters of sacred texts, 89, 101,
114; and Jangali movement, 24; marja'-i
taqlīd (source of emulation), 26, 28, 29, 53;
and Musaddiq, 24–25, 77; and the poor,
29–30, 31; under Reza Shah, 25–26, 28; role
in revolution, 23–24, 29–31, 36, 47, 216n55,
220n139; in rural areas, 103–4; Society
of Combatant Clerics (SCC), 67, 70, 112,
114, 124, 238n75; Special Clerical Courts,
101, 121; system of (vilāyat-i faqīh), 24,
29, 36, 53–54, 68, 69, 72, 90, 95, 98, 99, 110,
112, 114, 115, 125–26, 131, 216n58, 218nn96,97,
231nn188,189,198, 232n210, 233n227,
234nn229,231,232,233, 239n88; and tobacco
movement, 24
Clinton, Bill, 111
Cohen, Eliot, 211n4
College Faculty for Change (Egypt), 183
College of Women's Physical Education
(Iran), 75
Committee for the Defense of Workers'
Rights (Egypt), 183–84
Committee of Imdād Imām, 125

Construction Crusade, 125
Copts, 140, 141, 148, 175–76, 183, 185, 252n227
credit associations, 125
Cuban revolution, 8

Dabashi, Hamid, 16
Dabbagh, Marziyih, 72–73
Dabbaqh, Mona al-, 246n109
Daftar-i Tahkim va Vahdat-i Anjumanha-yi
Islami (DTV), 66–68, 69, 70, 108, 112, 122,
129, 132
Dahl, Robert, 212n8
Dajani, Basma al-, 244n57
Dante Alighieri, 93
Darwin, Charles, 29, 231n190
Dastgheib, Golnar, 224n66
Dastghiya, Gawhar, 72–73
Dastjerdi, Marziyih Wahid, 79, 224n69
Davis, James, 18
Dawalibi, Farid al-, 240n
Delbari, Reza, 108
Della Porta, Donatella, 253n11
Delta university, 39
democracy: and art of presence, 15, 201–5;
attitudes of Iranian intellectuals toward,
88, 90, 91, 94–97, 106, 111, 112, 134, 182,
191; definitions of, 4, 211nn4,8; and
foreign intervention, 198–200, 254n24;
relationship to Christianity, 5, 212nn11,16,
212nn13,16; relationship to Islam, 3–6, 9,
11–13, 48, 49–50, 55, 69, 70–71, 80, 87, 90, 113,
114–15, 131–36, 135, 187–89, 211nn4,5, 213n23,
239n84, 253n1; as religious democracy, 49,
96, 126, 132, 136, 175, 193, 232n203, 239n84;
separation of religion and state, 95–96,
102, 110, 189; and violent revolution,
200–201
Denoeux, Guilain, 43
Desouqui, 'Ali al-Din Hilal, 249n173
Diani, Mario, 253n11
Dihnamaki, Mas'ud, 116
Din, Nazira Zayn al-, 156
Diyab, 'Amr, 148, 152, 164, 243n53
Dowell, William, 18
drug use, 162
DTV. See Daftar-i Tahkim va Vahdat-i
Anjumanha-yi Islami
Durkheim, Émile, 20, 45

Ebadi, Shirin, 201
economic conditions: in Egypt, 16, 34–35,
37–38, 43, 44–45, 98–99, 138, 174, 214n1,

216n51; in Iran, 16, 17, 22, 25, 27–28, 52–53, 67, 68–69, 73–74, 95, 97, 98–99, 103, 104–5, 134, 214n1, 216n51, 233n218; and Islamism, 6–9, 34, 52–53; state intervention in economy, 17
economics, 91, 134
education: in Egypt, 34–35, 37, 38–39, 42, 45, 46, 68, 143, 154, 169, 170–71, 173–74, 195, 220n132, 249n176; in Iran, 25, 27, 29, 30, 31, 37, 41–42, 45, 50, 64, 66–71, 73, 81, 85, 97, 102–3, 104–5, 121–22, 125, 129, 130; madrasas, 25, 28; universities, 7, 8, 27, 30, 38–39, 50, 64, 66–71, 73, 81, 85, 99, 102–3, 108–9, 121–22, 125, 129, 130, 143, 169, 170, 203
Egypt: authoritarian rule in, 3, 12, 14–15, 18, 21, 32–33, 37, 38, 40, 46–47, 135, 138, 141, 143–45, 171, 177, 180–82, 184–85, 188, 191, 192–94, 197, 198, 204, 221n139, 241nn13,28, 242nn29,35,39, 250n193; al-Azhar, 12, 33, 37, 42, 45, 46, 137, 143, 144, 147, 149, 154, 155–56, 167, 168–70, 173, 176, 191, 192, 217n84, 219n114, 220n139, 243n45, 248n142, 249n170, 250n193, 252n227; British colonialism in, 37, 41; conspiracy theories in, 179–80; constitution of, 167, 242n37; economic conditions in, 16, 34–35, 37–38, 43, 44–45, 98–99, 138, 174, 214n1, 216n51; floods of 1994, 34, 44; vs. Iran, 11–12, 14–15, 16, 17–18, 21, 24, 29, 32, 36–37, 41–42, 45, 46–48, 50, 51, 63, 68, 98–99, 105, 135, 136–37, 138, 147, 150, 156–57, 161, 164, 173, 178, 182, 183, 186, 189–94, 195–96, 198, 204, 214n1, 216n51, 219n113, 220n139, 235n245; judiciary in, 143, 146, 171–72, 192, 195–96, 252n227; labor movement in, 197; land reform in, 139; law in, 33, 35, 145, 166–67, 168, 171–72, 173, 176, 177, 195–96, 242n37; liberal modernism in, 177–78; materialism in, 151, 153, 155, 161, 164–66, 245n75; middle class in, 16, 34–35, 37–38, 42, 98–99, 105, 147–48, 151, 155, 157, 163, 165–66, 184, 190, 191, 218n94, 219n113, 243n46, 244n63; military in, 46; Ministry of Awqāf, 33, 46, 144, 149, 168, 169, 220n114, 242n30, 248nn145,146; Ministry of Culture, 144, 169, 170, 252n224; Ministry of Education, 170–71, 180; Ministry of Information, 252n226; Ministry of the Interior, 141, 142, 166–67, 168, 241n24; Ministry of Youth, 173, 249n173; under Nasser, 35, 36, 37, 38, 40, 139, 166, 180–81, 183, 185, 197, 248n145; National Democratic Party (NDP), 46, 143, 146, 168, 182, 185, 186, 252n227; nationalism/nativism in, 12, 37,

38, 138, 165, 165–66, 174, 179–81, 182, 183, 191, 193, 197; Parliament, 137, 140, 143, 146, 169, 179, 185, 241n28; Personal Status Law, 145, 148; popular culture in, 33, 41, 46, 140, 148–49, 152–53, 154, 162, 167–68, 179, 243n53, 251n212; professionals in, 33–34, 35, 137, 143, 144, 147–48, 170–72, 179, 183, 220, 220n127, 242nn35,40, 243n46; public opinion regarding democracy, 254n27; relations with Israel, 35, 39, 99, 165, 179–80, 183–84, 197, 252n223; relations with United States, 165, 166, 179–80, 182, 183–84; the Sa'id, 39–40, 137, 138–39, 140–41, 218n91, 240nn3,4,11; secularism in, 41, 45–46; state media, 46, 143, 168, 172; Supreme Council for Islamic Affairs, 33, 168; Teacher Training College (Dar al-'Ulum), 45, 170; upper class in, 12, 149–50, 151–52, 153–61, 163, 165–66, 167, 190, 219n113, 245n75. See also education, in Egypt; intelligentsia, Egyptian; Mubarak, Hosni; Sadat, Anwar
Egyptian Anti-Globalization Group, 183–84
Egyptian Islamism, 9, 17–18, 20, 29, 32–36, 51, 135, 191–94; ahli (private mosques), 33; Hizb al-'Amal, 33; vs. Iranian post-Islamism, 11–12, 14–15, 16, 17–18, 21, 24, 50, 135, 136–37, 138, 156–57, 161, 182, 183, 186, 189–94, 195–96, 198, 204; Islamic Jihad, 32–33, 38, 39, 142, 241n17; Islamic private schools, 45; and the Islamic state, 137, 138, 145, 146, 167, 185, 186; Labor Party, 34, 40, 144, 146, 169, 217n84, 242n32, 243n42; lay preachers, 151–56, 159–60, 245n75; and middle class, 34–35, 37–38, 147–48, 151, 155, 157; morality and ethics in, 138, 139–40, 145–46; and negative integration, 43, 46; nongovernmental organizations (NGOs), 34, 43–45, 47, 143, 144, 146; and the poor, 34, 35–36; private voluntary organizations (PVOs), 43; and professionals, 33–34, 35, 44, 143, 144, 146, 170, 218n94, 242nn35,40; Radio Qur'an, 33; role of da'wa in, 12, 38, 39, 42, 137, 139–40, 142, 144, 145, 149, 152–53, 156, 169, 174; role of lay activists in, 36–38; social welfare services, 34, 43, 44, 45, 137, 139, 140, 155; and the state, 32–33, 38, 42, 43–44, 46–47, 48, 137, 138, 139, 140–42, 143–46, 155–56, 166–74, 177, 181–82, 191, 192–94, 195–96, 198, 204; and students, 137, 147, 170–71, 195; Sufi orders, 33, 47, 150; and upper class, 149–50, 151–52, 153–61, 167; Young Men's Muslim

Association, 45; *zakat* funding, 43, 44.
See also al-Jama'a al-Islamiyya; Muslim
Brotherhood; women, Egyptian
Egyptian Organization of Human Rights,
248n142
Egyptian Popular Committee for Solidarity
with the Palestinian Intifada (EPCSPI),
183–84
Egyptian Society for Culture and Dialogue,
176
Ehsani, Kaveh, 221n3, 254n31
Enayat, Hamid, 218n96
Erdogan, Recep Tayyip, 199
Eryan, 'Asam al-, 144, 145, 167, 175, 176, 177,
242nn35,37, 251n206, 253n234
Esposito, John, 211n5
European Union, 199
Ezzat, Heba Rauf, 157

Fadhlullah, Shaykh Muhammad, 232n210
Fahmi, Khaled, 252n224
Faludi, Susan, 77
Fandy, Mamoun, 240n4
Faraj, 'Abd al-Salam, 39
Fardin, 32
fascism, 5, 212n13
Fathi, Shirin, 155, 157, 159
Fatima (daughter of the Prophet), 72, 73
Fawwaz, Zaynab, 156
feminist theology, 4, 72–73, 77–78, 225n97
Fida'iyan, Marxist, 23
Fida'iyan-i Islam, 24, 118
Fida'iyan majority, 123
15th Khurdad, 111
Foran, John, 214n3
foreign domination, 7–8, 13, 24, 38, 42, 79, 87,
133; intervention, 198–200, 254n24
foreign investment, 96
Foucault, Michel, 51, 134, 231n190; on
governmentality, 254n29; on the power of
words, 6; on state power, 194
Foundation of the *Mustaz'afin*, 125
France: Suez crisis, 197
freedom: free-market economics, 67, 68, 86,
124, 161, 212n8; of the individual, 11, 49, 63,
65, 69, 70, 75, 114, 156–57; from occupation,
7–8, 213n19; of the press, 118–20
Freedom Movement, 29, 108, 111
free-market economics, 67, 68, 86, 124, 161,
212n8
Friedman, Milton, 53
Front for Islamic Resistance (Iran), 116

Front for Republicanism (Iran), 132
Front of al-Azhar Ulema (Jibhat al-Ulema
al-Azhar), 169–70, 219n114
Fu'ad, Muhammad, 243n53
Fuda, Faraj: To Be or Not to Be, 248n142
Furuhar, Daryush, 117

Galileo Galilei, 121; *Letter to Grand Duchess
Christina* (essay on religion as Queen of
Science), 93
Ganji, Akbar, 86, 87, 109, 112, 229n161, 234n233;
Republican Manifesto, 96; trial of, 120,
121, 238n66
Garmsar, 224n53
Garton Ash, Timothy, 115
gender relations, 2, 39, 40, 72–73, 104, 234n243;
child custody, 52, 71, 78, 79–80, 83, 226n99;
divorce rate, 80, 162–63; equality in, 4, 12,
49, 76–77, 82–83, 84, 90–91, 148, 156, 157, 176,
189, 201–2, 203, 228n135; extramarital sex,
60–61, 162, 165, 222n24; patriarchy, 3, 12, 77,
80, 82, 83, 155–57, 190, 192, 203, 204, 212n8,
227n130; polygamy, 52, 71, 72, 79, 80; right
to initiate divorce, 52, 71, 78, 79, 80, 82, 83,
148, 227n120; sex segregation, 50, 51–52,
57, 78, 137, 140, 190, 246n111; temporary
marriage (*mut'a*), 52, 60, 79, 226n116;
travel without male permission, 71, 148,
172; '*urfi* marriage, 148, 164, 165, 243n50,
246n116
Germany, 198; Social Democracy in, 20
Ghad Party, 182
Ghaffari, Hadi, 112
Ghannoushi, Rashed al-, 4, 12
Ghazlan, Mahmud, 252n252
Ghity, Muhammad al-: *A Scandal Called
Saida Sultana*, 251n212
Giddens, Anthony, 87, 159, 245n96
Gilman, Charlotte Perkins, 77
Giranpayih, Bahruz, 121, 128
globalization and Muslim societies, 3, 7, 18,
44–45, 48, 88, 102, 138, 165–66, 168, 173–74,
247n117
Goethe, Johann Gottfried von, 88
Goethe Institute, 23
Goldstone, Jack, 253n11
Golpaigani, Ayatollah Muhammad Reza,
232n210
Gougoush, 32, 41
Gramsci, Antonio, 134; on insurrection,
42; on passive revolution, 15, 48, 115, 116,
132–33, 138, 174, 190, 193, 194–95, 198; on

revolutionary reform, 115; on the state, 194–95; on true revolution, 21; on war of position, 20–21, 42, 43, 136–37, 138, 194–95
Great Britain: colonial rule in Egypt, 37; colonial rule in Jordan, 199; Islamic Research Center in London, 140; relations with Iran, 24, 25; Suez crisis, 197
Greece, 133, 199
Greiss, Sherine, 243n46
Griech-Polelle, Beth, 212n13
Gudarzi, Muhsin, 128
Gulen, Fetullah, 13
Gurr, Ted, 18
Gutierrez, G. A., 213n20

Habermas, Juergen, 87, 123, 134, 231n190
Habib, Kamal, 241n22
Habib, Rafiq, 176
Habibi, Shahla, 72, 81
hadīth, 4, 5, 72, 170, 174, 177, 212n17, 226n99
Hafez, Sabri, 178, 179, 252n225
Hafiz, Usama Ibrahim, 241n27, 249n177
Hajar, 'Ali al-, 148–49
Hajjariyan, Sa'id, 85, 97, 109, 112, 119, 120, 230n186, 234n233, 235n9; and Center for Strategic Studies (CSS), 94–95
Halliday, Fred, 17
Hambastigi Party, 112
Hamid, 'Ala': Distance in a Man's Mind, 248n142
Hamida, 129
Hamouda, Abdel: How Egyptians Joke about Their Leaders, 251n212
Hamza, Mustafa, 140
Hanafi, Hasan, 92, 137, 170
Haqq, Shaykh Jād al-, 169
Hasani, Mullah, 115, 237n43
Hashim, Ahmed 'Umar, 220n136
Hashim, Salih, 241n22
Hashimi, Firishtih, 72
Hashimi, Taha, 126
Hassan, Riaz, 243n45
hātif al-Islāmi, 152, 244n68
hay'ats (ad hoc religious establishments), 31
Hefny, Kadry, 251n203
Hegel, G. W. F., 88
Heikal, Muhammad Hasnein: Secret Negotiations, 251n212
Held, David, 87, 212n8
Hellow, Muhammad al-, 243n53
Herrera, Linda, 220n132
Hijazi, Ahmad 'Abd al-Mu'ti, 172

Hildegard of Bingen, 77
Hill, Christopher: God and the English Revolution, 93
hisba cases, 171–72, 177, 248n156
Hitler, Adolf: Mein Kampf, 212n13
Hizb al-Shari'a, 142
Hizb al-Wasat, 13, 47, 142, 175–76, 177, 186, 189
Hizbullah Cultural Front, 116
Hizbullah Student Union, 111
Hobbes, Thomas, 231n190, 254n30
Homi, Bhaba, 229n153
homosexuality, 4, 157, 167
Hudaybi, Hasan al-, 38
Hudaybi, Ma'mun al-, 144
Humam, Tal'at Yasin, 39
Hungary, 197
Huntington, Samuel, 214n20
Husayn, 'Adel, 40, 144
Husayn, Magdi, 146
Husayn, Qadriyya, 156
Husayniyyih-i Shuhadā, 93
husyniyyas (ad hoc religious establishments), 23, 93

Ibn Taymiyya, 38, 177, 178
Ibrahim, Najih, 240n10, 249n177
Ibrahim, Saad Eddin, 18, 180, 218n95
Ibrahimi, Amir Farshad, 116, 122, 221n7, 237nn54,55
Ibrahimi, Masarat Amir, 225n81
Ibtikar, Masumih, 86
Idarih Amakin, 75
identity politics, 9, 72
Idris, King, 199
ijtihād, 72, 101, 176
Ikhwan al-Muslimin. See Muslim Brotherhood
Imami, Sa'id, 117, 119, 121
Imara, Muhammad, 137, 177–78
India: Jami'at-i Islami, 13, 189; post-Islamism in, 13, 189; Subaltern Studies Group in, 229n153
individualism, 11, 14, 64, 104, 160, 162, 163, 164, 212n8
intelligentsia, Egyptian, 12, 41, 177–81, 183, 191, 252n224. See also religious intellectuals, Iranian
International Islamic Front to Fight the Jews and Crusaders (IIFFJC), 142
International Monetary Fund (IMF), 133, 197
Internet, 81, 120, 152, 168, 173, 183, 184, 188, 242n32
Iqbal, Muhammad, 88

Iran: Assembly of Experts, 53–54, 95, 101, 126, 127, 128, 231n188, 234nn231,232; Assembly of *Maslaha,* 101; Bureau of Women's Affairs, 76; Center for Strategic Studies (CSS), 94–95; Constitutional Revolution of 1905–1906, 24, 215n33; Constitution of the Islamic Republic, 53–54, 78, 127, 188, 193, 231n198, 234nn231,232; Council of Exigency, 107, 124; Council of Guardians, 53–54, 98, 101, 107, 113, 116, 119, 123, 124, 125, 127–28, 129–31; coup of 1953, 22, 23, 26–27; degree of religiosity in, 147; economic conditions in, 16, 17, 22, 25, 27–28, 52–53, 67, 68–69, 73–74, 95, 97, 98–99, 103, 104–5, 134, 214n1, 216n51, 233n218; vs. Egypt, 11–12, 14–15, 16, 17–18, 21, 24, 29, 32, 36–37, 41–42, 45, 46–48, 50, 51, 63, 68, 98–99, 105, 135, 136–37, 138, 147, 150, 156–57, 161, 164, 173, 178, 182, 183, 186, 189–94, 195–96, 198, 204, 214n1, 216n51, 219n113, 220n139, 235n245; emigration from, 99; Family Protection Law, 52, 71, 72; First Five-Year Plan, 98; Iraq war, 11, 51, 55, 59, 69, 71, 73, 75, 99, 115, 233n227; Jangali movement, 24; judiciary, 25, 53, 71, 77, 80, 82, 93, 100–101, 107, 116, 119–20, 123–24, 127, 128–29, 132, 133, 201–2, 239nn84,88; land reform, 27, 28; law in, 52, 53, 62, 71, 72, 79, 90, 100–101; materialism in, 28, 216n55; middle class in, 16, 22, 27, 28, 52, 54, 71, 73–74, 85, 92, 97, 98–99, 102, 104–5, 134, 135, 191; military in, 16, 106; Ministry of Culture, 85, 92–93, 107, 109, 118, 119, 131, 228n135; Ministry of Endowments (awqāf), 25, 28; Ministry of Foreign Affairs, 111, 123, 131; Ministry of Health, 74; Ministry of Higher Education, 131; Ministry of Intelligence, 85, 94, 117, 131; Ministry of Labor, 134; Ministry of the Interior, 107, 109, 123, 188; nationalism in, 24, 25, 26; *nuruz* in, 41; Pahlavi rule in, 3, 16, 17, 18, 21–32, 47, 52, 71, 83, 199, 214n2, 217n66, 218n97; Parliament/Majlis, 53, 76, 79, 80, 81, 98, 101, 107, 110, 112, 119–20, 121, 123–24, 128, 130–31, 224nn66,69, 226n119, 239n88; popular culture in, 31–32, 57, 59–60, 61–62; population growth in, 74, 225n84; professionals in, 27, 33–34, 44, 49, 74, 82, 98–99, 109, 143, 144, 146, 170, 218n94, 242nn35,40; Qajar period, 36; relations with Great Britain, 24, 25; relations with United States, 22, 23, 26–27, 96, 110, 111, 123, 131, 199, 232n202; secularism in, 28, 31–32,

41, 71, 76–77, 87, 92, 95–96, 111, 113, 131–32, 189, 198, 204, 225n93, 229n152, 230n182, 234n233; Shahriar, 221n12; Social and Cultural Council of Women, 76; Special Security Police, 121–22; state employees, 12, 49, 52, 94, 135, 230n182; state media, 106, 107, 117–18, 129; supreme leader (*faqih*), 53, 69, 70, 77, 90, 95, 98, 100–101, 106, 108, 113, 114, 115, 118, 119–20, 123, 124, 125, 126–27, 128, 129, 130, 132–33, 227n130, 234nn231,232, 239n88; tobacco movement, 24; trade unions in, 26; unemployed movement in, 20; working class in, 22, 27, 109, 235n12; during World War I, 24. *See also* clergy, Iranian; education, in Iran; Iranian post-Islamism; Iranian reform government; religious intellectual, Iranian; students, Iranian; women, Iranian; youths, Iranian

Iranian Cultural Revolution, 66–68, 85, 99, 229n161

Iranian post-Islamism, 10–15, 48, 142, 183, 189–94; vs. Egyptian Islamism, 11–12, 14–15, 16, 17–18, 21, 24, 50, 135, 136–37, 138, 156–57, 161, 182, 183, 186, 189–94, 195–96, 198, 204; vs. European Reformation, 84–85; global context of, 97, 102; and middle class, 71, 73–74, 85, 92, 97, 102, 104–5, 134, 135; nonviolent strategy of, 97, 132, 193; and professionals, 49, 74; as religious democracy, 49, 96, 126, 132, 136, 175, 193, 232n203, 239n84; and religious intellectuals, 12, 14, 49, 55, 61, 70, 84–97, 102, 106, 111, 112, 114, 118, 121, 126, 134, 182, 191, 193, 213n23, 228nn140,142,146, 229n152, 231n196, 232n203, 234n236; and social changes, 97, 98–99, 102–3, 136; and state employees, 12, 49, 94, 135, 230n182; and students, 11–12, 49, 55, 66–71, 84, 92, 94, 97, 120, 121–22, 191, 230n182, 231n190, 233n227; and urban public space, 55–58, 107; and women, 11, 12, 14, 49, 55, 57, 58, 65, 71–84, 90, 94, 97, 99, 102, 104, 108, 120, 182, 189–90, 225nn93,97, 227nn127,131, 235n244; and youths, 11–12, 14, 49, 55, 57, 58, 59–65, 84, 92, 97, 99, 100, 102, 104, 107, 135, 182, 190, 216n55, 219n113, 223n31, 235n245

Iranian reform government, 10, 14, 15, 36, 49, 106–35; and civil society, 109; election of 1997, 70–71, 97, 106, 108, 114–15, 196; and the Internet, 120; Khatami as president, 70–71, 97, 105, 109, 113, 122, 131, 133; loss of support for, 106, 129–31, 132, 135, 196, 239n96; opposition to, 13, 106, 113–31, 132–34, 193, 198; and Parliamentary election of 2000, 110, 112, 119–20, 123, 127; and Parliamentary election of 2004, 130–31; and the press, 109–10, 118–20; relations with Council of Guardians, 107, 113, 116, 119, 123, 124, 125, 127–28, 129–31; relations with judiciary, 116, 118, 119, 120–21, 123, 123–24, 128–29, 132, 133; and rule of law, 106, 127, 131, 132, 134; and Second of Khurdad Front, 107, 111–12; and students, 70–71, 107–8, 120, 121–22, 129, 130, 132, 135, 239n99; twin bills, 127–28; and women, 108, 120, 135. *See also* Iranian post-Islamism

Iranian revolution, 11–12, 14, 49, 182, 191–92; explanations of, 16–18, 20, 21–24, 29–31, 216n64; influence of, 47, 192; and religious intellectuals, 228n146; role of clergy in, 23–24, 29–31, 36, 47, 216n55, 220n139; and socioeconomic class, 17; students during, 66–67, 121, 221n13; women during, 71, 72, 83–84; youths during, 59

Iranian Students News Agency (ISNA), 108

Iraq: Ba'athism in, 3, 8, 199; invasion and occupation by US and Britain, 122, 128, 130, 183–84, 197–98, 200; war with Iran, 11, 51, 55, 59, 69, 71, 73, 75, 99, 115, 233n227

Isfahan, 62, 129, 234n243

Islam: *fiqh* (jurisprudence), 35, 90, 91, 100–101, 114, 176, 212n17, 226n107, 249n192; God's sovereignty in, 3–4, 90, 187; *hadīth*, 4, 5, 72, 170, 174, 177, 212n17, 226n99; the Hajj, 172; '*Id al-Adha* (New Year), 166, 168; interpretation of sacred texts, 4–6, 36, 77–78, 83, 84, 88–91, 101, 114, 143, 172, 174–75, 176, 177, 187–88, 190, 191, 201, 212n17, 225n97, 228n140; jihad, 38, 170, 174, 213n23; and modern science, 28–29, 86, 88, 172, 229n161; morality and ethics in, 2, 6–7, 8, 9, 12, 45, 55, 86, 90, 96, 102, 138, 139–40, 145–46, 149–50, 152, 153–54, 156, 158–59, 160–64, 167–69, 171–74, 177, 178, 190, 191, 192, 249n176, 252n226; Muharram, 61; obedience and obligation in, 7, 11, 13, 91, 114, 115, 126, 139–40, 149–50, 153, 154, 159, 161, 173, 177, 190; the Prophet, 36, 77, 101, 149, 174, 177, 178, 228n140, 248n248; Ramadan, 41, 46, 145, 151, 163, 185, 219n113; and reason, 86; relationship to authoritarian regimes, 3–4, 11, 12, 13, 14–15, 17, 42; relationship to democracy, 3–6, 9, 11–13, 48, 49–50, 55,

69, 70–71, 80, 87, 90, 113, 114–15, 131–36, 135, 187–89, 211nn4,5, 213n23, 239n84, 253n1; relationship to economic conditions, 6–7, 98–99; relationship to modernity, 4, 6–7, 11, 13; role in Muslim societies, 1–3, 10–15; saints in, 150; Shari'a, 5–6, 24, 33, 35, 42, 53, 72, 78, 79, 82, 90, 100–101, 113, 114, 145, 148, 157, 166–67, 168, 170, 171, 172, 174, 176, 177, 186, 189, 242nn37,40, 249n170; truth of, 2, 89–90, 92, 187–88, 230n169; *umma* (community of Muslim believers), 4, 36, 53, 95, 176; Western attitudes toward, 1–3, 9. *See also* Egyptian Islamism; Iranian post-Islamism; Islamism

Islami, Jam'iyat-i Mu'talifiyyih, 68

Islami, Sa'id, 117, 119, 121

Islamic Association of Doctors (Iran), 238n75

Islamic Associations of Bazaar Guilds, 124, 238n78

Islamic Center of Alumni of the Indian Subcontinent, 238n75

Islamic Jihad, Egyptian, 32–33, 38, 39, 142, 241n17

Islamic Labor Party (Iran), 134

Islamic Participation Front (IPF), 112

Islamic Party of Reform (Hizb al-Islamiyya al-Islah), 142

Islamic Republic Party, 76

Islamic Research Institute (Egypt), 169, 248n142, 250n193

Islamic Society of Academics (Iran), 238n75

Islamic Society of College Students (Iran), 238n75

Islamic Society of Engineers (Iran), 124

Islamic Society of Students (Iran), 67

Islamic Society of Teachers (Iran), 238n75

Islamic Society of Workers (Iran), 238n75

Islamism, 6–9; *Ansar-i Hizbullah*, 51, 58, 63, 66, 107, 113, 114, 116, 117, 118, 120, 121, 122, 124, 129, 133, 237nn54,55; *basijis*, 51, 55, 62, 63, 68, 113, 116, 121, 122, 237n55; and economic conditions, 6–9, 34, 52–53; and the Islamic state, 9, 10, 11, 12, 14, 36, 38, 42–43, 50–55, 72–73, 98, 99, 100–102, 125–26, 131, 136, 137, 138, 145, 146, 149, 186, 192–93, 218nn96,97, 233n227; Islamists' attitudes toward democracy, 3–4, 12, 114, 187; vs. liberation theology, 8; vs. post-Islamism, 10–15, 16, 17–18, 21, 24, 49–50, 76, 87, 97, 98, 108, 113, 125–26, 135, 136–37, 138, 156–57, 161, 178, 182, 183, 186, 189–94, 195–96, 198, 204, 213nn23,26;

Revolutionary Guards (Pāsdārān), 22,

50, 55, 58, 63, 68, 86, 113–14, 116, 117, 118, 120, 122, 123, 125, 133, 134, 237n55; and sacred texts, 5–6, 143; sex segregation, 50, 51–52, 57, 78, 137, 140, 190, 246n111; slogan "Islam is the solution," 91, 171, 177, 186, 243n42; and social welfare, 8, 9, 34, 43, 44, 45, 137, 139, 140, 155, 161; and students, 66–67; and urban public space, 50–52, 59, 62, 221n3; *vilāyat-i faqīh* in Iran, 24, 29, 36, 53–54, 68, 69, 72, 90, 95, 98, 99, 110, 112, 114, 115, 125–26, 131, 216n58, 218nn96,97, 231nn188,189,198, 232n210, 233n227, 234nn229,231,232,233, 239n88. *See also* Egyptian Islamism
Islamshahr, 98
Isma'il, Yahya, 170
Israel: Middle East peace process, 96, 232n202; Netanyahu, 142–43; 1967 war, 18, 35, 38, 99; occupation of Palestinian territories, 7–8, 12, 45, 145, 148, 179–80, 182, 183–84, 197, 198, 200, 252n223; relations with Egypt, 35, 39, 99, 165, 179–80, 183–84, 197, 252n223; relations with United States, 7–8; Sharon, 142–43

Jaber, Shaykh, 40, 140
Jala'ipur, Hamidreza, 85–86, 88, 93, 96, 109, 120, 228n145, 230n174, 231n196
Jama'a al-Islamiyya, al-, 32–33, 38–40, 138–43, 189, 219n104, 240n10, 250n195; assassination of Sadat, 32, 39, 40, 168, 219n105; in Asyut, 140, 240nn3,11; and the Egyptian state, 139, 140–42, 143, 146, 177, 193, 249n177; and Imbaba, 39–40, 137, 138–39, 140; Luxor massacre, 141–42, 180, 241n17; murder of Fudā, 248n142; and the Sa'id, 39–40, 137, 138–39, 140–41, 218n91, 240nn3,4,11; *Silsilat Tashih al-Mafāhim,* 174–75; violence renounced by, 142–43, 174–75, 177, 241nn26,27
Jama'āt al-Islamiyya, al-, 38–39
Jama'iyya al Islamiyya, 38
Jama'iyya Ansar al-Sunna al-Muhammadiyya, 178
Jame'y-i Mustaqil-i Danishjuyi, 68
Jami'ih-i Ta'limat-i Islami, 217n72
Jami'iyyat-i Mu'talifih-i Islāmi, 125, 238n78
Jannati, Ayatollah Ahmad, 116
Japan, 147, 198
Jibali, Tahani al-, 252n227
Jihad, al-, 32–33, 38, 39, 142, 241n17
jihad-i sāzandigi, 55
Jindi, Khalid al-, 149, 151, 152, 153–54, 160

Jordan, 213n19; attitudes toward democracy in, 254n27; authoritarian rule in, 3, 197, 199; Queen Ranya, 152

Kadivar, Muhsin, 86, 88, 90, 91, 93, 94, 101, 121, 230nn174,186, 231nn188,189, 238n67; on democracy, 91; prosecution of, 101, 121
Kani, Mahdavi-yi, 116
Kar, Mihrangiz, 80, 120
Karadj, 62
Karam, Azza, 245n84
Karāma group, 183
Karbaschi, Ghulam Husayn, 55–57, 112, 118, 215n39
Karguzarān Party, 112
Karrubi, Mehdi, 67
Kashan, 62
Kashani, Ayatollah Mostafavi, 24
Katuzian, Huma, 87
Kawakibi, 'Abd al-Rahman al-, 86, 251n207
Keddie, Nikki, 16–17
Kepel, Gilles, 10, 18, 213n23, 219n101
Keshavarzian, Arang, 239n78
Khalid, 'Amr, 149, 151–55, 159, 160, 164, 181, 244nn69,71
Khalkhali, Sadiq, 112
Khamenei, Ayatollah 'Ali, 48, 101, 234n229; and Association of Combatant Clergy (ACC), 67; on freedom of the press, 119; as Supreme Leader, 106, 108, 113, 115, 118, 119–20, 123, 124, 125, 126–27, 128, 129, 130, 132–33, 239n88
Khamenei, Rahbar, 93
Khan, Ihsanullah, 24
Khan, Mirza Kuchek, 24
Kharazi, Muhsin, 231n188
Khatami, Muhammad, 67, 83, 142, 228n142; on American democracy, 111; on democracy as protection of the minority, 97; foreign policy, 111, 123; as minister of culture, 85, 92–93; at Ministry of Intelligence, 117; as president, 70–71, 97, 105, 109, 113, 122, 131, 133; relations with Khamenei, 126; on religious democracy (*mardum sālāri-yi dīni*), 96, 175; on religious intellectuals, 85, 92; twin bills introduced by, 127–28, 129–30; on the West, 88
Khatami, Muhammad Reza, 112, 119
Khaz'ali, Ayatollah, 113, 114, 115
Khoiniha, Musavi, 94
Khomeini, Ayatollah Ruhollah, 85; charisma of, 53, 55, 69, 101; death of, 11, 55, 67, 232n202,

234n232; fatwa against Rushdie, 111; on
hukumat-i Islami (Islamic government),
36; before Iranian revolution, 23, 24–25,
26, 29–30, 32, 36, 218nn96,97; and legal
uniformity, 100–101; policy on veils, 71;
and the poor, 30, 216n60; on popular
culture, 32; unitarism (wahdāt kalamih)
of, 133; and vilāyat-i faqīh, 29, 36, 55, 95,
99, 100–101, 216n58, 218nn96,97, 231n198,
232n210, 234n229; on women, 83–84
Khomeini, Husayn, 131
Khoramabad, 98
Khosrokhavar, Farhad, 213n23
Khu'i, Ayatollah 'Abd al-Qasim Musavi,
232n210
Khuramābād: student movement national
congress in, 117, 118, 122
Kifaya movement, 12, 182–83, 184, 185–86, 193
Kim, Quee-Young, 18
Kis, Jonus, 197
Kishk, Shaykh, 33, 149
Korea, South, 133, 198–99
Kovel, Joel, 213n20
Kuhn, Thomas, 87
Kurdahi, George, 154
Kurds, 108; Kurdistan Democratic Party, 123

Labor House, 109, 235n12
Labor Party (Egypt), 34, 40, 144, 146, 169,
217n84, 242n32, 243n42
Lahiji, Shahla, 120
Lakatos, Imre, 87
Lankarani, Ayatollah Fadhel, 78–79
Lapidus, Ira, 41
Latin America: guerrilla movements in, 8;
liberation theology, 4, 8, 213n20; student
movements in, 66
law: in Egypt, 33, 35, 145, 166–67, 168, 171–72, 173,
176, 177, 195–96, 242n37; in Iran, 52, 53, 62,
71, 72, 79, 90, 100–101; rule of, 106, 127, 131,
132, 134. See also Islam, Shari'a
Lebanon, 213n19, 232n210; Hizbullah in, 13, 189;
labor movement in, 197
liberation theology, 4, 8, 213n20
Libya, 199
Lipset, Seymour Martin, 20
Liset, S., 212n11
literacy, 14, 202; among Iranian women, 27, 64,
73, 97, 103; Literacy Corps, 27
Lowry, Michael, 158, 212n16
Luqmaiyan, Husayn, 123–24
Luther, Martin, 5, 114, 129, 231n190; On the Jews

and Their Lies, 212n13
Luxemburg, Rosa, 97
Luxor massacre, 141–42, 180, 241n17

Machiavelli, Niccolò, 93
MacLeod, Arlene, 45
Mādi, Abul-'Ala, 175
Mafātih al-Jinān, 30
Mahjoub, 'Alireza, 235n12
Mahjub, 'Ali, 166–67
Mahmood, Mustafa, 46, 137; A Journey to
Paradise and Hell, 251n212
Mahmood, Saba, 245n80
mahr (bride price), 79
Mahruf, Najib, 172
maktabies, 53
Maktab-i Tashayu', 29
Malakian, Mustafa, 91, 93, 228n140
Mamdani, Mahmood: Good Muslims, Bad
Muslims, 254n24
Marshall, Susan, 17–18
Marx, Karl, 29, 87, 88, 134, 157–58, 231n190
Marxism, 23, 26, 69, 87, 194, 212n8, 216n55,
233n227, 254n30
Mashdad, 98
Mashhur, Mustafa, 42–43, 145, 175, 242nn34,40
mashrū'a, 24
Massey, Doreen, 63
Mas'ud, Khalid, 5, 212n17
Maw'ūd Cultural Front, 116
Mazahiri, Ayatollah, 79
MB. See Muslim Brotherhood
Mehrez, Samia, 178
Melucci, Alberto, 194; on cultural production,
195, 253n17
Meshkini, Ayatollah, 231n188
Mexico, 197; Chiapas, 205
middle class: in Egypt, 16, 34–35, 37–38, 42,
98–99, 105, 147–48, 151, 155, 157, 163, 165–66,
184, 190, 191, 218n94, 219n113, 243n46,
244n63; in Iran, 16, 22, 27, 28, 52, 54, 71,
73–74, 85, 92, 97, 98–99, 102, 104–5, 134, 135,
191; and Islamism, 6–9, 34
Migdal, Joel, 194
Milani, Mohsen, 17
Military Academy group (Egypt), 38
Milosovic, Slobodan, 130
Mirdamadi, Muhsin, 66, 86, 238n67
Moaddel, Mansoor, 16, 214n3
modernity: Muslim attitudes toward, 6, 46,
86, 88, 96, 191, 193; relationship to Islam,
4, 6–7, 11, 13

Morocco, 197–98, 213n19; *al-ʿAdl wa al-Ihsān* in, 9, 189; attitudes toward democracy in, 254n27; authoritarian rule in, 197, 199; labor movement in, 197; post-Islamism in, 9, 189

Morris, Benny, 211n4

motion pictures, 31, 33, 151, 165, 172–73, 179, 252n224

Mottahedeh, Roy, 216n59

Mozambique, 133

Mubarak, Hisham, 219n103

Mubarak, Hosni, 199; assassination attempt of 1995, 143; fifth term in office, 183, 184, 185; and Personal Status Law, 145; policy on Islam, 168, 249n170

Mubarak, Jamal, 184

Muhajirani, Ataʾullah, 93, 97, 107, 116, 118, 238n67

Muhammadi, Akbar, 122

Muhammadi, Majid, 94

Muhammadi, Manuchir, 122

Muhammad Reza Shah Pahlavi, 22–23, 24, 25, 26–27, 47, 52, 83, 97, 199

Muhammad the Prophet, 77, 149, 178, 248n248; Sunna, 36, 101, 174, 177, 228n140

Muhidin, ʿAlaʾ, 39, 140

Muhsin, Salahidin, 172

muhtasib, 174, 248n156

Muʿin, Mustafa, 235n2

Mujahidin-i Khalq Organization, 32, 86, 98, 115, 123

Mujahidin Inqilab-i Islami, 86

Mujahidin (Iran), 23

Mukhtari, Muhammad, 117

mulid festivals, 150–51

Munir, Muhammad, 148

Munson, Henry, 17

Muntazari, Ayatollah Husayn ʿAli, 86, 93, 98, 108–9, 113, 126, 232n210

Musa, ʿAbd al-Halim, 141

Musaddiq, Muhammad, 22, 24, 26, 29, 199

Mushārikat Front, 128, 134

Muslim Brotherhood, 13, 37–38, 39, 40–41, 46–47, 189, 217n84, 242nn32,34; and democracy, 185, 186; and the Egyptian state, 143–46, 167, 176, 185, 193, 221n139, 241n28, 241n29, 242nn35,39,40; and the Islamic state, 42–43, 137, 145, 167, 185, 186; Mashhur, 42–43, 145, 175; parliamentary activities of, 137, 143, 146, 185, 186, 241n28, 243n42, 253n234; and professionals, 33–34, 35, 44, 143, 144, 146, 170, 218n94, 242nn35,40;

relations with Kifaya, 184–85; relations with Labor Party, 14, 146, 243n42; and students, 137, 143, 184–85

Muslim societies: diversity of, 1–3; exceptionalism regarding, 1–3, 211n4; and globalization, 3, 7, 18, 44–45, 48, 88, 102, 138, 165–66, 168, 173–74, 247n117; middle class in, 8–9; in Middle East, 1–3, 8–9, 135, 254n22; role of Islam in, 1–3, 10–15

Muslim Student Followers of Imam Line, 66

Mustafa, Dalia Ahmed, 244nn67,69

Mustafa, Shukri, 38

Mutahhari, Ayatollah Murtaza, 28, 29, 30, 72, 85, 86, 216n55

Muʿtalifih, Jamʿiyyat-i, 114

Nabavi, Bahzad, 94, 132, 237n58

Nabavi, Ibrahim, 120, 121

Nafi, Bashir, 178, 251n208

Naguib, Rime, 246n107

Naquib, Sameh, 219n101

Nasif, Malak, 156

Nassef, Emad: *Girls for Export*, 251n212; *The Red File*, 251n212; *The War of the Whores*, 251n212; *Women from Hell*, 251n212

Nassef, Emad: *The Age of Fifi Abdou*, 251n212

National Alliance for Reform and Change (Egypt), 183

National Campaign Against the War in Iraq (Egypt), 183–84

National Center for the Study of Public Opinion (NCSPO) (Iran), 128

National Coalition for Democratic Transformation (Egypt), 183

National Democratic Party (NDP) (Egypt), 46, 143, 146, 168, 182, 185, 186

National Front (Iran), 26, 29, 66

nationalism, 8, 13, 198, 200; in Egypt, 12, 37, 38, 138, 165, 165–66, 174, 179–81, 182, 183, 191, 193, 197; in Iran, 24, 25, 26

Nawh, Mukhtar, 144

NDP. *See* National Democratic Party

negative integration, 20, 43, 46

neoliberalism, 43

Nepstad, Sharon E., 213n20

Netanyahu, Benjamin, 142–43

Nogarola, Isotta, 77

nongovernmental organizations (NGOs), 197; in Egypt, 33, 34, 140, 143, 144, 146, 161, 176, 182–84, 183; in Iran, 23, 30, 65, 81, 109, 120, 124, 216n64, 235n5, 238n75

Nubakhat, Munirih, 79, 224n69

Nuri, Abdullah, 93, 97, 107, 116, 216n58, 231n196, 234n236; on reason and faith, 88–89, 92; on religious truth, 89–90; trial of, 101, 121, 232n202, 238n67
Nuri, Ayatollah Ali Akbar Natiq, 58, 106
Nuri, Shaykh Fadlullah, 24

oil, 7, 26, 104, 133; price of, 27, 98
Olmsted, Frederick Law, 56–57
Open University, 64
Organization of Mujahidin of the Islamic Revolution (OMIR), 69–70, 94, 95, 112

Pahlavi dynasty. See Muhammad Reza Shah Pahlavi; Reza Shah Pahlavi
Pakistan: Islamism in, 9
Palestine, 96, 213n19, 232n202; Israeli occupation, 7–8, 12, 45, 145, 148, 179–80, 182, 183–84, 197, 198, 200, 252n223
Parsa, Misagh, 17
Parsons, Anthony, 16–17
passive revolution. See Gramsci, Antonio, on passive revolution
Pateman, C., 212n8
Paul, Gregory, 212n13
Payam-i Hajar, 75–76
Payam-i Zan, 75–76
Philippines, 133, 198–99
Pipes, Daniel, 253n1
Pizan, Christine de, 77
pluralism, 4, 5, 91, 131, 185, 186; in post-Islamism, 11, 13, 55, 101, 110, 113–14, 131, 175, 187, 188–89, 191, 193
Poland, 197; Solidarity, 19
political patronage, 124–25, 127
poor, the/lower class, 4, 52, 187; in Egypt, 34, 35–36, 137, 150, 157–58, 161, 163, 165, 184, 191, 214n1, 218n91; in Iran, 22, 30, 31, 52, 54, 56, 75, 134, 135, 191, 214n1, 216n60, 225n88, 227n131; Islamism and social welfare, 8, 9, 34, 43, 44, 45, 137, 139, 140, 155, 161; and liberation theology, 8
Popper, Karl, 87
Popular Campaign for Change (Egypt), 183
popular culture: in Egypt, 33, 41, 46, 140, 148–49, 152–53, 154, 162, 167–68, 179, 243n53, 251n212; in Iran, 31–32, 57, 59–60, 61–62
popular masses, 29–30, 95, 216n59; popular will, 4, 126, 177, 186, 187, 231n188, 234n232; umma (community of Muslim believers), 4, 36, 53, 95, 176
Portugal, 199

post-colonialism, 87–88, 191, 229n153
post-Islamism: defined, 10–11; vs. European Reformation, 84–85, 89, 114; vs. Islamism, 10–15, 16, 17–18, 21, 24, 49–50, 76, 87, 97, 98, 108, 113, 125–26, 135, 136–37, 138, 156–57, 161, 178, 182, 183, 186, 189–94, 195–96, 198, 204, 213nn23,26; pluralism in, 11, 13, 55, 101, 110, 113–14, 131, 175, 187, 188–89, 191, 193. See also Iranian post-Islamism
professionals, 8, 203; in Egypt, 33–34, 35, 137, 143, 144, 147–48, 170–72, 179, 183, 220, 220n127, 242nn35,40, 243n46; in Iran, 27, 33–34, 44, 49, 74, 82, 98–99, 109, 143, 144, 146, 170, 218n94, 242nn35,40
prostitution, 50, 59, 60, 61, 222n18
publications, Egyptian, 33, 178–79; Ahrar al-Hilwan, 218n84; Ahrar al-Saʿid, 218n84; al-Aharar, 218n84; al-Ahram, 179, 221n139, 243n50, 247n135; al-Ahram al-Arabi, 152, 180; al-Ahram al-Riaydi, 152; al-Ahrar, 218n84; al-ʿArabi, 182; al-Azhar, 217n84; al-Dustur, 182; al-Haqiqa, 218n84; al-Iʿtisām, 140; al-Jamaʿa al-Islamiyya, 40; al-Liwaʾ al-Islami, 46, 143, 168, 172, 220n137; al-Manar, 178; al-Manar al-Jadid, 178, 241n22; al-Misr al-Yowm, 182; al- Mujahid, 46; al-Mukhtar al-Islami, 217n84, 242n32; al-Murābitūn, 140; al-Musawwar, 241n26; al-Muslim al-Muʿasir, 217n84; al-Muslim al-Saqir, 218n84; Al-Muslimun, 217n84; al-Nur, 217n84, 218n84; al-Shaʿb, 144, 146, 241n22, 242n32; al-Tasawuf al-Islami, 217n84; al-Uruba, 218n84; al-Usrat al-ʿArabi, 218n84; al-Wafd, 148, 179, 247n135; al-Wasat, 218n84; ʿAqidati, 46, 168, 172–73, 217n84, 220n136, 221n139, 244n68; Kilāmāt Haqq, 40; Liwaʾ al-Islam, 143, 217n84, 218n84; Minbar al-Islam, 217n84; Minbar al-Sharq, 217n84, 242n32; Nahdit Misr, 182; Rawz al-Yusif, 180; Sawt al-Azhar, 168, 252n226; Shabab al-Aharar, 218n84
publications, Iranian, 97, 236n16; Abān, 119; Adinih, 87; Aftab, 236n18; Āftābgardan, 119; Akhbār, 119; al-Zahra, 227n127; ʿArūs, 227n127; Aryā, 119; Arzish, 119; ʿAsr-i Azādigān, 119; ʿAsr-i Mā, 69–70, 95; Ayāndigān, 30; Azād, 119; Azar, 70, 108; Bahar, 70, 86, 93; Bahman, 93; Bāmdād, 119; Bānū, 227n127; Banu, 227n127; Burish, 227n127; Farārāh, 93; Farhang-i Āfarīnesh, 58; Farzanih, 77, 81, 227n127; Fayziyyih, 116;

Gardawn, 87; Guftar-i Māh, 29; Guftugu, 87, 93; Haftih Namih-i Subh, 58; Hamsar, 227n127; Hamshahri, 56; Harīm, 116, 128; Hawzih va Danishgah, 91, 93; Hayat-i Naw, 129, 236n19, 238n78; Huquq-i Zan, 81; Huviyyat-i Khish, 70; Inqilāb-i Islāmi, 237n61; Intikhāb, 126; Irāndukht, 227n127; Iran-i Farda, 93; Irshād-i Niswān, 227n127; Itila'at, 23, 30; Itila'at Siyasi-Iqtisadi, 87; Jabhih, 116; Jalvih, 227n127; Jami'iyyih, 86, 109, 110, 119; Jami'iyyih Sālim, 119; Jins-i Duvvum, 81; Jumhuri-i Islami, 58, 110, 236n19; Kawkab, 227n127; Kayhan, 30, 70, 85, 110, 115, 116, 118, 128, 129, 236n19; Kayhan-i Farhangi, 92–93; Khānih, 119; Khurdad, 85; Kitab-i Naqd, 93; Kitab-i Zan, 81; Kitāb-i Zanān, 227n127; Kiyan, 69, 87, 90, 91, 92, 93, 100, 119, 230n182; Mahtab, 81, 227n127; Maktab-i Tashayu', 29; Malinih, 227n127; Ma'rifat, 91, 93; Mashriq, 114; Mawj, 118; Mi'raj, 227n127; Mushārikat, 119; Mutali'āt-i Zān, 227n127; Nada, 81, 227n127; Naqd va Nazar, 91, 93; Navid Ishahān, 119; Nishāt, 110, 119; Nūr-i Barān, 227n127; Nuruz, 86, 129, 238n67; Partaw va Sukhan, 116, 237n52; Payam-i Danishju, 58, 215n39; Payam-i Hajar, 81; Payam-i Zan, 227n127; Pigāh, 227n127; press permits, 109, 119; Pūshish, 227n127; Qarn-i 21, 227n127; Quds, 236n19; Rahburd, 95; Rah-i Naw, 86, 109; Rah-i Zaynab, 76; Rahruvan-i Sumayih, 227n127; Rayhanih, 81, 227n127; Rawnaq, 87; Risālat, 110, 126, 128, 129, 236n19, 237n51; Salam, 70, 86, 95, 119, 121; Shalamchih, 116; Shamīmi Nargis, 227n127; Shurūsh-Bānuvān, 227n127; Subh-i Imrūz, 110, 119; Subh-i Khānivadih, 109; Takāpū, 227n127; Tarh va Mūd, 227n127; Tavānā, 119; Taws, 86, 110, 119; Tūbā, 227n127; Yālithārāt, 116; Yās, 227n127; Yas-i Naw, 129, 239n96; Zan, 77, 110, 119, 227n127; Zanan, 77–78, 79, 81, 90, 93, 227n127; Zanān-i Farda, 227n127; Zanān-i Junūb, 227n127; Zān-i Imrūz, 227n127; Zan-i Ruz, 75–76, 81; Zan-i Sharqi, 227n127; Zan va Pazhūhish, 227n127
Puyandih, Muhammad Ghaffar, 117

Qabil, Ahmad, 121, 188
Qaddafi, Muammar al-, 199
Qaderi, Tahereh, 216n52
Qamar, Mustafa, 148, 243n53

Qardawi, Yusif al-, 173, 176, 250n192
Qasim, Safinaz, 157
Qaziyan, Husayn, 121
Qazvin, 224n53
Qowimi, Sayad al-: Rabb al-Zaman, 248n142
Quba Mosque, 23
Queen Boat case, 167
Qum, 23, 62; publishing in, 91; Seminary in, 30, 53, 78–79, 86, 91, 92, 93, 113, 116, 126, 226n107, 230n169, 237n55, 239n81; university in, 86
Qur'an, the, 41, 72, 145, 148, 161, 174; bey'a (allegiance) in, 91; human dignity (karāma) in, 89; interpretation of, 4, 5–6, 36, 77, 78, 83, 84, 88–91, 101, 114, 143, 172, 176, 187–88, 190, 191, 201, 212n17, 225n97, 228n140; Kahf: 46, 226n99; and reason, 88; S. 49:13, 77; shura (consultation) in, 4, 91, 175, 185; study groups, 46; Sura 4:34 Nis', 77, 78, 83
Qurban, Khalu, 24
Qutb, Sayyed, 38
Qutbzadih, Sadiq, 98

radio, 138, 173
Rafiqdust, Muhsin, 125
Rafsanjani, Faezeh, 75, 110
Rafsanjani, Hashemi, 53, 72, 81, 112, 134, 231nn198,199; and Association of Combatant Clergy (ACC), 67; and Center for Strategic Studies (CSS), 94–95; economic policies, 67, 95; policy on temporary marriage (mut'a), 60; postwar reconstruction policies, 11, 55–56
Rahim, Muhammad, 243n53
Rahnavard, Zahra, 72
Rajab, Sami, 46
Raraya, Salih, 38
Rauf, Heba, 76
Rawhaniyat-i Mubariz, 67
Rawls, John, 87
Reconstruction Party, 107
Reda, Rashid, 37, 178
Reja'i, Ms., 72–73, 76
religious intellectuals, Iranian, 12, 14, 49, 55, 61, 70, 84–97, 121, 213n23, 228nn142,146, 229n152; as alternative thinkers (digār-i andishān), 84, 126; attitudes toward democracy, 88, 90, 91, 94–97, 106, 111, 112, 134, 182, 191; attitudes toward foreign domination, 87; attitudes toward modernity, 86, 88, 96, 191, 193; attitudes toward rationality, 86, 88, 89, 90, 91,

92; attitudes toward revolution, 87; attitudes toward sacred texts, 88–91, 92, 114, 191, 228n140; attitudes toward separation of religion and state, 95–96, 102, 231n196, 232n203, 234n236; attitudes toward the West, 88; background of, 85–86, 94; defined, 85; in middle class, 85; republican theology developed by, 88–91, 118
republican theology, 88–91, 118
Reza'i, Muhsin, 58
Reza Pahlavi, 97
Reza Shah Pahlavi, 22, 25–26, 27, 28
rights, 12, 187; vs. duties, 11, 91, 139–40; human rights, 4, 23, 45, 86, 178, 180, 184, 189, 191, 199, 201, 213n23; of women, 76, 156, 175, 188
Rodinson, Maxim: *Muhammad,* 169
Roth, Guenther, 20
Roy, Olivier, 10, 213n26
Ruhami, Muhsin, 101, 121, 122
rule of law, 106, 127, 131, 132, 134
rural areas: economic conditions in, 103; education in, 103; employment in, 103; Iranian youths in, 54, 64, 221n12; mullahs in, 103–4
Rushdi, Usama, 241n17
Rushdie, Salman, 111
Russia, 24

Saad, Reem, 171; "Marriage Egyptian Style," 252n224
Sachedina, Abdul-Aziz, 123
Sa'd, Muhammad, 144
Sadat, Anwar, 38, 167, 172; assassination of, 32, 39, 40, 168, 219n105; economic policy (*infitāh*), 34–35, 161
Sa'dawi, Nawal al-, 172
Sadda, Huda, 245n87
Sadiqi, Hasan, 235n12
Sadriya, Mujtaba, 238n77
Saghiya, Hazem, 178
Sahabi, Yadollah, 86
Saharkhiz, Issa, 236n16
Said, Edward, 1, 178, 229n153
Sa'id, Samira, 243n53
Saidzadih, Sayyed Muhsen, 79, 90
Sajdi, Dana, 243n46
Salafis, 178, 213n23, 251n203
Salih, 'Abd al-Hasan, 240n11
Sanandaj, 236n23
Sani'i, Yusif, 112
Sarallah, 75

Sartre, Jean-Paul, 29
Saudi Arabia, 151, 244n63; authoritarian rule in, 3, 199; post-Islamism in, 13, 189; youths in, 63
SAVAK, 23, 27
Sawafi, Rahim, 113–14
Sazgara, Muhsin, 86
SCC. *See* Society of Combatant Clerics
Schimmel, Ann Mary, 123
Scholder, Klaus, 212n13
Schulze, Reinhard, 213n23
Schurman, Anna Maria von, 77
science, 28–29, 86, 89, 172, 229n161
secularism: in Egypt, 41, 45–46; in Iran, 28, 31–32, 41, 71, 76–77, 87, 92, 95–96, 111, 113, 131–32, 189, 198, 204, 225n93, 229n152, 230n182, 234n233
Seong, K., 212n11
September 11th attacks, 1, 9, 36, 111, 146, 173, 182, 188
Serri, Yasser al-, 140
Shabastari, Muhammad Mujtahid, 91, 92, 93, 96, 229n159, 230n186
Sha'bula, 179
Shahata, Shaykh Hasan Muhammad, 167
Shahid Avini Cultural Group, 116
Shahin, Shaykh 'Abd-al-Sabur, 168, 173; *Abi Adām,* 172
Shahin, Yusif: *al-Muhājir,* 172
Shahrudi, Ayatollah, 239nn84,88
Shahrur, Muhammad, 92
Shajarian, Muhammad Reza, 123
Shakar, Hani, 148–49
Shalamchih Cultural Group, 116
Shalbaf, Uzra, 227n121
Shamsulva'izin, Mashallah, 93, 109, 120, 228n146, 230n184
Sharaf, Ibrahim, 145
Sha'rawi, Shaykh, 150
Shari'ati, 'Ali, 29, 30, 32, 46, 72, 85, 86, 87, 90, 94
Shari'atmadari, Ayatollah Kazim, 98, 232n210
Shari'atmadari, Husayn, 237n47
Sharif, 'Ali Muhammad 'Ali, 249n177
Sharif University, 67–68
Sharon, Ariel, 142–43
Shawqiyyun, al-, 38
Shaykh, Shawki al-, 38
Sheiby, Menna al-, 244n63
Shihawi, Ahmad: *Wasiya fi 'Ishq al-Nisa',* 249n170
Shi'i Islam: *hawzehs,* 16, 23, 26, 30, 53, 78–79, 86, 91, 92, 93, 113, 116, 125, 126, 226n107,

230n169, 237n55, 239n81; Imam Husayn, 41; Muharram, 61; vs. Sunni Islam, 36, 167, 191; Twelfth Imam, 36, 53, 118. *See also* clergy, Iranian

Shiraz, 62, 98, 129

Shirazi, Ayatollah (Bahrain), 232n232

Shirazi, Ayatollah Hā'iri, 60

Shuja'i, Zahra, 83, 235n5

Shukri, Ibrahim, 40, 144

Shukri, Muhammad: *al-Khubz al-Hafi*, 169

Shulkami, Haniya, 245n75

Sid-Ahmed, Muhammad, 178, 179

Simmel, Georg, 164

Sirri, Yasir, 241n17

Smith, Christian, 213n20

Snow, David, 17–18

socialism, 6, 8, 19, 133; in Austria, 20; in Egypt, 38, 40; in Germany, 20

Socialist Party (Iran), 123

social justice, 4, 8

social movements: and art of presence, 201–5; and economic conditions, 196; institutions and value systems in, 18–19, 20; and integrative communities, 20; negative integration of, 20, 43, 46; and power of words, 6; relationship to political change/power, 13–15, 136, 138, 145–46, 166–74, 181–82, 186, 188, 191–97, 198, 202–4, 253n11; relationship to sacred texts, 4–6; vs. revolutionary insurrections/protest movements, 11–12, 14, 17–21, 24, 47, 136, 191–94, 200–201, 220n139; role of popular mobilization in, 17, 18–19, 22–23, 134–35, 136–37, 146, 181–83, 188, 194, 195, 196, 202, 203, 254n22; and socialization of the state, 14, 166–74, 181–82, 192, 198, 204

Society of Combatant Clerics (SCC), 67, 70, 112, 114, 124, 238n75

Society of Islamic Mu'talifih, 124

Society of Tehran Preachers, 238n75

Sorur, Ahmad Fathi, 170

Sousan, 32

South Africa: apartheid in, 199

Soviet Union, 133

Spain, 196, 199

Staniszkis, Jadwiga, 19

state employees, 8; in Iran, 12, 49, 52, 94, 135, 230n182

state media: in Egypt, 46, 143, 168, 172; in Iran, 106, 107, 117–18, 129

students, Egyptian, 68, 137, 143, 161–64, 170, 173–74, 191, 246n103; at American

University, 147, 169, 243n46, 244n71; at al-Azhar University, 221n139; and al-Jamaʿa al-Islamiyya, 38–39, 137; and Muslim Brotherhood, 137, 143, 184–85

students, Iranian, 14, 23, 26, 30, 224n58; *Daftar-i Tahkim va Vahdat-i Anjumanha-yi Islami* (DTV), 66–68, 69, 70, 108, 112, 122, 129, 132; Iranian Cultural Revolution, 66–68, 85; number of, 64, 102–3; and post-Islamism, 11–12, 49, 55, 66–71, 84, 92, 94, 97, 120, 121–22, 191, 230n182, 231n190, 233n227; publications by, 70, 108, 110, 118, 121, 215n39; and reform government, 70–71, 107–8, 120, 121–22, 129, 130, 132, 135, 239n99; during revolution, 66–67, 121, 221n113; from rural areas, 68; U.S. embassy seized by, 66, 86, 94; women among, 25, 52, 66, 68, 70–71

Sudan, 197–98; Darfur, 205; Islamism in, 9, 144

Sueirki, Rajab al-, 149

Suez Canal crisis, 197

Sufi orders, 33, 47, 150

Sultan, Jamal, 241n22

Sunni Islam: vs. Shi'i Islam, 36, 167, 191; and social change, 181. *See also* clergy, Egyptian

Surush, ʿAbd al-Karim, 87, 114, 213n23, 229n165, 230n174, 231n196, 234n236; on democracy, 91; influence of, 85, 86, 93, 120, 121; on rationality, 90, 92; on the religious state, 96; on the West, 88

Syria, 197–98

Sztompka, Piotr, 253nn15,17

Tabarzadi, Hashmatullah, 67, 70, 224n58, 233nn220,227

Tabataba'i, Allameh, 29

Tabataba'i, Shahin, 72

Tabriz, 23, 129

Taha, Rifa'i Ahmad, 140, 142

Tahiri, Ayatollah, 116

Tahrani, Khusra, 94

Tahtawi, Rifaʿ al-, 178

Tajbakhsh, Kian, 236n23

Tajik, Mohammad Reza, 94

Tajikistan: Hizb Tahrir, 189; Islamic Renaissance Party (IRP), 189

Tajzadeh, Mustafa, 94, 97, 188

Takfir wa al-Hijra, al-, 38, 218n91, 241n22

Taleqani, Aʿzam, 76

Taleqani, Mahmud, 29

Taliʿat al Fatah, 38

Taliqani, Aʿzam, 72, 73

Tantawi, Shaykh Muhammad, 167, 168–69, 170
tanwir (enlightenment), 177–78, 180
Taymuriya, 'Aysha, 156
Tehran, 129, 225n88; attitudes toward religion
    in, 99–100; Bahman Cultural Complex,
    56, 221n7; drug use in, 99; Karbaschi,
    55–57, 112, 118, 215n39; newspapers and
    periodicals in, 30; poverty in, 214n1;
    prostitution in, 50, 222n18; public space
    in, 50–52, 55–58, 215n39; universities in,
    23, 116, 117, 130, 224n53, 240n99; youths in,
    62, 221n12
Tehrani, Reza, 93
television: in Egypt, 138, 151, 152, 159, 162, 165,
    173, 184, 252n226; in Iran, 31–32, 33, 46, 103
Tharwat, Muhammad, 148–49
The Street is Ours (Egypt), 183
Third Worldism, 22, 85, 86, 88, 108
Thompson, E. P., 3
Tilly, Charles, 18
Tocqueville, Alexis de, 111
tolerance, 4, 12, 13, 87, 106, 113, 131, 134, 157, 187
Torres, J. C., 212n11
tourism, 117, 163, 167, 173, 175, 241n16; Luxor
    massacre, 141–42, 180, 241n17
Tudeh Communist Party, 26
Tunisia, 197; al-Da'wa Islamic Party, 12
Turkey, 135, 178; Ataturk, 25; and European
    Union, 199; Justice and Development
    Party, 9, 13, 189, 199; the military in, 199;
    post-Islamism in, 13, 181, 189; Rifah/
    Welfare Party, 13, 19, 189, 196; secularism
    in, 41; Virtue Party, 13, 189

Ulema Front. See Front of al-Azhar Ulema
    (Jibhat al-Ulema al-Azhar)
UN Convention on the Elimination of
    Discrimination Against Women, 79
United States: Christian right in, 253n1;
    invasion and occupation of Iraq, 122, 128,
    130, 183–84, 197–98, 200; Muslim attitudes
    toward, 7–8; Orientalist thought in, 3;
    relations with Afghanistan, 9, 123, 198,
    199; relations with Egypt, 165, 166, 179–80,
    182, 183–84; relations with Iran, 22, 23,
    26–27, 96, 110, 111, 123, 131, 199, 232n202;
    relations with Israel, 7–8; religion in,
    91–92, 147, 153; September 11th attacks, 1,
    9, 36, 111, 146, 173, 182, 188; World Trade
    Center bombing of 1993, 32, 142
urbanization, 8, 14, 18, 27, 97, 103, 202
Urumiyih, 129

Vargas llosa, Mario: Who Killed Palomino
    Molero, 248n142
veiling: of Egyptian women, 40, 45, 140,
    147–48, 151, 153, 154, 155, 160, 166, 171, 172,
    177, 243n47, 244n71, 252n226; of Iranian
    women, 25, 26, 51, 52, 55, 57, 61, 71, 72, 75, 76,
    79, 82, 189–90, 225n90
veterans of Iran-iraq war, 68, 86, 89, 98, 124
violence in Egypt, 140–43, 173–75, 219n104;
    Luxor massacre, 141–42, 180, 241n17;
    murder of Fuda, 248n142; Sadat
    assassination, 32, 39, 40, 168, 219n105; Taba
    bombing, 184
violence in Iran: political murders by
    Islamists, 110, 117, 120, 126, 237n61, 237n66;
    student congress in Khuramābād
    disrupted, 117, 118, 122; Tehran University
    dormitories ransacked in 1999, 116, 117, 118,
    121–22, 129
Voll, John, 211n5

Wafd party, 36, 243n42
Wahabism, 89, 169
Wahba, Caroline, 243n46
Wahba, Christine Emil, 243n46
Wahsh, Nabih al-, 171
WAIR. See Women's Association of the
    Islamic Revolution
war of position. See Gramsci, Antonio, on
    war of position
Wasat Party, al-. See Hizb al-Wasat
Wasil, Shaykh Nasr Farid, 172, 173
Weber, Max, 158
websites, 81, 120, 152, 173, 183, 184, 188, 242n32
Western culture: Muslim attitudes toward,
    6–7, 16, 17–18, 31–32, 44–45, 57, 60, 76, 86,
    88, 162, 165–66, 173–74, 179, 191, 205, 217n75,
    229n159
Western feminism, 72, 76, 77, 156–57, 212n8
Wilde, Oscar, 121
women, Egyptian, 42, 137, 175, 183; attitudes
    toward religion among, 76, 147–48,
    150, 155–61, 166, 172, 190, 243n47, 244n71,
    245nn84,94; halaqāt (religious gatherings)
    among, 149, 155, 159, 244n73, 245n80; as
    judges, 252n227; veiling of, 40, 45, 140,
    147–48, 151, 153, 154, 155, 160, 166, 171, 172, 177,
    243n47, 244n71, 252n226. See also gender
    relations
women, Iranian: in the arts and music, 73,
    74, 82, 202; attitudes toward religion
    among, 72–73, 75, 77–79, 83, 84, 156, 190, 201,

224nn66,69; collective identity of, 81, 104; education of, 25, 27, 52, 64, 66, 68, 70–71, 73, 77, 79, 81, 82, 83, 202, 227n121; employment for, 73–74, 75, 79, 82, 83, 104, 202; as judges, 71, 77, 80, 82, 83, 201–2; literacy among, 27, 64, 73, 97, 103; maternal impunity of, 81–82; in middle class, 71, 73–74, 99; nongovernmental organizations (NGOs) of, 81, 109, 235n5; during Pahlavi rule, 22, 27, 28, 52, 71, 72; in Parliament, 76, 79, 80; and post-Islamism, 11, 12, 14, 49, 55, 57, 58, 65, 71–84, 90, 94, 97, 99, 102, 104, 108, 120, 182, 189–90, 225nn93,97, 227nn127,131, 235n244; publications by, 77–78, 79, 81, 90, 109–10, 119, 227n12; public nagging by, 82; public presence of, 81–83, 84, 190, 202; and reform government, 108, 120, 135; restrictions on, 24, 51, 52, 55, 57, 61, 62, 70–71, 72, 75–76, 79, 83, 84, 99, 189–90; during revolution, 71, 72, 83–84; sports competition among, 74–75, 79, 82, 83, 202, 225n85, 235n5; suicide among, 80; veiling of, 25, 26, 51, 52, 55, 57, 61, 71, 72, 75, 76, 79, 82, 189–90, 225n90. *See also* gender relations
Women's Association of the Islamic Revolution (WAIR), 72, 76
Women's Week Festival, 81
Woolf, Virginia, 77
Workers' Councils (*shura-yi kārgarān*), 134
Workers' Party (Iran), 112
World Bank, 133
World Value Survey (WVS), 254n27

Yazdi, Ayatollah Misbah, 92, 114, 116, 215n43, 231n188, 237n52
Yemen, 197–98; labor movement in, 197
Younis, Wesam, 243n47
youths, Egyptian, 34, 63, 137, 167–68, 249n171; accommodating innovation among, 163–64, 190; attitudes toward parents, 235n245; attitudes toward religion among, 42, 150, 151–52, 161–64, 165, 190, 219n113; and al-Jama'a al-Islamiyya, 39–40; sexuality among, 162, 246n109; and violence, 173–74
youths, Iranian: attitudes toward parents among, 235n245; attitudes toward religion among, 28, 61, 63, 73, 100, 161, 190, 216n55, 219n113, 223n31; collective identity of, 64–65, 190, 222n19; girls, 59, 60, 64; and music, 57, 60; nongovernmental organizations (NGOs) among, 65, 109; number of, 64; during Pahlavi rule, 22, 27, 29, 30, 41–42; and post-Islamism, 11–12, 14, 49, 55, 57, 58, 59–65, 84, 92, 97, 99, 100, 102, 104, 107, 135, 182, 190, 216n55, 219n113, 223n31, 235n245; in rural areas, 54, 64, 221n12; sexuality among, 60–61, 222n24; Valentine's Day among, 60; youth centers (*khānih-i javānān*), 31
Youths for Change (Egypt), 183
Yugoslavia, 130
Yunasi, 'Ali, 237n56
Yusra, 172

Zam, Muhammad Ali, 222n18
Zanan-i Iran, 81
Zaqzuq, Mahmud, 242n30
Zarafshan, Naser, 117
Zawahiri, Ayman al-, 38, 39, 142, 241n17
Zayat, Muntasir al-, 141–42, 249n177
Zeinab (granddaughter of the Prophet), 72
Zibakalam, Sadiq, 229n161
Zighal, Malika, 221n139
Zuhdi, Karam, 39, 240n10
Zumur, 'Abud al-, 39, 139, 240n10
Zumur, Tariq al-, 240n

Stanford Studies in Middle Eastern and Islamic Societies and Cultures

Joel Beinin, *Stanford University*
Juan R. I. Cole, *University of Michigan*

Robert Vitalis, *America's Kingdom: Myth-Making on the Saudi Oil Frontier*
2006

Jessica Winegar, *Creative Reckonings: The Politics of Art and Culture in Contemporary Egypt*
2006

Joel Beinin and Rebecca L. Stein, editors, *The Struggle for Sovereignty: Palestine and Israel, 1993–2005*
2006